Lecture Notes in Computer Science 15342

Founding Editors

Gerhard Goos
Juris Hartmanis

AF173727

The series Lecture Notes in Computer Science (LNCS), including its subseries Lecture Notes in Artificial Intelligence (LNAI) and Lecture Notes in Bioinformatics (LNBI), has established itself as a medium for the publication of new developments in computer science and information technology research, teaching, and education.

LNCS enjoys close cooperation with the computer science R & D community, the series counts many renowned academics among its volume editors and paper authors, and collaborates with prestigious societies. Its mission is to serve this international community by providing an invaluable service, mainly focused on the publication of conference and workshop proceedings and postproceedings. LNCS commenced publication in 1973.

Pari Delir Haghighi · Michal Greguš ·
Gabriele Kotsis · Ismail Khalil
Editors

Information Integration and Web Intelligence

26th International Conference, iiWAS 2024
Bratislava, Slovak Republic, December 2–4, 2024
Proceedings, Part I

 Springer

Editors
Pari Delir Haghighi 🆔
Monash University
Clayton, VIC, Australia

Michal Greguš 🆔
Comenius University in Bratislava
Bratislava, Slovakia

Gabriele Kotsis 🆔
Johannes Kepler University
Linz, Austria

Ismail Khalil 🆔
Johannes Kepler University
Linz, Austria

ISSN 0302-9743   ISSN 1611-3349 (electronic)
Lecture Notes in Computer Science
ISBN 978-3-031-78089-9   ISBN 978-3-031-78090-5 (eBook)
https://doi.org/10.1007/978-3-031-78090-5

This Springer imprint is published by the registered company Springer Nature Switzerland AG
The registered company address is: Gewerbestrasse 11, 6330 Cham, Switzerland

If disposing of this product, please recycle the paper.

Preface

We are delighted to present the proceedings of the 26th International Conference on Information Integration and Web Intelligence (iiWAS 2024), which was held at the faculty of Management, Comenius University, Bratislava, Slovakia from 2–4 December 2024.

The proceedings of iiWAS 2024 consist of two volumes and include papers which highlight cutting-edge research across a diverse array of topics, each addressing crucial aspects of today's evolving digital landscape. This collection brings together scholars, practitioners, and industry professionals to explore innovative solutions and emerging trends in fields such as web intelligence, machine learning, natural language processing, blockchain, recommender systems, healthcare technology, and more.

iiWAS 2024 received a total of 92 paper submissions. From these, the Program Committee selected 27 as regular papers, resulting in an acceptance rate of 29%. Additionally, 25 papers were accepted as short papers to showcase pioneering research and innovative projects across various disciplines. These short papers highlight early-stage research, novel ideas, and preliminary findings, fostering meaningful discussions and potential collaborations.

The single-blind peer review process provided evaluation of each submitted paper by at least three reviewers. Their assessment not only served the purpose of quality control for the conference but also contained valuable comments for the authors and inspiring ideas for improvement or further research.

We would like to sincerely thank our Program Committee members and external reviewers for their critical and motivating reviews.

As we move further into the digital era, the ability to seamlessly integrate vast amounts of data, build intelligent systems, and extract meaningful insights has never been more essential. This conference reflected the progress made in achieving these goals and provided a platform to explore how the convergence of technologies is reshaping various industries. The topics covered in this volume range from cutting-edge methodologies for similarity search and sequence indexing to personalized recommender systems, AI-driven transparency in blockchain, and real-world applications of machine learning in health, climate, and human behavior.

The breadth of work compiled here speaks to the interdisciplinary nature of information integration, as the participants have drawn from a wide spectrum of domains to propose solutions to complex problems. Contributions on digital transformation, knowledge graphs, data privacy, and sustainability address some of the most pressing challenges of our time, while novel approaches to conversational agents, recommendation systems, and human-computer interaction show how intelligent systems can enhance our daily lives.

We also placed a strong emphasis on real-world applications, such as digital forensics, peer review systems, and personalized healthcare, underscoring the vital role of AI and web intelligence in improving societal outcomes. Notably, several papers reflect on the ethical considerations and long-term sustainability of these technologies, demonstrating the community's commitment to responsible innovation.

We would like to express our gratitude to all authors for their contributions and to the reviewers for their insightful feedback, which has helped shape these proceedings. Special thanks go to the conference organizing committee at the faculty of Management, Comenius University, Bratislava, Slovakia for their dedication and hard work in bringing this event to fruition.

We extend our heartfelt gratitude to our keynote speakers: Toshiyuki Amagasa from the University of Tsukuba, Japan; Antonio Liotta from the Free University of Bozen-Bolzano, Italy; and Martin Homola from the Faculty of Mathematics, Physics and Informatics, Comenius University in Bratislava, Slovakia for their exceptional presentations. Their insights were enlightening and deeply resonated with our participants, making their contributions one of the event's highlights.

We hope that this volume will serve as a valuable resource for researchers, developers, and professionals working at the intersection of web intelligence and information integration. May the insights and discoveries contained in these proceedings inspire further collaboration, exploration, and innovation in the years to come.

December 2024

Pari Delir Haghighi
Michal Greguš
Gabriele Kotsis
Ismail Khalil

Organization

Program Committee Chairs

Pari Delir Haghighi   Monash University, Australia
Michal Greguš   Comenius University Bratislava, Slovakia

Steering Committee

Gabriele Kotsis   Johannes Kepler University Linz, Austria
Ismail Khalil   Johannes Kepler University Linz, Austria
Peter Štarchoň   Comenius University Bratislava, Slovakia
Syopiansyah Jaya Putra   Universitas Islam Negeri, Indonesia
Dirk Draheim   Tallinn University of Technology, Estonia

Program Committee Members

Akiyo Nadamoto   Konan University, Japan
Anne Kayem   University of Exeter, UK
Atsuhiro Takasu   National Institute of Informatics, Japan
Bala Srinivasan   Monash University, Australia
Barbara Catania   University of Genoa, Italy
Bernardo Breve   University of Salerno, Italy
Chulyun Kim   Sookmyung Women's University, South Korea
Dan Johansson   Umeå University, Sweden
Deborah Dahl   Conversational Technologies, USA
Devis Bianchini   University of Brescia, Italy
Dion Goh   Nanyang Technological University, Singapore
Donjet Bislimi   Universum International College, Kosovo
Edgar Weippl   SBA Research & University of Vienna, Austria
Elio Masciari   University of Naples Federico II, Italy
Emanuele Storti   Università Politecnica delle Marche, Italy
Erich Schikuta   University of Vienna, Austria
Francesc D. Muñoz-Escoí   Universitat Politècnica de València, Spain
Gaetano Cimino   University of Salerno, Italy
Geomar André Schreiner   Universidade Federal da Fronteira Sul, Brazil
Giovanna Guerrini   University of Genoa, Italy
Harald Wahl   University of Applied Sciences Technikum Wien, Austria

Xiaohui (Vincent) Wang	City University of Hong Kong, China
Yasuhiko Morimoto	Hiroshima University, Japan
Yoshiyuki Shoji	Aoyama Gakuin University, Japan
Yousuke Watanabe	Nagoya University, Japan
Zaher Al Aghbari	University of Sharjah, UAE

External Reviewers

Anand Kumar	Amazon Inc., USA
Emanuelle Cavalleri	University of Milan, Italy
Jin Lu	University of Georgia, USA
Srijita Das	University of Michigan – Dearborn, USA
Yijun Duan	Kyoto Institute of Technology, Japan
Zhengquan Li	University of Michigan – Dearborn, USA

Organizers

Abstracts of Keynote Talks

Harnessing Large Language Models for Entity Processing in Resource-Constrained Environments

Toshiyuki Amagasa

University of Tsukuba, Japan

Abstract. Data preprocessing, particularly named-entity recognition (NER) and entity matching (EM), has long posed significant challenges in data engineering. While traditional methods have made strides, the advent of large language models (LLMs) has ushered in a new era of possibilities, potentially surpassing conventional approaches in both NER and EM tasks. However, the practical application of LLMs faces several hurdles, most notably the constraints of limited training data and computational resources.

This talk explores these challenges and discusses strategies to leverage the power of LLMs for entity processing within resource-limited settings. We will delve into 1) the current landscape of NER and EM in data preprocessing, 2) the transformative potential of LLMs in these areas and real-world constraints hampering LLM adoption, and 3) promising approaches to optimize LLM performance under resource limitations.

Towards Explainable AI-Powered Malware Detection

Martin Homola

Comenius University Bratislava, Slovakia

Abstract. Malware analysis has become more and more challenging due to the rapid evolution of attack techniques, and an ever-increasing volume of new malware samples. Indeed, traditional signature-based approaches struggle with this load and machine learning has steadily gained ground in this application area due to its effectiveness and classification power. However, much as in other domains, malware experts lack the confidence and trust in opaque machine learning models that provide classification of the sample but few or no justifications to support and explain such decisions. The lecture will delve into the novel explainable AI methods and techniques and illustrate their benefits and the trade-offs in the malware detection use case.

Contents – Part I

Machine Learning in Healthcare, Climate Change, and Human Behavior

Sequence and Similarity Search Techniques

Knowledge Graphs, Databases, and Ontologies

Contents – Part II

Human-Computer Interaction, Music Therapy, and User-Centric Systems

Environmental and Geological Data Science

Web Intelligence, Language Models, and AI-Based Question Answering

RUVA – A Radical Universal Visual Annotation for Web-Based Language Learning

Werner Winiwarter[✉] (iD)

Faculty of Computer Science, University of Vienna, Währingerstraße 29,
1090 Vienna, Austria
werner.winiwarter@univie.ac.at
https://ufind.univie.ac.at/en/person.html?id=6309

Abstract. In this paper, we introduce a novel language representation, which we have built on five cornerstones: radical construction grammar, uniquely identifiable concepts, visualization, Uniform Meaning Representation, and Interlinear Morphemic Glossing. The resulting annotation is perfectly suited for multilingual applications, in particular second language acquisition. We have integrated the representation into our Web-Based Language Learning environment, which allows to design engaging annotation tasks by using augmented browsing technology. As first use case, we focus on Japanese language learning because of the growing popularity at our university and the particular challenges posed by this difficult language.

Keywords: Cognitive linguistics · Language representation · Annotation · Visualization · Web-Based Language Learning · Japanese

1 Introduction

Due to the worldwide manga craze we have witnessed an unprecedented increasing demand for Japanese language courses at our university. As a consequence, we have received an urgent call for additional technological support to assist the colleagues from our language department.

In previous collaborations [52] we have created solutions for Japanese language learning integrated into a Web-Based Language Learning environment, which enabled the study of Japanese Web pages through augmented browsing technology and included gamification and visualization elements. In particular, we developed a sentence representation, which we enhanced with images and uniquely identifiable concepts [51]. The pictorial representations proved to be extremely beneficial for memory and retention.

Therefore, in this current work, we take one step further by using only visual elements in the semantic level of our representation. We retrieve all images from

P. Delir Haghighi et al. (Eds.): iiWAS 2024, LNCS 15342, pp. 3–18, 2025.
https://doi.org/10.1007/978-3-031-78090-5_1

Wikimedia Commons, either through the *Wikidata image property* or our image database [50], which currently contains over 3,500 images that have been manually annotated with semantic tags and links to *WordNet* synsets [35].

To obtain a purely visual interlingual semantic representation, we also replace thematic role names with expressive emojis and use color-coding to indicate concept types, role inversions, etc. As unique concept identifiers we use *PropBank* rolesets [41], *WordNet* synsets, or *Wikipedia* page titles.

Whereas our previous semantic representations were based on the popular *Abstract Meaning Representation* (AMR) [2], only recently its successor, the *Uniform Meaning Representation* (UMR) [46], has been developed. It extends AMR in several directions, especially towards multilinguality and document-level annotations that cover intersentential dependencies.

Another essential feature of UMR is its sound theoretical foundation by building on *radical construction grammar* [9,11], which was created in the context of linguistic *typology* [10], i.e. the study and classification of languages according to their structural characteristics. Radical construction grammar considers word classes and other syntactic structures as language-specific and construction-specific [12] and rejects the notion of syntactic relations altogether by replacing them with semantic relations.

Consequentially, we have also reframed our research work based on UMR and radical construction grammar. In our annotation tasks, the language students visually build up the syntactic structure bottom-up starting from the morphemic level until they finalize the construction of the complete sentence. At the morphemic level we complete our representation by using *Interlinear Morphemic Glossing* to map Japanese morphemes either to English morphemes or grammatical category labels according to the *Leipzig Glossing Rules*[1].

The remainder of this paper is organized as follows. In Sect. 2, we discuss some relevant related work and offer a brief background on Japanese to assist the reader with understanding several essential language-specific issues. Section 3 provides an overview of our system architecture, before we present the RUVA annotation in detail in Sect. 4 using several illustrative examples. Finally, we describe the user interaction during our annotation tasks in Sect. 5 and finish the paper in Sect. 6 with some thoughts on future work.

2   Related Work

After the first global LLM hype, their severe limitations soon became painfully apparent. This has led to a renewed interest in *neuro-symbolic* approaches [47] and a resurgence of activity in the field of *cognitive linguistics* [13]. One influential subarea is *construction grammar* [45], which is actually a broad family of theories with the common denominator that they view *constructions* as the basic units of language, which are pairings of *form* and *meaning*. They all reject the separation of lexical items and grammatical rules, instead both are regarded as constructions. As a consequence, the traditional lexicon is replaced by a *constructicon* [15], a multidimensional association network of constructions.

---

[1] https://www.eva.mpg.de/lingua/tools-at-lingboard/glossing_rules.php.

The annotation of sentences with *meaning representations* has established itself in the last decade as a thriving research field in computational linguistics (see [1]). The most influential and most actively promoted approach has been AMR. There are many parsers available, the best[2] parser being at the moment [30]. The *SPRING* [3] parser can be tried via a Web interface[3], which also offers a nice visualization. One point of criticism concerning AMR's reliance on numbered, not directly interpretable core arguments, is addressed by the *WISeR* meaning representation [17], which maps them to thematic roles. For UMR, there has been a first workshop in 2024 for the kick-off of UMR parser development[4].

Whereas *Interlinear Morphemic Glossing* has been neglected for quite some time by natural language processing research, it has a long tradition in linguistics and typology. Only recently, there have been some efforts by computational linguists to extend and formalize the Leipzig Glossing Rules [38] and to automate interlinear glossing, e.g. [43,53]. There has even been a first shared task on this topic in 2023 [19].

Multimodal enhancements of lexical resources have also a long history but only recently gained new momentum due to the strong interest in research on visual question answering (VQA) [32] or multimodal large language models (MLLMs) [4]. One example of an attempt towards a multimodal semantic representation is *VoxML* [42]. Regarding the mapping of images to WordNet synsets, there exists the well-known *ImageNet* collection, which maps about 1,000 images to each synset [14]. Another effort to assign cliparts to synsets was discontinued after illustrating only 581 synsets [6]. A much more influential resource is *Wikipedia*, which has been increasingly enhanced with visual representations. However, the number of images provided varies widely across language versions. The most comprehensive recent effort is certainly *BabelNet* [39] with the annotation tool *Babelfy* [37] and the latest *BabelPic* [8] dataset targeting non-concrete concepts.

Japanese is an agglutinative SOV language with topic-comment sentence structure. Phrases are exclusively head-final and compound sentences are strictly left-branching. The most noticeable characteristics for language students are the missing articles, no distinction between singular and plural, no gender, no conjugation for person, a complex system of honorifics, and a high level of ambiguity, e.g. by omitting the subject or using zero anaphora.

There exist many excellent reference grammars, e.g. [25,26], and a lot of research activity on Japanese linguistics: see [22] for an introduction; for a recent comprehensive overview we recommend [23]. There are also a wealth of typological studies of Japanese, e.g. [24,44].

One of the main obstacles for getting proficient in Japanese is the complex writing system (see [34,36,40]). It uses a combination of logographic *kanji* and two syllabaries *hiragana* and *katakana*. Kanji are adopted Chinese characters, since 2010 Japanese students are required to learn 2,136 so-called *jōyō kanji* in primary and secondary school. Most kanji have more than one reading depending on the context. The readings are generally divided into *Sino-Japanese readings*,

---

[2] https://paperswithcode.com/task/amr-parsing/latest.

[3] http://nlp.uniroma1.it/spring/.

[4] https://umr4nlp.github.io/web/UMRParsingWorkshop.html.

which are close to Chinese pronunciations at the time of adoption into Japanese, and *native readings*, which are pronunciations of Japanese words conveying the meaning of the kanji.

There exist several *romanization* systems, i.e. using Latin script to write Japanese. The most widely used one is the *Hepburn romanization*, it again has several variants, the most common one being *Revised Hepburn* (see [29]). There are many romanization tools, the most easily accessible one is *Pykakasi*[5] based on the *kakasi*[6] library.

The most important lexical resource for Japanese is the *Japanese Multilingual dictionary* (JMdict) [7], which can be searched online in combination with many other lexical resources via the *Online Japanese Dictionary Service* (WWWJDIC)[7]. Another very useful online service is *Honyaku Star*[8]. It references numerous dictionaries and corpora and shows translations in context. Honyaku Star includes currently over 2 million translations. Japanese is also part of the *Open Multilingual Wordnet* (OMW) [5], which makes it possible to assign Japanese words to English synsets. OMW is easily accessible via the *NLTK* toolkit[9].

The most prolific linguistic tool for Japanese is certainly the *CaboCha* dependency parser [27], which includes the *MeCab* part-of-speech and morphological analyzer [28]. More recently, trained pipelines have been added to the popular natural language toolkit *SpaCy*[10], another similar solution is *UniDic2UD*[11].

3   System Architecture

Figure 1 highlights the main components of our Web-Based Language Learning environment. The language students can access the learning server through a Web browser by using augmented browsing enabled through *Chrome extension APIs*[12], and the *jQuery*[13] and *jQuery UI*[14] libraries. Whenever a student loads a new Japanese Web document, it is automatically analyzed and segmented into individual sentences. An event handler is assigned to each sentence. If a student clicks on a sentence, it is transferred to the server via *XMLHttpRequests* in *JSON* format.

The language learning server is implemented in *SWI-Prolog* [49], which is not only a natural choice for language processing tasks but also provides a scalable Web server solution [48] and libraries for efficiently handling RDF/XML files.

---

[5] https://pypi.org/project/pykakasi/.
[6] http://kakasi.namazu.org/.
[7] http://wwwjdic.se/cgi-bin/wwwjdic.cgi?1C.
[8] http://honyakustar.com/.
[9] https://www.nltk.org/.
[10] https://spacy.io/models/ja.
[11] https://github.com/KoichiYasuoka/UniDic2UD.
[12] https://developer.chrome.com/docs/extensions/reference/api.
[13] https://jquery.com/.
[14] https://jqueryui.com/.

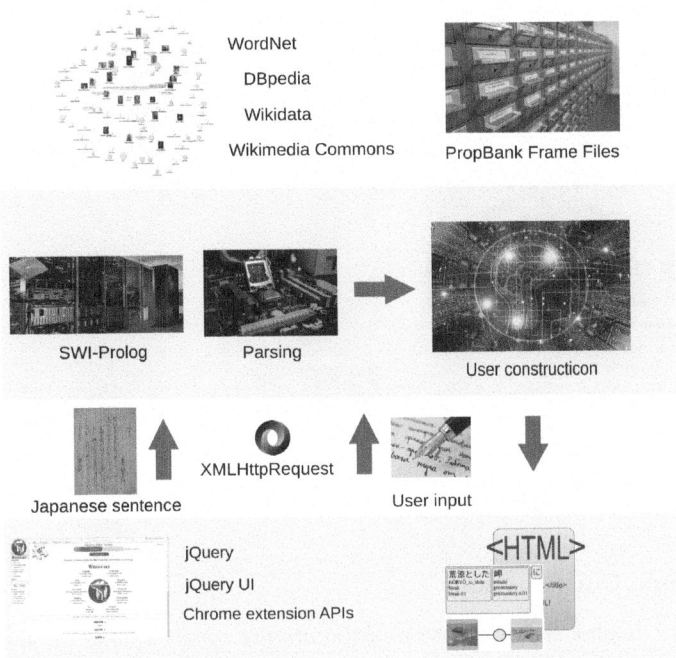

Fig. 1. System architecture

The server parses the sentence by using the linguistic knowledge stored in the *user constructicon* and dynamically generates an HTML page with the annotated sentence, which is opened in a new tab in the student's browser. The user can now add new information to the annotation, which is again sent to the server leading to an update of the constructicon, a reparsing of the sentence, and an actualization of the HTML page. As external resources we use *PropBank Frame Files*, *WordNet*, *DBpedia* [31], *Wikidata*, and *Wikimedia Commons*.

4 RUVA

In this section we introduce the RUVA language representation by using an illustrative example sentence. It is the second sentence from the Japanese translation[15] of the 1833 tale "The Invisible Girl"[16] by Mary Shelley, which we retrieved from *Wikisource*. The original sentence reads as "... narrate, as concisely as I can, how I was surprised on visiting what seemed a ruined tower, crowning a bleak promontory overhanging the sea, that flows between Wales and Ireland..." (the complete original sentence is actually over 4 times longer).

We start our explanations in Sect. 4.1 with atomic constructions, move on to phrases in Sect. 4.2, and then finish with clauses in Sect. 4.3.

---

[15] https://ja.wikisource.org/wiki/透明少女.
[16] https://en.wikisource.org/wiki/The_Invisible_Girl.

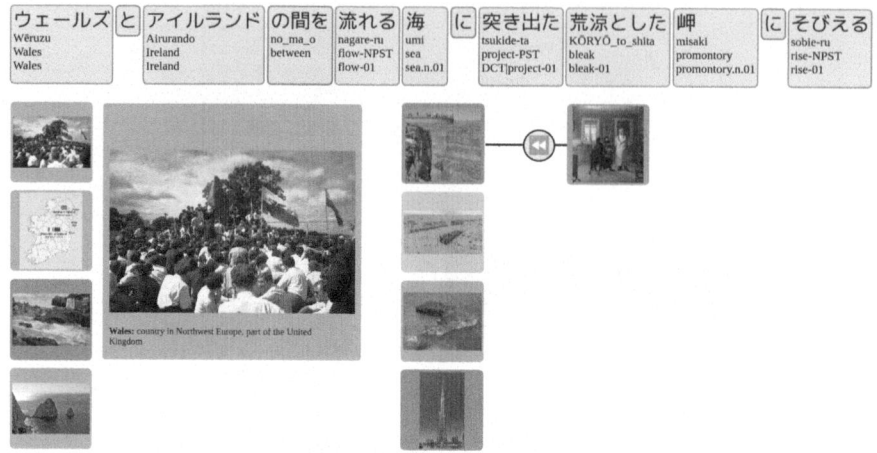

Fig. 2. Example of atomic constructions (Color figure online)

4.1   Atomic Constructions

In Fig. 2, we display the annotation of the *atomic constructions* for the first half of our example sentence (the five concepts in the middle of the figure are actually below the other four concepts on the left, we just shifted them to make the figure more compact). The boxes at the top represent the atomic constructions and show their *canonical trilinear representations*. They consist of three lines: the *transliterations* using Revised Hepburn romanization, the *Interlinear Morphemic Glosses* (IMGs), and the *idiomatic translations* to concepts.

For instance, the first word ウェールズ is mapped to the *Wikipedia page title* `Wales`, leading to the display of the corresponding visual concept representation on the left side of the figure as starting point to assemble the *meaning representation* part of our annotation. The background color magenta indicates that the *semantic class* is `object`, which includes persons, animals, and physical objects of various kinds. If the user hovers with the mouse over the concept, the Wikipedia page title is shown as tooltip and the corresponding construction in the linear representation at the top is painted in the same background color to establish the alignment between the two parts of the sentence representation. By clicking on the concept image, the user can open an enlarged version with the concept label and the *Wikidata description*.

The border color of the construction represents the *information packaging* function. The color magenta signals the function `reference`, i.e. it indicates what the speaker is talking about. In radical construction grammar, a *construction* (cxn) is always a pairing of semantic content and information packaging function. In this case, we have the prototypical combination, hence the same color, resulting in a `referent expression` with the prototypical use as *head* of a *referring phrase*[17]. This construction label is also shown as tooltip.

---

[17] All definitions can be looked up in the comprehensive glossary of terms in [11].

The next word と ("to") is a member of a short list of very common parti-cles. As each of them has many different syntactic functions and no independent semantic content, it is not necessary to add any annotation for such monosyl-labic words. The expression の間を consists of three words, indicated by the underscore characters in the transliteration, and is also used like a postposition, therefore we only add the IMG "between" but no idiomatic translation.

The word 流れる is the dictionary form of a Japanese verb, it consists of two morphemes: the stem 流れ and the ending る, indicated by a hyphen and the grammatical category NPST (non-past) in the IMG. It is translated to the *PropBank roleset* flow-01. This is the prototypical pairing of an action, i.e. a relational, dynamic, and transitory concept, and predication, which con-veys what the speaker is asserting about the referents in a particular utterance. Therefore, both are painted in cyan. The resulting construction is a predicate, prototypically used as *head* of a *clause*.

海 is an example of a mapping to a *WordNet synset*, namely sea.n.01. 突き出た is the past tense (PST) of the verb 突き出る. The past tense is modeled in the meaning representation as a BEFORE ( ) relation to the *special concept* DCT (document creation time), colored in orange, indicating the present moment. This sequence of concepts is written in the idiomatic translation with a vertical bar. As can be seen, we do not need arrowheads to indicate the direction of the relation because we always place the dependent to the right of the head. The role name is shown as tooltip.

Finally, the expression 荒涼とした acts like an adjective and is translated to bleak-01, therefore, we have again a prototypical pairing between the semantic class property (relational, 1-dimensional, usually scalar and stable concept) and the information packaging function modification, which provides additional information about the referent and enriches the specification of the referent for the hearer. In this case both are colored in green and we result in a modifier, i.e. prototypically the *head* of an *attributive phrase*. The use of uppercase in the transliteration indicates Sino-Japanese readings for the kanji.

4.2 Phrases

By using atomic constructions as elements, we can assemble *complex construc-tions*. The first main type are phrases: constructions used for reference or mod-ification. Figure 3 shows the second half of our example sentence, which contains some interesting cases of phrases. The word 廃墟 is semantically an action, namely ruin-01, which is packaged as referent expression. It is modified by the expression のような. It is a *hedge*, i.e. it expresses ambiguity, probability, cau-tion, or indecisiveness. Therefore, this represents a new information packaging function called admodification, which is defined as qualifying a modifier, usu-ally via semantically expressing degree or hedging of the property denoted by the modifier. We use the color teal for admodification, the resulting construction is then simply called an admodifier. At the same time, the admodifier のような changes the information packaging function of the referent expression 廃墟 to

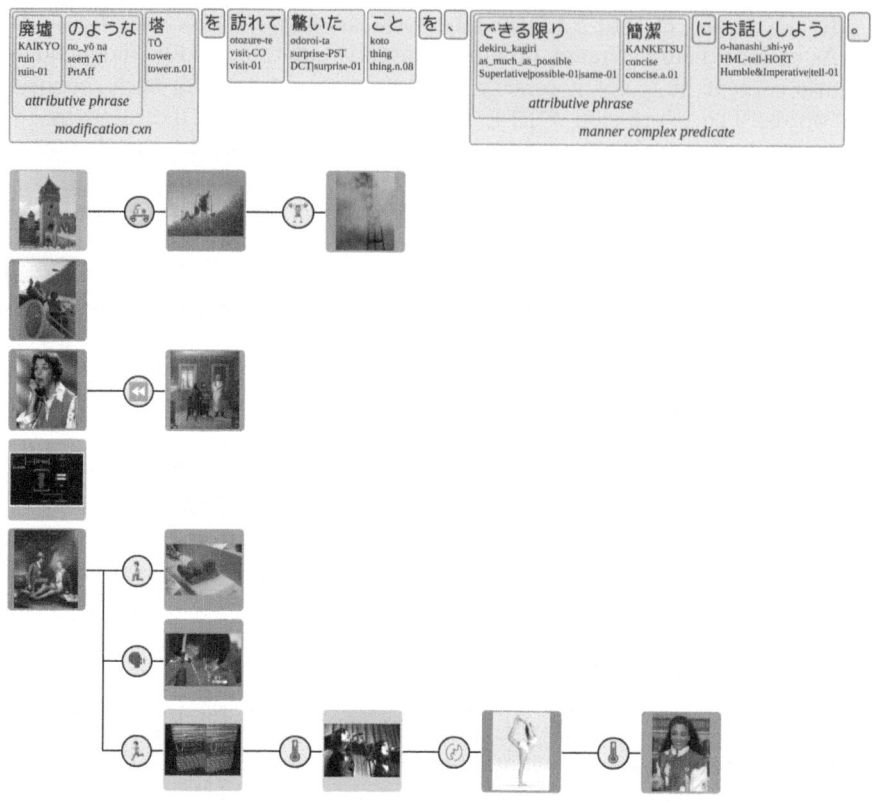

Fig. 3. Example of phrases

modification, which is also indicated by the grammatical category AT (attributor) in the IMG. Therefore, we result in an **attributive phrase**, a construction that performs the act of modification. Together with the referent expression 塔, we arrive in a second step at a **modification cxn**, a construction that consists of a referent expression and dependent attributive phrases.

In the meaning representation, the admodifier is mapped to the special concept **PrtAff**, which represents the *modal strength* value *partial strength* with *affirmative polarity*. The corresponding role is called **MODSTR** (🌡). The action **ruin-01** is linked to the object **tower.n.01** by the *inverse relation* **UNDERGOER-OF** (🚐), which is indicated by the background color.

The word 訪れて is a coordinative form of the Japanese verb 訪れる, the ending indicates the coordinator (CO) function. It is a `deranked predicate`, i.e. it is part of a complex predicate construction but does not recruit the predicate construction in a simple predicate. This way it can act like a conjunction as coordinator; it is color-coded in brown.

The second attributive phrase consists of the modifier 簡潔 and the expression できる限り, which is an `equative cxn` acting as admodifier. An equative construction has the semantic function of assigning the identical position on a gradable predicative scale to two referents, the `comparee` and the `standard`. In the meaning representation this is modeled by the concept `same-01` and the STANDARD (☝) `possible-01` with the DEGREE (🌡) `Superlative`; the comparee is missing. The equative cxn is then linked to the concept `concise.a.01` again with the role 🌡 .

Finally, the predicate of the sentence is an `imperative-hortative cxn`, which expresses the speech act which requests that the action expressed in the propositional content of the imperative-hortative be carried out, prototypically by the addressee but possibly by other persons. In particular, hortative is used for a first person. In the expression お話ししよう, the hortative (HORT) is expressed by the final ending. In addition, this form – especially the prefix お – indicates humble (HML) level of politeness. In the meaning representation this is modeled by two relations, using "&" in the idiomatic translation. The first one is the relation with the role POLITE (🧎) to the special concept `Humble`, the second one is the relation with the role MODE (🧎) to `Imperative` (which subsumes hortative). The attributive phrase is combined with the imperative-hortative cxn to create a `manner complex predicate`, i.e. a complex predicate in which the stative component describes a state that holds of the event denoted by the main predicate. In the meaning representation this is depicted as a MANNER (🏃) relation between `tell-01` and `concise.a.01`.

4.3 Clauses

The second group of complex constituents are `clauses`, i.e. constructions that perform the function of predication. In Fig. 4 we show again the first part of our sentence, this time with a complete structural analysis. The meaning representation continues from Fig. 3. In the upper half it starts from `thing.n.08` and ends with `ruin-01` (with only the concept `PrtAff` missing as we already covered it in Fig. 3) and `rise-01`. From the latter the representation continues in the lower half on the left with the concept `promontory.n.01`. The three only partially visible phrases reach till 訪れて, 驚いた, and the end of the sentence.

The first clause on the left is a `path event cxn`. It describes motion of a *figure* along a spatial path relative to a *ground*. It is modelled in the meaning representation by two PATH-BETWEEN (∧) relations from `flow-01` to the two locations `Wales` and `Ireland`. The most frequent clause type used in this sentence is the `relative clause cxn`. This construction is defined by the function of modifying a referent with an action concept. It consists of the dependent `relative`

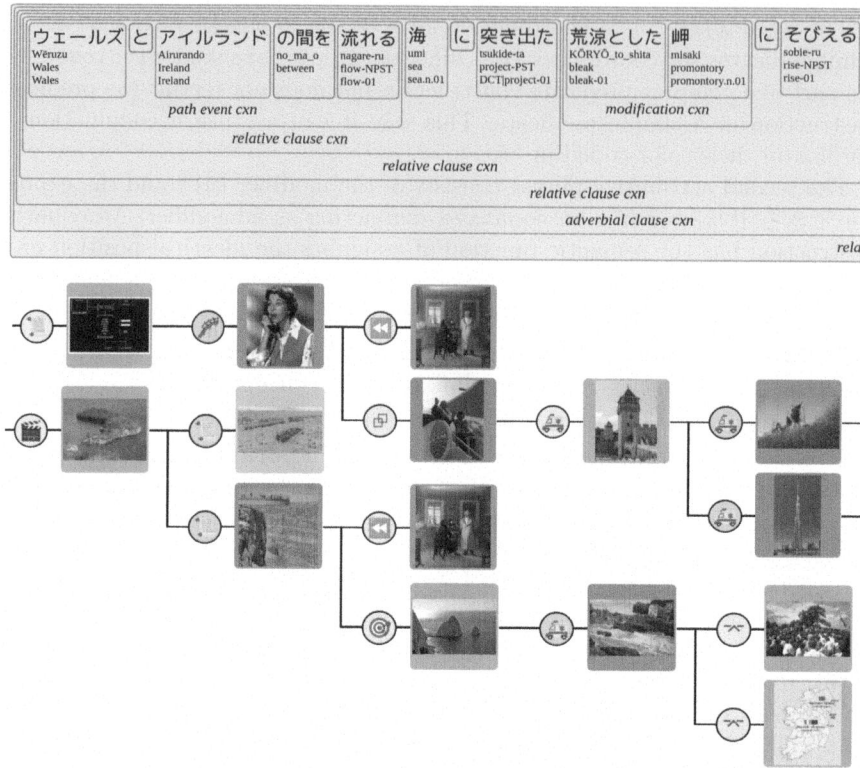

Fig. 4. Example of clauses

clause, which denotes the event that is used to modify the `relative clause head` referent in the `matrix clause`.

The meaning representation of the first relative clause construction contains a new role type `GOAL` ( ) between `project-01` and `sea.n.01`. At the next level, `promontory.n.01` is linked to `bleak-01` and `project-01` via `THEME-OF` ( ) relations, and to `rise-01` by a *START* ( ) relation, which indicates the location from which the motion originates.

The deranked predicate 訪れて (see Sect. 4.2) leads to a deranked relative clause cxn and at the next level to an `adverbial clause` cxn, which is a complex sentence construction with a figure-ground information packaging of the relation between the events denoted by the two clauses. It consists of a matrix clause and an adverbial dependent clause. In this case, it is a *temporal relation* with a partial or full overlap between child and parent, which is depicted in the meaning representation by an `OVERLAP` ( ) relation between `surprise-01` and `visit-01`. The final clause is again a relative clause cxn with the role `STIMULUS-OF` ( ) between `thing.n.08` and `surprise-01`.

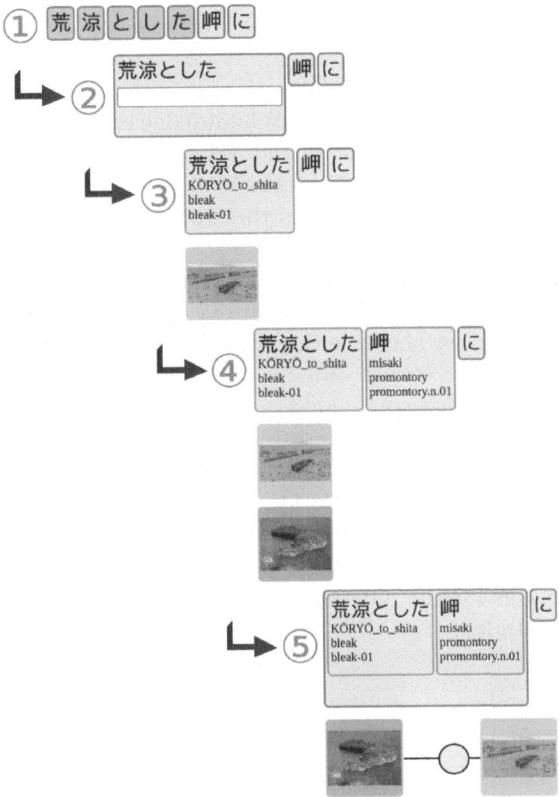

Fig. 5. Example of user interaction (Color figure online)

5 User Interaction

After we have worked out the details of the RUVA formalism in Sect. 4, we now take a closer look at the user interaction. As a first showcase implementation, we have developed an annotation task for language students, in which we ask them to follow the same line of reasoning we used for the presentation of our approach. In Fig. 5, we can observe one simple example of the workflow involved in annotating a sentence from a Japanese Web page. At the beginning of their training, the students start from scratch with a completely empty user constructicon.

We first display the sentence as a simple list of Japanese characters, which is the starting point to assemble the complete annotation step-by-step following a bottom-up strategy. As Step ① in Fig. 5, the user can create words and expressions by drawing a box with the cursor to select characters, which are highlighted in orange. As soon as the user releases the mouse button, the display changes to ②. Now the student is supposed to enter the correct transliteration, the IMG, and the idiomatic translation. At all user input steps, the level of support can be increased by offering select menus or suggestions. This is achieved by accessing the external resources in Fig. 1 as well as the language-specific tools and lexicons mentioned in Sect. 2.

Whenever the user adds some information, it is stored in the constructicon, and can be used to learn rules to apply this knowledge to new examples. Context-sensitive rules are learnt automatically and adjusted incrementally for each new item. We also store the number of times the student was exposed to this item so we can choose the number of repetitions the student has to perform before the item is inserted automatically.

After entering all the data, the complete atomic construction including the visualization of the concept is displayed in ③. We encourage the students to change the default image by choosing their own favorite images to personalize the learning experience and to collect valuable data about the observed multimodal associations in the constructicons.

In ④, the user has completed the annotation of the first two constructions. By selecting both of them with the mouse, we end up in ⑤, i.e. with a new complex construction and a new relation between the two concepts. The last thing the student has to do is to input a label for the new construction and a role for the new relation. Again, assistance can be offered for these two annotation steps. Also the emojis for the different roles can be altered to suit the personal preferences of the student.

6   Conclusion

In this paper, we have presented the RUVA sentence representation, a novel approach based on radical construction grammar and UMR. In stark contrast to the predominant *Universal Dependencies* [33] paradigm in computational linguistics, the *universals* in RUVA are concepts and constructions. This leads to a powerful formalism, which successfully addresses the challenge of efficiently mapping the diversity of human languages. The renunciation of word classes and syntactic categories results in a flexible model that can treat many complex phenomena including multi-word and idiomatic expressions in a natural way.

Based on this sound theoretical foundation, we have developed a Web-Based Language Learning solution for Japanese, which offers engaging annotation exercises. We intend to have our system soon ready for more widespread experimental use in language classrooms to obtain valuable feedback regarding usability and functionality, which is also essential for issue tracking and system stabilization. Once we have reached the desired level of maturity, we plan to make the environment available on GitLab.

To demonstrate the applicability of our approach to under-resourced languages, we have recently started a new research project for the Albanian language. We have also already initiated activities to simplify the representation for novice language learners by adapting design principles and experience from the field of *Augmentative and Alternative Communication* (AAC) [21]: in particular we will experiment with the use of *Open AAC Symbols*[18] for visualization. To

---

[18] https://www.openaac.org/symbols.html.

further improve the readability of long and complex sentences, we will add the ability to easily collapse and expand parts of a sentence in the display.

A more ambitious and long-term research target will be the extension of RUVA to incorporate also the document-level representation of UMR for modelling intersentential dependencies. We will also experiment with different user interaction modalities with varying degrees of automatic linguistic analysis and annotation. In addition, we will consider other application scenarios for additional target user groups, e.g. students of translation studies, literature studies, or linguistics. In particular, conducting psycholinguistic experiments with RUVA represents a fascinating challenge for future work. We are very curious about the results of analyzing the user constructicon data, which we will collect from the students. We will also look at the task of consolidating the individual user constructicons to create integrated resources for future instructional use.

Finally, we also want to address the important research question of an optimal interaction with LLMs [18]. While currently LLMs excel at end-to-end machine translation tasks, they still lack the cognitive faculties to truthfully model and annotate all the complexities of natural language [16,20]. We see a strong potential of user constructicons to correctly model the idiolect of a person acquired through past language exposure. Therefore, they could represent one cornerstone for building the next generation of AI.

References

1. Abend, O., Rappoport, A.: The state of the art in semantic representation. In: Proceedings of the 55th Annual Meeting of the ACL (Volume 1: Long Papers), pp. 77–89 (2017). https://doi.org/10.18653/v1/P17-1008
2. Banarescu, L., et al.: Abstract Meaning Representation for sembanking. In: Proceedings of the 7th Linguistic Annotation Workshop and Interoperability with Discourse, pp. 178–186 (2013)
3. Bevilacqua, M., Blloshmi, R., Navigli, R.: One SPRING to rule them both: symmetric AMR semantic parsing and generation without a complex pipeline. In: Proceedings of the AAAI Conference on Artificial Intelligence (AAAI 2021), pp. 12564–12573 (2021)
4. Bewersdorff, A., et al.: Taking the next step with generative artificial intelligence: the transformative role of multimodal large language models in science education. arXiv:2401.00832 (2024)
5. Bond, F., Paik, K.: A survey of wordnets and their licenses. In: Proceedings of the 6th Global WordNet Conference (GWC 2012), pp. 64–71 (2012)
6. Bond, F., et al.: Enhancing the Japanese WordNet. In: Proceedings of the 7th Workshop on Asian Language Resources (ALR7), pp. 1–8 (2009)
7. Breen, J.: JMdict: a Japanese-multilingual dictionary. In: Proceedings of the Workshop on Multilingual Linguistic Resources, pp. 71–79 (2004)
8. Calabrese, A., Bevilacqua, M., Navigli, R.: Fatality killed the cat or: BabelPic, a multimodal dataset for non-concrete concepts. In: Proceedings of the 58th Annual Meeting of the ACL, pp. 4680–4686 (2020)
9. Croft, W.: Radical Construction Grammar: Syntactic Theory in Typological Perspective. Oxford University Press (2001)

10. Croft, W.: Typology and Universals. Cambridge Textbooks in Linguistics, Cambridge University Press (2002)
11. Croft, W.: Morphosyntax: Constructions of the World's Languages. Cambridge Textbooks in Linguistics, Cambridge University Press (2022)
12. Croft, W.: Word classes in radical construction grammar. In: The Oxford Handbook of Word Classes. Oxford University Press (2023)
13. Croft, W., Cruse, D.A.: Cognitive Linguistics. Cambridge Textbooks in Linguistics, Cambridge University Press (2004)
14. Deng, J., et al.: ImageNet: a large-scale hierarchical image database. In: 2009 IEEE Conference on Computer Vision and Pattern Recognition (CVPR) (2009)
15. Diessel, H.: The Constructicon: Taxonomies and Networks. Elements in Construction Grammar, Cambridge University Press (2023)
16. Ettinger, A., et al.: "You are an expert linguistic annotator": limits of LLMs as analyzers of abstract meaning representation. arXiv:2310.17793 (2023)
17. Feng, L., et al.: Widely interpretable semantic representation: frameless meaning representation for broader applicability. arXiv:2309.06460 (2023)
18. Feng, Z., et al.: Trends in integration of knowledge and large language models: a survey and taxonomy of methods, benchmarks, and applications. arXiv:2311.05876 (2023)
19. Ginn, M., et al.: Findings of the SIGMORPHON 2023 shared task on interlinear glossing. In: Proceedings of the 20th SIGMORPHON Workshop on Computational Research in Phonetics, Phonology, and Morphology, pp. 186–201 (2023)
20. Groschwitz, J., et al.: AMR parsing is far from solved: GraPES, the Granular AMR Parsing Evaluation Suite (2023)
21. Hall, N., et al.: Fundamentals of AAC: A Case-Based Approach to Enhancing Communication. Plural Publishing Inc. (2023)
22. Hasegawa, Y.: Japanese: A Linguistic Introduction. Cambridge University Press (2015)
23. Hasegawa, Y. (ed.): The Cambridge Handbook of Japanese Linguistics. Cambridge Handbooks in Language and Linguistics, Cambridge University Press (2018)
24. Iwasaki, S.: Japanese. John Benjamins (2013)
25. Kaiser, S., et al.: Japanese: A Comprehensive Grammar. Routledge (2013)
26. Kamermans, M.: An Introduction to Japanese - Syntax. SJGR Publishing, Grammar & Language (2010)
27. Kudo, T., Matsumoto, Y.: Japanese dependency analysis using cascaded chunking. In: CoNLL 2002: Proceedings of the 6th Conference on Natural Language Learning 2002 (COLING 2002 Post-Conference Workshops), pp. 63–69 (2002)
28. Kudo, T., Yamamoto, K., Matsumoto, Y.: Applying conditional random fields to Japanese morphological analysis. In: Proceedings of the 2004 Conference on Empirical Methods in Natural Language Processing, pp. 230–237 (2004)
29. Kudo, Y.: Modified Hepburn romanization system in Japanese language cataloging: where to look, what to follow. Cataloging Classif. Q. **49**(2), 97–120 (2011). https://doi.org/10.1080/01639374.2011.536751
30. Lee, Y.S., et al.: Maximum Bayes Smatch ensemble distillation for AMR parsing. In: Proceedings of the 2022 Conference of the North American Chapter of the ACL: Human Language Technologies, pp. 5379–5392 (2022)
31. Lehmann, J., et al.: DBpedia - a large-scale, multilingual knowledge base extracted from Wikipedia. Semantic Web **6**(2), 167–195 (2015)
32. Lerner, P., Ferret, O., Guinaudeau, C.: Cross-modal retrieval for knowledge-based visual question answering. arXiv:2401.05736 (2024)

33. de Marneffe, M.C., et al.: Universal dependencies. Computational Linguistics **47**(2), 255–308 (2021). https://doi.org/10.1162/coli_a_00402
34. Matsumoto, H.: Peak learning experiences and language learning: a study of American learners of Japanese. Lang. Cult. Curriculum - LANG CULT CURRIC **20**, 195–208 (2007)
35. Miller, G.A.: WordNet: a lexical database for English. Commun. ACM **38**(11), 39–41 (1995)
36. Mori, Y.: Review of recent research on kanji processing, learning, and instruction. Jpn. Lang. Lit. **48**(2), 403–439 (2014)
37. Moro, A., Raganato, A., Navigli, R.: Entity linking meets word sense disambiguation: a unified approach. Trans. ACL (TACL) **2**, 231–244 (2014)
38. Mortensen, D.R., et al.: Generalized glossing guidelines: an explicit, human- and machine-readable, item-and-process convention for morphological annotation. In: Proceedings of the 20th SIGMORPHON workshop on Computational Research in Phonetics, Phonology, and Morphology, pp. 58–67 (2023)
39. Navigli, R., et al.: Ten years of BabelNet: a survey. In: Proceedings of IJCAI 2021, pp. 4559–4567 (2021)
40. Paxton, S.: Kanji matters in a multilingual Japan. J. Rikkyo Univ. Lang. Center **42**, 29–41 (2019)
41. Pradhan, S., et al.: PropBank comes of Age—Larger, smarter, and more diverse. In: Proceedings of the 11th Joint Conference on Lexical and Computational Semantics, pp. 278–288 (2022). https://doi.org/10.18653/v1/2022.starsem-1.24
42. Pustejovsky, J., et al.: The development of multimodal lexical resources. In: Proceedings of the Workshop on Grammar and Lexicon: Interactions and Interfaces (GramLex), pp. 41–47 (2016)
43. Samardžić, T., Schikowski, R., Stoll, S.: Automatic interlinear glossing as two-level sequence classification. In: Proceedings of the 9th SIGHUM Workshop on Language Technology for Cultural Heritage, Social Sciences, and Humanities (LaTeCH), pp. 68–72 (2015). https://doi.org/10.18653/v1/W15-3710
44. Taoka, C.: Aspect and argument structure in Japanese. Ph.D. thesis, University of Manchester (2000)
45. Ungerer, T., Hartmann, S.: Constructionist Approaches: Past, Present, Future. Elements in Construction Grammar, Cambridge University Press (2023)
46. Van Gysel, J.E.L., et al.: Designing a uniform meaning representation for natural language processing. KI - Künstliche Intelligenz **35**, 343–360 (2021)
47. Wan, Z., et al.: Towards cognitive AI systems: a survey and prospective on neuro-symbolic AI. arXiv:2401.01040 (2024)
48. Wielemaker, J., Huang, Z., Van Der Meij, L.: SWI-Prolog and the Web. Theory Pract. Logic Program. **8**(3), 363–392 (2008)
49. Wielemaker, J., et al.: SWI-Prolog. Theory Pract. Logic Program. **12**(1–2), 67–96 (2012)
50. Winiwarter, W., Wloka, B.: VISCOSE – a kanji dictionary enriched with VISual, COmpositional, and SEmantic information. In: 7th Workshop on Cognitive Aspects of the Lexicon (CogALex-VII) (2022)
51. Wloka, B., Winiwarter, W.: AAA4LLL – Acquisition, annotation, augmentation for lively language learning. In: 3rd Conference on Language, Data and Knowledge (LDK2021) (2021)

52. Wloka, B., Winiwarter, W.: DARE – a comprehensive methodology for mastering kanji. In: 23rd International Conference on Information Integration and Web Intelligence (iiWAS2021), pp. 427–435 (2021)
53. Zhao, X., et al.: Automatic interlinear glossing for under-resourced languages leveraging translations. In: Proceedings of the 28th International Conference on Computational Linguistics, pp. 5397–5408 (2020). https://doi.org/10.18653/v1/2020.coling-main.471

CLOR-QA: Cross-Lingual Open-Retrieval Question Answering Model with Dynamic Database Integration

Sonia Khetarpaul[(✉)] , Vedanta Vivek Patil , Mitra Abhi Sura,
Shrey Sharma, and Pooja Singh

Department of Computer Science and Engineering,
Shiv Nadar Institution of Eminence, Delhi NCR, India
{sonia.khetarpaul,vp433,ms139,ss989,pooja.singh}@snu.edu.in

Abstract. In this diverse world, language barriers pose significant challenges in sectors such as tourism and medicine, affecting the efficiency in communication and information availability. In context of tourism, diverse linguistic norms often affect tourist experience and satisfaction. This paper proposes a novel solution to address information scarcity and asymmetry - a Cross-Lingual Open retrieval Question Answering (CLOR-QA) system. This model, trained on English, Chinese, Vietnamese, Arabic, and German, facilitates cross-lingual information retrieval, enabling users to access data in languages different from the query language by integrating a cross-lingual approach into the question-answering system. The user can access the multilingual data entered in real time to get prompt responses through the proposed CLOR-QA model, this system utilizes Helsinki-NLP model to bridge gaps between different languages. Moreover, it integrates BERT-based QA models customized for each language, enhancing precision in extracting answers by effectively capturing language-specific intricacies. The CLOR-QA system offers a promising solution to overcome language barriers by improving the accessibility of cross-lingual information.

Keywords: Cross Lingual · Natural Language Processing · Information Retrieval

1 Introduction

These days information comes in many forms and languages. To make it accessible to everyone, we need systems that can understand and respond to questions in different languages. It bridges the gap between different languages and provides a smooth flow of information from one language to another. The term 'cross-lingual' in CLOR-QA denotes its ability to interpret and respond to queries in multiple languages, thus bridging the gap between people who speak different languages. "Open retrieval" refers to finding and accessing information from various sources. This highlights the model's versatility and cross-lingual processing

ⓒ The Author(s), under exclusive license to Springer Nature Switzerland AG 2025
P. Delir Haghighi et al. (Eds.): iiWAS 2024, LNCS 15342, pp. 19–31, 2025.
https://doi.org/10.1007/978-3-031-78090-5_2

prowess, enabling seamless knowledge retrieval across language barriers. This paper talks about the development of a real-time cross-lingual open retrieval question answering with dynamic database integration system (CLOR-QA), a novel approach to tackle information scarcity and asymmetry.

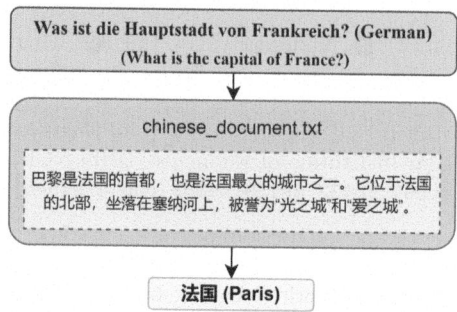

Fig. 1. Overview of CLOR-QA. If a question is given in L_1 (german), the model finds the answer in L_2 (chinese) and returns the answer in the desirable language.

This model leverages the Helsinki-NLP's Opus-MT models [13] for translation in our cross lingual open retrieval question-answering (QA) model. Specifically, we employed these pre-trained models to facilitate seamless translation between languages, enabling users to interact with the QA system in their preferred language. Figure 1 shows the overview of CLOR-QA.

1.1   Motivation and Contributions

CLOR-QA makes it possible to access wide pools of information without any constraints and even accept real time uploads for a more personalized response. This approach majorly impacts the travel and medical sector, but is not restricted to them. It offers advantages such as tailoring the model to organization-specific needs, ensuring better understanding and retrieval of multilingual content, and maintaining data privacy by keeping sensitive information within the organization. LLMs these days use centralized servers, there's a risk of sensitive linguistic data being stored and accessed, compromising user privacy and confidentiality, whereas we can have CLOR-QA model running locally without any external connection. The following are the key contributions of the paper:

1. A language to language cross lingual functionality with real time response with negligible processing time.
2. Capability to incorporate user defined documents into the system without requiring retraining and generate answers in real time.
3. Running locally to ensure user privacy and confidentiality without any external requirement.

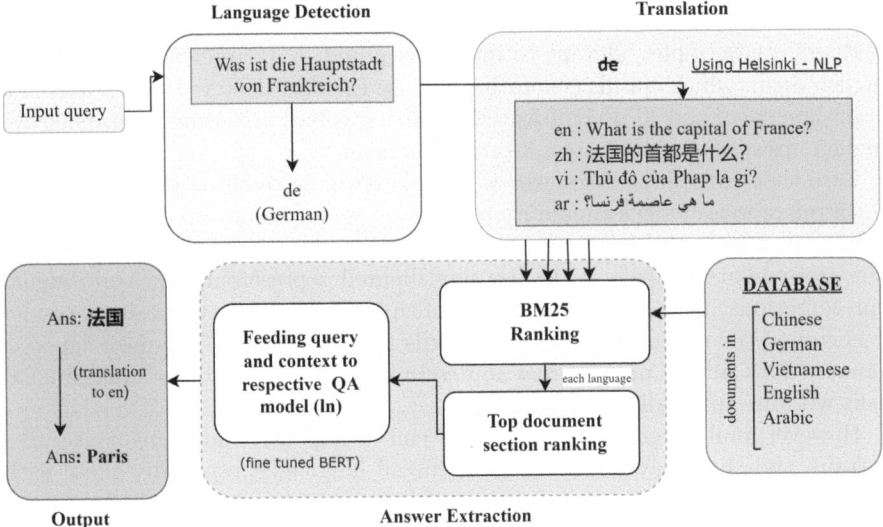

Fig. 2. Overall process of CLOR-QA

To enhance the accuracy and relevance of our QA model, we utilized T5 model [1] to generate a curated dataset for training and verification. This dataset played a pivotal role in fine-tuning our model, ensuring its proficiency in understanding and responding to user queries across diverse languages.

The combination of Helsinki-NLP's Translation capabilities and T5-generated QA datasets forms a foundation for the cross-lingual functionality of our model.

2   Related Work

Cross-lingual Question Answering (QA) has got significant attention in the recent years with the emergence of NLP systems capable of working with multiple languages, can understand and generate responses. The authors (Asai et al.) in [9] introduced the Cross-lingual Open-Retrieval Question Answering (XOR QA) framework, which has further catalyzed research efforts in this domain.

The authors evaluate a variety of approaches on XOR QA and find that the best performing approaches use a combination of machine translation and cross-lingual pre-trained models. In the XOR QA framework, there are three separate tasks that take place to facilitate cross-lingual document retrieval and question answering.

The tasks include XOR-Retrieve, which focuses on retrieving English Wikipedia paragraphs relevant to questions posed in a target language, XOR-English Span, which entails generating concise English answers to questions in a target language, and XOR-Full Answer, which involves providing comprehensive English answers to questions in a target language.

Zero-shot cross-lingual transfer was explored in research by (Chen et al.) [2] which refers to a model's capability to perform well on a task in a new language without requiring additional training on that language. One way to achieve zero-shot cross-lingual transfer is to use multilingual representations. Multilingual representations, trained on text from multiple languages gave positive results by encoding the semantic meaning of words and phrases in a language-agnostic manner. This allows multilingual representations to be used for cross-lingual tasks without any additional training.

However, multilingual representations can be expensive and time-consuming to train, and they may not be suitable for all languages, especially those with limited resources.

Large-scale knowledge bases (KBs) such as Freebase [8] and DBpedia [7] store huge amounts of structured knowledge. These KBs support a variety of natural language processing tasks, including question answering over knowledge base (KBQA), where models exploit the knowledge related to the questions and precisely identify the answers by reasoning through various KB relations.

In [17] by Zhang, C, the author focused on cross-lingual KBQA (xKBQA), which aims to answer questions over a KB in another language. The paper discusses supervised baselines, which utilize established methods for translating non-English data into English for evaluation, as well as zero-shot baselines.

A significant challenge in xKBQA is the lack of large-scale xKBQA datasets. Such datasets are quite expensive to annotate since the annotators are expected to be multilingual and have background knowledge about KBs. As a result, even the largest xKBQA dataset so far contains only a few hundred questions [5].

CLOR-QA takes inspiration from XOR-Full Answer [9] by using fine tuned BERT models to return the answers in target language, where the document from which retrieval is done can be of some other language. The use of knowledge bases [17] xKBQA for CLOR-QA can further extend its capabilities to act on untrained data from other languages using multilingual representations [2].

3   Methodology

The proposed framework features a pipeline (Fig. 2) that consists of three steps to get the answer in the desired language. Algorithm 1 also clearly depicts the basic functioning of the CLOR-QA model.

1. *Building database:* The user submits the documents for the model. These documents are stored within folders; the text from each document is then extracted and stored as a text file and segregated based on the language present. In document preprocessing the text is cleaned and all reads and writes are performed using UTF-8 such that no exceptions occur while the model

is running due to unrecognized Unicode characters. Non-ASCII characters, if present, are handled to avoid issues with text processing.

2. *Language detection and translation:* Language of the given input is identified using a standalone language identification (LangID) tool [4]. The query is translated to other languages except the detected language to act as input for answer extraction later. Query translation is done by leveraging Helsinki translators [13], the user queries are translated into the five supported languages: English, Chinese, German, Vietnamese, and Arabic. This allows a comprehensive search to be performed on the entire document corpus the user provides.

3. *Answer extraction:* As mentioned above, the user provided query is converted into the target languages using Helsinki transformers. Then BM25 [15] a well-known ranking algorithm for document ranking is used, to find the most relevant document upon which the document is subdivided into sections and ranked. The highest ranked section is passed to BERT [14] as the context for the query, the specific BERT QA model for that language then gives the most probable answer span. This approach retrieved the relevant documents and then extracted accurate answers from those documents without running BERT on other lower ranked documents where the probability of finding the desired answer was very low. This is further explained in the following subsection.

3.1   Answer Extraction

The following steps collectively form the architecture of this cross-lingual model, as shown in (Fig. 2) and in (Algorithm 1), leveraging techniques in information retrieval and natural language processing for effective multilingual query handling. The steps involved in answer extraction are:

1. *Text Tokenization*: It is achieved by breaking down the text into smaller units. Text tokenization is needed for the BM25 ranking to be done. In this way, each document's text is transformed into a list of tokens or words, which allows for a more granular analysis of the text.

2. *Implementation of BM25*: Document retrieval using BM25 relies on the utilization of the BM25 Okapi algorithm. The TREC [12] developed this variant of the popular BM25 algorithm. It includes additional parameters to ensure greater accuracy and allows the ranking of the documents to be done based on their relevance to the user's query. The ranking is based on how likely the answer for a given query will be in them-the highest-ranked document from each supported language.

3. *Training BERT models*: A question-answering pipeline is initialized for each language by training the base BERT models on QA pairs on SQuaD2.0, deQuAD 2.0 and WebQA datasets from the respective languages. Then we

have a QA model for each of the five languages capable of answering questions. Separate models prioritize contextual understanding and accuracy of the model instead of building one multilingual model. The pipeline is fed both the query and the context obtained in the earlier steps.

4. *Context search*: In this final step of each of the selected top documents is divided into sections, and they are then ranked similarly to what was done by the document retrieval algorithm used earlier. The section with the highest rank is then fed to the respective language's BERT model, , English [11], Vietnamese [18], Arabic [21], Chinese [20] and German [10] as context for the user's query (the model will find the answer span within this context and return the answer).

An **in-hand translator** is also built that integrates the Helsinki NLP model, a transformer-based language model. The translation capability is provided to enhance the translation function's efficiency for cases when the user is dealing with multilingual contexts.

Algorithm 1. CLOR-QA Model

Require: Query *query*
Ensure: Answer for each language
1: $id \leftarrow$ identify_language
2: **for each** *lang* **in** *lang.keys()* **do**
3:    load_docs(*lang*)
4: **end for**
5: $Question_{diffLang} \leftarrow query$
6: $Q \leftarrow Question_{diffLang}$
7: **for each** *lang* **in** *lang.keys()* **do**
8:    **if** $lang \neq id$ **then**
9:       $words \leftarrow En\_De(Q, lang, id)$ {Encoder and Decoder}
10:      $Question_{diffLang} \leftarrow words$
11:   **end if**
12: **end for**
13: $tokenized\_text, ans \leftarrow \{\}, \{\}$
14: $t\_text \leftarrow tokenized\_text$
15: **for each** *lang* **in** *doc.keys()* **do**
16:   $t\_text[lang] \leftarrow token\_docs(lang)$
17:   $bm25\_score, text\_top \leftarrow top\_doc(lang, Q, t\_text)$
18:   $answer \leftarrow get\_ans(text\_top, Q)$
19: **end for**
20: **return** answer

The above code as shown in Algorithm 1 begins by identifying the language of the query and loading relevant documents for each language. The query is then prepared and differentiated for each language, undergoing encoding and decoding processes to ensure cross-lingual understanding. After this, the documents are tokenized and retrieved, with BM25 scoring used to rank their relevance to the query. Finally, answers are extracted from the top-ranked documents for each language, resulting in a comprehensive set of answers tailored to the user's query in real-time.

4   Performance Evaluation and Results

The CLOR-QA model was tested on custom dataset based upon passages from Wikipedia pages of different countries [24]. 100 queries of different languages were tested for documents other than the input language. Figure 3 shows some sample selected questions, relevant passages, and answers in different languages from the dataset. The user has the capability to ask question in one language (L1), like Chinese, to documents written in another language (L2), such as German, and receive accurate answers in the respective language. Such flexibility empowers users to access relevant information effortlessly, irrespective of language differences.

Question	Answer	Relevant Passage
What is paris known for?	其丰富的历史、文化和艺术	总之，巴黎是一个充满活力、充满魅力的城市，无论你对历史、艺术、美食还是时尚感兴趣，都会让你流连忘返。
巴黎以什么闻名?	Their rich history, their culture, and their art.	Paris ist eine mehrsprachige Stadt und obwohl Französisch die offizielle Sprache ist
thủ đô của bhutan là gi?	Thimphu	Capital of Bhutan is Thimphu.
Wie viele Provinzen gibt es in China?	23	China comprises 23 provinces (China considers Taiwan its 23rd province)

Fig. 3. Sample questions, relevant passages, and answers in different languages from the dataset

After achieving promising results, conducting an evaluation of the model's performance becomes essential to validate it's efficiency and get a feedback to identify where it might be lacking. The evaluation process involves a two-step approach:

1. A T5, a text-to-text transformer, is employed to generate question-answer pairs based on the provided text.
2. The question-answering mechanism (CLOR-QA) is utilized to determine answers for each generated question. This mechanism is designed to extract relevant information based on the input text. These answers are matched with generated answers to perform an evaluation using different methods.

The CLOR-QA model has been evaluated using a set of 100 questions, with 25 questions in each of the four languages: German (de), English (en), Chinese (zh), and Vietnamese (vi). The model has been intentionally not provided any QA pairs with answers in the Arabic (ar) documents, but it has still been evaluated on a total of 100 questions to demonstrate the comparatively low score, showing its performance for detecting true negatives.

4.1   Initializing the T5 Model and Question Generation

With the help of user-provided documents, corpus of question-and-answer pairs for evaluation are generated. The given (Algorithm 2) outlines the execution of this approach. The documents are accessed, and their text is cleaned and formatted.

QA Generation: T5 model is initialized to generate the QA pairs based on the provided corpus. The question generation is done by isolating keywords using the T5 model as potential answers and leveraging the same model again to build questions using the entire paragraph and the keyword to generate the question.

Data structuring: The obtained question and keyword are then converted into a structured JSON with the question generated and the keyword as the answer as shown in Algorithm (2). This format includes paragraphs and QA pairs for each document. The questions and answers generated by the T5 model are organized and associated with the corresponding document and the paragraphs from which they were generated.

Performance optimization : To optimize the performance with the QA Data, the model weights for the T5 model are cached to ensure efficient processing in subsequent steps.

Algorithm 2. Question Generation

Require: *QA_Generation*
Ensure: Question-answer pairs *qa_pairs*
1: $model\_name \leftarrow' t5 - base'$
2: **for each** language **in** languages.keys() **do**
3:      $input\_id \leftarrow$ token_encode(*text*)
4:      $output\_id \leftarrow$ model_gen(*text*)
5:      **for** *ids* in *output_id* **do**
6:          $questions \leftarrow$ token_decode(*ids*)
7:      **end for**
8:      **for** *q* in *questions* **do**
9:          *qa_pairs.append(q, text)*
10:     **end for**
11: **end for**
12: **return** *qa_pairs*
13: Save data $\leftarrow$ JSON File

The above algorithm showcases the process of generating QA pairs using 't5-base' model, and iterates over each language specified in a dictionary. For each language, the input text is encoded into numerical IDs, and the model generates question IDs based on this input. These question IDs are then decoded into human-readable questions. After this, a QA pair is formed by combining the question with the original input text for each decoded question. Finally, the algorithm returns the list of generated QA pairs, optionally allowing for the data to be saved to a JSON file. This process enables the automatic creation of QA pairs across multiple languages, from a given data corpus given by the user.

The questions of the QA pairs is then fed in place of the user input, and the answer is scored based on its similarity to the provided answer. The T5 model was used as we felt that using T5 for answer span identification and question generation would bring bias to the model.

4.2   Precision, Recall and F1 Score

Precision, recall, and F1 scores were calculated for each language based on the model's performance on the 100 questions. Given that none of the answers to the 100 questions were present in the model's training data.

Interpretation: The results reveal that all languages (German, English, Chinese, Vietnamese) achieved high precision, recall, and F1 scores across all three metrics as shown by the bar graph plotted in Fig. 4.

The comparatively low score for Arabic aligns with expectations, given that the model was not provided answers for any of its questions during training, emphasizing the importance of having relevant training data for optimal model performance.

4.3   Semantic Similarity Metric: DistilUSE

To assess the semantic similarity between the generated and actual answers, we leverage the *distiluse-base-multilingual-cased-v2 model* [16]. This multilingual sentence embedding model converts both the generated and actual answers into vectors. Since, we can have a multilingual database, among the languages, the CLOR-QA model supports.

Table 1. Similarity Scores

Query	English	German	Chinese	Vietnamese	Arabic
English	0.98	0.84	0.74	0.87	0.82
German	0.92	0.96	0.67	0.78	0.71
Chinese	0.86	0.79	0.92	0.68	0.63
Vietnamese	0.84	0.82	0.72	0.94	0.64
Arabic	0.72	0.02	0.59	0.04	0.89

For this, we have taken sample questions of all 5 languages and the database is manually modified with respect to the sample questions, this is done to make sure every combination of query language and the document language (that contains the answer) is considered for a better evaluation.

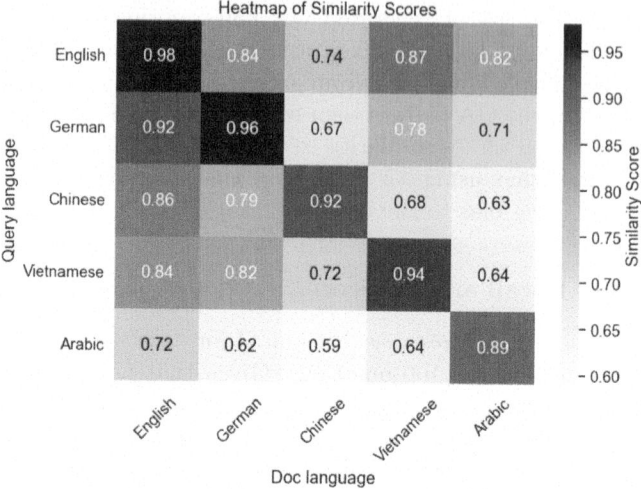

(a) Similarity scores for all 5 languages

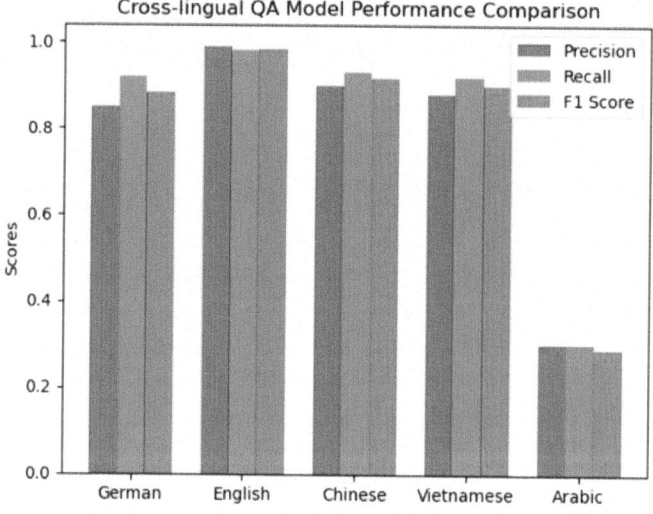

(b) Precision, Recall, and F1 score for all 5 languages

Fig. 4. Evaluation

Sentence Embedding and Mean-Pooling: The sentence embedding of both the generated and actual answers are created using distiluse-base-multilingual-cased-v2. These embedding are then mean-pooled to generate representative vectors for each answer.

Cosine Similarity Computation: The similarity score between the vectors of both the generated and actual answers are computed using cosine similarity.

This metric provides a quantitative measure of the semantic similarity between the generated and actual answers.

By employing this comprehensive evaluation metric, we ensure a nuanced assessment of our question-answering system's performance, considering both the question generation and answer extraction aspects, while leveraging advanced techniques in semantic similarity measurement. A heat map (Fig. 4) was created based on the data, using varying shades of colors to represent differences in the corresponding similarity scores.

Average Similarity Score: Values in the heat map (Fig. 4) represent the average similarity scores for 20 questions in each language (except Arabic). Scores range from 0.0 (low similarity) to 1.0 (high similarity).

Interpretation: (Fig. 4) and Table 1 provides an overview of the average similarity scores between questions and documents in each language. German, English, Chinese, and Vietnamese languages show relatively higher average similarity scores, indicating better matches.

If the query and documents are from the same language, the similarity percentages are 98%, 96%, 92%, 94% and 89% respectively for english, german, chinese, vietnamese and arabic. For cross lingual cases the similarity percentages can be seen in Table 1. Arabic language has a lower average similarity score, suggesting lower overall similarity with the arabic language documents.

The poor results for Arabic in cross-lingual models can be attributed to its complex morphology, including extensive use of affixes and root patterns, which complicate accurate translation and alignment with languages having simpler morphological structures. Additionally, the script and bidirectional text rendering pose technical challenges for models primarily designed around left-to-right scripts. We can enhance cross-lingual performance for Arabic by using specialized QA models designed to handle its unique linguistic features and script, as shown in ArabicaQA [23] by (Abdallah et al.).

5   Limitations

While CLOR performs exceptionally well for cross lingual tasks, a lot of things can be worked on to improve this further. Currently, this model doesn't incorporate entity recognition and linking techniques. The enhancement in [3] by (Tedeschi et al.) enriches the answer generation process with contextually relevant information, enhancing the system's understanding of complex content.

In this model, incorporating any new language means having translations from that language to all the other pre-existing ones and fine tuning QA model for it. This can be made more efficient by merging a pre-trained multilingual model like XLM-R with zero-shot transfer learning for cross-lingual question answering [6]. This approach can expand the system's capabilities to answer questions in languages it has never been directly trained on, showcasing adaptability and generalization.

6   Conclusion

In this paper, we proposed a cross lingual open-retrieval question answering model (CLOR-QA). This model has been trained on 5 languages English, Chinese, Vietnamese, Arabic and German. CLOR-QA helps the user to retrieve information from an other language when the asked question can be from some other language. The research done concluded that the results are better if the documents and queries pertain to a homogeneous subject instead of a wide range of diverse subjects as the answers can be more easily ranked and fed to the model. Experimental results on a varied user defined document database showcase that the model has good performance for cross lingual tasks. This can further be worked on for even better results which will solve many problems which require cross lingual functionality.

References

1. Raffel, C., et al.: Exploring the limits of transfer learning with a unified text-to-text transformer. T5. **21**, 1–67 (2020). https://jmlr.org/papers/volume21/20-074/20-074.pdf
2. Chen, G., et al.: Zero-shot cross-lingual transfer of neural machine translation with multilingual pretrained encoders. In: Proceedings of the 2021 Conference on Empirical Methods in Natural Language Processing (2021). https://doi.org/10.18653/v1/2021.emnlp-main.2
3. Tedeschi, S., Conia, S., Cecconi, F., Navigli, R.: Named entity recognition for entity linking: what works and what's next. In: Entity, pp. 2584–2596 (2021). https://aclanthology.org/2021.findings-emnlp.220/
4. langid (2016). https://pypi.org/project/langid/
5. Usbeck, R., Gusmita, R.H., Ngomo, A.-C.N., Saleem, M.: 9th challenge on question answering over linked data (QALD-9). Data, 58–64 (2018). http://ceur-ws.org/Vol-2241/paper-06.pdf
6. Choi, H., Kim, J., Joe, S., Min, S.-J., Gwon, Y.: Analyzing zero-shot cross-lingual transfer in supervised NLP tasks. Zero Shot (2021). https://doi.org/10.1109/icpr48806.2021.9412570
7. Auer, S., Bizer, C., Kobilarov, G., Lehmann, J., Cyganiak, R., Ives, Z.G.: DBPedia: a nucleus for a web of open Data. In: In: Aberer, K., et al. (eds.) The Semantic Web. ISWC ASWC 2007 LNCS, vol. 4825, pp. 722–735. Springer, Heidelberg (2007). https://doi.org/10.1007/978-3-540-76298-0_52
8. Bollacker, K.D., Evans, C., Paritosh, P., Sturge, T., Taylor, J.: Freebase. KB (2008). https://doi.org/10.1145/1376616.1376746
9. Asai, A., Kasai, J., Clark, J.H., Lee, K., Choi, E., Hajishirzi, H.: XOR QA: cross-lingual open-retrieval question answering. XOR QA (2021). https://doi.org/10.18653/v1/2021.naacl-main.46
10. Xu, F.: deutsche-telekom/bert-multi-english-german-squad2 · Hugging Face (2021). https://huggingface.co/deutsche-telekom/bert-multi-english-german-squad2
11. Alexaapo: BERT based pretrained model using SQuAD 2.0 dataset for question-answering (2021). https://github.com/alexaapo/BERT-based-pretrained-model-using-SQuAD-2.0-dataset

12. Robertson, Stephen & Walker, Steve & Jones, Susan & Hancock-Beaulieu, Micheline & Gatford, Mike. Okapi at TREC-3. (1994)
13. Helsinki-NLP (Language Technology Research Group at the University of Helsinki) (2021). https://huggingface.co/Helsinki-NLP
14. Paulmelki: This project aims at creating a search engine based on BERT language model. (GitHub) (2021). https://github.com/paulmelki/BERT_BM25_InformationRetrieval
15. Whissell, J.S., Clarke, C.L.A.: Improving document clustering using Okapi BM25 feature weighting. Inf. Retrieval J. **14**(5), 466–487 (2011). https://doi.org/10.1007/s10791-011-9163-y
16. Reimers, N., Gurevych, I.: Sentence-BERT: sentence embeddings using siamese BERT-networks. In: Proceedings of the 2019 Conference on Empirical Methods in Natural Language Processing (2019). http://arxiv.org/abs/1908.10084
17. Zhang, C.: Cross-lingual question answering over knowledge base as reading comprehension (2023). https://arxiv.org/abs/2302.13241
18. Pandya, H.A., Ardeshna, B., Bhatt, B.S.: Cascading adaptors to leverage English data to improve performance of question answering for low-resource languages (2021). https://arxiv.org/abs/2112.09866
19. google-bert/bert-base-chinese · Hugging Face (no date). https://huggingface.co/bert-base-chinese
20. Liu, Y., et al.: RoBERTa: a robustly optimized BERT pretraining approach.(2019). https://arxiv.org/abs/1907.11692
21. Ahmed, Z.: ZeyadAhmed/AraElectra-Arabic-SQUADV2-QA · Hugging face (2022). https://huggingface.co/ZeyadAhmed/AraElectra-Arabic-SQuADv2-QA
22. Zhao, Z., et al.: UER: an open-source toolkit for pre-training models. EMNLP-IJCNLP **2019**, 241 (2019)
23. Abdallah, A., et al.: ArabicaQA: a comprehensive dataset for arabic question answering.(2024). https://arxiv.org/abs/2403.17848
24. Wikipedia (2024). https://simple.wikipedia.org/wiki/List_of_countries

Financial News Classification Using Language Learning Models and Reinforcement Learning

William Jones Beckhauser[✉] and Renato Fileto

Department of Informatics and Statistics, Federal University of Santa Catarina,
Florianópolis, Santa Catarina, Brazil
beckhauserwilliam@gmail.com, r.fileto@ufsc.br

Abstract. This study examines the application of Reinforcement Learning (RL) in conjunction with Large Language Models (LLMs) for the multi-label classification of financial news. The research evaluates models of different scales, including GPT-4, Llama3 8B, and Llama3 70B, across two scenarios: (1) classification using only the query and corpus without RL, and (2) classification incorporating RL. A dataset consisting of 111,000 financial news articles was constructed through web scraping, with a sample of 1,000 articles manually labeled into three impact categories: weak, semi-strong, and strong. The experimental results demonstrate that smaller models, such as Llama3 8B, exhibit improved accuracy and coverage when RL is applied. However, larger models like GPT-4 displayed reduced performance under RL, suggesting challenges in adapting larger architectures for this task.

Keywords: Large Language Model · Reinforcement Learning · Multi-label Classification

1 Introduction

The classification of financial news is an important task for various economic agents [8], as information from news outlets directly influences investment decisions and asset movements in financial markets [7]. Governments, financial institutions, and investors use this information to monitor trends and anticipate market movements [1]. Given the vast amount of data continuously generated, it becomes necessary to develop efficient and accurate methods for processing and classifying this news to support decision-making [11].

Recently, Large Language Models (LLMs), such as GPT [9], Llama [5], and Gemini [13], started to become widely used for natural language processing tasks, such as text classification [14], information extraction [2], and text summarization [6]. These models have shown good results in various contexts, but their applicability to specific scenarios, such as financial news analysis and classification, still faces limitations. A particular challenge is adapting these models to improve accuracy in more abstract contexts [3], such as classifying the

P. Delir Haghighi et al. (Eds.): iiWAS 2024, LNCS 15342, pp. 32–37, 2025.
https://doi.org/10.1007/978-3-031-78090-5_3

news impact. This challenge can be addressed through Reinforcement Learning (RL) [10].

This paper proposes an investigation into the combination of RL and LLMs for the multi-label classification of financial news. The study involves construct-ing a corpus of 111,000 financial news articles obtained through web scraping, of which a sample of 1,000 articles was manually classified. The aim is to evaluate how RL can be used to improve the performance of language models, particularly in categorizing news into three impact classes (Weak, Semi-Strong, Strong), and to compare the effectiveness of RL in models of different sizes, such as Llama3 (8B and 70B) and GPT-4.

The contributions of this paper include: (i) the analysis of the integration between RL and LLMs in multi-label classification of financial news; (ii) the construction of a dataset with 111,000 financial news articles, named FIN111K; and (iii) a comparative evaluation of models of different sizes, with an emphasis on the benefits of using RL in smaller models (Llama3 8B).

2 Data Collection

The data used in this research were extracted via web scraping, encompass-ing titles and summaries of financial news from leading online portals in the sector. In selecting data sources, we adopted specific criteria for choosing elec-tronic journals. We opted for sources that provided information beyond titles and news descriptions, including publication dates, without requiring subscription or access restrictions, available in English, and relevant to the financial sector. We identified three main journals for the study, as described in previous research [12]: **The Economist**[1], **Financial Times**[2], and **Investors Chronicle**[3].

We used the BeautifulSoup library to extract news articles by analyzing the HTML content of the magazines. We defined search criteria using CSS selectors to locate relevant HTML elements. A loop was implemented to iterate through the identified elements and extract information from each news item. In cases where the journals used buttons to load more content, we employed the Python Selenium library. The results are available via GitHub[4].

During the collection process, we obtained a total of 140,652 news articles, distributed as follows: 19,333 from The Economist, 58,583 from Financial Times, and 62,736 from Investors Chronicle. After data cleaning, which included nor-malizing dates, removing duplicates, and deleting empty records, we consolidated a dataset of 111,000 financial news articles, which we named FIN111K.

For our experiments, we randomly selected 1,000 news articles using the random library, which were subsequently classified into three impact categories commonly used in the financial market: weak, semi-strong, and strong [4].

---

[1] Available at https://www.economist.com/.
[2] Available at https://www.ft.com/.
[3] Available at https://www.investorschronicle.co.uk/.
[4] https://github.com/WilliamBeckhauser/FIN111K.

3   Methodology

This section details the process of integrating LLMs with a RL agent for the classification of financial news, as show in Fig. 2. The process is structured into three main stages: prompt generation, LLM configuration, and validation with the RL agent. In the first stage, prompts are generated from the inputs, organized, and formatted to guide the LLM in the classification task. In the next stage, we adjust LLM parameters such as temperature and the number of output tokens to control the model's behavior and adapt the responses to the task requirements. Finally, the RL agent validates the LLM's outputs by checking if they match the labels in the annotated corpora. When discrepancies occur, the agent provides up to five iterations of corrective feedback, adjusting the responses until they align with the expected labels.

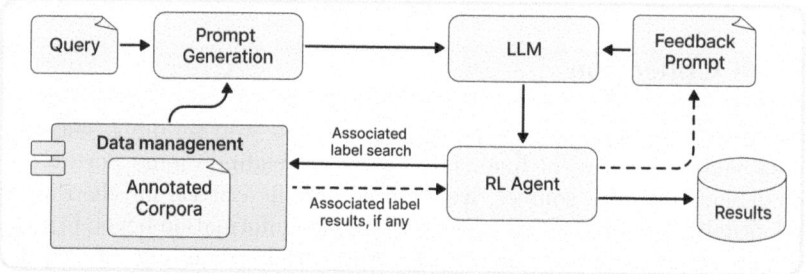

Fig. 1. Process for classifying financial news using LLM and RL.

3.1   Prompt Generation

The prompt generation phase processes two types of input: the query and the news itself, originally stored in the annotated corpus. The query defines the model's behavior, through the"System" parameter, and the instruction, which specifies the task to be performed, the context, and the expected output - in this case, the classification of the financial news into one of three categories: weak, semi-strong, or strong.

The information to be sent to the LLM to classify each news is organized in a prompt. Figure 2 illustrates a prompt, where the instructions, the context, and the output indicator are derived from the query, while the input data come from the annotated corpus.

3.2   LLM

In this stage, we adjusted the LLM settings and made an API call to send our prompt, which was generated in the Prompt Generation step. We modified

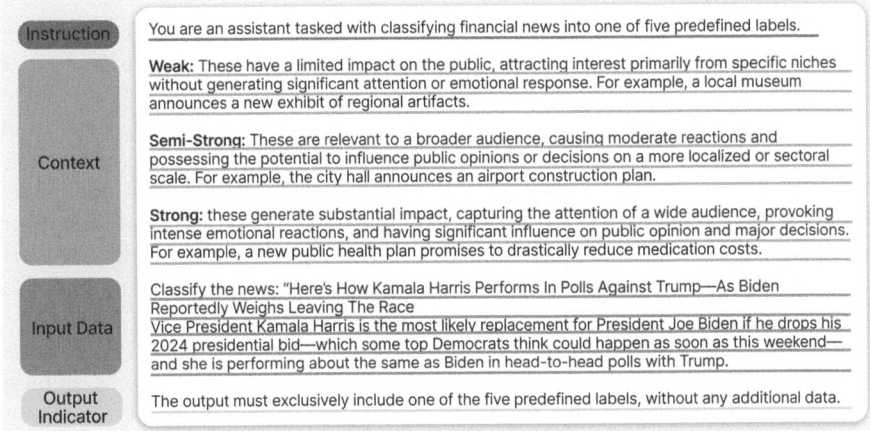

Fig. 2. Prompt Structure for Classifying Financial News

parameters such as temperature and the number of output tokens. The temperature setting affects the level of randomness in the model's results, with lower values producing more deterministic outputs and higher values providing greater variability. The number of output tokens is set to ensure that the responses are concise and maintain the appropriate length. For classification tasks with short labels, described with just one or two words, we set a maximum of 10 tokens per response. API calls using Llama3 models (8b and 70B) were made through the Deepinfra API[5], while GPT (4o) was accessed via the OpenAI API[6].

3.3 RL Agent

The RL agent performs a two-step validation process. The first step checks if the classification generated by the LLM matches one of the predefined categories in the system. If the classification does not align with any of the established labels, the agent provides feedback to adjust the LLM's output until it conforms to the expected categories.

In the second step, if the LLM's classification matches the predefined labels, the RL agent cross-references the result with the Annotated Corpus, which contains previously validated labels. The agent compares the LLM's classification with the labels present in the corpus. In case of a discrepancy between the LLM's output and the corpus label, the agent provides feedback, consisting of corrections that identify the discrepancy and indicate the correct label. This validation and feedback cycle can be repeated until the output aligns with the corpus label or up to five times (parameter) per document to be classified. The feedback cycles allow the model to adjust iteratively.

---

[5] https://deepinfra.com/models.

[6] https://platform.openai.com/docs/models.

4   Experiment

This section describes the experiments conducted for multi-label classification of financial news. The dataset was tested in two distinct scenarios: (1) classification using only the query and corpus, without the involvement of the RL agent; and (2) classification using the RL agent. In this experiment, a total of 1,000 news items were used, with 80% allocated for training with RL and 20% for model evaluation. The model parameters were set to produce a maximum of 10 output tokens, with the temperature ranging from 0.1 to 0.3, where 0.1 yielded the best performance. A detailed description of the experiments and the dataset employed can be accessed on GitHub[7].

As shown in Table 1, the Llama3 8B model combined with RL yielded the best overall performance, achieving 89% precision (an increase of 38% points) and 85% coverage (an increase of 26% points). These results indicate significant improvement compared to the same model without RL.

Table 1. Multi-label Classification Results of Financial News Using LLM and RL.

Model	Accuracy	Precision	Coverage	F1-Score
Llama3 8B	70%	51%	59%	53%
Llama3 70B	71%	64%	61%	61%
GPT-4o	80%	84%	79%	**79%**
Llama3 8B + RL	**87%**	**89%**	**85%**	**79%**
Llama3 70B + RL	79%	83%	78%	77%
GPT-4o + RL	73%	71%	73%	71%

On the other hand, the GPT-4o model combined with RL showed a slight reduction in both precision and coverage compared to GPT-4o without RL, which can be attributed to the model's lower flexibility, possibly preferring to rely on its initial training configurations.

The consistency in coverage and precision for Llama3 70B + RL suggests that the effectiveness of the RL agent may vary depending on the size and complexity of the underlying model. While the largest Llama model (70B) showed modest improvements with RL, the smallest one (8B) benefited more significantly.

5   Conclusion and Future Work

This study analyzed the use of LLM combined with RL for the classification of financial news. The combination resulted in performance improvements in smaller-scale models, such as Llama3 8B, suggesting a direction for further investigation. For future work, we plan to incorporate Retrieval-Augmented Generation (RAG) techniques to expand the context in prompt generation, in addition to conducting experiments with a greater diversity of models and sample sizes.

---

[7] https://github.com/WilliamBeckhauser/FIN111K.

Acknowledgements. This work was supported by a 2022 CNPq Universal grant, FAPESC grant 2021TR1510, the Print CAPES-UFSC Automation 4.0 Project, and by the Céos project, financed by the Public Ministry of Santa Catarina State (MPSC).

References

1. Ashtiani, M.N., Raahemi, B.: News-based intelligent prediction of financial markets using text mining and machine learning: a systematic literature review. Expert Syst. Appl. **217**, 119509 (2023)
2. Biswas, A., Talukdar, W.: Robustness of structured data extraction from in-plane rotated documents using multi-modal large language models (LLM). J. Artif. Intell. Res. (2024)
3. Chang, Y., et al.: A survey on evaluation of large language models. ACM Trans. Intell. Syst. Technol. **15**(3), 1–45 (2024)
4. Fama, E.F.: Efficient capital markets: a review of theory and empirical work. J. Financ. **25**(2), 383–417 (1970)
5. Gao, P., et al.: LLaMA-adapter v2: parameter-efficient visual instruction model. arXiv preprint arXiv:2304.15010 (2023)
6. Jin, H., Zhang, Y., Meng, D., Wang, J., Tan, J.: A comprehensive survey on process-oriented automatic text summarization with exploration of LLM-based methods. arXiv preprint arXiv:2403.02901 (2024)
7. Kamal, S., Sharma, S., Kumar, V., Alshazly, H., Hussein, H.S., Martinetz, T.: Trading stocks based on financial news using attention mechanism. Mathematics **10**(12) (2022). https://doi.org/10.3390/math10122001
8. Li, Y., Wang, S., Ding, H., Chen, H.: Large language models in finance: a survey. In: Proceedings of the fourth ACM International Conference on AI in Finance, pp. 374–382 (2023)
9. Liu, X., et al.: GPT understands, too. AI Open (2023)
10. Rita, M., Strub, F., Chaabouni, R., Michel, P., Dupoux, E., Pietquin, O.: Countering reward over-optimization in LLM with demonstration-guided reinforcement learning. arXiv preprint arXiv:2404.19409 (2024)
11. Samadova, N.: Information sources of economic competence analysis of economic subjects and their classification. Academia Repository **4**(12), 278–283 (2023)
12. Strauß, N.: Framing sustainable finance: A critical analysis of op-eds in the financial times. Int. J. Bus. Commun. **60**(4), 1427–1440 (2023)
13. Team, G., et al.: Gemini: a family of highly capable multimodal models. arXiv preprint arXiv:2312.11805 (2023)
14. Zhang, Y., et al.: Pushing the limit of LLM capacity for text classification. arXiv preprint arXiv:2402.07470 (2024)

ExtractGPT: Exploring the Potential of Large Language Models for Product Attribute Value Extraction

Alexander Brinkmann[1]([📧]) [ID], Roee Shraga[2] [ID], and Christian Bizer[1] [ID]

[1] University of Mannheim, 68131 Mannheim, Germany
{alexander.brinkmann,christian.bizer}@uni-mannheim.de
[2] Worcester Polytechnic Institute, Worcester Polytechnic Institute, Worcester, USA
rshraga@wpi.edu

Abstract. E-commerce platforms require structured product data in the form of attribute-value pairs to offer features such as faceted product search or attribute-based product comparison. However, vendors often provide unstructured product descriptions, necessitating the extraction of attribute-value pairs from these texts. BERT-based extraction methods require large amounts of task-specific training data and struggle with unseen attribute values. This paper explores using large language models (LLMs) as a more training-data efficient and robust alternative. We propose prompt templates for zero-shot and few-shot scenarios, comparing textual and JSON-based target schema representations. Our experiments show that GPT-4 achieves the highest average F1-score of 85% using detailed attribute descriptions and demonstrations. Llama-3-70B performs nearly as well, offering a competitive open-source alternative. GPT-4 surpasses the best PLM baseline by 5% in F1-score. Fine-tuning GPT-3.5 increases the performance to the level of GPT-4 but reduces the model's ability to generalize to unseen attribute values.

Keywords: Information Extraction · Product Attribute Value Extraction · Large Language Models · E-commerce

1 Introduction

Online shoppers often filter and compare products using criteria such as brand, color, or screen size to find products that fit their needs [14]. However, many vendors only provide textual product descriptions [17,30]. To enable a precise faceted search for products, attribute-value pairs need to be extracted from these textual product descriptions [25,29]. Figure 1 shows an example offer for a toothbrush set including attribute-value annotations. In the figure, attribute names are marked with colored boxes. Attribute values are underlined.

State-of-the-art techniques for attribute value extraction (AVE) often rely on pre-trained language models (PLMs) [3,17,22,25,30] such as BERT [4]. However, these methods require large amounts of task-specific training data and

© The Author(s), under exclusive license to Springer Nature Switzerland AG 2025
P. Delir Haghighi et al. (Eds.): iiWAS 2024, LNCS 15342, pp. 38–52, 2025.
https://doi.org/10.1007/978-3-031-78090-5_4

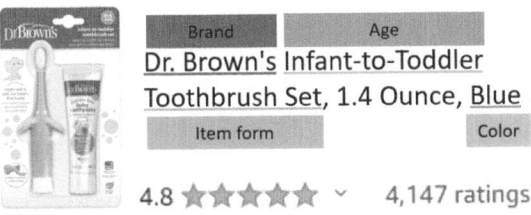

Fig. 1. An example product title with tagged attribute-value pairs. Vendors include product attribute values in the title to enhance visibility.

struggle to generalize to unseen attribute values. Large language models (LLMs) like GPT-3.5 [11], GPT-4 [10] and Llama-3 [5] have proven effective in mitigating these shortcomings for various natural language processing tasks [2,20]. This paper proposes and evaluates prompt templates for instructing LLMs to extract attribute values in zero-shot and few-shot scenarios. We test different approaches to represent the target attributes for the zero-shot scenario. In the few-shot scenario, we evaluate three methods for using training data: (i) providing example attribute values, (ii) selecting in-context demonstrations, and (iii) fine-tuning the LLM. We compare the performance of the best prompt template/LLM combination with state-of-the-art PLM-based methods fine-tuned with varying amounts of training data. The contributions of the paper are as follows:

1. We propose different prompt templates for instructing LLMs about the target attribute schema of the AVE task. The templates cover use cases with and without task-specific training data.
2. Our experiments show that LLMs require a small set of task-specific training data for picking example values and/or demonstrations to reach decent performance.
3. Our comparison of the different approaches to use training data shows that providing demonstrations is more effective than providing example values.
4. We show that GPT-4 outperforms all other LLMs with a top average F1 score of 85%. The best open-source LLM, Llama-3-70B, has an F1 score only 3% lower than GPT-4's top score, making it a strong open-source alternative.
5. Comparing LLMs and PLMs, we show that LLMs are more training data-efficient. Given the same amount of training data, GPT-4 achieves a 5% higher average F1 score and is 19% better with unseen values than the best PLM-based method AVEQA.
6. Our experiments show that a fine-tuned GPT-3.5 model has a similar performance as GPT-4 but loses some of its ability to generalize to unseen attribute values.

The paper is structured as follows. First, we review related work. Next, we describe the experimental setup (Sect. 3) before delving into prompt engineering. We introduce zero-shot prompt engineering (Sect. 4) as well as in-context learning and fine-tuning (Sect. 5) to evaluate the usage of task-specific training data. Lastly, we compare LLM- and PLM-based methods in Sect. 6. The code and data for replicating our experiments are available online[1].

2   Related Work

Attribute Value Extraction. The goal of AVE is to extract specific attribute values from unstructured text, such as product titles and descriptions, based on a pre-defined target schema, which represents a set of target attributes. Early works used domain-specific rules to extract attribute-value pairs [16,27] from product descriptions. Initial learning-based methods required extensive feature engineering and did not generalize to unknown attributes and values [7,13,21]. Recent approaches use BiLSTM-CRF architectures, with OpenTag [29] and its extension SU-OpenTag [22] utilizing BERT [4] for encoding. AdaTag [23] employs BERT [4] and a mixture-of-experts module for AVE. Recently, many works approach AVE as a question-answering task, using different PLMs to encode the target attribute, product category, and product title [15,17,25]. The PLM-based models SU-OpenTag, AVEQA and MAVEQA serve as baselines for our experiments. OA-Mine [28] employs BERT [4] to mine for unknown attributes and values. Brinkmann et al. use LLMs to extract and normalize attribute values [1]. LLM-ensemble employs an ensemble of LLMs for AVE [6]. Other works deal with AVE from multiple modalities like texts and images [18,30].

Information Extraction Using LLMs. LLMs have successfully been used for information extraction tasks in other application domains: Wang et al. [19] and Parekh et al. [12] employed OpenAI's LLMs to extract structured data about events from unstructured text. Goel et al. [8] combine LLMs with human expertise to annotate patient-related information in medical texts. Khorashadizadeh et al. [9] explore in-context learning for LLMs to generate knowledge graphs from text.

3   Experimental Setup

Our main research question is how to instruct an LLM to extract the values of the attributes mentioned in the target schema. This section presents our setup to approach this question experimentally, including datasets, LLMs, and evaluation metrics.

3.1   Datasets

We use the benchmark datasets OA-Mine [28] and AE-110K [22], which have been used by related work [17,24,25]. Both datasets consist of English product offers with annotated attribute-value pairs. The MAVE [25] dataset is not considered, because its attribute-value pairs are annotated using an ensemble

---

[1] https://github.com/wbsg-uni-mannheim/ExtractGPT.

of fine-tuned AVEQA models [17] and are not manually verified, hence during human-inspection we found numerous annotation errors [31]. Other datasets used in the related work are not publicly available [23,29].

OA-Mine. We use the human-annotated product offers of the OA-Mine dataset[2] [28]. The subset includes 10 product categories, with up to 200 product offers per category. Each category has between 8 and 15 attributes, resulting in a total of 115 unique attributes. Attributes with the same name but different product categories are treated as distinct attributes. We do not apply any further pre-processing to the subset of OA-Mine.

AE-110K. The AE-110K dataset[3] comprises triples of product titles, attributes and attribute values from the AliExpress Sports & Entertainment category [22]. Product offers are derived by grouping the triples by title. The subset contains 10 categories, with up to 400 offers per category. For each category, 6 to 17 attributes are known, resulting in a total of 101 unique attributes.

Training/Test Split. The subsets OA-Mine and AE-110K are split into training and test sets in a 75:25 ratio, stratified by product category to ensure the presence of all attributes in both sets. To evaluate the impact of the amount of training data on LLM performance, we create small and large training sets for OA-Mine and AE-110K. The large training sets include all available training data. For the small training set, 20% of the product offers per category are sampled from the available training data. Table 1 presents statistics for OA-Mine and AE-110K.

Table 1. Statistics for OA-Mine and AE-110K.

	OA-Mine			AE-110K		
	Small Train	Large Train	Test	Small Train	Large Train	Test
Attribute-Value Pairs	1,467	7,360	2,451	859	4,360	1,482
Unique Attribute-Value Pairs	1,120	4,177	1,749	302	978	454
Product Offers	286	1,452	491	311	1,568	524

Example Extractions. Table 2 shows example product offer titles, target attributes and attribute values from the datasets. The attribute values are underlined in the titles. The lower part of the table shows the attribute values extracted by GPT4 using the prompt templates list, json-val and json-val-dem which will be introduced in Sects. 4 and 5. The extraction of attribute values is either correct (✓) or incorrect (×).

---

[2] https://github.com/xinyangz/OAMine/tree/main/data.
[3] https://raw.githubusercontent.com/lanmanok/ACL19_Scaling_Up_Open_Tagging/master/publish_data.txt.

Table 2. Example product offers, attribute-value pairs and extracted attribute values for the two datasets OA-Mine and AE-110k.

Dataset	OA-Mine	OA-Mine	AE-110k
Category	Vitamin	Coffee	Guitar
Attribute	Net Content	Flavor	Body Material
Title	NOW Supplements, Vitamin A (Fish Liver Oil) 25,000 IU, Essential Nutrition, <u>250</u> Softgels	Cafe Du Monde Coffee Chicory, 15-Ounce (Pack of 3)	Factory customization Acoustic Guitar Sitika Solid Spruce Vintage Sunburst high-quality
Target Value	250	Coffee Chicory	Solid Spruce
list	n/a ×	n/a ×	Sitika Solid Spruce ×
json-val	250 Softgels ×	n/a ×	Solid Spruce ✓
json-val-dem	250 ✓	Coffee Chicory ✓	Solid Spruce ✓
	(a)	(b)	(c)

3.2 Large Language Models

This paper evaluates the proprietary LLMs GPT-3.5 and GPT-4 as well as the open-source LLMs Llama-3-8B and Llama-3-70B [5]. Table 3 lists the LLMs with the exact model name, number of parameters, and access via API or number of GPUs for running the LLM locally. We access GPT-3.5 and GPT-4 through the OpenAI API. The open-source models Llama-3-8B[4] and Llama-3-70B[5] are publicly available and were run on local GPUs. The temperature parameter of all LLMs is set to 0 to reduce the randomness. We use up to four NVIDIA RTX A6000 GPUs to run the open-source LLMs and fine-tune the PLM-based baselines.

Table 3. List of evaluated LLMs.

LLM	Exact Name	Model Size	API/GPUs
GPT-3.5 [11]	gpt-3.5-turbo-0613	175B	API
GPT-4 [10]	gpt-4-0613	unknown	API
Llama-3-8B	Meta-Llama-3-8B-Instruct	8B	1
Llama-3-70B	Meta-Llama-3-70B-Instruct	70B	4

3.3 Evaluation Metrics

We report the F1-score, calculated by categorizing predictions into five groups as per previous works [17,22,23,25]. The five categories are NN (no predicted

---

[4] https://huggingface.co/meta-llama/Meta-Llama-3-8B-Instruct.

[5] https://huggingface.co/meta-llama/Meta-Llama-3-70B-Instruct.

value, no ground truth value), NV (predicted value, no ground truth value), VN (no predicted value, ground truth value), VC (predicted value matches ground truth value), and VW (predicted value does not match ground truth value). The F1-score is derived from the precision $(P = VC/(NV + VC + VW))$, recall $(R = VC/(VN + VC + VW))$, and the formula $F1 = 2PR/(P + R)$.

4   Zero-Shot Prompt Engineering

This section discusses a zero-shot scenario, meaning that no training data is available. The main research question in this scenario is: how to describe the target schema to the LLMs, specifically, how to define which attributes should be extracted. First, we introduce the structure of our prompt templates. Afterwards, we analyze the representation of the target schema along two dimensions: the level of detail of the attribute descriptions and the format in which the target schema is presented.

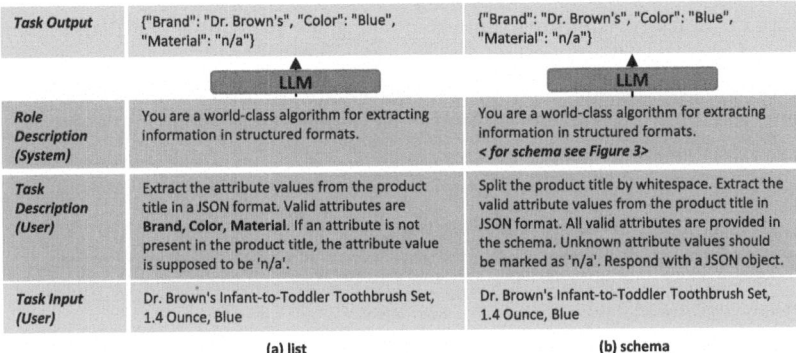

Fig. 2. Zero-shot prompt templates `list` and `schema`.

4.1   Prompt Templates

Prompt design is key for having LLMs reach a high performance [26]. Thus, we create various prompt templates to systematically analyze different target attribute representations. All templates instruct the LLM to simultaneously extract attributes from product titles, leveraging synergies between them. Each template consists of four chat messages: role description (blue), task description (blue), task input (green) and task output (grey), as shown in Fig. 2. The role description outlines the LLM's behaviour. The task description provides AVE instructions, including pre-processing the product title, formatting the response as JSON, and marking absent attributes as n/a. The task input contains the product title. Role and task description are static whereas task input and task output change with each extraction. The chat prompt template combines role description, task description, and task input, with each message having a specific type: `system` for the role description, and `user` for the task description and input. The LLM's response, the task output, is supposed to be a JSON document adhering to the target schema, enabling the evaluation of the task output.

4.2   Representation of the Target Schema

This section investigates how different target schema representations affect the performance of LLMs on the attribute value extraction task. The representations are evaluated based on two dimensions: (i) level of detail and (ii) representation format. Depending on the level of detail an attribute in the target schema is described by its name, a description, and example values. We evaluate four representation formats:

- `list` enumerates the attribute names as illustrated in Fig. 2 (a).
- `textual` articulates names (green), descriptions (red) and example values in plain text as depicted in Fig. 3 (a).
- `compact` densely combines names (green), descriptions (red) and example values (blue) as shown in Fig. 3 (b).
- `json` represents names (green), descriptions (red) and example values (blue) using the JSON schema vocabulary[6] as depicted in Fig. 3 (c).

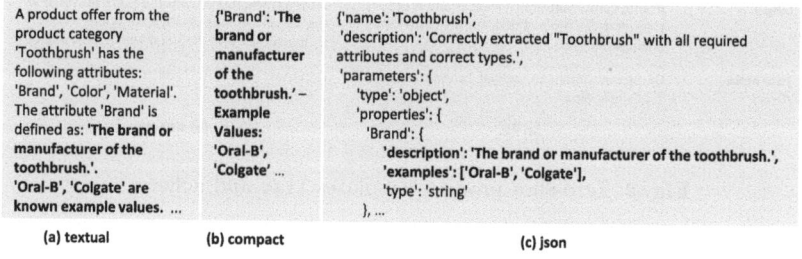

(a) textual   (b) compact   (c) json

Fig. 3. Target schema representation formats (a) `textual`, (b) `compact` and (c) `json`.

The product category determines the set of attributes in the target schema. On average, OA-Mine and AE-110k define 10 attributes per product category. For demonstration purposes, Fig. 2 and Fig. 3 display a subset of the attributes for the 'toothbrush' category. The `schema` prompt template integrates the `textual`, `compact` and `json` schema representations into the role description as seen in Fig. 2. We generate attribute descriptions using GPT-3.5 since the original datasets do not provide descriptions. In the zero-shot scenario, example values are absent as they need to be selected from training data. Section 5.1 covers the use of example values.

---

[6] https://json-schema.org/.

Table 4. F1-scores for zero-shot prompt templates. The highest F1-score per dataset is marked in bold.

Model	OA-Mine				AE-110K			
	list	textual	compact	json	list	textual	compact	json
GPT-3.5	63.3	62.7	65.1	64.8	61.4	61.3	**63.6**	61.5
GPT-4	**69.1**	68.9	68.8	68.1	56.3	55.5	53.7	62.1
Llama-3-8B	62.9	65.2	64.6	43.2	57.8	57.7	58.1	22.0
Llama-3-70B	67.3	64.3	63.9	49.9	58.9	52.0	56.0	30.0

As shown in Table 4, overall, GPT-3.5, GPT-4 and the Llama-3 LLMs achieve zero-shot F1-scores above 60%. None of the target schema representations has a clear advantage over the other representations across all LLMs. The `json` representation is difficult to interpret for all open-source, while for GPT-3.5 and GPT-4 this drop in performance is not observed. Once we add example values in Sect. 5, GPT-3.5 and GPT-4 benefit most from the `json` representation.

5 Using Training Data

This section explores the scenario where training data is available. We investigate using the training data for (i) adding example values to the target schema representations, (ii) sampling demonstrations for in-context learning, and (iii) fine-tuning GPT-3.5.

5.1 Example Values

This section explores the effect of adding attribute values from the training set to the target schema representations introduced in Section 4. The evaluation is conducted in two steps. First, we compare the representation formats `textual`, `compact`, and `json` with example values (`val`) to the best representation without example values (`compact`). Second, we assess how different amounts of sampled attribute values affect the performance of the best representation. By default, up to 10 unique values are randomly sampled for each attribute from the training set. If less than 10 unique values are found, all available values are retrieved.

Target Schema Representations. Table 5 shows the impact of adding attribute values to the target schema representations. The average F1 performance of GPT and Llama-3 LLMs increases by 5% to 16% compared to the `compact` representation without attribute values. OpenAI's LLMs perform best with the *json* representation, while Llama-3 LLMs excel with the *compact* representation.

Amount of Example Values. We now evaluate the impact of the number of unique example values sampled from the training set on the performance of GPT-3.5 and GPT-4. Samples of 3, 5, and 10 example values per attribute

Table 5. F1-scores for prompt templates with example values. The highest F1-score per dataset is marked in bold.

Model	OA-Mine				AE-110K			
	0-val	10-val			0-val	10-val		
	compact	compact	textual	json	compact	compact	textual	json
GPT-3.5	65.1	60.7	61.4	69.8	63.6	55.0	40.5	**74.4**
GPT-4	68.8	64.8	66.4	**75.0**	53.7	53.5	46.5	70.1
Llama-3-8B	64.6	67.5	70.9	25.5	58.1	69.9	70.6	20.3
Llama-3-70B	63.9	71.1	73.0	70.3	56.0	66.0	64.0	50.0

are taken. For each configuration, we calculate the total number of sampled unique attribute values (Unique) and the percentage of test set attribute values included in the sampled set (Seen). Table 6 shows that providing too few (3) or too many (10) example values harms GPT-3.5's performance, while GPT-4 maintains consistent F1-scores, peaking with 5 example values. The sampled attribute values represent only 6% to 28% of all unique test set values, indicating that simply looking up these values is not enough to achieve F1-scores above 70%. Both models derive general patterns from the `json-val` target schema representation. Including example values increases the number of tokens and associated costs. Comparing costs per 1k extracted attribute-value pairs of GPT-3.5 and GPT-4 to the shortest `list` prompt template, `json-val` prompts are three times more expensive.

Table 6. F1-scores for prompt templates with example values. The highest F1-score per dataset is marked in bold.

Prompt	OA-Mine				AE-110K			
	Unique	Seen	GPT-3.5	GPT-4	Unique	Seen	GPT-3.5	GPT-4
list	0	0%	63.3	69.1	0	0%	61.4	56.34
json-3-val	283	6%	74.4	74.81	172	20%	66.6	69.49
json-5-val	429	9%	74.0	74.55	222	24%	69.7	72.76
json-10-val	719	13%	69.8	75.02	271	28%	74.4	70.08

5.2 In-Context Demonstrations

This section examines the impact of adding in-context learning demonstrations from the training set to the prompt templates from three perspectives: (i) the number of demonstrations selected, (ii) the effect of training set size on LLM performance, and (iii) a comparison of GPT and Llama-3 LLMs.

Prompt Templates. The prompt templates list and the schema, as introduced in Sect. 4, are extended to include demonstrations (dem). Figure 4 illustrates this extension. Each demonstration (light blue) consists of a task input and a task output. The demonstrations are added to the chat prompt following the role and task description (blue). The task description (blue) is then repeated, followed by the task input (green). Task input and output of the demonstration are of the message types user and assistant, respectively.

Role Description (System)	You are a world-class algorithm for extracting information in structured formats.
Task Description (User)	Extract the attribute values from the product title in a JSON format. Valid attributes are **Brand, Color, Material**. If an attribute is not present in the product title, the attribute value is supposed to be 'n/a'.
Demonstration – Task Input (User)	Quip Kids Electric Toothbrush Set - Electric toothbrush with multi-use cover (Green)
Demonstration –Task Output (Assistent)	{"Brand": "Quip", "Color": "Green", "Material": "n/a"}
Task Description (User)	Extract the attribute values from the product title in a JSON format. Valid attributes are **Brand, Color, Material**. If an attribute is not present in the product title, the attribute value is supposed to be 'n/a'.
Task Input (User)	Dr. Brown's Infant-to-Toddler Toothbrush Set, 1.4 Ounce, Blue

Fig. 4. Prompt template for in-context learning.

Amount of Demonstrations. The first dimension we explore is the number of demonstrations selected from the training set. We evaluate GPT-3.5 using the prompt template list-dem with 3, 10 and 15 demonstrations. To find semantic similarity demonstrations, the product titles of the training demonstrations are embedded using OpenAI's embedding model text-embedding-ada-002[7]. The embedded demonstrations with the greatest cosine similarity to the embedded task input are considered to be semantically similar. Table 7 shows that the highest F1-score of 79.9% is achieved with 10 demonstrations, which is 2% better than with 3 demonstrations. Usage fees for hosted LLMs like GPT-3.5 depend on the number of tokens in the input prompts. Increasing the number of tokens by adding demonstrations can significantly raise usage fees. The right columns in Table 7 illustrate the cost for extracting one thousand attribute values based on December 2023 OpenAI usage fees[8]. Using 10 demonstrations is twice as expensive as using 3, and using 15 demonstrations increases the cost further without improving the F1-score.

Amount of Training Data. We evaluate the training data efficiency of LLMs by assessing the list-dem prompt with 10 demonstrations from both small (S) and large (L) training sets for all LLMs. For GPT-4, we also report results for

---

[7] https://platform.openai.com/docs/guides/embeddings/.

[8] https://openai.com/pricing.

Table 7. F1-scores and extraction cost of the `list-dem` prompt template with different amounts of demonstrations. The highest F1-score per dataset is marked in bold.

	OA-Mine		AE-110K		Average	
	F1	$ for 1k A/V pairs	F1	$ for 1k A/V pairs	F1	$ for 1k A/V pairs
3	77.0	0.0746	79.1	0.0664	78.1	0.0705
10	**77.5**	0.1558	**82.2**	0.1259	**79.9**	0.1408
15	76.9	0.2133	82.2	0.1643	79.6	0.1888

Table 8. F1-scores for selecting demonstrations from either the small training set (S) or the large training set (L). The highest F1-score per dataset is marked in bold.

Prompt	Model	OA-Mine		AE-110K		Average	
		S	L	S	L	S	L
list-dem	GPT-3.5	77.5	77.7	82.2	82.3	79.9	80.0
	GPT-4	78.2	78.0	80.4	82.6	79.3	80.3
	Llama-3-8B	79.0	77.9	81.7	81.8	80.4	79.8
	Llama-3-70B	81.8	81.5	84.0	84.1	82.9	82.8
json-val-dem	GPT-4	80.2	**82.2**	85.5	**87.5**	82.8	**84.9**

the `json-val-dem` prompt, as GPT-4 benefits from extended attribute representation and demonstrations. Table 8 shows a marginal F1-score gain when demonstrations are sampled from the larger training set. GPT-4 gains 2% with the large training set using the `json-val-dem` prompt, achieving the best average F1-score of 85%. In the following, we refer to the combination of the `json-val-dem` prompt and GPT-4 as ExtractGPT.

Comparison to Llama-3 LLMs. Table 8 also reports results for Llama-3-8B and Llama-3-70B. The best-performing open-source LLM, Llama-3-70B, is only 2% worse than GPT-4, making it a competitive alternative if sufficient GPUs are available. Llama-3-8B is a more compute-efficient option, with an average F1-score only 3% lower than Llama-3-70B. All LLMs achieve higher F1-scores on AE-110K than on OA-Mine, indicating that OA-Mine is more challenging than AE-110K. This is because OA-Mine has four times more unique attribute values than AE-110k and 82% of the unique values in OA-Mine's test set are unseen, compared to 71% in AE-110K.

5.3   Fine-Tuning

In this section, we evaluate the impact of fine-tuning on the AVE performance of GPT-3.5. First, we compare the fine-tuned GPT-3.5 models with Extract-GPT from Sect. 5.2. Second, we examine if fine-tuning imparts general knowledge useful for extracting attribute values from products not in the training set.

Procedure. GPT-3.5 is fine-tuned using the training sets of OA-Mine and AE-110K. The training records are formatted with `list` and `json-val` templates, generating role descriptions, task descriptions, and task inputs, with task outputs containing attribute-value pairs. For `json-val`, 10 example values per attribute are sampled from the training set. These pre-processed datasets are uploaded to OpenAI's fine-tuning API[9] and GPT-3.5 is fine-tuned for three epochs on these datasets using the OpenAI's default parameters.

Performance. We evaluate the F1-scores and extraction costs of fine-tuned models compared to ExtractGPT. Table 9 shows that fine-tuned GPT-3.5 models achieve similar F1-scores to ExtractGPT, averaging 85%. Fine-tuned GPT-3.5 models significantly reduce API usage costs. Extracting 1k attribute-value pairs costs up to 70 times more with ExtractGPT than with the fine-tuned GPT-3.5 models. Considering fine-tuning and extraction costs, it is more cost-effective to fine-tune GPT-3.5 with the `list` prompt on the large training set, starting with about 500 attribute-value pairs, than to use ExtractGPT.

Table 9. F1-scores and the extraction cost ($ for 1k A/V pairs) of fine-tuned GPT-3.5 models and GPT-4. The highest F1-score per dataset is marked in bold.

Prompt	LLM	OA-Mine		AE-110k	
		F1	$ for 1k A/V pairs	F1	$ for 1k A/V pairs
json-val-10-dem	GPT-4	82.2	6.4411	87.5	6.3123
list	ft-GPT-3.5	83.6	0.2600	85.7	0.2643
json-val	ft-GPT-3.5	84.5	1.2307	86.0	0.9709

Generalization. The following analysis examines whether fine-tuned GPT-3.5 models can generalize to products and their attribute values not included in the training data. This is a crucial requirement due to the constant emergence of new products. We test this by applying the two models fine-tuned on OA-Mine to AE-110k, and vice versa. These four fine-tuned models are compared to a plain GPT-3.5 as a baseline. The results in Table 10 indicate the fine-tuned models perform, on average, 17% worse than the plain GPT-3.5, suggesting they may not generalize well and may lose some general language comprehension skills. Based on these observations, we identify two scenarios for users employing GPT-3.5 or GPT-4 for AVE: (i) For frequent AVE on a known set of products, the lower token usage fee of the fine-tuned model justifies the fine-tuning cost. (ii) For infrequent AVE with constantly changing products, ExtractGPT is recommended.

---

[9] https://platform.openai.com/docs/guides/fine-tuning.

Table 10. F1-scores of the fine-tuned GPT-3.5 models transferred to the other dataset.

Dataset	Model	list	json-val
OA-Mine	GPT-3.5	63.3	69.8
	ft-GPT-3.5 on AE-110k	43.7	53.9
AE-110K	GPT-3.5	61.4	74.4
	ft-GPT-3.5 on OA-Mine	46.2	55.9

6   Comparison to PLM-Based Baselines

This section compares the performance of ExtractGPT to the PLM-based baselines SU-OpenTag[10] [22], AVEQA [17], and MAVEQA[11] [25]. To assess training data efficiency, we fine-tune the baseline methods on both the small (S) and large (L) training sets. We ensure a fair comparison to ExtractGPT by using the same training sets for in-context learning.

Absolute Performance. Table 11 shows the F1-scores of the fine-tuned PLM-based baselines and ExtractGPT. The best average F1-score of SU-OpenTag and AVEQA is 6% lower than the average performance of ExtractGPT.

Table 11. F1-scores of PLM baselines and GPT-4 on all and unseen attribute-value pairs in the test sets. The highest F1-score per dataset is marked in bold.

	All Attribute-Value Pairs						Unseen Attribute-Value Pairs					
	OA-Mine		AE-110K		Average		OA-Mine		AE-110k		Average	
	S	L	S	L	S	L	S	L	S	L	S	L
SU-OpenTag	55.1	73.9	70.6	85.5	62.8	79.7	42.0	58.4	32.0	40.9	37.0	49.6
AVEQA	67.0	78.7	76.8	80.9	71.9	79.8	56.6	65.0	49.8	49.3	53.2	57.2
MAVEQA	23.1	65.7	57.7	76.8	40.4	71.3	18.8	42.6	6.2	24.9	12.5	33.7
Extract-GPT	80.2	**82.2**	85.5	**87.5**	82.8	**84.9**	**76.4**	74.7	**68.8**	59.1	**72.6**	66.9

Training Data-Efficiency. Comparing PLM-based baselines fine-tuned on small and large training sets reveals a performance gap of 8% to 31%, indicating their need for large amounts of training data. In contrast, ExtractGPT shows only a 2% performance gap between small and large training sets. Notably, ExtractGPT using the small training set outperforms all PLM-based methods using the large training set, despite having a training set five times smaller.

Unseen Attribute Values. Our final analysis examines how PLM-based models and ExtractGPT perform with unseen attribute values. This is crucial for

---

[10] https://github.com/hackerxiaobai/OpenTag_2019/tree/master.
[11] https://github.com/google-research/google-research/tree/master/mave.

handling new products in e-commerce. We compare performance differences on test set attribute values not included in the training sets. OA-Mine has 1,607 and 1,073 unseen pairs, while AE-110K has 572 and 414, depending on the training set size. Table 11 shows that all methods struggle with unseen values because lower F1-scores compared to the scenario with all attribute-value pairs are achieved. ExtractGPT is more robust, achieving an average F1-score 19% higher than the best PLM-based method, AVEQA, on the small training set.

7 Conclusions

This paper explores the use of Large Language Models (LLMs) for product attribute value extraction (AVE). It evaluates various zero-shot and few-shot prompt templates with different LLMs. The best overall performance was achieved by GPT-4, with an F1-score of 85%, using a prompt incorporating schema knowledge, attribute descriptions, and demonstrations. Notably, GPT-4's performance is only 3% higher than the performance of Llama-3-70B, an open-source LLM, highlighting its competitiveness. Our experiments showed that LLMs are more training data efficient for AVE compared to PLMs. Given the same training data, GPT-4 surpassed the best PLM-based methods by 6% in F1-score and proved more robust to unseen attribute values. Fine-tuning GPT-3.5 increased its performance close to GPT-4's, but reduced GPT-3.5's ability to generalize to new product attribute values not included in the training data.

References

1. Brinkmann, A., Baumann, N., Bizer, C.: Using LLMs for the extraction and normalization of product attribute values. In: ADBIS, pp. 217–230 (2024)
2. Brown, T., Mann, B., Ryder, N., et al.: Language models are few-shot learners. In: NeurIPS, vol. 33, pp. 1877–1901 (2020)
3. Chen, W.T., Shinzato, K., Yoshinaga, N., et al.: Does named entity recognition truly not scale up to real-world product attribute extraction? In: EMNLP, pp. 152–159 (2023)
4. Devlin, J., Chang, M.W., Lee, K., et al.: BERT: pre-training of deep bidirectional transformers for language understanding. In: NAACL, pp. 4171–4186 (2019)
5. Dubey, A., Jauhri, A., Pandey, A., et al.: The LLaMA 3 herd of models (2024). arXiv:2407.21783 [cs]
6. Fang, C., Li, X., Fan, Z., et al.: LLM-Ensemble: optimal large language model ensemble method for e-commerce product attribute value extraction (2024). arXiv:2403.00863 [cs]
7. Ghani, R., Probst, K., Liu, Y., et al.: Text mining for product attribute extraction. In: ACM SIGKDD Explorations Newsletter, vol. 8, pp. 41–48 (2006)
8. Goel, A., Gueta, A., Gilon, O., et al.: LLMs accelerate annotation for medical information extraction. In: ML4H, pp. 82–100 (2023)
9. Khorashadizadeh, H., Mihindukulasooriya, N., Tiwari, S., et al.: Exploring in-context learning capabilities of foundation models for generating knowledge graphs from text. In: TEXT2KG | BiKE, vol. 3447, pp. 132–153 (2023)

10. OpenAI: GPT-4 technical report (2023). arXiv:2303.08774 [cs]
11. Ouyang, L., Wu, J., Jiang, X.: Training language models to follow instructions with human feedback. In: NeurIPS, vol. 35, pp. 27730–27744 (2022)
12. Parekh, T., Hsu, I.H., Huang, K.H., et al.: GENEVA: benchmarking generalizability for event argument extraction with hundreds of event types and argument roles. In: ACL, pp. 3664–3686 (2023)
13. Putthividhya, D., Hu, J.: Bootstrapped named entity recognition for product attribute extraction. In: EMNLP, pp. 1557–1567 (2011)
14. Ren, Z., He, X., Yin, D., et al.: Information discovery in e-commerce: half-day SIGIR 2018 tutorial. In: SIGIR, pp. 1379–1382 (2018)
15. Shinzato, K., Yoshinaga, N., Xia, Y., et al.: Simple and effective knowledge-driven query expansion for QA-based product attribute extraction. In: ACL, pp. 227–234 (2022)
16. Vandic, D., van Dam, J.W., Frasincar, F.: Faceted product search powered by the Semantic Web. Decis. Support Syst. **53**(3), 425–437 (2012)
17. Wang, Q., Yang, L., Kanagal, B., et al.: Learning to extract attribute value from product via question answering: a multi-task approach. In: SIGKDD, pp. 47–55 (2020)
18. Wang, Q., Yang, L., Wang, J., et al.: SMARTAVE: structured multimodal transformer for product attribute value extraction. In: EMNLP, pp. 263 – 276 (2022)
19. Wang, X., Li, S., Ji, H.: Code4Struct: code generation for few-shot event structure prediction. In: ACL, vol. 1, pp. 3640–3663 (2023)
20. Wei, J., Tay, Y., Bommasani, R., et al.: Emergent abilities of large language models. TMLR (2022)
21. Wong, Y.W., Widdows, D., Lokovic, T., et al.: Scalable attribute-value extraction from semi-structured text. In: ICDMW, pp. 302–307 (2009)
22. Xu, H., Wang, W., Mao, X., et al.: Scaling up open tagging from tens to thousands: comprehension empowered attribute value extraction from product title. In: ACL, pp. 5214–5223 (2019)
23. Yan, J., Zalmout, N., Liang, Y., et al.: AdaTag: multi-attribute value extraction from product profiles with adaptive decoding. In: ACL|IJCNLP, pp. 4694–4705 (2021)
24. Yang, L., Wang, Q., Wang, J., et al.: MixPAVE: mix-prompt tuning for few-shot product attribute value extraction. In: ACL, pp. 9978–9991 (2023)
25. Yang, L., Wang, Q., Yu, Z., et al.: MAVE: a product dataset for multi-source attribute value extraction. In: WSDM, pp. 1256–1265 (2022)
26. Zamfirescu-Pereira, J., Wong, R.Y., Hartmann, B., et al.: Why johnny can't prompt: how non-AI experts try (and fail) to design LLM prompts. In: CHI, pp. 1–21 (2023)
27. Zhang, L., Zhu, M., Huang, W.: A framework for an ontology-based e-commerce product information retrieval system. JCP **4**(6), 436–443 (2009)
28. Zhang, X., Zhang, C., Li, X., et al.: OA-Mine: open-world attribute mining for e-commerce products with weak supervision. In: WWW, pp. 3153–3161 (2022)
29. Zheng, G., Mukherjee, S., Dong, X.L., et al.: OpenTag: open attribute value extraction from product profiles. In: SIGKDD, pp. 1049–1058 (2018)
30. Zhu, T., Wang, Y., Li, H., et al.: Multimodal joint attribute prediction and value extraction for E-commerce product. In: EMNLP, pp. 2129–2139 (2020)
31. Zou, H.P., Samuel, V., Zhou, Y., et al.: ImplicitAVE: an open-source dataset and multimodal LLMs benchmark for implicit attribute value extraction (2024). arXiv:2404.15592 [cs]

Feature Extraction for Claim Check-Worthiness Prediction Tasks Using LLM

Yuka Teramoto[1]([✉]), Takahiro Komamizu[2], Mitsunori Matsushita[3], and Kenji Hatano[1]

[1] Doshisha University, 1–3 Tatara-Miyakodani, Kyotanabe, Kyoto 610–0394, Japan
`teramoto@mil.doshisha.ac.jp, khatano@mail.doshisha.ac.jp`
[2] Nagoya University, Furo, Chikusa, Nagoya, Aichi 464–8603, Japan
`taka-coma@acm.org`
[3] Kansai University, 2-1-1 Ryozenji, Takatsuki, Osaka 569–1095, Japan
`m_mat@kansai-u.ac.jp`

Abstract. This study explores the use of Large Language Models (LLMs) for Claim Check-Worthiness Prediction (CCWP), a crucial pre-screening task in fact-checking. We predict the time between a claim's occurrence and verification by analyzing data from fact-checking organizations. The results show that validation time is the same between the top 25% and bottom 75% of total checklist condition fulfillment claims. That is, further optimization is needed for LLMs to perform effective CCWPs.

Keywords: Fact-checking · Claim Check-Worthiness Prediction task (CCWP) · Large Language Models (LLMs) · Misinformation

1 Introduction

The rapid spread of misinformation can lead to significant societal disruptions, highlighting the importance of effective fact-checking mechanisms. In the fact-checking process, claims are reported by citizens and categorized by organizations, which then prioritize verification. Claim Check-Worthiness Prediction (CCWP) is a crucial task for prioritizing claims for screening. Because, a large number of fact-checking candidates are gathered at fact-checking centers, each with varying societal impacts. Fact-checking is a complex and sensitive task that can take days to weeks and places a significant burden on individuals. Furthermore, the rapid completion of CCWP is performed, the more effectively the impact of misinformation can be mitigated [10].

Computational assistance can enhance efficiency by helping prioritize information for verification. This study investigates whether LLMs can assist in the pre-screening phase based on criteria set by human experts. Previous studies have suggested that LLM and human collaboration are practical for enhancing

P. Delir Haghighi et al. (Eds.): iiWAS 2024, LNCS 15342, pp. 53–58, 2025.
https://doi.org/10.1007/978-3-031-78090-5_5

the efficiency of fact-checking tasks [3, 11]. These papers insist that humans must handle the critical and sensitive aspects of the validation process because LLMs can introduce biases, hallucinations, and amplification of inaccurate data [8].

In this study, we investigate and report on the ability of LLMs in the human-in-the-loop fact-checking approach by using a structured checklist, focusing on claim checks. Specifically, we investigate whether the judgments made by LLMs according to the checklist are useful in identifying which claims should be urgently judged true or false. The use of checklists can produce the following effects: The impact of incorrect outputs is subdivided by dividing the forecasting task into tasks for evaluation in a checklist. It also reduces the difficulty of individual tasks and facilitates human verification of outputs.

We use assessments made by LLMs based on the checklist for predicting time lag between a claim's occurrence and the completion of a fact-checking task. Current CCWP methods use a binary variable to represent the need for verification, but the verification value is continuous. Additionally, existing data are unsuitable for validation in LLMs due to data leakage risks. This study uses data from actual fact-checking organizations to design a new task that predicts the days between a claim's occurrence and its verification.

2   Related Works

Many previous studies have tackled the tasks of CCWP [4]. In recent years, the check-worthiness tasks have attracted significant attention. CLEF-2024 Check-That! lab provides a dataset designed for check-worthiness tasks and a competition opportunity for state-of-the-art methods. According to the report from the organizers of CheckThat! lab [2], methods using transformer-based models have increased in prevalence over the past few years.

Recently, researchers have dealt with comprehensive fact-checking tasks, including CCWP, collecting evidence, and determining veracity using LLMs [9]. Comprehensive fact-checking is essential to social unrest and public health issues. Therefore, caution should be exercised in using LLMs, because LLMs contain biases and can amplify these biases [8]. Moreover, LLMs can produce hallucinations that deviate from facts, and the mechanisms of these hallucinations are not fully understood [5]. Furthermore, existing researches [7,9] using LLMs still need to examine data leakage rigorously. Because the LLMs' training data may already include publicly available datasets for detecting claim check-worthy tasks and related information. On the other hand, when solving comprehensive or partial fact-checking tasks using LLMs in the real world, LLMs have already been trained, and they must also handle claims that arise subsequently.

3   Proposed Method

As Fig. 1, this study explores practical methods for incorporating LLMs into the manual fact-checking process. Specifically, we examine whether LLMs can execute CCWP, a preliminary step of the fact-checking process. In numerous

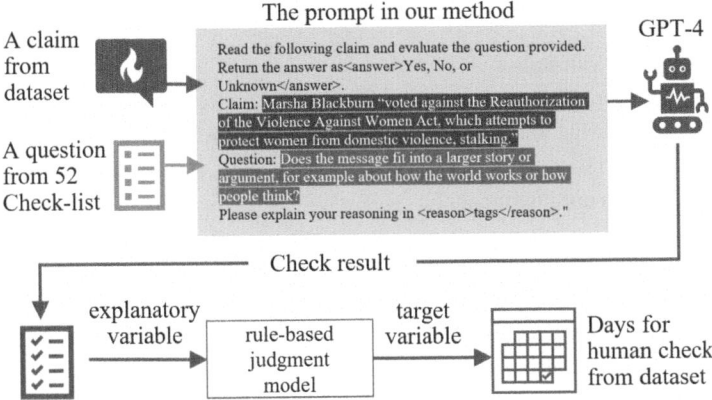

Fig. 1. Our proposed method

previous studies, the CCWP label has been represented as a Boolean value indicating whether a claim holds a checkable value. This approach was used because CCWP functioned as an initial screening process to determine whether fact-checkers should verify a reported claim. In contrast, our study envisages a new secondary screening exercise that assigns further priority to claims of assured importance that were deemed worthy of verification in the primary screening and survived the selection process. As a result, we have not made direct comparisons with existing studies. Existing check-value determination methods are likely to determine that all the data in this study are check-value. To use a simple metaphor, our task is to determine the rank of diamonds, not to separate stones from diamonds.

We use a structured checklist outlining human fact-checkers' steps to prioritize claims. Moreover, we considered the following two points to evaluate the practical application in real-world scenarios rigorously. First, we designed a new task to predict how quickly claims submitted to fact-checking organizations were addressed. Second, to demonstrate the effectiveness of LLMs on claims not included in their training data, we evaluated only claims that emerged after the cutoff date of the LLM's training data. We made the LLM execute the checklist-based claim evaluations, quantified the results, and assessed its ability to prioritize the fact-checking tasks. Sehat et al. created a 52-item checklist to determine the priority of fact-checking [12]. This checklist was developed based on a fact checking survey of human experts Examples of the questions are shown in Table 1. Fact-checkers respond to each item with "Yes," "No," or "Unknown." The higher the number of "Yes" responses, the more urgent it is to fact-check the corresponding claim.

This paper assumes that LLMs will likely perform comparably to humans on some of these questions in Sect. 2. Indeed, even in behavioral economics, it is known that LLMs can mimic human impressions and value judgments [6,14]. We observed the checklists and hypothesised that two types of these questions

Table 1. Examples of questions used to determine the priority of fact-checking

Question Category	Example
External information	Is there a lack of high quality information that is publicly accessible and refuting the message's claim?
Impressions from the text	Does the message directly call audience members to share the content further?

exist: those that ask for external information relevant to the claim and those that ask for characteristics or impressions derived from the text. The former includes items such as the characteristics of the claim's issuer and whether there have been any official announcements related to the claim. The latter includes whether the claim makes statements about global trends or contains aggressive bias against specific groups. The latter group of questions pertains to human impressions and value judgments derived from the text, which LLMs can likely replicate sufficiently. On the other hand, the former questions might be influenced by external factors. Examples of such external factors include the context of the documents accessible to the LLM and the structure of the websites where the claims are found. Therefore, there may be differences in the accuracy of LLM responses. There may be cases where the distinction between them is ambiguous. Therefore, we will treat these questions without distinguishing between them in our experiment.

This study uses the Fact-Check Insights dataset distributed by Duke University[1] to rigorously evaluate LLMs' responses in a zero-shot scenario. Standard benchmark datasets [2,13] for CCWP have limitations when using data beyond the cutoff date of the training data for GPT-4. The metadata of the Fact-Check Insights dataset includes the date when the claim was verified and the date when the fact-check article was published. By calculating the difference between these dates, we can determine how many days it took to address a claim in the real world. This study uses this number of days is used as the target variable. Figure 2 shows the prompt used when inputting to the LLM. Following the precedent set by prior research using LLMs as annotators [6], the response sections are structured with tags. The sentences following "Claim:" and "Question:" will be modified. For reviewing the claim, it is necessary to answer the 52 questions created in prior research [12]. Therefore, 52 different prompts will be created for each claim.

We use GPT-4 [1][2] for evaluation. There are three reasons for this choice:

1. The cutoff date of the model's training data is known.
2. Its outputs are relatively stable.
3. It is a model capable of obtaining sufficient claim data that emerged after the cutoff date from the Fact-Check Insights dataset.

---

[1] "Fact-Check Insights", https://www.factcheckinsights.org/, Last accessed on July 20, 2024.

[2] MODEL NAME: gpt-4-turbo, TRAINING DATA: Up to Dec. 2023.

4   Experimental Results

The Fig. 2 show simple aggregations of our analyses. A high number of "Yes" responses indicates that the complaint requires a prompt response. Therefore, we used the 25th percentile as the threshold to divide the total number of "Yes" into top and bottom groups because the 25th percentile represents the third quartile.

The response types are categorized into four groups: "Yes", "No", "Unknown", and "Error". Specifically, the number of instances classified as "Yes" is 3,328, "No" is 38,730, "Unknown" is 30,869, and "Error" is 113. This data is crucial for understanding how citizen reports on specific claims are categorized and which categories appear most frequently. Notably, the overwhelming number of instances classified as "No" indicates that many claims are evaluated negatively. As Fig. 2, the data for the bottom 75% of the respondents with a small number of "Yes" responses are often answered in a short time, but the high dispersion of the data shows

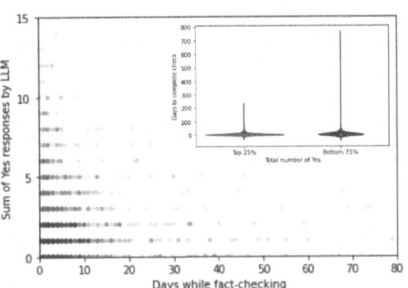

Fig. 2. The red section shows the top 25% of claims with the most "Yes" responses from the LLM checklist. The violin plot illustrates the distribution of checking days. (Color figure online)

a tendency for the respondents to take a long time to answer the questions. As Fig. 2, the fact-checkers are quicker to deal with claims with a high number of "Yes" responses from LLMs. However, it should be noted that a low number of "Yes" responses does not necessarily mean a low priority. Fact-checkers also responded to the bottom 75% of groups in a short time. We believe that adding other features to consider and increasing the complexity of the model is a potentially effective approach. Conversely, for the data with a large number of Yes responses, the number of days required is mostly lower than for the data with a small number of Yes responses, and the variation in the number of days is also smaller. Therefore, a large number of "Yes", is likely to be one of the conditions for a claim to be highly urgent.

5   Conclusion and Future Challenges

We developed scenarios for using LLMs in the fact-checking processes, considering the LLM's training data cutoff date and evaluating post-cutoff claims. Our analyses show that irrespective of the time to check, CLAIMs rarely meet the checklist conditions in determining LLM. To improve our method, we plan to develop a weighted model, analyze the impact of individual checklist items, and refine our classification system to identify critical claims better. By addressing these issues, we aim to create a more effective system for identifying and addressing urgent claims.

This work was partly supported by JST RISTEX #JPMJRS23L2 and Tateishi Science and Technology Foundation Research Grant C #237018 and the Grants-in-Aid for Academic Promotion, Graduate School of Culture and Information Science, Doshisha University.

References

1. Achiam, J., et al.: GPT-4 technical report. arXiv preprint arXiv:2303.08774 (2023)
2. Barrón-Cedeño, A., et al.: The CLEF-2024 CheckThat! Lab: check-worthiness, subjectivity, persuasion, roles, authorities, and adversarial robustness. In: Goharian, N., et al. (eds.) Advances in Information Retrieval: 46th European Conference on Information Retrieval, ECIR 2024, Glasgow, UK, March 24–28, 2024, Proceedings, Part V, pp. 449–458. Springer Nature Switzerland, Cham (2024). https://doi.org/10.1007/978-3-031-56069-9_62
3. Das, A., Liu, H., Kovatchev, V., Lease, M.: The state of human-centered NLP technology for fact-checking. Inf. Process. Manage. 60(2), 103219 (2023)
4. Hassan, N., Li, C., Tremayne, M.: Detecting check-worthy factual claims in presidential debates. In: Proceedings of the 24th ACM International on Conference on Information and Knowledge Management, pp. 1835–1838 (2015)
5. Ji, Z., et al.: Survey of hallucination in natural language generation. ACM Comput. Surv. 55(12), 1–38 (2023)
6. Leng, Y.: Can LLMs mimic human-like mental accounting and behavioral biases? SSRN 4705130 (2024)
7. Li, X., Zhang, Y., Malthouse, E.C.: Large language model agent for fake news detection. arXiv preprint arXiv:2405.01593 (2024)
8. Neumann, T., Lee, S., De-Arteaga, M., Fazelpour, S., Lease, M.: Diverse, but Divisive: LLMs can exaggerate gender differences in opinion related to harms of misinformation. arXiv preprint arXiv:2401.16558 (2024)
9. Quelle, D., Bovet, A.: The perils and promises of fact-checking with large language models. Front. Artif. Intell. 7, 1341697 (2024)
10. Rastogi, S., Bansal, D.: A review on fake news detection 3T's: typology, time of detection, taxonomies. Int. J. Inf. Secur. 22(1), 177–212 (2023)
11. Schmitt, V., et al.: Evaluating Human-Centered AI Explanations: introduction of an XAI evaluation framework for fact-checking. In: Proceedings of the 3rd ACM International Workshop on Multimedia AI against Disinformation, pp. 91–100 (2024)
12. Sehat, C.M., Li, R., Nie, P., Prabhakar, T., Zhang, A.X.: Misinformation as a harm: structured approaches for fact-checking prioritization. Proc. ACM Hum.-Comput. Interact. 8(CSCW1), 1–36 (2024)
13. Shaar, S., et al.: Findings of the NLP4IF-2021 shared tasks on fighting the COVID-19 infodemic and censorship detection. arXiv preprint arXiv:2109.12986 (2021)
14. Wang, Y., Cai, Y., Chen, M., Liang, Y., Hooi, B.: Primacy effect of ChatGPT. In: Proceedings of the 2023 Conference on Empirical Methods in Natural Language Processing, pp. 108–115 (2023)

Training Data for Dialogue Generation Considering Philosophies

Masaya Sueyoshi$^{(\boxtimes)}$, Tetsuya Kitahata, and Akiyo Nadamoto

Konan University, Okamoto 8–9–1 Higashinada–ku, Kobe, Japan
{m2324003,s2171036}@s.konan-u.ac.jp, nadamoto@konan-u.ac.jp

Abstract. With the advancement of generative AI, research on dialogue generation has rapidly progressed. This dialogue generation not only enables interactions with fictional AIs but also facilitates dialogues with historical people, providing new avenues for communication. When generating dialogues with historical people, it is essential to consider their philosophies, which reflect their thoughts and life views. Currently, dialogue generation that considers personas has been realized; however, personas merely represent the personality or character of the dialogue partner and differ from philosophies. Therefore, this study proposes a method for dialogue generation that considers historical people's philosophies. As an initial step, this paper proposes a method for constructing training data that considers these philosophies.

Keywords: Dialogue Generation · Philosophy · LLMs

1 Introduction

With the advancement of generative AI, research on dialogue generation has rapidly progressed. Dialogue generation is widely utilized in the business sector, with practical applications in Q&A and customer support systems. Research that considers the persona in dialogue generation is attracting attention. Here, "persona" refers to the personality or character the AI embodies during the dialogue. For example, a friendly and easy-to-understand Grandpa Professor or a friendly customer support AI. However, it is important to note that the persona only represents the personality or character of the AI dialogue partner, and current generative AI does not consider the AI dialogue partner's thoughts or life views. On the other hand, individuals possess their philosophies, encompassing their thoughts, values, and life views. Particularly, great people who have left behind famous quotes often have unique philosophies. Generative AI has made it possible to engage in dialogues with deceased individuals and historical people, creating new forms of communication. However, current dialogues with such statistics do not consider their philosophies and are limited to generating dialogues based on superficial personas. For example, in a dialogue with Einstein AI, considering his persona as a curious, friendly, and humorous individual, the following interaction can be generated:

© The Author(s), under exclusive license to Springer Nature Switzerland AG 2025
P. Delir Haghighi et al. (Eds.): iiWAS 2024, LNCS 15342, pp. 59–66, 2025.
https://doi.org/10.1007/978-3-031-78090-5_6

User : Professor Einstein, could you briefly explain the theory of relativity?

Einstein AI : Hello! I'm glad you're interested in the theory of relativity. Simply put, the theory of relativity is the idea that time and space are not absolute but change depending on the observer's movement. For example, the speed of light is the same for everyone, but the flow of time and the extent of space can change based on the observer's speed. It's a bit strange but fascinating, isn't it?

In this example, Einstein's philosophy of scientific inquiry, emphasis on observation and experimentation, and critical thinking are not included. Therefore, this study proposes a dialogue generation method that considers not the persona but the philosophy of the dialogue partner. Extracting individual philosophies from people is generally challenging. Therefore, in this study, we propose a method to extract the philosophy of a great person who left many documents from his or her documents and generates dialogues using the philosophy of the great person. This method allows users to engage in more realistic and meaningful dialogues with historical documents. In this research, we focus on Hachisaburo Hirao, the founder of our university(Konan University), a Japanese politician, entrepreneur, and educator who was active from 1866 to 1945 and left behind numerous writings. By leveraging his extensive literature, we aim to construct dialogue generation that not only solves problems but also allows users to learn new insights from the philosophies of great people. This paper outlines the initial steps of this endeavor, including the methods for constructing the dataset and the techniques for training the model.

2   Related Work

There are many studies about dialogue generation methods with large-scale language models. Odede et al. [6] develop the chatbot system, that proposing GPT-3.5 embedding to create a chatbot to fulfill information needs about courses of interest to university affiliates and improve their search. Liu et al. [4] develop a chatbot that contains emotional nuances in conversations. Zhao et al. [9] develop a conversational model to engage in smooth and natural dialogues. Montagna et al. [5] propose an architecture to develop a chatbot system with LLM to support chronic patients. Ashby et al. [1] are developing dialogues with a computer in games that consider the player's characteristics. Li et al. [3] propose a model for generating empathetic expression in dialogue systems. Zhao et al. [8] propose a model to implement persgenerate persona-aware response from d textual features and Emoji usage patterns. Han et al. [2] propose a persona-consistent dialogue generation model with contrastive learning. Xu et al. [7] propose the less egocentric personalized dialogue generation model. These studies aim to improve the performance of existing LLMs. However, our research aims to generate a dialogue with the philosophy, which is a different point from others.

3   Generating Training Data

3.1   Datasets

In this study, we use Hachisaburo Hirao's diary, which he wrote from 1913 to 1945. He wrote diaries about his experiences and his feelings and impressions of them. We consider that we can extract his philosophy from the diaries. This diary consists of the date, weather, and text. It consists of 18 volumes and was written between 1913 and 1945. In this study, we use ten volumes, specifically 9 through 18, written between 1927 and 1945.

These periods were before and during World War II, and characteristics of the Japanese language used "old kanji characters" and "historical kana usage". These features distinguish old Japanese writing from modern writing. The shape of the old kanji character is different from today's. Historical Kana Usage is that the kana syllabary in pre-war texts adhered to historical dialogues, which differ from modern kana usage. Examples include "ifu(say in English)" instead of the modern "iu". Additionally, there are differences in the usage of particles and auxiliary verbs. For example, the term "tari" in historical kana usage indicates the completion of an action in modern Japanese. Another example is "seri", where "se" represents "suru" (to do) and "ri" indicates the completion of an action in contemporary usage. This makes it challenging to accurately interpret the content using the original old Japanese language for documents. Therefore, we have to convert Hirao's diary, written in old Japanese, into modern Japanese.

3.2   Translating Training Data of Hirao Diaries

We translate diaries into contemporary Japanese using ChatGPT-4o[1]. However, the current version of ChatGPT-4o can only partially perform these translations. Therefore, for entries that cannot be translated automatically, we have to translate the passage of them manually.

The procedure for converting contents with historical Japanese into modern Japanese is as follows. Currently, we create a database for old and modern kanji called OM-database.

1. Input the content with historical Japanese into the ChatGPT-4o prompt.
2. Verify the output to ensure accurate translation. If the translation is correct, use the output as part of the dataset.
3. If the translation is incorrect, convert the old characters to modern characters. If the word exists in the OM-database, it will be converted automatically. Manual dialogue is necessary if the word does not exist in the OM-database. Subsequently, to automate this process in the future, store the pair of old and modern characters in the OM-database.
4. Using the diary entries converted to modern characters, input the content into the ChatGPT-4o prompt.

---

[1] https://openai.com/chatgpt/.

Table 1. Philosophy tag list

Tag	Subtag	Attribute	Value	Meaning
Behavior				The passage of human behavior.
	Basis			Indicate the basis for the action. Represent it as a nested Behavior tag.
Speech				The passage of speech.
		subject	The person in the document	The speech is the person who is writing the document.
			Another person	The speech is by another person.
Thought				The passage of thought.
	Word-of-wisdom	subject	The person in the document	The word of wisdom is the word of the person who is writing the document.
			Another person	The word of wisdom is the word of another person.

As a result, training data comprised 182,487 sentences, and 9,493,968 words were generated. Due to the presence of 396 types of archaic Kanji characters in the training data, 21 of which could not be translated automatically, manual translation was required. ChatGPT-4o is capable of automatically converting all historical kana usage.

3.3 Philosophy Tags for Training Data

It would be beneficial to have tags indicating that a particular passage of a diary pertains to philosophy. However, it is challenging for annotators to identify and mark philosophical content within the diary clearly. Therefore, we propose a set of tags specifically for philosophy, designed to annotate content that may contain philosophical elements with easily understandable tags. Therefore, after converting the diary from archaic Japanese into modern language, each sentence is tagged as shown in Table 1 to reflect the dialogue generated with philosophy. We call the tags "Philosophy tags". The diary is broadly divided into weather, the author's behavior, thoughts, and references to others' statements.

These behaviors, statements, and thoughts are identified for extracting the author's philosophy. In this process, facts and behaviors unrelated to the author's philosophy are not tagged.

Furthermore, dialogue texts that consider the author's philosophy are generated by assigning weights to the tokens of those tagged sentences during training.

3.4 Training of the LLM

In this study, we use LLM for Japanese, youri-7b-chat of Llama-2-Chat[2]. We conducted fine-tuning of the Large Language Model (LLM) using the generated training data. The model's parameters are the batch size is 16, the number of epochs is 8, the learning rate is 0.0002, and the optimizer is AdamW.

---

[2] https://huggingface.co/rinna/youri-7b-chat.

4   Experiment

In this paper, before implementing the proposed tagging method, we conducted experiments to evaluate how fine-tuning with Hirao's diary can generate dialogues incorporating Hirao's philosophy. We performed a comparative experiment using our proposed method, which fine-tuning Hirao's diary with the baseline mod,el which is the non-fine-tuned Llama-2-Chat.

Condition of Experiment
We experimented with five university students who had some understanding of the Hirao Philosophy and who were attending Konan University, which was estaHirao establish experiment focused on three primary themes: (1) the seven precepts of Hirao's philosophy, (2) topics related to Konan University, and (3) general dialogue with the students. experimental procedure was as follows:

1. Participants selected three precepts from the themes in (1) and engaged in a dialogue about them.
2. Participants discussed the three themes in (2).
3. Participants engaged in dialogues about the three themes in (3).

Each dialogue consisted of two turns, resulting in a total of ninedialoguese. Following each dialogue, participants completed a questionnaire nine times in total. The questionnaire included the following items:

– Is this dialogue consistent? (Consistency)
– Is this dialogue logical? (Logic)
– Is this dialogue coherent? (Coherence)
– Did you discover anything new in this dialogue? (Novelty)

The questionnaire responses were recorded using a four-point Likert scale: "4. Very much", "3. Yes", "2. No", and "1. Not at all".

Results and discussion
Fig. 1 shows the results. In the consistency, the Hirao's precepts learned with fine-tuning have better values than those without fine-tuning. This may be due to the focused themes and the dialogue generated through fine-tuning on those themes. Similarly in Logicality, only the theme of Hirao's precepts Learned with fine-tuning have better value than those without fine-tuning. In summary, we find that the fine-tuning using Hirao's diary results in better consistency and logic specifically in dialogues about Hirao's precepts.

Conversely, regarding coherence, responses indicating that the dialogues were broken outnumbered those indicating coherence, irrespective of the presence or absence of fine-tuning. This suggests that the dialogues generated by the initial dialogue model are inherently flawed. We intend to generate dialogues using other models in the future and compare the results.

In terms of novelty, the results with fine-tuning are more novel than those without fine-tuning in the cases of Hirao's precepts and Konan University. By fine tuning Hirao's diary, the dialogue system was able to provide new insights to

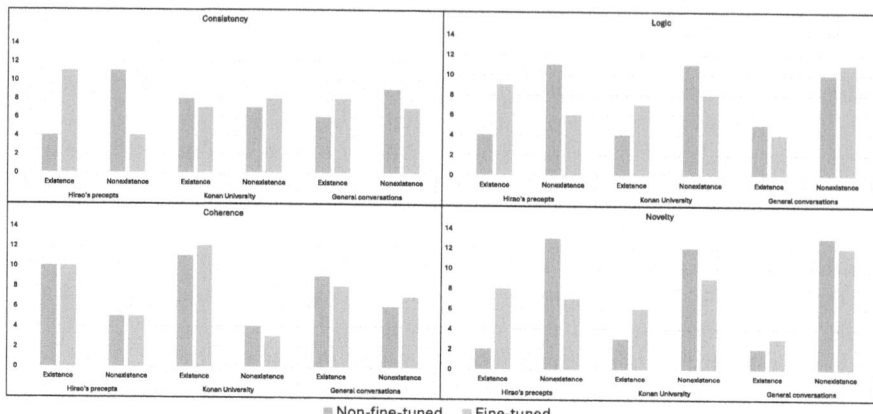

Fig. 1. Results of the experiments

Table 2. Example of the results of experiments

Themes	Hirao's precepts		Konan University		General dialogues	
Model	Non-fine-tuned		Non-fine-tuned	Fine-tuned	Non-fine-tuned	Fine-tuned
Input	What does 'Genius exists in everyone, and it is different in each individual' mean?		Why was Konan University founded?		I can't stop browsing at SNS and YouTube lately.	
Output	Innate talent is something that isn't immediately apparent at birth.	Innate qualities exist in everyone, and they are just different for each person.	It was founded in 1951.	The main reason was likely to support Japan's economic and social recovery after the war.	That doesn't sound good.	While these sites have a lot of information, relying too much on them can make it hard to control your time, which isn't very good.
Input	Could you explain a bit more?	That's a profound thought.	Can you tell me the reason?	How is that related?	I know. I feel like I'm wasting my time.	Yeah, I know. But I just end up watching them anyway.
Output	I'm sorry, I can't explain it any further.	Yes, it is.	To enhance the education of the general public.	The only way to recover many of the things lost during the war was to strengthen industries, which required a large number of young people. Educating them was essential for this purpose.	Yeah, that's not great.	That's why it's important to manage your time.

the participants. In conclusion, fine-tuning enables the From the Table 2 shows the example of the resilts.

From the Table 2, the dialogue with fine-tuning convey the spirit of Hirao. In particular, as the dialogue about the thema of the Konan university, people feels like a dialogue with Professor Hirao himself.

5   Conclusion

In this paper, we propose a method for constructing training data that reflects historical people's philosophies as an initial step in researching a dialogue generation method that incorporates philosophical elements. Specifically, we introduced a method for translating ancient documents into modern languages and a philosophy tag for dialogue generation that considers philosophical elements. As a preliminary experiment of the proposed method, we conducted a feasibility study on dialogue generation that considers the author's philosophy using diaries translated into modern language without employing tags. The experimental results indicate that fine-tuning alone is insufficient for generating dialogues incorporating the author's philosophy. Future experiments will use a dialogue generation model that accounts for the weight of tags in the proposed method. Additionally, we will propose a philosophy-aware dialogue generation method utilizing various techniques, such as Retrieval-Augmented Generation (RAG).

Acknowledgements. This work was partially supported by Research Institute of Digital Twin at Konan University.

References

1. Ashby, T., Webb, B.K., Knapp, G., Searle, J., Fulda, N.: Personalized quest and dialogue generation in role-playing games: a knowledge graph- and language model-based approach. In: Proceedings of the 2023 CHI Conference on Human Factors in Computing Systems (2023)
2. Han, Z., Zhang, S., Zhang, X.: Persona consistent dialogue generation via contrastive learning. In: Companion Proceedings of the ACM Web Conference 2023, pp. 196–199. WWW '23 Companion (2023)
3. Li, X., Wang, G., Wang, Y., Zhou, Q.: Mixed knowledge-enhance empathetic dialogue generation. In: Proceedings of the 2023 International Conference on Electronics, Computers and Communication Technology, pp. 77–81 (2024)
4. Liu, C., et al.: Speak from heart: an emotion-guided LLM-based multimodal method for emotional dialogue generation. In: Proceedings of the 2024 International Conference on Multimedia Retrieval, pp. 533–542. ICMR '24, Association for Computing Machinery (2024)
5. Montagna, S., Ferretti, S., Klopfenstein, L.C., Florio, A., Pengo, M.F.: Data decentralisation of LLM-based chatbot systems in chronic disease self-management. In: Proceedings of the 2023 ACM Conference on Information Technology for Social Good, pp. 205–212 (2023)

6. Odede, J., Frommholz, I.: Jaybot – aiding university students and admission with an LLM-based chatbot. In: Proceedings of the 2024 Conference on Human Information Interaction and Retrieval, pp. 391–395 (2024)

7. Xu, C., Li, P., Wang, W., Yang, H., Wang, S., Xiao, C.: COSPLAY: concept set guided personalized dialogue generation across both party personas. In: Proceedings of the 45th International ACM SIGIR Conference on Research and Development in Information Retrieval, pp. 201–211. SIGIR '22, Association for Computing Machinery (2022)

8. Zhao, S., et al.: PEDM: a multi-task learning model for persona-aware emoji-embedded dialogue generation. ACM Trans. Multimedia Comput. Commun. Appl. **19**(3s) (2023)

9. Zhao, Y., Cheng, B., Huang, Y., Wan, Z.: FluGCF: a fluent dialogue generation model with coherent concept entity flow. IEEE/ACM Trans. Audio Speech Lang. Process. **32**, 853–867 (2024)

Finding Adequate Additional Layer of Auxiliary Task in BERT-Based Multi-task Learning

Takuto Kitamura$^{(\boxtimes)}$ (ID) and Yu Suzuki (ID)

Gifu University, Gifu, Japan
kitamura.takuto.f6@s.gifu-u.ac.jp, suzuki.yu.r4@f.gifu-u.ac.jp

Abstract. We find adequate additional layers of auxiliary tasks for BERT-based multi-task learning. Multi-task learning is a method for improving the accuracy of machine learning model by adding auxiliary tasks. Previous studies propose multi-task learning models with auxiliary tasks added to different layers. Our research question is which layer is effective for adding auxiliary tasks to improve accuracy because the answer is still unknown. The aim of this study is to find adequate additional layer of auxiliary tasks that maximizes model accuracy. We use a BERT-base model consisting of twelve layers of Transformer and experiment with seven datasets. Our experimental results show that changing the additional layer of auxiliary tasks improves *macro-F*1 by up to 5.1% (*p-value* = 0.019). Moreover, our findings suggest that the insertion of auxiliary tasks into layers with the main task's characteristics increases accuracy.

Keywords: BERT · Multi-Task Learning · Machine Learning · Deep Learning · Natural Language Processing

1 Introduction

Multi-task learning [3] is a method to improve main tasks' accuracy by adding auxiliary tasks. Several studies [1,2,4,12] suggest that auxiliary tasks that provide hints for solving main tasks will improve main tasks' accuracy. The addition of auxiliary tasks can provide features that cannot be obtained by solving a single task alone to a machine learning model. As a result, the model can enhance its generalization performance.

Multi-task learning has been studied from various perspectives, such as the optimal combination of tasks and how to efficiently learn multiple tasks simultaneously. A large body of studies investigated what auxiliary tasks improve the accuracy of the main task. For example, Barnes et al. [1] said that adding a negation recognition task as the auxiliary task improves the accuracy of the sentiment analysis. Cheng et al. [4] reported that adding a name extraction task as the auxiliary task improves the accuracy of the name error detection task.

P. Delir Haghighi et al. (Eds.): iiWAS 2024, LNCS 15342, pp. 67–83, 2025.
https://doi.org/10.1007/978-3-031-78090-5_7

On the other hand, few studies examined which layer is best for adding auxiliary tasks. Søgaard and Goldberg [9] reported that adding the POS-tag prediction as the auxiliary task in the lower layer improves the accuracy of the main task in multi-task learning LSTM. Hashimoto et al. [6] proposed a multi-task learning model that combines multiple tasks, considering the hierarchical structure of classical language processing tasks. However, studies have yet to comprehensively investigate which layers are effective for adding auxiliary tasks to improve accuracy in the multi-task learning model.

This study aims to find an additional layer of the auxiliary task that maximizes the accuracy of the multi-task learning model. Some studies [6,9] suggest that learning low-level tasks in the model's earlier layers and high-level tasks in the later layers offers benefits. Low-level tasks are word-level tasks, such as a part-of-speech(POS) prediction task, while high-level tasks are semantic tasks, such as chunking and textual entailment. In addition, several studies [7,11] show that BERT has surface information such as POS at the lower layers and semantic information at the higher layers. Based on these findings, we propose a hypothesis: Adding the POS-tag prediction task in the lower layers of BERT improves the accuracy of the main task. In other words, we can maximize the accuracy of the multi-task learning model when we add auxiliary tasks to the layers that match the characteristics of the auxiliary task.

Our study conducts experiments on a BERT-base model [5] consisting of twelve layers of Transformer. We use seven datasets written in English (E) or Japanese (J): RTE (E), MRPC (E), CoLA (E), SST2 (E), Livedoor corpus (J), Rakuten dataset (J), and Twitter dataset (J). Our experiments use the POS-tag prediction task as the auxiliary task. We change the additional layer of auxiliary tasks and conduct experiments. Experimental results show that changing the additional layer of auxiliary tasks leads to a maximum *macro-F1* improvement of 5.1%. Contrary to the previous study's assertion, the results indicated that sometimes it is better to learn low-level tasks, such as POS-tag prediction, in the later layers of the model.

Our main contributions are the following:

- We reveal that changing the additional layer of the auxiliary tasks can improve *macro-F1* by up to 5.1% (*p-value* = 0.019).
- Our results suggest that the layer suitable for adding the auxiliary task is more dependent on the characteristics of the main task than those of the auxiliary task.

2 Related Work

Multi-task learning is a method for improving the accuracy of a model by solving multiple tasks simultaneously and utilizing information obtained from other tasks. Transfer learning [8] and multi-task learning are similar from the perspective of improving learning efficiency and generalization by using the domain knowledge and information from related tasks or domains. Multi-task learning has been studied not only in the field of NLP, but also in various other fields, such as imaging.

Recent studies report what auxiliary tasks are effective in improving the performance of multi-task learning. Wu et al. [12] show that training a Named Entity Recognition (NER) task simultaneously improves the performance of an intent classification task for medical questions. This study proposes a bidirectional LSTM and an Attention layer combined with a multi-task learning model. They use Word2Vec as a word embedding vector pre-trained on an online medical corpus. They create a dataset for the NER task by annotating six items such as disease name, treatment method, and body part by multiple doctors. Using the proposed model, $F - score$ and $Recall$ in the NER task are comparable to BERT, and $Precision$ is better than BERT. The proposed model also outperforms BERT on all evaluation metrics in the intent classification task.

Benayas et al. [2] show that training the intent classification and NER tasks simultaneously improves the performance of those tasks in a natural language understanding engine for conversational agents. This study proposes a hard parameter sharing model based on Transformers such as BERT and RoBERTa. They propose a model combining hard-parameter sharing with soft-parameter sharing. The combined model incorporates a mechanism to convert parameters obtained from the intent classification and NER tasks into parameters considering both tasks using Hadamard and matrix products.

Several studies have examined auxiliary task layers in multi-task learning. Søgaard and Goldberg [9] report that when learning auxiliary tasks, such as POS tagging, learning these tasks in the lower layer is better than the higher layer. This study proposes a three-layer multi-task learning model using bidirectional LSTM. This study uses a chunking or CCG super tagging task as the main task and POS tagging as the auxiliary task. They report that the auxiliary task trained in the third or the first layer improves the $F\text{-}score$ of the main task, but the auxiliary task trained in the first layer improves the $F\text{-}score$ more than when trained in the third layer.

Hashimoto et al. [6] propose a hierarchical multi-task learning model that combines multiple tasks. This study uses word-level tasks such as POS tagging and chunking, syntactic-level tasks such as dependency parsing, and semantic tasks such as semantic relational estimation and textual entailment. Its study reports that it is better to add tasks considering the linguistic hierarchy in the following order: word level, syntactic level, and semantic level. They demonstrate best or competitive results in multiple tasks.

In addition, several studies analyze which features are acquired and at which layers by BERT. Several studies [7, 11] investigate the linguistic representations captured by each layer of BERT using a probing task. Probing is an NLP task to assess how well a model understands specific linguistic, semantic, and syntactic features. This task can measure the extent to which the model grasps subject-verb agreement, POS identification, and more complex concepts. Jawahar et al. [7] show that BERT has superficial information in the lower layer, syntactic information in the middle layer, and semantic information in the higher layer.

Tenney et al. [11] show that BERT learns multiple NLP tasks hierarchically, including POS-tag tagging, coreference, and relation classification.

Previous studies [6,9] experiment with a multi-task learning model that is not pre-trained. These studies report that adding the auxiliary task to the lower layers in LSTM improves accuracy. However, which layer of a pre-trained model is better in terms of adding auxiliary tasks is not well studied. Our study differs from the above studies in two aspects. One aspect is that an exhaustive survey of additional layers of auxiliary tasks. The other aspect is that our experiment is conducted on a pre-trained model.

3   Model Construction

Sections 3.1 and 3.2 introduce how to construct our Multi-Task Learning Model (MTLM) and the baseline Single-Task Learning Model (STLM), and training method. Figure 1 shows the structure of our MTLM. This figure shows the MTLM with auxiliary task added to the third layer of BERT. We build and experiment with the MTLM and STLM described below. In this experiment, we fine-tune the MTLM and STLM as in the normal model. However, only the backpropagation differs from the typical model. Code 1.1 shows the backpropagation of the MTLM and STLM. Section 3.3 describes the main and auxiliary tasks. This section describes the loss function for the two tasks.

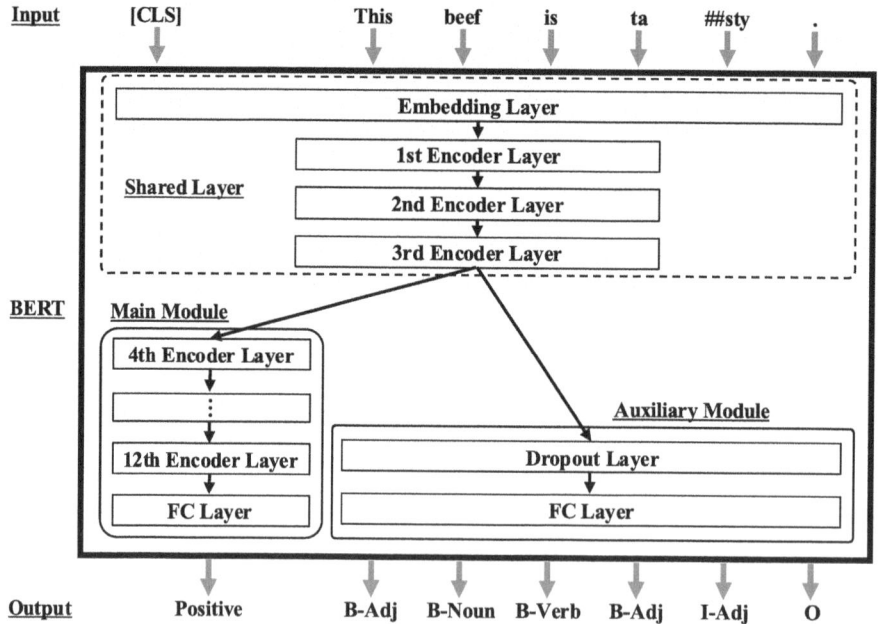

Fig. 1. An overview of our Multi-Task Learning Model (MTLM).

3.1   MLTM; Multi-task Learning Model

We use Fig. 1 to illustrate our MTLM. The MTLM refers to a model that learns the main task with the main module and the auxiliary task with the auxiliary module. This MTLM predicts the main task at the twelfth layer and the auxiliary task at the third layer. Our MTLM has one input: tokenized text data. The MTLM has two outputs: a class label to which the input text data belongs and a POS tag of the tokenized text data.

This model shares the encoder layers up to the third layer of BERT. In this example, our MTLM architecture splits into main and auxiliary modules from the third encoder layer onwards. The position of the layers that are shared or branched changes depending on the auxiliary task additional layer. The main module uses the [CLS] token to classify the class of input text. The auxiliary module classifies the POS tag to which each token belongs. The MTLM predicts both the auxiliary tasks and main tasks concurrently. Therefore, the MTLM has one input and multiple outputs. We set the parameters in the third and twelfth layers of BERT and the additional FC layer trainable. We use BERT's pre-trained parameters for all layers except those mentioned.

We define the loss function L_t of the MTLM as follows: $L_t = L_m \cdot \lambda_m + L_a \cdot \lambda_a$, where L_m is the loss function of the main task and λ_m is the weighting parameter of L_m. L_a is the loss function of the auxiliary task and λ_a is the weighting parameter of L_a. Section 3.3 describes L_m and L_a. In MTLM, we adjust the importance of each task in the model by weighting the losses between tasks. We use λ for the weighting of Loss.

code 1.1. Loss Backward

```
1   # Reset the gradient.
2   optimizer.zero_grad()
3   # Start an automatic mixed precision.
4   with torch.amp.autocast(device_type = "cuda", dtype = torch.float16):
5       # Input to the BERT and get the main and auxiliary outputs.
6       output_main, output_auxiliary = bert_base_model(inputs)
7       # Calculate the main and auxiliary task loss.
8       L_m = criterion_main(output_main, label_main)
9       L_a = criterion_auxiliary(output_auxiliary, label_auxiliary)
10      # Change the total loss depending on the model_type.
11      if model_type == "MTLM":
12          L_t = L_m * λ_m + L_a * λ_a
13      elif model_type == "STLM":
14          L_t = L_m
15  # Scale the total loss and do backpropagation.
16  scaler.scale(L_t).backward()
17  # Update the model's parameters.
18  scaler.step(optimizer)
19  # Update scaler.
20  scaler.update()
```

Code 1.1 is a code for backpropagation. We use this code to illustrate the backpropagation in the MTLM. The MTLM predicts the main task with the main module and the auxiliary task with the auxiliary module, and calculates the loss of two tasks. The MTLM does backpropagation for the main and auxiliary tasks. This case corresponds to where the mode_type is MTLM in the Code 1.1.

Main Module. We add the fully connected (FC) layer to the twelfth layer of BERT. The input size of the FC layer added in the twelfth layer is 768 dimensions, and the output size of the FC layer is p dimensions because the main task is a p-class classification task.

Auxiliary Module. We add a dropout layer and an FC layer to the third layer of BERT. The probability ρ to initialize the dropout layer's output is $\rho = 0.1$. The FC layer's input size via the dropout layer is 768 dimensions, and the output size is $2q + 1$ dimensions. We build the MTLM of the auxiliary module based on the following two websites[1,2].

3.2   STLM; Single-Task Learning Model (Comparison Model)

The STLM refers to a model that learns the main task only with the main modules of the MTLM. The STLM has the same structure as the MTLM and two outputs for a single input. The STLM can predict the auxiliary task but does not learn its task. We set the parameters in the third and twelfth layers of BERT and the additional FC layer trainable. Setting the STLM to be trainable with the same parameters as the MTLM allows us to compare it with the MTLM. If the number of trainable parameters or layers is different, we can not eliminate the effect of increasing the number of trainable parameters.

We define the loss function L_t as follows: $L_t = L_m \cdot \lambda_m$. The STLM predicts the main task with the main module, and calculates the loss of the main task. The STLM does backpropagation for the main task but does not perform backpropagation for the auxiliary task. This case corresponds to where the mode_type is STLM in the Code 1.1.

3.3   Task Definition

Section 3.3 describes the definitions of the main and the auxiliary tasks. In addition, this section describes how to assign labels for use in the auxiliary task to text data.

Main Task. is to classify the labels preassigned to the various datasets. This task is a p-class prediction task. The cross-entropy loss function of the main task L_m is defined as follows: $L_m = -\sum_{i=1}^{p} y_i \log \hat{y}_i$, where p is the number of classes, y_i is the true label of the main task, and $\hat{y}_i$ is the FC layer's output in the main module of the model. The MTLM predicts positive if the input sentence is *"This beef is tasty."* when solving the main sentiment classification task.

---

[1] https://huggingface.co/transformers/v3.5.1/_modules/transformers/modeling_bert.html.

[2] https://huggingface.co/learn/nlp-course/chapter7/2.

Auxiliary Task is the POS-tag classification task. This task is a $2q+1$-class the prediction task because we use BIO tags. The cross-entropy loss function of the auxiliary task L_a is defined as follows: $L_a = -\sum_1^j \sum_{k=1}^{2q+1} y_k \log \hat{y_k}$, where $2q+1$ is the number of the POS tags, and j is the number of tokens of the input text. y_k is the true label of the auxiliary task, and $\hat{y_k}$ is the FC layer's output in the auxiliary module of the model. The MTLM predicts [B-Adj, B-Noun, B-Verb, B-Adj, I-Adj, O] if the input sentence is *"This beef is tasty."* when solving the auxiliary task.

The morphological analyzer generates the POS tags using the auxiliary task to the text data. In Japanese datasets, the morphological analyzer MeCab[3] assigns the POS tags used in the auxiliary task. The dictionary used in MeCab is ipadic-NEologd[4]. In English datasets, the morphological analyzer in the NLTK[5] assigns the POS tags used in the auxiliary task. We use POS tags such as nouns, verbs, adjectives, adverbs, conjunctions, particles, and auxiliary verbs. The analyzer assigns the POS tags according to the IOB2 format. The analyzer assigns the B-Noun and I-Adj for the POS-tag used in our experiments. Alternatively, the analyzer assigns the O-tag for the other POS.

4 Experiments

Section 4.1 shows the details of the datasets used in the experiments. We use Japanese and English datasets. Section 4.2 describes the experimental conditions, such as hyperparameters and early stopping. Sections 4.3–4.5 describe the results and discussion. In this study, we carry out three types of evaluation experiments. We use BERT, a deep learning model for natural language processing, in the experiments. The pre-trained model used in the experiments on the Japanese dataset is a BERT-base model[6] from Tohoku University. The pre-trained model used in the experiments on the English dataset is a BERT-base model[7] from Google. We fine-tune these BERT models in our experiments.

4.1 Datasets

In our study, we conduct experiments to determine the impact of the auxiliary task on the main task. We need to compare results on various datasets. Therefore, the experiments use Japanese and English datasets with different domains.

GLUE[8] is an English dataset. This dataset contains English sentences collected from news, Wikipedia, books and articles. We use RTE, MRPC, CoLA, and SST2 included in GLUE in this case. The main task of RTE is to recognize

---

[3] https://github.com/SamuraiT/mecab-python3.
[4] https://github.com/neologd/mecab-ipadic-neologd/blob/master/README.ja.md.
[5] https://www.nltk.org.
[6] https://huggingface.co/tohoku-nlp/bert-base-japanese-char-whole-word-masking.
[7] https://huggingface.co/google-bert/bert-base-uncased.
[8] https://huggingface.co/datasets/nyu-mll/glue.

textual entailment for pairs of sentences, and classify the sentences into two parts: entailment and not_entailment. The main task of MRPC is to determine the equivalence of pairs of sentences, and classify the sentences into two parts: equivalent and not_equivalent. The main task of CoLA is to classify sentences based on their grammatical correctness, and classify the sentences into two parts: acceptable and unacceptable. The main task of SST2 is a sentiment classification of movie reviews, and classify the sentences into two parts: positive and negative.

Livedoor Corpus[9] is provided by Ronwit Inc.. Each column in the dataset consists of URLs, dates, titles, and Japanese text data of Livedoor news. The main task of the Livedoor corpus is to provide a 9-class classification task for news articles.

Rakuten Dataset[10] is provided by Research Data Repository[11]. In this Rakuten Ichiba dataset, we deal with reviews from 2015 to 2019 about food products. The main task of the Rakuten dataset is to classify the reviews into a 5-class sentiment: positive, weak positive, neutral, weak negative, and negative.

Twitter Dataset [10][12] is provided by The Suzuki laboratory in Gifu University. This dataset consists of the ID of the message and the labels put on the tweet by several crowd workers. The main task of the Twitter dataset is to classify a 3-class sentiment for the tweet: positive, neutral, and negative.

4.2   Experimental Condition

In our experiments, the maximum length of tokens that BERT can handle is 500, and the batch size is 32. The optimizer in our experiments is Adam. The learning rate of trainable BERT parameters is $5 \cdot 10^{-5}$ and that of the additional FC layer is $1 \cdot 10^{-4}$. This experiment set λ_m to 1, and λ_a to 0.5.

We utilize early stopping to prevent overfitting. If the minimum value of the loss function in the validation data does not update for ten epochs, we stop training and save the model. In a preliminary experiment, if the minimum value of the loss function in the validation data does not update for 100 epochs, we stop training and save the model. We conclude that ten epochs are sufficient because the result of ten epochs and 100 epochs are the same.

4.3   Experiment 1: Find Adequate Layers for Adding Auxiliary Task

This experiment is the evaluation of the MTLM and the STLM. The purpose of this experiment is to investigate which layer of BERT is suitable for learning the auxiliary task to improve the accuracy of the main task.

---

[9] https://www.rondhuit.com/download.html#ldcc.

[10] Rakuten Group, Inc. (2020): Rakuten Ichiba data. Informatics Research Data Repository, National Institute of Informatics. (dataset).https://doi.org/10.32130/idr.2.1.

[11] https://www.nii.ac.jp/dsc/idr/en/.

[12] https://www.db.info.gifu-u.ac.jp/sentiment_analysis/.

Table 1. Comparison Results in F-value between the MTLM and the STLM.

Dataset Name	RTE	MRPC	CoLA	SST2	Livedoor	Rakuten	Twitter
Dataset Size	2.49k	3.67k	8.55k	67.3k	7.4k	25k	30k
1st layer	**3.539**	**2.188**	**3.594**	0.071	0.677	0.337	-0.101
	(0.027)	(0.004)	(0.011)	(0.200)	(0.248)	(0.262)	(0.596)
2nd layer	**2.834**	**3.216**	**4.057**	0.166	-0.349	**1.187**	0.370
	(0.046)	(0.005)	(0.001)	(0.153)	(0.507)	(0.019)	(0.192)
3rd layer	**3.954**	**2.320**	**3.261**	0.133	**1.165**	0.443	0.201
	(0.033)	(0.024)	(0.005)	(0.186)	(0.049)	(0.325)	(0.309)
4th layer	**3.477**	1.373	**3.435**	0.129	0.208	0.447	0.331
	(0.040)	(0.081)	(0.005)	(0.284)	(0.704)	(0.111)	(0.202)
5th layer	**4.083**	**2.392**	**1.387**	0.053	0.865	**0.965**	0.027
	(0.013)	(0.008)	(0.039)	(0.380)	(0.060)	(0.003)	(0.896)
6th layer	2.470	**3.236**	**1.871**	0.075	0.550	-0.080	**0.440**
	(0.085)	(0.032)	(0.034)	(0.172)	(0.149)	(0.780)	(0.044)
7th layer	**4.678**	1.835	**2.459**	0.057	**1.540**	0.803	0.472
	(0.018)	(0.157)	(0.002)	(0.570)	(0.037)	(0.166)	(0.059)
8th layer	**5.085**	**2.640**	**1.610**	**0.292**	0.461	0.808	0.597
	(0.019)	(0.043)	(0.029)	(0.034)	(0.326)	(0.112)	(0.073)
9th layer	**3.300**	**2.894**	**2.523**	0.127	0.732	0.545	**0.641**
	(0.007)	(0.023)	(0.013)	(0.187)	(0.134)	(0.285)	(0.031)
10th layer	3.029	**4.107**	**2.093**	0.032	**0.971**	0.438	0.280
	(0.074)	(0.003)	(0.025)	(0.523)	(0.011)	(0.466)	(0.266)
11th layer	**2.743**	2.389	2.062	**0.187**	0.849	**0.955**	**0.639**
	(0.023)	(0.051)	(0.098)	(0.345)	(0.079)	(0.035)	(0.081)
12th layer	0.927	**3.123**	**2.070**	0.183	0.573	0.283	0.201
	(0.404)	(0.016)	(0.012)	(0.083)	(0.070)	(0.354)	(0.138)
Max-Min	4.158	2.734	2.670	0.260	1.889	1.268	0.742

Experimental Procedure and Content. At first, we label the text data using the method described in Sect. 3.3. We split all text data into ten pieces for cross-validation. The ratio of the data quantity in the training, validation, and test data is 8:1:1.

Secondly, we construct the MTLM and the STLM described in Sect. 3. We train the two models using the same training and validation data. We utilize early stopping.

Finally, the two models make inferences using the same test data. At this point, we compare the *macro-F*1 of the main task between the MTLM and the STLM. We measure the significance of the difference in *macro-F*1 between the two models using the paired two-sample t-test. We use *macro-F*1 for evaluation instead of *Accuracy* because some datasets are imbalanced. The significance level α is set to 0.05.

Results. Table 1 shows an overview of the experimental and test results. The 1st layer row shows the difference in the 10-run *macro-F*1 average values between the MTLM trained with the auxiliary task added to the first layer and the baseline STLM. The RTE or MRPC columns show the results for each dataset. The Max-Min row shows the difference between the most and least accurate cases. The Dataset Size row shows the dataset size for each dataset used to train and infer the model. The numbers in parentheses indicate *p-value*. We test whether the difference in *macro-F*1 between the MTLM and the STLM is significant with the paired two-sample t-test. The bolded numbers indicate results where the *macro-F*1 of the MTLM is higher than that of the STLM, the *p-value* is below a significance level α, and a significant difference is detected. The underlined text indicates the top 2 items with *macro-F*1 improvements.

This table shows that changing the additional layer improves the *macro-F*1 of the main task. This table shows a significant difference between the two groups in one or more additional layers on all datasets. What stands out in the table is the result on RTE, CoLA, and Livedoor. Result shows a change in *macro-F*1 of 5.085%(*p-value* = 0.019) on RTE, 4.107%(*p-value* = 0.003) on MRPC, and 1.540%(*p-value* = 0.037) on Livedoor by changing the layer to which the auxiliary task is added. On the other hand, we find that the *macro-F*1 of the main task decreases depending on the additional layer of the auxiliary task. Interestingly, adding the auxiliary task to the second layer on Livedoor reduced accuracy by 0.349%, and adding the auxiliary task to the first layer on Twitter reduced accuracy by 0.101%.

The Max-Min rows for the English data set show 4.16% for RTE, 2.73% for MRPC, 2.67% for CoLA, and 0.26% for SST2. The Max-Min rows for the Japanese data set show 1.89% for Livedoor, 1.27% for Rakuten, and 0.74% for Twitter. As the dataset size increases, the Max-Min values become smaller.

Discussion. The seven datasets used in this study have different characteristics. Our experiments use Japanese and English datasets. Some datasets include sentences written by experts, such as books and news, and sentences written by ordinary people, such as tweets and reviews. We find that the POS-tag prediction improves the *macro-F*1 of the main task without dependence on the characteristic of the dataset.

As the dataset size increases, the Max-Min values become smaller. We observe the above trend for both the Japanese and English datasets. It is generally known that multi-task learning is particularly effective when the dataset size is small. Our results are consistent with the previous findings.

CoLA is the task that determines the correctness of the grammar. As shown in underlined text, the accuracy of the MTLM improves by adding the auxiliary task in the first or second layer. SST2 is the sentiment analysis task, and RTE is the entailment recognition task. As shown in underlined text, adding the auxiliary task in the eighth or eleventh layer on SST2 and the seventh or eighth layer on RTE improves the accuracy. These results show two findings below. First, adding a low-level task, such as POS-tag prediction, in the lower layers of the model is not always a good idea. Second, the accuracy of MTLM is affected by the characteristic of the main task, not the characteristic of the auxiliary task. In other words, for the syntactic main task, such as grammatical analysis, adding the auxiliary task in lower layers is advisable, whereas for the semantic main task, such as sentiment analysis, adding the auxiliary task in higher layers is considered beneficial.

4.4 Experiment 2: Comparison of MLTM and SLTM

Table 2. $macro$-$F1$ of the auxiliary task

Dataset Name	RTE	MRPC	CoLA	SST2	Livedoor	Rakuten	Twitter
1st layer	61.81	70.81	85.29	73.45	89.25	85.96	83.25
2nd layer	72.22	77.74	87.84	79.35	90.38	88.72	84.71
3rd layer	74.58	80.55	88.75	81.48	93.04	91.93	88.76
4th layer	74.54	80.58	88.79	82.87	93.07	92.04	88.52
5th layer	74.45	81.12	88.97	84.30	93.40	92.40	88.81
6th layer	74.47	80.86	88.55	84.42	93.61	92.42	88.76
7th layer	72.82	79.76	88.30	84.42	93.06	92.30	88.62
8th layer	73.76	79.68	88.11	84.01	93.49	92.49	89.03
9th layer	71.09	78.20	87.28	83.48	93.21	92.54	89.28
10th layer	69.13	77.30	85.98	82.78	93.00	92.58	89.22
11th layer	68.41	75.83	85.72	81.71	92.41	92.57	89.02
12th layer	71.59	77.80	85.57	80.81	92.35	92.81	89.06

Table 3. Spearman's rank correlation coefficient

Dataset Name	RTE	MRPC	CoLA	SST2	Livedoor	Rakuten	Twitter
r_s	0.301	−0.147	−0.203	−0.308	−0.014	−0.175	0.329

In experiment 2, we compare the accuracy of the main and auxiliary tasks. The purpose of this experiment is to investigate whether the auxiliary task affects the main task.

Experimental Procedure and Content. Using the model constructed in the first experiment, we calculate the accuracy of the main task and the auxiliary task on the test data. We use the seqeval library to calculate the accuracy of the auxiliary task. We use the spearman module in the Python library scipy to calculate the relationship between the accuracy of these tasks.

Results. Table 2 shows the *macro-F*1 of the auxiliary task. The underlined text shows the highest *macro-F*1 of the auxiliary task. The RTE column shows the *macro-F*1 of the auxiliary task on RTE. The 1st layer row shows the 10-run *macro-F*1 average values of the auxiliary task on the MTLM trained with the auxiliary task added to the first layer. These results show the auxiliary task's *macro-F*1 of the MTLM with the auxiliary task added in the first layer to the auxiliary task's *macro-F*1 of the MTLM with the auxiliary task added in the twelfth layer. Table 3 shows a relationship between the difference between the MTLM and the STLM and the *macro-F*1 of the auxiliary task. The correlation coefficient r_s is Spearman's rank correlation coefficient.

If the *macro-F*1 of the main task improves when the *macro-F*1 of the auxiliary task improves, the correlation coefficient r_s approaches 1. Conversely, if the *macro-F*1 of the main task improves when the *macro-F*1 of the auxiliary task decreases, the correlation coefficient r_s approaches -1. For the English dataset, Table 3 shows that the highest correlation coefficient r_s is 0.301 on RTE and the lowest r_s is -0.308 on SST2. For the Japanese dataset, the second experimental result shows that the highest correlation coefficient r_s is 0.329 on Twitter and the lowest r_s is -0.175 on Rakuten.

Discussion. Result shows r_s in the range of -0.3 to 0.3. The correlation coefficients for the English dataset range from -0.308 to 0.301. Those values for the Japanese dataset range from -0.175 to 0.329. There is some variation among the datasets or characteristics of tasks, but none of the correlation coefficients are notably high. Correlation coefficient indicates a lack of association between the difference of MTLM and STLM and the *macro-F*1 of the auxiliary task because r_s is close to zero.

Table 3 at the 1st layer row shows the *macro-F*1 of the auxiliary task is the lowest for all datasets when the auxiliary task is added in the first layer. However, looking at the 1st layer row in Table 1, the *macro-F*1 improves significantly on some datasets. On CoLA, the *macro-F*1 of the auxiliary task is lowest when the auxiliary task is added to the first layer, while the metric of the main task improves significantly. On Rakuten, the *macro-F*1 of the auxiliary task is lowest when the auxiliary task is added to the first layer, while the metric of the main task does not improve significantly.

The best *macro-F*1 of the auxiliary task depends on the datasets. On CoLA, the auxiliary task *macro-F*1 is the best when the auxiliary task is added to the fifth layer, while the main task's metric improves significantly. On Rakuten, the auxiliary task *macro-F*1 is the best when the auxiliary task is added to the twelfth layer, while the main task metric is not significantly improved. In some cases, the accuracy of the main task improves even when the auxiliary task has the best or the lowest *macro-F1*. This observation suggests that adding the auxiliary task to the layer that can learn the auxiliary task well does not affect improving the *macro-F1* of the main task.

4.5   Experiment 3: Visualization of BERT Results

This experiment is a visualization of BERT model's Attention. Attention indicates a decision-making basis of the Transformer model during inference. The purpose of this experiment is to compare the impact on Attention of changing the additional layer of the auxiliary task. We compare Attention between the various models to see how the basis for judgements has changed.

Fig. 2. Attention Visualization between the MTLM(8) and the STLM(8) on RTE.

Experimental Procedure and Content. This experiment uses the model created in first Experiment. In this experiment, we do not train the model, but only infer from the test data. At this time, we visualise Attention of BERT model.

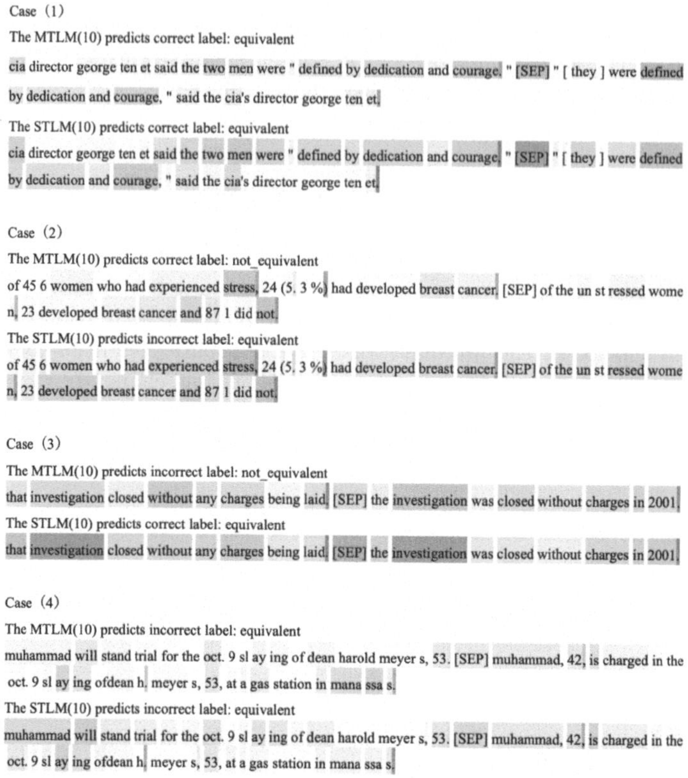

Case (1)

The MTLM(10) predicts correct label: equivalent

cia director george ten et said the two men were " defined by dedication and courage, " [SEP] " [they] were defined by dedication and courage, " said the cia's director george ten et

The STLM(10) predicts correct label: equivalent

cia director george ten et said the two men were " defined by dedication and courage, " [SEP] " [they] were defined by dedication and courage, " said the cia's director george ten et

Case (2)

The MTLM(10) predicts correct label: not_equivalent

of 45 6 women who had experienced stress, 24 (5, 3 %) had developed breast cancer, [SEP] of the un st ressed wome n, 23 developed breast cancer and 87 1 did not

The STLM(10) predicts incorrect label: equivalent

of 45 6 women who had experienced stress, 24 (5, 3 %) had developed breast cancer, [SEP] of the un st ressed wome n, 23 developed breast cancer and 87 1 did not

Case (3)

The MTLM(10) predicts incorrect label: not_equivalent

that investigation closed without any charges being laid, [SEP] the investigation was closed without charges in 2001

The STLM(10) predicts correct label: equivalent

that investigation closed without any charges being laid, [SEP] the investigation was closed without charges in 2001

Case (4)

The MTLM(10) predicts incorrect label: equivalent

muhammad will stand trial for the oct. 9 sl ay ing of dean harold meyer s, 53. [SEP] muhammad, 42, is charged in the oct. 9 sl ay ing ofdean h, meyer s, 53, at a gas station in mana ssa s.

The STLM(10) predicts incorrect label: equivalent

muhammad will stand trial for the oct. 9 sl ay ing of dean harold meyer s, 53. [SEP] muhammad, 42, is charged in the oct. 9 sl ay ing ofdean h, meyer s, 53, at a gas station in mana ssa s.

Fig. 3. Attention Visualization between the MTLM(10) and the STLM(10) on MRPC.

We average the Attention values, which each token gives the [CLS] token, of the 12 Self-Attention tokens in the final layer. We refer to this value as V_a. This value V_a ranges from 0 to 1. We multiply these values by 255 to correspond to a 256-step RGB scale as follows: $(R, G, B) = (255, 255 \times (1 - V_a), 255 \times (1 - V_a))$. A high Attention value indicates a dark red color. The dark red area is the model strongly focus on them. On the other hand, a low Attention value indicates a light red color. The light red area is the model weakly focus on them.

Results. We call the MTLM with the auxiliary task added in the 8th layer as MTLM(8) and the STLM with the trainable 8th layer as STLM(8). In case (1), a model(A) and a model(B) predict correctly. In case (2), a model(A) predicts correctly, but a model(B) predicts incorrectly. In case (3), a model(A) predicts incorrectly, but a model(B) predicts correctly. In case (4), a model(A) and a model(B) predict incorrectly.

Figure 2 shows an Attention visualization on RTE. Case(2) of Fig. 2 shows that both models focus on **media, down, points**, but Attention is slightly different. Both models focus on **always, dow**, and **up**. For the other cases of Fig. 3, there is no difference between the words that models focus on. Attention is similar.

Figure 3 shows an Attention visualization on MRPC. Case(1) of Fig. 3 shows that both models focus on **[SEP], were**, but Attention is different. Case(3) of Fig. 3 shows that both models focus on **investigation, [SEP]**, but Attention is different. Case(4) of Fig. 3 shows that both models focus on **muhammad, [SEP]**, but Attention is different.

Discussion. Figure 2 compares MTLMs to STLMs on RTE. A comparison of Attention between the MTLM and the STLM shows no significant difference in the focus areas of the models. Figure 3 compares MTLMs to STLMs on MRPC. Attention comparison result between the MTLM and STLM reveals that there are differences in what the models focus on. We find that the influence of the auxiliary task on Attention, the basis for the model's judgement, varies depending on the main task.

We can interpret Attention as the basis for the model's judgement. The reason why the accuracy of the main task improves, that is, the model changes its judgement appears in Attention. In other words, we believed that the improvement in accuracy of the main task due to the addition of the auxiliary task could be attributed to changes in the area the model focuses on, changes in Attention. The results of this experiment show that the influence on Attention is task-dependent. The improvement of the main task can not be explained by changes in the basis for model judgement. In other words, we determine that the improvement of the main task may not have been caused by a change in Attention.

Experiment 2 shows no correlation between the accuracy of the main and auxiliary tasks. These results mean that the auxiliary task does not affect the accuracy of the main task, namely based on the model's judgements. Attention is not the only basis for model's judgement. We think that another factor could be changes in model weights. In the future, we will visualize the model weights and investigate the causes.

5 Conclusion

In multi-task learning, which auxiliary tasks are effective in improving the accuracy of the main task have been extensively studied. However, there is little research on which layer is suitable for adding the auxiliary task to improve the accuracy of the main task. An objective of our study is to identify the optimal additional layer of auxiliary tasks in the multi-task learning model using BERT.

Experimental results show that the POS-tag prediction improves the accuracy of the main task without dependence on the characteristic of the dataset. The results also indicate that even with the same auxiliary task, the optimal layer for its addition to improve the accuracy of the main task can vary depending on the main task. Furthermore, results suggest that the layer to which the auxiliary task should be added depends on the characteristic of the main task. We find that adding the auxiliary task to lower layers seems beneficial for the main task like syntactic task, whereas adding its task to higher layers appears to be advantageous for the main task like semantic task.

As a prospect, we would like to conduct additional experiments in other pre-trained models. In addition, it is necessary to investigate which layer is better to improve the accuracy of the main task when adding auxiliary tasks other than syntactic tasks, such as POS-tag prediction.

Acknowledgment. This work was supported in part by JSPS Grant-in-Aid for Scientific Research 24K03044 and 23K28383. In this paper, we used "Rakuten Dataset" (https://rit.rakuten.com/data_release/) provided by Rakuten Group, Inc. via IDR Dataset Service of National Institute of Informatics.

References

1. Barnes, J., Velldal, E., Øvrelid, L.: Improving sentiment analysis with multi-task learning of negation. Nat. Lang. Eng. **27**(2), 249–269 (2021)
2. Benayas, A., Hashempour, R., Rumble, D., Jameel, S., Amorim, R.C.D.: Unified transformer multi-task learning for intent classification with entity recognition. IEEE Access **9**, 147306–147314 (2021)
3. Caruana, R.: Multitask learning. Mach. Learn. **28**(1), 41–75 (1997)
4. Cheng, H., Fang, H., Ostendorf, M.: Open-domain name error detection using a multi-task RNN. In: Proceedings of the 2015 Conference on Empirical Methods in Natural Language Processing, pp. 737–746 (2015)
5. Devlin, J., Chang, M.-W., Lee, K., Toutanova, K.: BERT: pre-training of deep bidirectional transformers for language understanding. In: Proceedings of the 2019 Conference of the North American Chapter of the Association for Computational Linguistics: Human Language Technologies, Volume 1 (Long and Short Papers), pp. 4171–4186, Minneapolis, Minnesota, June 2019. Association for Computational Linguistics (2019). https://doi.org/10.18653/v1/N19-1423, https://aclanthology.org/N19-1423
6. Hashimoto, K., et al.: A joint many-task model: Growing a neural network for multiple NLP tasks. In: Proceedings of the 2017 Conference on Empirical Methods in Natural Language Processing, p. 1923. Association for Computational Linguistics (2017)
7. Jawahar, G., Sagot, B., Seddah, D.: What does bert learn about the structure of language? In: ACL 2019-57th Annual Meeting of the Association for Computational Linguistics (2019)
8. Sinno Jialin Pan and Qiang Yang: A survey on transfer learning. IEEE Trans. Knowl. Data Eng. **22**(10), 1345–1359 (2009)
9. Søgaard, A., Goldberg, Y.: Deep multi-task learning with low level tasks supervised at lower layers. In: Proceedings of the 54th Annual Meeting of the Association for Computational Linguistics (Volume 2: Short Papers), pp. 231–235 (2016)
10. Suzuki, Yu.: Filtering method for twitter streaming data using human-in-the-loop machine learning. J. Inf. Process. **27**, 404–410 (2019)

11. Tenney, I., Das, D., Pavlick, E.: BERT rediscovers the classical NLP pipeline. In: Proceedings of the 57th Annual Meeting of the Association for Computational Linguistics, pp. 4593–4601 (2019)
12. Chaochen, W., Luo, G., Guo, C., Ren, Y., Zheng, A., Yang, C.: An attention-based multi-task model for named entity recognition and intent analysis of Chinese online medical questions. J. Biomed. Inform. **108**, 103511 (2020)

Blockchain, Peer Reviews, and Digital Transparency

Ponzi Scheme Detection and Prevention in Blockchain Platforms Using Machine Learning: A Systematic Literature Review

Karen Esther Castro Severiche, Agnes Wahlqvist Odenman,
and Amin Jalali[✉]

Department of Computer and Systems Sciences,
Stockholm University, Stockholm, Sweden
{kaca2255,agwa4324}@su.se, aj@dsv.su.se

Abstract. A Ponzi scheme is an investment fraud in which existing investors are paid with funds collected from new investors, which causes significant financial losses. This fraudulent activity also exists in blockchain-enabled platforms, but it can be detected and prevented through the application of machine learning techniques. This paper aims to identify and report solutions to detect and prevent Ponzi schemes on blockchain-enabled platforms. The research follows a Systematic Literature Review methodology following the PRISMA 2020 guidelines. The data collected during this study was recorded and stored in the Open Science Framework, ensuring transparency, reproducibility, and supporting future research endeavors. In the end, 49 papers were identified through a process of screening and snowballing. These papers are further studied to report publication trends, applied algorithms, and the reported challenges. The findings indicate a rising global trend in the use of machine learning to detect and prevent Ponzi schemes, particularly since 2017, with China and India leading the way. Ethereum and Bitcoin are the most frequently utilized platforms, while the combination of Support Vector Machine, Random Forest, and Extreme Gradient Boosting emerges as the effective approach. Data imbalance, data quality issues, and computational limitations are identified as key challenges in this field.

Keywords: Machine learning · Bitcoin · Ethereum · Blockchain · cryptocurrency · Fraud detection · Cybercrime

1 Introduction

A Ponzi scheme is a type of investment fraud in which existing investors are paid with funds collected from new investors [1], which can cause significant financial losses. This type of fraud can happen in any financial system, including blockchain - a distributed, decentralized network for recording transactions [2]. As the market for decentralized cryptocurrencies based on blockchain-enabled platforms is growing, identifying such frauds becomes more important. These

P. Delir Haghighi et al. (Eds.): iiWAS 2024, LNCS 15342, pp. 87–102, 2025.
https://doi.org/10.1007/978-3-031-78090-5_8

platforms are decentralized, storing huge amounts of transactions, so they need to detect and prevent Ponzi schemes in an automated way.

Several studies investigated how Ponzi schemes can be detected and prevented automatically using different machine learning algorithms. As this area is new, there is a lack of a comprehensive study in the form of a systematic literature review showing the current state of the art for Ponzi scheme detection and prevention.

Therefore, this paper intends to identify peer-reviewed studies that applied machine learning to detect and prevent Ponzi Schemes on blockchain-enabled platforms. Identifying these studies enables discovering the publication trends, the algorithms used to train the models and the challenges and limitations in identifying Ponzi schemes in blockchain-enabled platforms through machine learning. Therefore, we pose these research questions for this study:

- **RQ1. Publication trends:** What are the publication trends in detecting and preventing Ponzi schemes using machine learning on blockchain-enabled platforms?
- **RQ2. Training algorithms:** What are the most used machine learning algorithms in training models for detecting and preventing Ponzi schemes on blockchain-enabled platforms?
- **RQ3. Challenges & limitations:** What challenges are encountered when applying machine learning techniques to Ponzi scheme detection and prevention on blockchain-enabled platforms?

To address these questions, we conducted a Systematic Literature Review (SLR), which is the first study in this area to the best of our knowledge. 49 papers are identified as a result of screening and snowballing based on which the research questions are answered. The remainder of this paper is organized as follows. Section 2 gives a short background on the topic. Section 3 elaborates on the research methodology. Section 4 presents and discusses the result. Section 5 concludes the paper and introduces future research.

2   Background

Ponzi schemes, sometimes referred to as high-yield investment programs (HYIP), are types of scams that pay early investors with money from new ones, creating the illusion of a successful investment through high returns [3].

Figure 1 shows a simple fictitious example of how a Ponzi scheme network can grow. This example starts with a schemer who invites first-level investors by promising a 40% return per month. Imagine each investor only pay 5 coins, and the network starts with 2 investors getting onboarded. In the first month, the schemer gains 10 coins. Some of these networks promise a return if each investor introduces their friends who also invest in the business. Let's imagine that each investor brings two investors to the network. We will have 4 new investors in the second month. The schemer can pay each of the first-level investors from money that (s)he receives from second-level investors in the second month. This means

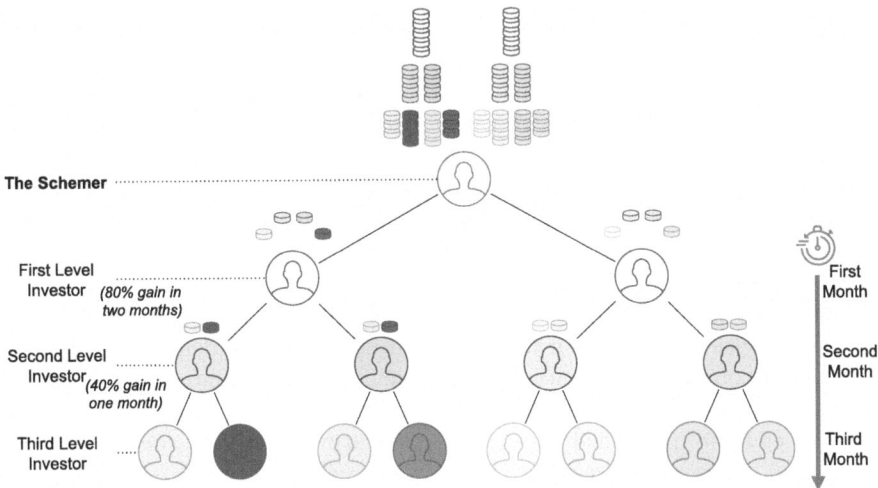

Fig. 1. A fictitious example of Ponzi schemes where each investor gains 40% each month which are funded by onboarding new investors.

that first-level investors will receive 2 coins, and the schemer will have 26 coins. In the third month, if the network can grow as fast as before, the investors will receive 2 more coins, and the schemer will collect 54 coins.

This business eventually falls apart when investors stop joining the scheme, leaving subsequent investors empty-handed. Therefore, a scheme organizer's main task is to recruit new investors with promises of investing their money in opportunities generating high returns to keep the scheme going. The name originates from Charles Ponzi, who in the 1920 s promised investors a return of 50%, claiming the profit came from international mail coupons but instead using funds from new investors [4]. The Ponzi scheme has been around for a long time, most likely even before the 1920 s, but it has now found its way into the digital world, specifically the cryptocurrency market and blockchain.

The history of blockchain can be traced back to 2008 [5], when Satoshi Nakamoto published a report on a system to make transactions without the need for third parties [6]. The importance of the system was not limited to introducing a new currency, called Bitcoin, but it also introduced a distributed ledger technology, called the blockchain. As a result, blockchain systems have been used in a wide range of rapidly expanding application scenarios. Transparency, robustness, auditability, and security are inherent characteristics of blockchain architecture.

The use of blockchain has not remained limited to cryptocurrencies. Smart contracts are one example of how blockchain is being used in fields other than cryptocurrencies. These contracts are pieces of software that govern the exchange of resources (including money and services) between participants [7]. Smart contracts enable anonymous parties to carry out trusted transactions and agreements [8]. Ethereum is a blockchain-based decentralized open-source software platform that also supports smart contracts [9].

As a side effect, the blockchain market has attracted cybercriminals and provided opportunities for scams to take place. Many investment frauds can be identified by recognizing investment offers too simply good to be true returns with characteristics including guaranteed and overly-consistent returns, along with risks being low or nonexistent. Pyramid schemes, advance fee schemes, market manipulation fraud(or "pump and dump"), and Ponzi schemes are a few examples of such frauds.

As blockchain provides transparency and auditability, detecting and preventing such activities is possible if machines can be trained to identify that behavior. When it comes to systematic literature reviews on the matter, the following reviews seem to be closest related to the topic:

Vacca et al. [8] published a systematic literature review on smart contracts focusing on software engineering tools, techniques, and practices intended to address the unique challenges posed by smart contracts and blockchain development. Furthermore, it attempts to identify potential future research directions as well as unresolved issues. Ponzi schemes are only addressed as one of the fraud issues for blockchain-based software in this work. Badawi & Jourdan [10] focused their systematic literature review on the threats and defenses related to cryptocurrencies, along with their respective scales and efficiencies. In the study, the Ponzi scheme is mentioned as one of the types of threats, and it goes on to further discuss how datasets for research on detection have been collected, as well as referencing studies on detection mechanisms with high detection rates such as Bartoletti et al. [11] as aforementioned.

The current study will build on previous research by focusing entirely on Ponzi schemes, which existing works did not appear to do to the same extent.

3   Methodology

Systematic Literature Review (SLR) is used as the research methodology in this study, where we followed PRISMA (Preferred Reporting Items for Systematic Reviews and Meta-Analyses) 2020 guidelines [12] adopting PRISMA 2020 checklist [12], Explanation and Elaboration document [13] and flow diagram [12]. All data are stored in the Open Science Framework (OSF) during the study [14]. OSF is a tool enabling storing research data while doing the research to support openness, integrity, and reproducibility of the result [15][1].

Figure 2 shows the PRISMA flow diagram which is adopted for this study. The PRISMA flow diagram contains three main phases, i.e., *identification*, *screening*, and *included*, which represent the identification of records that can answer the research question, screening identified records to exclude unrelated ones, and including the final records for the study. These are visualized as vertical boxes on the left side of the figure. The flow diagram is configured as two

---

[1] The repository is available here: https://osf.io/k92hc.

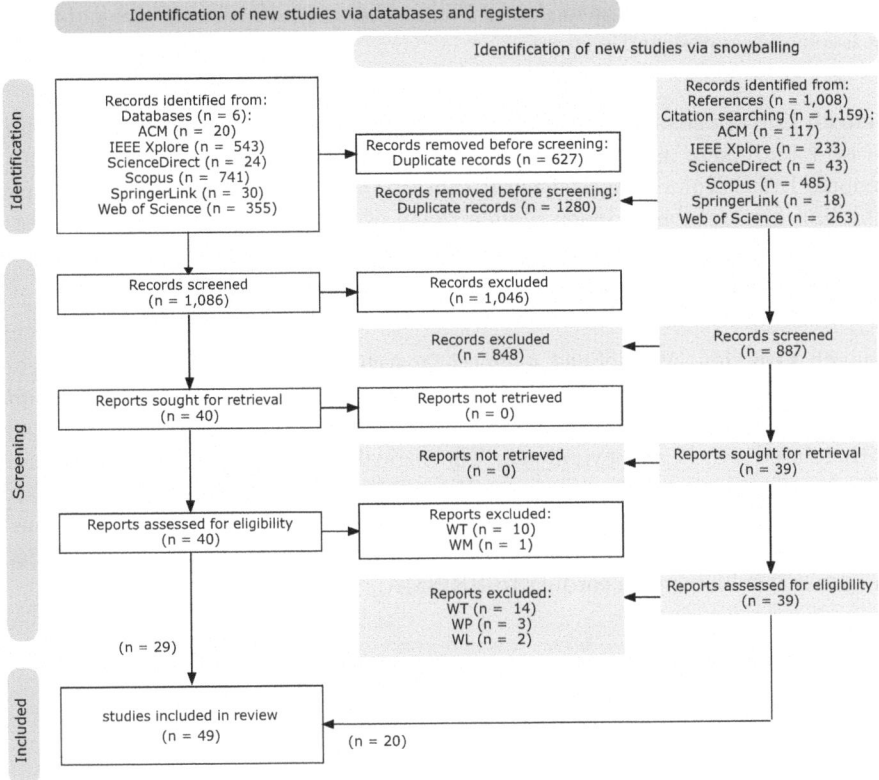

Fig. 2. The adopted Prisma flow diagram shows the data collection steps and the number of selected papers in each step.

main sequential steps, i.e., i) identifying included records by querying databases, ii) identifying records related to included records through snowballing.

3.1 Identification of New Studies

In this step, we identified included records by querying databases and excluding unrelated works in the screening phase.

Inclusion and Exclusion Criterion. To evaluate the relevancy and the quality of sources, we defined the inclusion and exclusion criteria as specified here. The inclusion criteria is defined as i) when multiple papers report on the same study, only the most recent paper will be included, ii) studies applying machine learning or data mining techniques for detecting Ponzi schemes are only included, iii) published peer-reviewed papers and articles are only included. The exclusion criteria is defined to exclude records when i) access to the full text is not possible, ii) they are not written in English, iii) they do not apply machine learning or data mining techniques to detect Ponzi schemes, and iv) they are published as Books, keynotes, and posters.

Search Databases. We chose the following databases to search related articles as we found them as main forums in the preliminary search: Web of Science, Scopus, IEEE Xplore, ACM Digital Library, ScienceDirect, and SpringerLink. The first two databases index a wide range of academic peer-reviewed papers. The other databases are also included as they are used mostly in this field to publish papers.

Search Queries. We defined a generic search query and adopted it based on each database if needed. The generic search query is defined as the composition of the key terms associated with the first research question of this study, along with related words and synonyms. The logical search query for all databases allowing such long queries (Scopus, Web of Science, ACM Digital Library, and SpringerLink) are performed as shown in Table 1. The search terms are defined to be generic to target all possible relevant articles where they can be excluded in systematic filtering, according to PRISMA.

Table 1. The generic search query used in this study.

("machine learning" OR "artificial intelligence" OR "data mining")
AND
(ponzi OR "ponzi scheme" OR hyip OR "high-yield investment program" OR scam OR fraud)
AND
(cryptocurrency OR blockchain OR ethereum OR decentralization OR "smart contracts" OR investment OR transaction)
AND
(detection OR detect OR discover OR spot OR identify OR uncover OR recognize OR find OR notice OR prevention OR prevent OR impediment)

The search terms were found by looking through keywords and index terms of related studies as well as by searching for synonyms for the purpose of not missing any relevant studies during the search process. Each term in the columns was included in the query and divided by the logical operator "OR", combining them into a single group. Each group was then combined using the "AND" conjunction creating the final search query, which generated a list of references that were saved and screened for duplicates, all recorded in the OSF repository [14].

For the search, it was necessary to find the appropriate field, such as title, abstract, and keywords, to apply the search string to all databases that allow such specifications. Searching in a single field does not always yield all relevant publications. As a result, only the title, abstract, and keywords of publications were included in the search where possible (Scopus, Web of Science, ACM Digital

Library, and ScienceDirect). A filter was also applied where possible to limit the results to studies in English and only include papers that meet the inclusion criteria.

For IEEE Xplore, some terms were cut due to query length restrictions, and the query was prepared for searching all metadata fields due to it not being possible to apply the query to multiple specific fields at the same time. For SpringerLink, no limits were applied to the search because it doesn't allow for title-abstract-keyword searches, and for ScienceDirect, the boolean connectors in queries are limited to 8; therefore, the query was shortened. As a result, we identified 1713 papers with 627 duplications, which feeds the screening phase of the first step with 1086 papers.

Screening Identified Records. The first two authors acted as reviewers and independently screened titles and abstracts of identified studies. They voted on whether to include or exclude each study based on specific inclusion and exclusion criteria by reading the titles and abstracts. All the votes are available in the OSF repository [14]. Additionally, the first two authors thoroughly read all the included papers, compiled the data, and drafted the paper. The third author played the role of a judge, resolving any conflicts that arose and providing supervision and guidance throughout the research process. As a result, 1046 papers were excluded, leaving a total of 40 papers for analysis.

The full text of these 40 papers was obtained, and both reviewers screened them, voting on their inclusion or exclusion according to the predetermined criteria to ensure inter-rater agreement. The relevant studies were carefully documented, and reasons for excluding studies at this stage were recorded.

The reasons used for excluding papers were: i) *Wrong Theme (WT)*: studies not relating to Ponzi schemes (corresponds to the third exclusion criterion), ii) *Wrong Method (WM)*: studies not applying machine learning or data mining techniques (corresponds to the third exclusion criterion), iii) *Wrong Publication type (WP)* (corresponds to the fourth exclusion criterion), and iv) *Wrong Language (WL)*: corresponds to the second exclusion criterion.

Among the initial 40 papers, 10 were excluded due to the wrong theme, and 1 is excluded due to the wrong method, which resulted in 29 papers being included in the second step.

4   Result and Discussion

This section presents the study's result, where the outline is defined following the defined research questions. Table 2 shows all included papers, the type of fraud that they detect or prevent, the platforms, and reported challenges.

In this table, these acronyms are used. PS: Ponzi scheme, NDR: Non-Representative data, CC: Computational Constraints, LD: Lack of Data, OD: Outdated Data, B: Bias, LA: Limited Accuracy, LP: Limited Performance. The term "Not Specified" for the platform is used to show if i) the platform is not mentioned or ii) it is not the only used platform. These three categories are marked as disjoint sets.

Table 2. Challengeouse, Platform & Fraud Types addressed by papers (acronyms are defined at beginning of Sect. 4).

Paper	Fraud Type			Platform			Reported Challengesous						
	PS	PS&Others	Not Specified	Bitcoin	Etherum	Not Specified	NRD	CC	LD	OD	B	LA	LP
[16]	+			+			+					+	+
[17]		+		+			+					+	+
[18]	+			+			+		+			+	
[19]	+			+									
[20]	+			+				+					+
[21]		+		+					+		+	+	+
[11]	+			+									
[22]	+			+				+				+	+
[23]	+			+			+					+	
[24]	+			+									
[25]	+			+									
[26]	+			+			+				+	+	
[27]	+			+			+					+	
[28]	+			+			+			+			
[29]		+		+					+		+	+	
[30]	+			+									
[31]	+				+								
[32]		+			+								
[33]	+				+								
[34]		+			+		+					+	
[35]	+				+								
[36]	+				+								
[37]	+				+		+						+
[38]	+				+								
[39]		+			+		+					+	
[40]		+			+								
[41]		+			+								
[42]	+				+		+					+	
[43]		+			+								
[44]	+				+								
[45]	+				+				+		+		
[46]	+				+		+		+	+	+		
[47]	+				+		+						+
[48]	+				+		+	+				+	+
[49]	+				+		+					+	
[50]		+			+				+				+
[51]	+				+								
[1]	+				+				+		+	+	
[52]	+				+			+	+				+
[53]	+				+								
[54]		+			+								
[55]		+			+								
[56]	+				+								
[57]	+				+		+					+	
[58]		+			+				+		+	+	+
[59]		+				+							
[60]		+				+	+						+
[61]	+					+							
[62]		+				+			+				

4.1   Publication Trends

We identified 49 papers that were published by researchers from different geographical locations.

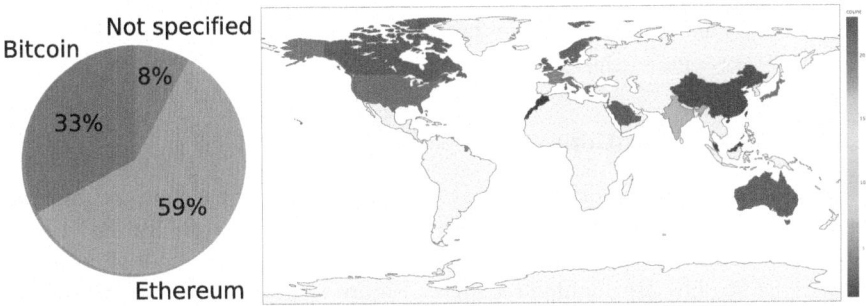

(a)   Publications   per platform

(b)   Geographical   distribution   based   on   the   authors' affiliations

Fig. 3. Percentages of papers based on the Authors' Geographical location (affiliation) and applied Platform

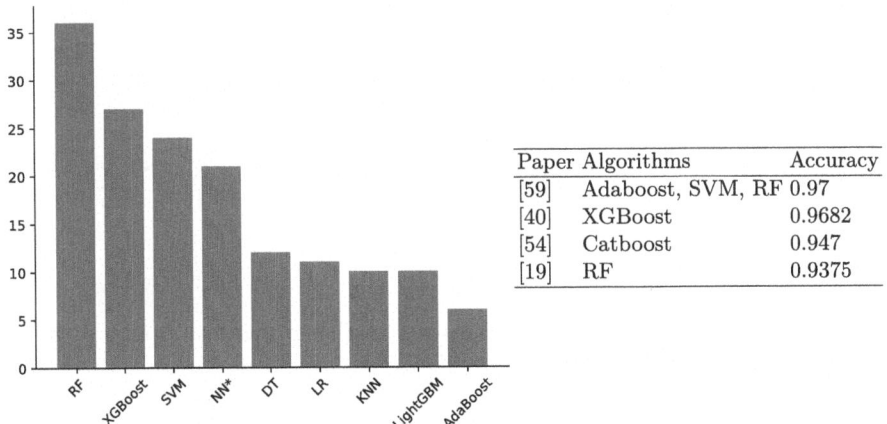

Paper	Algorithms	Accuracy
[59]	Adaboost, SVM, RF	0.97
[40]	XGBoost	0.9682
[54]	Catboost	0.947
[19]	RF	0.9375

Fig. 4. The most common used algorithms (shown in the bar chart) & top-reported accuracies in studies (shown in the table).

The right side of Fig. 3 shows the distribution of the authors geographical locations, indicating efforts on a global scale to tackle these problems. China leads with 23, followed by India (9 papers), France (4 papers), the United States, Italy, Greece, and Japan (3 papers), and the United Kingdom, Israel, Norway,

Saudi Arabia, Sweden, Denmark, Canada, and Australia (2 papers). Morocco, Malta, Malaysia, the Netherlands, and Taiwan each contributed one.

We also identified that the solutions are developed and tested on different platforms, where Ethereum is the most popular platform, with 59% of the papers claiming to detect fraud in the system. 33% of papers reported Bitcoin as their platform, and around 8% of the papers did not mention the platform. Bitcoin has been used as a platform at the beginning, yet recently there has been more focus on Ethereum, as shown in the left side of Fig. 3.

4.2   Training Algorithms

There are numerous algorithms used for the training phase in the included papers. As a result, listing them all is not feasible. The full list is available in the OSF repository [14]. Instead, the most commonly used algorithms among the various studies are highlighted here. Figure 4 shows the list of most commonly used algorithms on the left side. It also lists four top-reported accuracies in all included studies. The common algorithms are:

1. Random forest (RF) was the most commonly used classifier, used in 36 papers.
2. The XGBoost was implemented in 27 papers.
3. The SVM method was used by 24 of the papers, making it the third most used technique.
4. The fourth most widely used technique identified in the review was Neural Networks (NN). To encompass the various names used in the papers, NN is used as a representative term. This umbrella term encompasses different types of neural networks, such as Convolutional Neural Networks (CNN) and Artificial Neural Networks (ANN), among others.

The other most commonly used algorithms were Decision Tree (DT) classification algorithm, Logistic Regression (LR), K-nearest Neighbor (KNN), Light-GBM, and AdaBoost. More details can be found in our OSF Repository [14].

4.3   Challenges

We have identified three main categories of challenges in the studies such as non-representative data, poor data quality, and computational constraints. A combination of these categories can be observed, as reported, in most of the studies. As sub-categories, we could identify bias, limited performance, and limited accuracy. Note that not all papers acknowledged challenges and/or limitations in their research.

The problem of non-representative data was a frequent occurrence where data imbalance was reported as a challenge in the papers. This problem was reported by papers [18,34,60], and [37]. Ponzi scheme contracts are in the minority in the dataset when compared to other contracts, making the data non-representative. One paper [31] recorded 386 smart Ponzi schemes out of 3239 non-Ponzi schemes, while paper [20] revealed that only 120 of 24197 illicit addresses were Ponzi schemes. The dataset in paper [56] contained information on 386 smart Ponzi schemes and 3239 non-Ponzi schemes. The methods used to collect the data varied; for example, paper [56] gathered their data by using datasets provided in previous studies, whereas Bartoletti et al. [11] manually selected their data from forums and websites; however, many of the sources for extraction were shared. Some authors used datasets from previous studies to gather their sample data, i.e., Fan et al. [56], and Chen et al. [42].

Seventeen papers from the list of selected studies reported that their dataset had a class imbalance problem. To tackle the problem of an imbalanced dataset, some papers reported on the use of various oversampling techniques to augment the minority class as reported in papers [1,21,31,35,36,38,41,44,50,61], and [56]. However, it is also stated that the use of these techniques is restricted to the assumption that the local space between any two positive instances is positive or belongs to the minority class, which may not always be true when the training data is not linearly separable [63].

Furthermore, the fact that the dataset model used to train the algorithm is not based on real examples but on those generated by the oversampled technique could be considered a limitation.

A different difficulty encountered was a lack of data, as in papers [18,21, 48,50,52], and [58]. Data scarcity becomes more apparent in studies that use LightGBM as this requires a large amount of data to perform well, as described in paper [50]. Authors of papers [45,46], and [1] reported that their data was out of date, and as malicious contracts changed over time to avoid detection, the techniques implemented suffered, limiting final performance. The long training time was also a problem, as mentioned by papers [22,48], and [52], as well as computational constraints as in paper [21,29,58]. Paper [21] reported that not all of the data used to train the prediction model included all of the data that is inherently available on the Bitcoin blockchain.

Limited performance was the case for paper [26], where authors encountered classification errors, resulting in illegal businesses being classified as legal.

5   Conclusion

This paper presents an overview of studies on the impact of machine learning in detecting and preventing Ponzi schemes through conducting a systematic literature review. It presents 49 papers and how they are included. It also compiles and present the publication trends, top most used algorithms, and top reported accuracies, and challenges and limitations in this area.

Random forest is identified as the most frequently mentioned technique, where 36 papers employ it in their studies. It outperformed other techniques for detecting and preventing Ponzi schemes, according to the results reported. Other popular techniques are XGBoost (used by 27 papers), SVM (used by 24 papers), and neural networks (used by 21 papers).

These categories are identified as the most common challenge, i.e., non-representative data (data imbalance), poor data quality, and computational constraints. In addition, three sub-categories are identified, i.e., bias, limited performance, and limited accuracy.

When compared to other contracts, Ponzi scheme contracts are in the minority in the dataset. To address the issue of an imbalanced dataset, some papers reported on the use of various oversampling techniques to augment the minority class; however, the fact that the dataset used to train the model is not based on real examples but on those generated by the oversampling technique may be regarded as a limitation.

Different issues that arose were a lack of data, the data used was out of date, there was a long training time, and there were computational constraints. LightGBM, for instance, requires a large amount of data to perform well, so selecting the appropriate method is dependent on the data itself. Studying the type of data available to work with should go hand in hand with the method used to limit the problems mentioned.

By considering the results listed above, it can be concluded that machine learning in different variations can be used with good results to detect and prevent Ponzi schemes by training models using real-world examples of Ponzi schemes. The fact that a limited number of examples exist means that using machine learning to detect Ponzi schemes might require additional preparation of the dataset in order to prevent bad results caused by data imbalance.

A possible direction for future studies would be to extend the analysis result of identified approaches. In addition, the research questions can be broaden to address e.g. how attackers are changing tactics. Another question to answer could also be which types of features are used to train models and perform well with different machine learning techniques to detect Ponzi schemes.

References

1. Wang, L., Cheng, H., Zheng, Z., Yang, A., Zhu, X.: Ponzi scheme detection via oversampling-based long short-term memory for smart contracts. Knowl.-Based Syst. **228**, 107312 (2021)
2. Monrat, A.A., Schelén, O., Andersson, K.: A survey of blockchain from the perspectives of applications, challenges, and opportunities. IEEE Access **7**, 117134–117151 (2019)
3. Moore, T., Han, J., Clayton, R.: The postmodern Ponzi scheme: empirical analysis of high-yield investment programs. In: Keromytis, A.D. (ed.) Financial Cryptography and Data Security, pp. 41–56. Springer, Berlin, Heidelberg (2012). https://doi.org/10.1007/978-3-642-32946-3_4
4. Darby, M.: In Ponzi we trust. Smithsonian **29**(9), 134–147 (1998)
5. Nakamoto, S., Bitcoin, A.: A peer-to-peer electronic cash system. Bitcoin, **4**(2), 15 (2008). https://bitcoin.org/bitcoin.pdf
6. Nakamoto, S.: Bitcoin: a peer-to-peer electronic cash system. Decentralized Bus. Rev. (2008)
7. de Haro-Olmo, F.J., Varela-Vaca, Á.J., Álvarez-Bermejo, J.A.: Blockchain from the perspective of privacy and anonymisation: A systematic literature review. Sensors **20**(24), 7171 (2020)

8. Vacca, A., Di Sorbo, A., Visaggio, C.A., Canfora, G.: A systematic literature review of blockchain and smart contract development: techniques, tools, and open challenges. J. Syst. Softw. **174**, 110891 (2021)
9. Chen, T., et al.: Understanding ethereum via graph analysis. ACM Trans. Internet Technol. (TOIT) **20**(2), 1–32 (2020)
10. Badawi, E., Jourdan, G.-V.: Cryptocurrencies emerging threats and defensive mechanisms: a systematic literature review. IEEE Access **8**, 200021–200037 (2020)
11. Bartoletti, M., Pes, B., Serusi, S.: Data mining for detecting bitcoin Ponzi schemes. In: 2018 Crypto Valley Conference on Blockchain Technology (CVCBT), pp. 75–84. IEEE (2018)
12. Page, M.J., et al.: The PRISMA 2020 statement: an updated guideline for reporting systematic reviews. Int. J. Surg. **88**, 105906 (2021)
13. Page, M.J., et al.: PRISMA 2020 explanation and elaboration: updated guidance and exemplars for reporting systematic reviews. BMJ 372 (2021)
14. Odenman, A.W., Castro, E., Jalali, A.: Impact study of machine learning in Ponzi scheme detection and prevention: a systematic literature review (2022). https://osf.io/k92hc/
15. Foster, E.D., Deardorff, A.: Open science framework (OSF). J. Med. Library Assoc. JMLA **105**(2), 203 (2017)
16. Al-Hashedi, K.G., Magalingam, P., Maarop, N., Samy, G.N., Manaf, A.A.: A conceptual model to identify illegal activities on the bitcoin system. In: Abdullah, N., Manickam, S., Anbar, M. (eds.) Advances in Cyber Security: Third International Conference, ACeS 2021, Penang, Malaysia, August 24–25, 2021, Revised Selected Papers, pp. 18–34. Springer Singapore, Singapore (2021). https://doi.org/10.1007/978-981-16-8059-5_2
17. Yin, H.S., Vatrapu, R.: A first estimation of the proportion of cybercriminal entities in the bitcoin ecosystem using supervised machine learning. In: 2017 IEEE International Conference on Big Data (Big Data), pp. 3690–3699. IEEE (2017)
18. Lin, Y.-J., Wu, P.-W., Hsu, C.-H., Tu, I.-P., Liao, S.-W.: An evaluation of bitcoin address classification based on transaction history summarization. In: 2019 IEEE International Conference on Blockchain and Cryptocurrency (ICBC), pp. 302–310. IEEE (2019)
19. Toyoda, K., Mathiopoulos, P.T., Ohtsuki, T.: A novel methodology for HYIP operators' bitcoin addresses identification. IEEE Access **7**, 74835–74848 (2019)
20. Tian, H., Li, Y., Cai, Y., Shi, X., Zheng, Z.: Attention-based graph neural network for identifying illicit bitcoin addresses. In: Dai, H.-N., Liu, X., Luo, D.X., Xiao, J., Chen, X. (eds.) Blockchain and Trustworthy Systems: Third International Conference, BlockSys 2021, Guangzhou, China, August 5–6, 2021, Revised Selected Papers, pp. 147–162. Springer Singapore, Singapore (2021). https://doi.org/10.1007/978-981-16-7993-3_11
21. Harlev, M.A., Sun Yin, H., Langenheldt, K.C., Mukkamala, R., Vatrapu, R.: Breaking bad: de-anonymising entity types on the bitcoin blockchain using supervised machine learning (2018)
22. Nerurkar, P., Busnel, Y., Ludinard, R., Shah, K., Bhirud, S., Patel, D.: Detecting illicit entities in bitcoin using supervised learning of ensemble decision trees. In: Proceedings of the 10th International Conference on Information Communication and Management, pp. 25–30 (2020)
23. Li, Y., Cai, Y., Tian, H., Xue, G., Zheng, Z.: Identifying illicit addresses in bitcoin network. In: Zheng, Z., Dai, H.-N., Fu, X., Chen, B. (eds.) BlockSys 2020. CCIS, vol. 1267, pp. 99–111. Springer, Singapore (2020). https://doi.org/10.1007/978-981-15-9213-3_8

24. Eloul, S., Moran, S.J., Mendel, J.: Improving streaming cryptocurrency transaction classification via biased sampling and graph feedback. In: Annual Computer Security Applications Conference, pp. 761–772 (2021)
25. Toyoda, K., Ohtsuki, T., Mathiopoulos, P.T.: Multi-class bitcoin-enabled service identification based on transaction history summarization. In: 2018 IEEE International Conference on Internet of Things (iThings) and IEEE Green Computing and Communications (GreenCom) and IEEE Cyber, Physical and Social Computing (CPSCom) and IEEE Smart Data (SmartData), pp. 1153–1160. IEEE (2018)
26. Nerurkar, P., Bhirud, S., Patel, D., Ludinard, R., Busnel, Y., Kumari, S.: Supervised learning model for identifying illegal activities in bitcoin. Appl. Intell. **51**, 3824–3843 (2021)
27. Elbaghdadi, A., Mezroui, S., El Oualkadi, A.: SVM: an approach to detect illicit transaction in the bitcoin network. In: Ben Ahmed, M., Rakıp Kara, İ, Santos, D., Sergeyeva, O., Boudhir, A.A. (eds.) SCA 2020. LNNS, vol. 183, pp. 1130–1141. Springer, Cham (2021). https://doi.org/10.1007/978-3-030-66840-2_86
28. Singh, A., Gupta, A., Wadhwa, H., Asthana, S., Arora, A.: Temporal debiasing using adversarial loss based GNN architecture for crypto fraud detection. In: 2021 20th IEEE International Conference on Machine Learning and Applications (ICMLA), pp. 391–396. IEEE (2021)
29. Chaudhari, D., Agarwal, R., Shukla, S.K.: Towards malicious address identification in bitcoin. In: 2021 IEEE International Conference on Blockchain (Blockchain), pp. 425–432. IEEE (2021)
30. Toyoda, K., Ohtsuki, T., Mathiopoulos, P.T.: Identification of high yielding investment programs in bitcoin via transactions pattern analysis. In: GLOBECOM 2017-2017 IEEE Global Communications Conference, pp. 1–6. IEEE (2017)
31. Fan, S., Fu, S., Xu, H., Cheng, X.: AL-SPSD: anti-leakage smart Ponzi schemes detection in blockchain. Inf. Process. Manage. **58**(4), 102587 (2021)
32. Xing, C., Chen, Z., Chen, L., Guo, X., Zheng, Z., Li, J.: A new scheme of vulnerability analysis in smart contract with machine learning. Wireless Netw., 1–10 (2020)
33. Aljofey, A., Jiang, Q., Qu, Q.: A supervised learning model for detecting Ponzi contracts in Ethereum blockchain. In: Tian, Y., Ma, T., Khan, M.K., Sheng, V.S., Pan, Z. (eds.) Big Data and Security: Third International Conference, ICBDS 2021, Shenzhen, China, November 26–28, 2021, Proceedings, pp. 657–672. Springer Singapore, Singapore (2022). https://doi.org/10.1007/978-981-19-0852-1_52
34. Liu, L., Tsai, W.-T., Bhuiyan, M.Z.A., Peng, H., Liu, M.: Blockchain-enabled fraud discovery through abnormal smart contract detection on Ethereum. Futur. Gener. Comput. Syst. **128**, 158–166 (2022)
35. Zhang, Y., Kang, S., Dai, W., Chen, S., Zhu, J.: Code will speak: early detection of Ponzi smart contracts on Ethereum. In: 2021 IEEE International Conference on Services Computing (SCC), pp. 301–308. IEEE (2021)
36. He, X., Yang, T., Chen, L., et al.: CTRF: Ethereum-based Ponzi contract identification. Security Commun. Netw. 2022 (2022)
37. Jung, E., Le Tilly, M., Gehani, A., Ge, Y.: Data mining-based Ethereum fraud detection. In: 2019 IEEE international conference on blockchain (Blockchain), pp. 266–273. IEEE (2019)
38. Zhang, Y., Yu, W., Li, Z., Raza, S., Cao, H.: Detecting Ethereum Ponzi schemes based on improved LightGBM algorithm. IEEE Trans. Comput. Soc. Syst. **9**(2), 624–637 (2021)

39. Agarwal, R., Barve, S., Shukla, S.K.: Detecting malicious accounts in permissionless blockchains using temporal graph properties. Appl. Netw. Sci. **6**(1), 1–30 (2021)
40. Kumar, N., Singh, A., Handa, A., Shukla, S.K.: Detecting malicious accounts on the Ethereum blockchain with supervised learning. In: Cyber Security Cryptography and Machine Learning: Fourth International Symposium, CSCML 2020, Be'er Sheva, Israel, July 2–3, 2020, Proceedings 4, pp. 94–109. Springer, Cham (2020). https://doi.org/10.1007/978-3-030-49785-9_7
41. Poursafaei, F., Hamad, G.B., Zilic, Z.: Detecting malicious Ethereum entities via application of machine learning classification. In: 2020 2nd Conference on Blockchain Research & Applications for Innovative Networks and Services (BRAINS), pp. 120–127. IEEE (2020)
42. Chen, W., Zheng, Z., Cui, J., Ngai, E., Zheng, P., Zhou, Y.: Detecting Ponzi schemes on Ethereum: towards healthier blockchain technology. In: Proceedings of the 2018 World Wide Web Conference, pp. 1409–1418 (2018)
43. Farrugia, S., Ellul, J., Azzopardi, G.: Detection of illicit accounts over the Ethereum blockchain. Expert Syst. Appl. **150**, 113318 (2020)
44. Peng, J., Xiao, G.: Detection of smart Ponzi schemes using opcode. In: Zheng, Z., Dai, H.-N., Fu, X., Chen, B. (eds.) BlockSys 2020. CCIS, vol. 1267, pp. 192–204. Springer, Singapore (2020). https://doi.org/10.1007/978-981-15-9213-3_15
45. Sun, W., Xu, G., Yang, Z., Chen, Z.: Early detection of smart Ponzi scheme contracts based on behavior forest similarity. In:: 2020 IEEE 20th International Conference on Software Quality, Reliability and Security (QRS), pp. 297–309. IEEE (2020)
46. Ibba, G., Pierro, G.A., Di Francesco, M.: Evaluating machine-learning techniques for detecting smart Ponzi schemes. In: 2021 IEEE/ACM 4th International Workshop on Emerging Trends in Software Engineering for Blockchain (WETSEB), pp. 34–40. IEEE (2021)
47. Chen, W., Zheng, Z., Ngai, E.C.-H., Zheng, P., Zhou, Y.: Exploiting blockchain data to detect smart Ponzi schemes on Ethereum. IEEE Access **7**, 37575–37586 (2019)
48. Bian, L., Zhang, L., Zhao, K., Wang, H., Gong, S.: Image-based scam detection method using an attention capsule network. IEEE Access **9**, 33654–33665 (2021)
49. Chen, Y., Dai, H., Yu, X., Hu, W., Xie, Z., Tan, C.: Improving Ponzi scheme contract detection using multi-channel TextCNN and transformer. Sensors **21**(19), 6417 (2021)
50. Aziz, R.M., Baluch, M.F., Patel, S., Ganie, A.H.: LGBM: a machine learning approach for Ethereum fraud detection. Int. J. Inf. Technol. **14**(7), 3321–3331 (2022)
51. Shen, X., Jiang, S., Zhang, L.: Mining bytecode features of smart contracts to detect Ponzi scheme on blockchain. CMES-Comput. Model. Eng. Sci. **127**(3) (2021)
52. Lou, Y., Zhang, Y., Chen, S.: Ponzi contracts detection based on improved convolutional neural network. In: 2020 IEEE International Conference on Services Computing (SCC), pp. 353–360. IEEE (2020)
53. Yu, S., Jin, J., Xie, Y., Shen, J., Xuan, Q.: Ponzi Scheme Detection in Ethereum Transaction Network. In: Dai, H.-N., Liu, X., Luo, D.X., Xiao, J., Chen, X. (eds.) Blockchain and Trustworthy Systems: Third International Conference, BlockSys 2021, Guangzhou, China, August 5–6, 2021, Revised Selected Papers, pp. 175–186. Springer Singapore, Singapore (2021). https://doi.org/10.1007/978-981-16-7993-3_14

54. Zhou, J., Yan, S., Zhang, J.: Prediction and analysis of illegal accounts on Ethereum based on CatBoost algorithm. In: 2022 International Conference on Big Data, Information and Computer Network (BDICN), pp. 63–67. IEEE (2022)

55. Voronov, T., Raz, D., Rottenstreich, O.: Scalable blockchain anomaly detection with sketches. In: 2021 IEEE International Conference on Blockchain (Blockchain), pp. 1–10. IEEE (2021)

56. Fan, S., Xu, H., Fu, S., Xu, M.: Smart Ponzi scheme detection using federated learning. In: 2020 IEEE 22nd International Conference on High Performance Computing and Communications; IEEE 18th International Conference on Smart City; IEEE 6th International Conference on Data Science and Systems (HPCC/SmartCity/DSS), pp. 881–888. IEEE (2020)

57. Hu, T., Liu, X., Chen, T., Zhang, X., Huang, X., Niu, W., Lu, J., Zhou, K., Liu, Y.: Transaction-based classification and detection approach for Ethereum smart contract. Inf. Process. Manage. **58**(2), 102462 (2021)

58. Agarwal, R., Thapliyal, T., Shukla, S.K.: Vulnerability and transaction behavior based detection of malicious smart contracts. In: Meng, W., Conti, M. (eds.) Cyberspace Safety and Security: 13th International Symposium, CSS 2021, Virtual Event, November 9–11, 2021, Proceedings, pp. 79–96. Springer International Publishing, Cham (2022). https://doi.org/10.1007/978-3-030-94029-4_6

59. Bhowmik, M., Chandana, T.S.S., Rudra, B.: Comparative study of machine learning algorithms for fraud detection in blockchain. In: Computing Methodologies and Communication (ICCMC), pp. 539–541. IEEE (2021)

60. Bartoletti, M., Lande, S., Loddo, A., Pompianu, L., Serusi, S.: Cryptocurrency scams: analysis and perspectives. Ieee Access **9**, 148353–148373 (2021)

61. Fan, S., Fu, S., Xu, H., Zhu, C.: Expose your mask: smart Ponzi schemes detection on blockchain. In: 2020 International Joint Conference on Neural Networks (IJCNN), pp. 1–7. IEEE (2020)

62. Poursafaei, F., Rabbany, R., Zilic, Z.: SIGTRAN: signature vectors for detecting illicit activities in blockchain transaction networks. In: Karlapalem, K., et al. (eds.) PAKDD 2021. LNCS (LNAI), vol. 12712, pp. 27–39. Springer, Cham (2021). https://doi.org/10.1007/978-3-030-75762-5_3

63. Wang, J., Xu, M., Wang, H., Zhang, J.: Classification of imbalanced data by using the smote algorithm and locally linear embedding. In: 2006 8th International Conference on Signal Processing, vol. 3. IEEE (2006)

Cross-Chain Personal Data Exchange on EVM Platforms: Enhancing Transparency, and Equity

M. N. Triet, L. K. Bang$^{(\boxtimes)}$, H. V. Khanh, T. N. Anh, T. L. Nhi,
P. T. Nghiem, H. G. Khiem, and T. B. Nam

FPT University, Can Tho, Vietnam
trietnm3@fe.edu.vn, banglkce160155@fpt.edu.vn

Abstract. The pervasive distribution of personal data across digital platforms has magnified issues related to privacy, security, and equitable value distribution, necessitating robust management frameworks. Traditional centralized data management systems often compromise individual privacy and control, favoring large corporations. Blockchain technology, recognized for its decentralization, immutability, and transparency, introduces a significant shift towards more secure and user-empowering data management practices. This paper proposes a blockchain-based model for personal data exchange, utilizing Ethereum Virtual Machine (EVM)-compatible platforms to implement cross-chain functionality that enhances transparency and equity in data transactions. By employing smart contracts and Non-Fungible Tokens (NFTs), the system allows users to maintain control over their data and ensures fair compensation. The platform is evaluated across multiple EVM-supported environments, including Binance Smart Chain, Polygon, Fantom, and Celo, to assess operational efficiencies and economic viability. The findings suggest that blockchain integration offers a scalable and flexible approach, setting a new standard for personal data transactions in the digital economy.

Keywords: Blockchain Data Integrity · Privacy in Digital Trade · Cross-Chain Technology · EVM-Compatible Platforms · Smart Contract · NFT

1 Introduction

In the evolving landscape of digital economies, the management and trading of personal data have emerged as central issues, intricately linked to privacy, security, and equitable value distribution [3,14]. The widespread distribution of personal data across various digital platforms necessitates robust frameworks that ensure secure and equitable management. Traditionally, personal data management has been predominantly centralized, favoring large corporations and data brokers at the expense of individual privacy and control [13]. This model has often resulted in a lack of transparency and inadequate compensation for

P. Delir Haghighi et al. (Eds.): iiWAS 2024, LNCS 15342, pp. 103–109, 2025.
https://doi.org/10.1007/978-3-031-78090-5_9

data owners, sparking a critical need for revised approaches that prioritize user empowerment and data security [15].

The advent of blockchain technology offers promising solutions to these challenges. Blockchain's inherent characteristics of decentralization, immutability, and transparency provide a novel framework for personal data management. For instance, protocols like the Ocean Protocol facilitate a Web3 data economy, enabling data owners to maintain control over their assets and monetize their data while preserving privacy [8]. Additionally, the application of blockchain technology extends to various domains, including healthcare, where it enhances data privacy and security, and supports robust data management systems [4]. Despite the advancements in blockchain applications for personal data management, current implementations often focus on specific sectors or use-cases, such as healthcare data management or decentralized data marketplaces [5,16]. These implementations highlight the versatility of blockchain but also underscore the need for a comprehensive platform that addresses the broader spectrum of personal data management challenges across different industries.

Our proposed system, built on EVM-compatible platforms, leverages the principles of blockchain to enhance transparency and equity in personal data transactions. By employing smart contracts and NFT, our system enables users to tokenize their personal data and control the terms of its usage, thereby ensuring fair compensation and maintaining robust security measures. The cross-chain functionality of our platform further facilitates a flexible and scalable environment for data trading, overcoming the limitations of single blockchain networks. This paper is structured to first review existing blockchain-based personal data management approaches, drawing on literature that illustrates both the advancements and the limitations of current technologies [17]. We then detail our proposed model, focusing on its architecture, functionalities, and the benefits it offers over traditional data trading systems. A thorough evaluation of the system across several EVM-supported platforms-*Binance Smart Chain, Polygon, Fantom*, and *Celo*-is presented, highlighting the operational efficiencies and adapting to the challenges posed by different blockchain environments. Moreover, the cost analysis section of this paper explores the economic implications of deploying our system, considering transaction fees.

2   Related Work

The intersection of blockchain technology and personal data management offers a critical examination of how digital identities and data can be managed more securely and equitably. In their exploration of the Web3 data economy, McConaghy et al. [8] describe the Ocean Protocol, which provides mechanisms for data to be published and consumed through datatokens. Khiem et al. [4] address privacy enhancements on Android platforms using a hybrid architecture that incorporates blockchain to manage sensitive data, enhancing both security and user control.

Besides, Son et al. [16] and Le et al. [5] propose blockchain-based frameworks for emergency access in patient-centered healthcare systems. While not deployed on EVM-based platforms, these systems leverage the permissioned Blockchain Hyperledger Fabric to manage sensitive health records securely, utilizing smart contracts to facilitate appropriate access during emergencies. This methodology underscores the broader applicability of blockchain in sensitive data management contexts, ensuring security and confidentiality.

The valuation and trading of personal data in digital marketplaces also benefit from the application of blockchain technology. Molina et al. [10] and Robinson et al. [12] discuss models for personal data marketplaces, emphasizing the empowerment of data generators through decentralized architectures that enhance privacy and data rights. These models propose frameworks for evaluating risks and licensing data, which align with broader economic and privacy considerations. Lipman [6] and Charitsis [1] critique current data management practices, discussing the challenges and implications of data commodification under communicative and surveillance capitalism paradigms. Further, Purtova [11] and Malgieri [7] delve into the fundamental aspects of personal data ownership and valuation. They advocate for a reevaluation of personal data as a resource tied to power dynamics within data markets, suggesting enhanced awareness of data value among individuals. Lastly, Fallatah [2] and Moiso et al. [9] explore Personal Data Stores (PDS) and the concept of a "Bank of Individuals' Data" (BID). These models aim to place individuals at the center of data control, enabling effective management and monetization of personal data. These discussions collectively underscore the evolving nature of personal data as both an economic and privacy-centric commodity in the digital age.

3   Approach

In the proposed model, preseted in Fig. 1, we describe a model for managing and trading personal data using blockchain technology. This model emphasizes a systematic approach where personal data is handled as NFTs to ensure transparency and equity in data transactions. At the outset, the process involves the tokenization of personal data. Data owners convert their personal data into

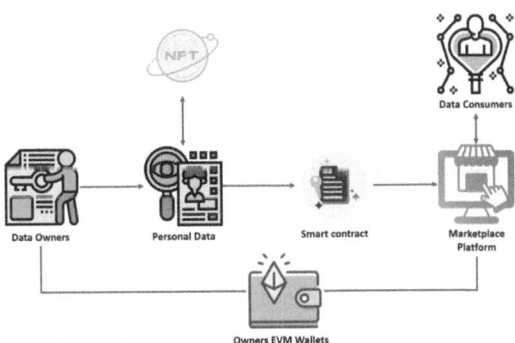

Fig. 1. Cross-Chain Personal Data Exchange

NFTs, effectively creating a digital representation of their data on the blockchain. This step is crucial as it not only secures the data through cryptographic means but also ensures that each piece of data is uniquely identifiable and owned, thereby preventing unauthorized duplication and use. Following tokenization, data owners deploy smart contracts on the EVM-supported blockchain platforms such as BNB Chain, Fantom, Celo, and Polygon. These smart contracts are programmed with specific terms that govern the access and usage of the data, including the pricing and sharing policies. By setting these terms on the blockchain, data owners can automate the enforcement of their policies, ensuring that they retain control over their data.

Once the smart contracts are in place, the tokenized data (a.k.a NFTs) is listed on a marketplace platform. This platform serves as an intermediary where data owners and potential data consumers can connect. Here, the data is made discoverable to potential buyers or consumers, facilitating a market-driven approach to data exchange. The purchase process is initiated when a data consumer selects an NFT on the marketplace. This action triggers the associated smart contract, which manages the transaction process. The smart contract automatically handles the transfer of payment from the consumer's wallet to the data owner's wallet. This payment transfer is executed in cryptocurrency, and the transaction details are recorded on the blockchain, providing a transparent and immutable ledger of the transaction. Finally, once the transaction is successfully processed, the smart contract grants the data consumer access to the data. This access is typically granted on-chain, where the consumer can securely download or interact with the data directly from the blockchain. This system not only simplifies the process of data trading but also enhances the security and transparency of personal data transactions, aligning with the paper's focus on enhancing transparency and equity in the digital data economy.

4   Evaluation

The evaluation of our proposed system for cross-chain personal data exchange is conducted across several EVM-supported blockchain platforms, each chosen for their distinct characteristics and performance metrics. The platforms under examination include *Binance Smart Chain, Polygon, Fantom,* and *Celo.* These platforms were selected due to their robust support for EVM, which is critical for ensuring the interoperability and functionality of the smart contracts that underpin our data token model.

Table 1. Transaction fee

	Contract Creation	Create NFT	Transfer NFT
BNB	0.0273134 BNB ($18.66)	0.00109162 BNB ($0.75)	0.00057003 BNB ($0.39)
Fantom	0.00957754 FTM ($0.001)	0.000405167 FTM ($0.000)	0.0002380105 FTM ($0.000)
Polygon	0.006840710032835408 MATIC($0.000)	0.000289405001852192 MATIC($0.000)	0.000170007501088048 MATIC($0.000)
Celo	0.007097844 CELO ($0.004)	0.0002840812 CELO ($0.000)	0.0001554878 CELO ($0.000)

The comparative analysis, shown in Table 1, is vital for stakeholders to understand the economic efficiency of deploying blockchain solutions for personal data exchanges in varying blockchain environments. Firstly, BNB emerges as the most expensive among the evaluated platforms in terms of transaction fees. The cost for creating a contract on this platform is considerably higher at $18.66, which might be attributed to its higher throughput and extensive network usage. Similarly, the fees for creating and transferring an NFT are $0.75 and $0.39, respectively. These values, although significantly lower than the contract creation cost, are still substantial when compared to the other platforms. This cost structure makes BNB Smart Chain suitable for users who prioritize network speed and reliability but may be less appealing for those looking to minimize transaction costs. Fantom, on the other hand, offers an extremely low-cost structure. The fees for contract creation, NFT creation, and NFT transfer are nearly negligible, each costing $0.001 or less. This pricing strategy enhances Fantom's attractiveness for developers and users engaged in high-volume, low-margin operations, such as frequent trading and management of NFTs. Polygon also exhibits very low transaction costs, similar to those of Fantom, with the fees for all activities under scrutiny rounding to nearly zero dollars. This near-zero fee structure is particularly advantageous for applications that require high transaction throughput without incurring significant costs, making Polygon an excellent choice for scalable and cost-effective blockchain operations. Celo provides a middle ground in terms of cost, with fees slightly higher than Fantom and Polygon but much lower than BNB Smart Chain. The fees for contract creation, NFT creation, and transfer on Celo are $0.004, $0.000, and $0.000, respectively.

5   Conclusion

This paper has explored the integration of blockchain technology in personal data management, emphasizing the need for systems that enhance transparency, security, and user control. Our proposed model leverages the unique attributes of blockchain, including decentralization and immutability, to foster a data management environment where personal data is not only secure but also managed in a manner that promotes equity and fairness. The use of smart contracts and NFTs enables users to assert control over their data, ensuring that they are adequately compensated for its use. The cross-chain functionality of our platform addresses the limitations of single blockchain networks, offering flexibility and scalability for data transactions. Through the evaluation of the system across various EVM-supported platforms, we have demonstrated that each platform brings unique benefits and challenges, affecting the system's performance and economic feasibility. The analysis of transaction fees, burn fees, and gas limits has further highlighted the financial implications of deploying blockchain solutions for data management on a large scale.

References

1. Charitsis, V., et al.: Creating worlds that create audiences: theorising personal data markets in the age of communicative capitalism (2018)
2. Fallatah, K.U., et al.: Personal data stores (PDS): a review. Sensors **23**(3), 1477 (2023)
3. Hoang, N.M., Son, H.X.: A dynamic solution for fine-grained policy conflict resolution. In: Proceedings of the 3rd International Conference on Cryptography, Security and Privacy, pp. 116–120 (2019)
4. Khiem, H.G., et al.: Applying blockchain technology for privacy preservation in android platforms. In: Zhang, Y., Zhang, L.-J. (eds.) Web Services – ICWS 2023: 30th International Conference, Held as Part of the Services Conference Federation, SCF 2023, Honolulu, HI, USA, September 23–26, 2023, Proceedings, pp. 47–61. Springer Nature Switzerland, Cham (2023). https://doi.org/10.1007/978-3-031-44836-2_4
5. Le, H.T., et al.: Patient-chain: patient-centered healthcare system a blockchain-based technology in dealing with emergencies. In: Shen, H., et al. (eds.) Parallel and Distributed Computing, Applications and Technologies: 22nd International Conference, PDCAT 2021, Guangzhou, China, December 17–19, 2021, Proceedings, pp. 576–583. Springer International Publishing, Cham (2022). https://doi.org/10.1007/978-3-030-96772-7_54
6. Lipman, R.: Online privacy and the invisible market for our data. Penn St. L. Rev. **120**, 777 (2015)
7. Malgieri, G., Custers, B.: Pricing privacy-the right to know the value of your personal data. Comput. Law Secur. Rev. **34**(2), 289–303 (2018)
8. McConaghy, T.: Ocean Protocol: Tools for the Web3 Data Economy. In: Tran, D.A., Thai, M.T., Krishnamachari, B. (eds.) Handbook on Blockchain, pp. 505–539. Springer International Publishing, Cham (2022). https://doi.org/10.1007/978-3-031-07535-3_16
9. Moiso, C., Minerva, R.: Towards a user-centric personal data ecosystem the role of the bank of individuals' data. In: 2012 16th International Conference on Intelligence in Next Generation Networks, pp. 202–209. IEEE (2012)
10. Molina, V., et al.: A conceptual marketplace model for IoT generated personal data. arXiv preprint arXiv:1907.03047 (2019)
11. Purtova, N.: The illusion of personal data as no one's property. Law Innov. Technol. **7**(1), 83–111 (2015)
12. Robinson, S.C.: What's your anonymity worth? Establishing a marketplace for the valuation and control of individuals' anonymity and personal data. Digit. Policy Regul. Govern. **19**(5), 353–366 (2017)
13. Son, H.X., Chen, E.: Towards a fine-grained access control mechanism for privacy protection and policy conflict resolution. International J. Adv. Comput. Sci. Appl. **10**(2) (2019)
14. Son, H.X., Hoang, N.M.: A novel attribute-based access control system for fine-grained privacy protection. In: Proceedings of the 3rd International Conference on Cryptography, Security and Privacy, pp. 76–80 (2019)
15. Son, H.X., et al.: Towards a mechanism for protecting seller's interest of cash on delivery by using smart contract in hyperledger. Int. J. Adv. Comput. Sci. Appl. **10**(4) (2019)

16. Son, H.X., Le, T.H., Quynh, N.T.T., Huy, H.N.D., Duong-Trung, N., Luong, H.H.: Toward a blockchain-based technology in dealing with emergencies in patient-centered healthcare systems. In: Bouzefrane, S., Laurent, M., Boumerdassi, S., Renault, E. (eds.) Mobile, Secure, and Programmable Networking: 6th International Conference, MSPN 2020, Paris, France, October 28–29, 2020, Revised Selected Papers, pp. 44–56. Springer International Publishing, Cham (2021). https://doi.org/10.1007/978-3-030-67550-9_4

17. Zichichi, M., et al.: Decentralized personal data marketplaces: how participation in a DAO can support the production of citizen-generated data. Sensors **22**(16), 6260 (2022)

Incentivize Peer Review Without Rewarding: Using OSS-Like Citation Pull Request

Chiaki Miura[1]([envelope])[iD] and Kensuke Ito[2][iD]

[1] Giant - Collaborative Development Platform for Science, Bunkyo, Japan
`t.miura@gnt.place`
[2] Endowed Chair for Blockchain Innovation, The University of Tokyo, Bunkyo, Japan
`k-ito@g.ecc.u-tokyo.ac.jp`

Abstract. Scholarly communication is experiencing significant growth in publication volume. However, due to a lack of incentives, the current peer review system struggles to secure a sufficient number of diverse referees. Learning from the recent success in Open-Source Software (OSS) development, several alternative review models have been proposed, though none have focused on the mechanisms behind contribution-driven development. We introduce *Push Citation*, which combines a reversed citation with a revision to prior articles. Citation metrics incentivize article owners to perform reviews and encourage contributors to make suggestions. An experiment on workload balancing demonstrates that Push Citation is robust against the increasing demand for reviews and the uneven distribution of the burden. Potential drawbacks and counter-measures are also discussed.

Keywords: Incentivize Peer Review · Open Science · Open-Source Software · Scholarly Communication

1 Introduction

Peer review plays a crucial role in shaping scholarly research. However, the exponential increase in paper submissions has not been accompanied by a corresponding increase in the availability of reviewers, resulting in a significant bottleneck in the publication process. The current peer review system has faced several criticisms [1], including inconsistency between reviewers, a low capacity to detect flaws, and susceptibility to biases such as the reviewee's race [2], gender [3], or institutional favoritism [4]. Although many recent innovations in review systems address the issues of unreliability and bias, the root of the peer review crisis is the challenge of securing a sufficient and diverse pool of reviewers [5]. This issue is based on the need for more incentives for researchers to actively participate in peer review. To date, there has not yet been an effective way to incentivize reviewers. One of the few exceptions is Gasparyan (2015) [6], who investigated

P. Delir Haghighi et al. (Eds.): iiWAS 2024, LNCS 15342, pp. 110–124, 2025.
https://doi.org/10.1007/978-3-031-78090-5_10

optimal ways to reward reviewers. However, it is known that providing explicit rewards to reviewers can lower the overall quality of their reviews [7] and sometimes even undermine their motivation [8]. This growing disconnect underscores the crucial need for a scalable and efficient review system capable of handling the rapidly increasing volume of academic research.

To address this issue, we propose *Push Citation*, which combines reversed citation with the revision of previous research. The basic notion in our model is similar to post-publication peer review, where every submission is immediately published and undergoes future screening. However, unlike post-publication peer review, authors curate works from the literature collection so that they can submit to the works to which they can contribute the most. By altering the manuscript of the literature, he or she suggests the improvement and proposes citing their work. The owner or owners of the literature then review his suggestion. By accepting his work, they can automatically update their work. This peer-to-peer review mechanism, similar to code reviews in software development, leverages the unique insights and expertise of the cited authors. Inspired by pull requests in OSS development, it establishes a reciprocal incentive between the reviewer and the contributor (Fig. 1).

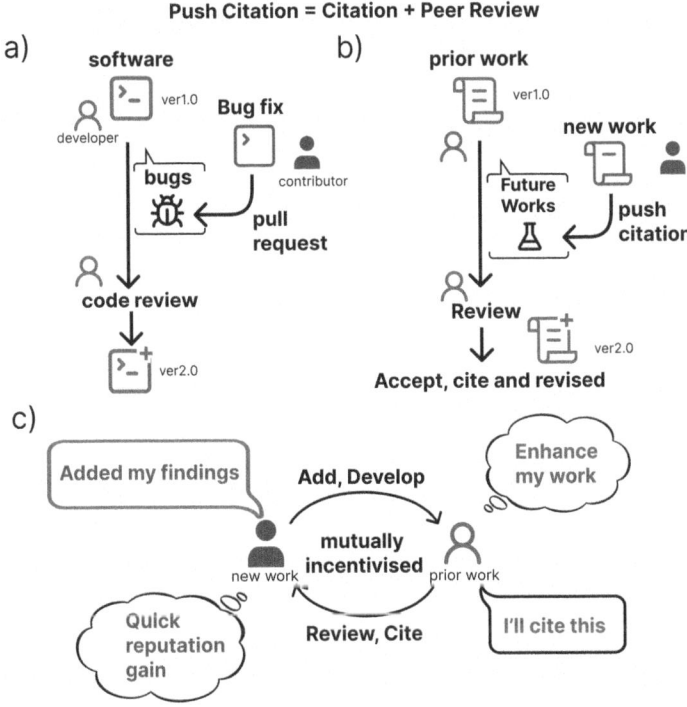

Fig. 1. a) Merge requests allow anyone to contribute to existing software. b) Pushing citations requires the revision of prior work. c) Push Citation incentivizes the author of prior works to review and the author of new works to propose revisions.

This paper consists of five sections, starting with this introduction. Section 2 discusses related works, Sect. 3 introduces the details of Push Citation, Sect. 4 presents experimental results, and Sect. 5 concludes with future research directions.

2 Related Works

Our proposal is related to three research topics in the field of web engineering: *incentives in peer review*, *incentives in Open-Source Software (OSS) development*, and *GitHub-style peer review*.

2.1 Incentives in Peer Review

Peer review is defined as "the process of subjecting an author's scholarly manuscript to the scrutiny of others who are experts in the same field" and its role is to evaluate the soundness, significance, and fit [9]. Despite its critical role, the peer review process faces numerous challenges, with a significant issue being the lack of sufficient incentives for participation. It is reported that 84.8% of researchers across the field "think institutions should more explicitly require and recognize peer review contributions" [10] along with the systematic problem reported from multiple disciplines [11,12]. Given its dependence on voluntary efforts, peer review places a significant burden on researchers, potentially leading to scalability issues, as discussed in Sect. 1. Various solutions have been proposed to address these incentive problems, particularly through the provision of rewards to reviewers [6,13]. However, this approach remains controversial because it can lead to strategic behavior among reviewers, potentially compromising the objectivity and quality of the review process [7]. For more information on the discussion of incentives in peer review, refer to existing comprehensive survey papers [5,14].

Our proposal aims to address these issues by leveraging the principles of OSS development.

2.2 Incentives in OSS Development

The development of OSS is a unique phenomenon characterized by the voluntary contributions of developers worldwide [15] Platforms such as *GitHub* [16] have become the central hubs of these activities, facilitating the easy submission of updates to repositories. Incentive structures in OSS development have been extensively investigated, especially from an economic perspective. Reputation has been identified as a key factor motivating contributors. Seminal studies by Lerner and Tirole [17,18] have explored the dynamics of how reputational incentives shape participation and contribution patterns in the OSS community.

Our proposal builds on this concept by integrating reputation-based incentives, similar to those in OSS development, into the academic peer review process. This approach suggests a promising path for enhancing participation and improving the quality of scholarly reviews.

There is an ongoing debate on what motivates scientists. However, considering scientific endeavor as a competitive process [19] aimed at producing increasingly impactful work, citation is perhaps the most compelling motivation. Although scientists tend to cite more frequently cited papers [20] and more recent papers [21], there is growing evidence that citation metrics, if properly normalized and interpreted [22–24], can be instrumental in fostering a healthy understanding of the validity, significance and relevance of a paper.

Scholarly communication is a cyclical process that builds on previous achievements while publishing new findings. The authors carefully select papers that best convey and support their discoveries [25]. The long-term impact of a paper is significantly influenced by how well it references promising papers that will attract numerous citations in the future [26].

Thus, citation functions as a distributed peer review mechanism for previous works. Reviewing a paper aligns with advancing one's own research when evaluating proposed revisions and improvements.

2.3 GitHub-Style Peer Review

The concept of incorporating OSS development principles into academic peer review is not entirely new. Examples include *The Journal of Open-Source Software* [27], which employs merge requests for peer review in computer science, and proposals [28] advocating for paragraph-level paper review similar to code review. These methods are commonly known as GitHub-style peer review [5], leveraging using OSS development platforms for post-publication review.

Our proposal is novel because it aims to transform the structure of peer review itself. Unlike existing practices where new papers cite existing ones and reviewers are third parties, our approach introduces a model where improvements are directly proposed (pushed) to existing papers (repositories). In this model, the reviewers are the maintainers of the repositories that receive the push. The key features of OSS development include i) open contribution by anyone, ii) repository maintainers can expect functional improvements as a form of review compensation, and iii) the ability to trace developers' contributions down to individual lines of code. While existing methods typically focus only on the first characteristic, our approach leverages all three to enhance academic peer review.

3   Model

Both traditional citation, referred to as *pull* citation in this paper, and Push Citation can be modeled as networks of peers and articles. In these networks, each peer represents a researcher who owns one or more articles, and each article is a node. An article consists of two main components: the manuscript and the references. The manuscript describes the research, including the main text, figures, tables, and data. The references list the connections between the current article and prior research. Using these references, we can construct a citation network $G(V, E)$, enabling various bibliometric analyses [21,29–31].

In this section, we provide a detailed definition and explanation of Push Citation.

3.1 Definition of Push Citation

Push Citation is a system where peers propose citations, with each proposal referred to as a push. For clarity in the following discussion, we assume that each article is allocated to only one peer and do not consider coauthorship[1]. The citation network consists of n articles $v_i \in V (i = 1, 2, ...n)$ and edges $e_{ij} \in E$. Each edge e_{ij} signifies that article v_i cites article v_j.

Push citation contributes to the same citation network as traditional citations but in reverse(Fig. 2 a). For instance, consider article v_i. In traditional *pull* citation, the owner of v_i creates the edge e_{ij} by adding one or more articles to the reference. However, in Push Citation, owners of other articles v_j propose the citation e_{ij} to v_i. The proposing owner of article v_j is called a contributor, and their citation proposal s_{ji} is called a *push*, similar to OSS pushes (Fig. 2)[2].

Push citation follows a structured procedure. A contributor creates an article and proposes a citation push, and an article owner reviews and integrates the push. First, a peer writes a manuscript and collects data, which can encompass various forms of knowledge, such as excerpts from a database [32], code [33], paragraphs, or experimental procedures [34]. The contributor submits pushes to existing articles, modifying the manuscripts of the corresponding article for each push. Each article owner evaluates the incoming push. If the owner accepts the proposed changes to their article's manuscripts, they finalize the updated version and establish the citation edge e_{ij}. If the owner declines the push, no changes are made, and no edge is created, indicating rejection of the push.

Citation metrics provide incentives for article owners to review pushes and merge articles that are relevant and beneficial. Every researcher strives to maximize the impact of their work. Owners review pushes to keep their works current because accepting incorrect or irrelevant results could decrease their article's credibility. This process also motivates young researchers in the field to push their work toward established articles, seeking early recognition and building their reputation. Push citation integrates emerging research into established contexts, facilitating easier engagement with the latest discussions while also allowing researchers to introduce potentially groundbreaking innovations in their own articles.

It is crucial to emphasize that Push Citation does not aim to replace traditional peer review methods but rather to supplement them. It provides an

---

[1] Considering coauthorship, we can build a bipartite network of peers and articles. Most of the following discussion applies equally to this case without major modifications.

[2] To be more precise, a pushed citation is a *citation pull request* from the OSS point of view because the peer proposes the owner pull the proposed article to the owner's reference. Here, we have a little confusing terminology. However, we stick to using push instead of pull because the citation proposal is initiated by whoever proposes it.

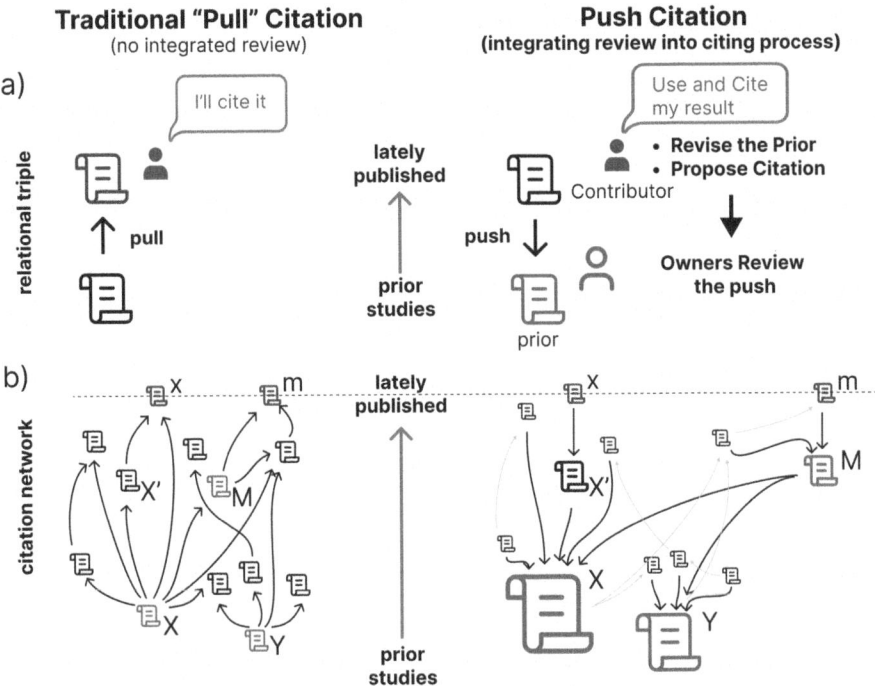

Fig. 2. Scholarship is a network of knowledge. Each arrow connecting articles depicts a flow of knowledge. Articles are arranged vertically according to their publication dates. (a) In traditional 'pull' citation, owner peer of newer article decides which article to cite. Meanwhile, in Push Citation, she revise a prior article based on her own findings, and propose to cite her article, integrating them into the manuscript of the prior. (b) To illustrate the difference between pull citation and *Push Citation*, we have constructed two example citation networks using identical sets of research reports. X and Y represent two distinct schools of thought in the field, and M had a methodological contribution that can be used for the assessment of the theories. Three articles are thought to be as a canonical literature in the field. The articles x and m are enhancements of the prior research X', one of the variations of X, and M, respectively. Push Citation network clearly reflect the complete scope of research while traditional citation count can only measure the monotonous "significance" of a paper. X' can eventually receive more focused and sophisticated developmental support, potentially overtaking X to become the most established theory.

additional, more agile layer of evaluation, thereby improving the overall quality and timeliness of scholarly communication. Push Citation addresses the challenges of scalability and efficiency that are currently limiting traditional peer review processes.

3.2   Alignment: Academia and Software Development Practices

Distributed software development involves constructing applications using code previously created by other peers. Academic citations share a similar structure, and current practices align closely with many aspects of distributed software development. Here, we highlight some of these parallels (Table 1), comparing current academic practices with their counterparts in distributed software development technology.

Table 1. The emerging technology and culture in academia align well with practices in OSS

Academia	Emerging trends in academia	OSS development
Versioning	*F1000Research* [35], *arXiv* [36]	Branch, Fork, Semantic Versioning
Machine aided review	*OpenReview* [37], *ScreenIT* [38], Explainable autonomous review generation [39]	Continuous Integration (CI)
Facile dissemination of alert and Retraction-free revision	*RetractionWatch* [40], Quantitative analysis of peer-review innovation effect [41]	Bug detection with package dependency network [42], Package reliability assessment [43]
Reviewer assignment problem [44]	Knowledge-graph based,	Reviewer assignment problem [45, 46]
Clarify contribution statements	*Contributor Roles Taxonomy (CRediT)* [47]	Contribution profile, commit messages, and Issues

Versioning. Preprints has not only expedited scholarly communication but also made it traceable. Comparing manuscripts on arXiv with their corresponding version-of-record papers has shown that peer review often results in minimal changes to the manuscript in numerous cases(initially published on arXiv in 2016) [48]. This has sparked constructive debates on the true role of peer review and has spurred various innovations in the review system in recent years [5].

On an OSS development platform like GitHub, developers use branches and forks to enhance version control. Branching is used to manage various development contexts, while forking allows developers to create personal copies for independent modifications. In Push Citation, proposals are initiated by the contributor pushing changes rather than the recipient pulling them.

Discussions often diverge even when based on the same theory, and resolution is frequently a matter of time. Branching, forking, and Push Citation mechanisms can help these controversies and facilitate a comprehensive understanding of the entire discussion.

Machine-Aided Review and Continuous Integration (CI), along with fine-grained citation index databases and platforms for openly accessible review comments [37], have enabled comparisons of fraud detection capabilities across multiple peer review systems [49, 50]. Many automated review systems now assist busy professors and conference chairs. Numerous computer science conferences employ conference management tools, and machine-aided review covers aspects such as ethics statements , obligations for open code , figure accessibility , evaluation of misreported p-values or sample size calculations , and identification of retracted papers' citations. The use of the ScreenIT [38] pipeline during the surge of COVID-19-related preprints is one of the most notable successes in integrating these processes into preprints.

CI involves the unit testing stages in the software release process. Each software owner implements a series of code tests, including linting and automated bug detection, before proceeding with code review. OSS developer's community is eager to maintain the out-of-the-box template for maintainers.

Machine-aided reviews [51] can be integrated as part of continuous integration processes. All pushes pass automated test criteria before being submitted for review in the target article. Existing disciplinary societies can develop test templates for article owners.

Retraction and Bug Detection with Package Dependency Networks emphasize reproducibility as a cornerstone of scientific integrity, yet achieving it remains challenging. While retracting invalid papers is a self-regulating mechanism in academia, editors and reviewers often hesitate owing to concerns about damaging authors' reputations or potentially undermining significant findings. Furthermore, despite retractions, many papers continue to cite retracted studies [52].

Relying on vulnerable packages (reusable code developed by other programmers) is a critical issue in software development. Recent research on OSS has highlighted essential metrics for reliable packages. Most programming languages include package managers to organize dependencies, and OSS package dependency networks undergo rigorous evaluation for robustness against failures [42, 43]. Alerts regarding vulnerabilities are often broadcasted in days, sometimes even hours [53].

With Push Citation, there is no longer a need to prominently display retraction notices. Instead, peers can push patches to articles. Push Citation can assess the acceptance and rejection rates of pushes, reflecting the significance or validity of the article. This incremental evaluation includes a measured approach to retraction and a process of improvement without damaging reputations.

Owing to space limitations, we were unable to cover several important aspects that merit examination in aligning academia with the OSS community. These include such as reviewer assignment problems and scalable contribution metrics. These topics will be addressed in a future report.

4   Calculation

Dealing with a workload that surpasses one's capacity is one of the most challenging aspects of peer review. In the following sections, we will formalize and assess the burden of pushes in the peer review process.

4.1   Formal Expression

Each article v_i has a specific processing capacity c_i, indicating the number of pushes it can handle per unit of time. When the rate of push exceeds this capacity, maintaining the quality of peer review becomes unsustainable. We can formalize this criterion as follows:

$$\frac{\Delta|s_{ji}|}{\Delta t} < c_i$$

Article citation counts demonstrate a fat-tailed distribution, highlighting a significant disparity in citation frequencies. This phenomenon is influenced by *preferential attachment*, where the likelihood of an article being cited increases with its current number of citations. Essentially, the rate at which new connections (or citations) accumulate for a node per unit of time is proportional to its current degree (total citation count). Similarly, in OSS platforms, the distribution of pull requests across repositories also exhibits a fat-tailed pattern [54]. Therefore, it is reasonable to assume that the number of pushes received by each article in the citation network will exhibit a similar preferential attachment. Consequently, the number of subsequent pushes received by an article is proportional to the cumulative number of previous push acceptances.

$$\frac{\Delta|s_{ji}|}{\Delta t} \propto e_{ij}$$

If the capacity remains constant, an article that receives many pushes will inevitably attract even more in the future, potentially leading to breakdowns. Therefore, strategies are needed to enhance an article's peer review capacity without disproportionately increasing the burden on individual reviewers.

In OSS development, repository owners appoint maintainers–comanagers of the repository–to distribute the workload with the owner. Maintainers are typically selected from core contributors who have made significant improvements to the application through diligent maintenance. When core contributors accept invitations to become maintainers, they assume responsibilities for code review. Similarly, promising researchers who have successfully made accepted pushes can be invited to participate as maintainers in the peer review process (Fig. 3). We assume probabilities p_a and $p_m \in [0, 1]$ for an article to accept an incoming push and for a maintainer to join an article, respectively. On average, $\frac{\Delta|s_{ji}|}{\Delta t} \cdot p_a \cdot p_m$ new maintainers join article v_i.

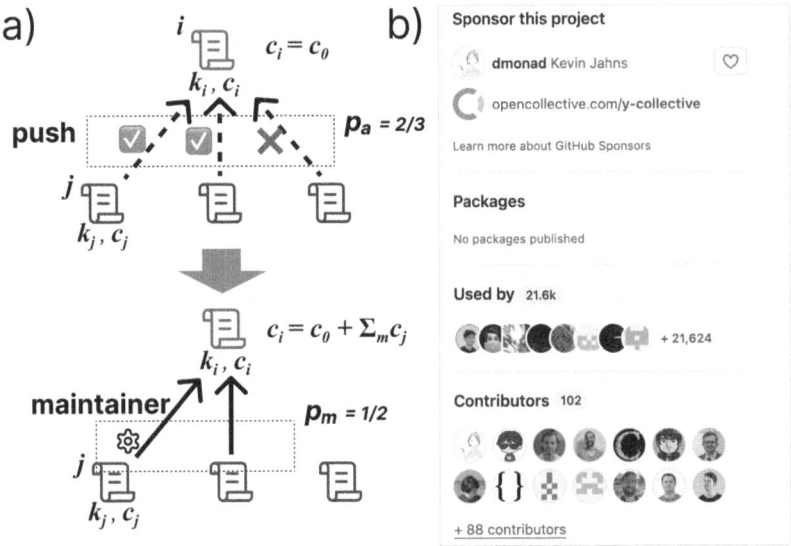

Fig. 3. a) Each push has a probability p_a of being accepted, and among accepted pushes, there is a probability p_m that they are added by maintainers. Each maintainer contributes their capacity to the prior research they are involved in. b) A snapshot from a example GitHub repository "yjs". Prominent repositories involves several degrees of participation, with each called such as user, contributor, moderator and administrator. We refer to maintainers meaning an invited moderator.

Each article has the same base capacity c_0, and maintainers recursively add capacity to the contributing article,

$$c_i = c_0 + \sum_{v_j \in M_i} c_j$$

where M_i is a set of maintainers of v_i.

4.2 Simulation

We simulated discrete values of p_a and p_m, ranging from $(0,1)$. At $t = 0$, we have a pre-defined network with 300 nodes and 300 edges constructed using preferential attachment. At each time step t, the number of nodes in the network $N(t) = f(t)$. We chose $f(t) = t^2$ for our simulation rather than an exponential function. This choice is based on reports indicating that the number of publications in a journal tends to remain relatively stable, with new publications typically targeting the established research area covered by the journal.

We performed ten simulations for each pair of p_a and p_m, measuring the relative remaining capacity of each article $c_i - \frac{\Delta|s_{ji}|}{\Delta t}$. In most cases, all articles had sufficient capacity to handle additional reviews. The graph shows that the mean relative remaining capacity exceeds 10% over the simulated time window (Fig. 4).

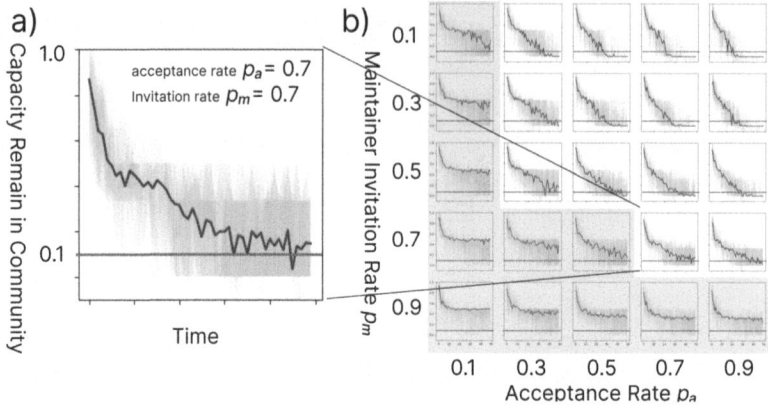

Fig. 4. Aggregated results from 10 simulations. The blue area represents the 98th percentile of relative remaining review capacity at each time step, while the solid line indicates the averaged mean. We have highlighted the *safe* setting in red, indicating that the mean remaining capacity will never be lower than 20% during the considered timesteps. All calculations assume $c_0 = 1$. (Color figure online)

5   Conclusion

In this paper, we introduced Push Citation, a mechanism to incentivize reviewers without resorting to direct rewards. Inspired by the structure of OSS development, this system allows improvements to be directly proposed to existing papers (repositories) rather than generating new papers by citing existing ones. In this model, reviewers function as maintainers of these repositories. Our experiments confirm the scalability of this approach.

Our proposal addresses the need for incentives for reviewers in the current peer review system. However, several challenges need to be addressed to enhance the practicality of this proposal, including the following.

Conflict of Interest. pertains to "concerns that competing interests may bias research methods and the interpretation of data and conclusions [55]." This issue is already a significant concern in existing peer review systems but becomes more pronounced in Push Citation, where repository maintainers themselves determine whether to accept or reject a push. For example, maintainers may reject a valid push that contradicts the repository's claims or accept a less substantiated push that aligns with their own claims. Transparency is crucial for addressing these biases. The reasons behind such reject/accept must be transparent to the community. Evidence from the open-review process suggests that transparency encourages more careful deliberation by reviewers.

Spamming, defined as "the act of spreading unsolicited and unrelated content [56]," poses a risk in the context of Push Citation. There is a concern that individuals may intentionally flood the network with low-quality or irrelevant pushes, leading to congestion. Traditional methods, such as imposing a small cost for each push, could effectively mitigate this issue. This cost includes monetary or computational resources [57]. Additionally, limiting the number of pushes an account can make in a specified period could be another solution. However, this approach may potentially increase vulnerability to Sybil attacks.

Sybil Attacks involve "the forging of multiple identities [58]." In Push Citation, this could involve the creation of multiple accounts used them to mutually push content, artificially inflating the perceived value or agreement with a repository. Moreover, time-frame anti-spamming may potentially vulnerable to the Sybil attack. A direct countermeasure is to verify identities and maintain a one-to-one correspondence between individuals and accounts. *ORCID* [59] is one of the tools for such identity authorization [60].

Scalability. as discussed in Sect. 4, clearly indicates that there is a critical threshold for the maintainer invitation rate to maintain an adequate review quality. To ensure effective maintenance, the invitation rate for maintainers should ideally be kept above 50% when the acceptance rate is higher than 0.5. This invitation rate is overwhelmingly high given that long-time contributors on GitHub, who have contributed consistently for over a year, comprise only 12% of successful pull requests [46],

However, although acceptance rate may largely vary depending on field and recognition of the venue, an average conference do not accept more than a half of submission. Also, it is important to note that the simulation was conducted under specific conditions, mainly due to computational resource constraint. Each peer is required to make only one push per article, which artificially inflates the apparent acceptance rate in our calculation. One advantage of Push Citation is that even if the acceptance rate is low, it does not require additional cost of refereeing to publish the articles. By integrating process automation from OSS development into academic reviewing, we envision an academic *copilot* that assists researchers in writing well-structured paragraphs that effectively convey their ideas. This machine-aided writing tool would facilitate faster composition of review comments for owners and maintainers, thereby enhancing the initial capacity c_0 for each reviewer.

Addressing these challenges will be crucial for making the proposed system more practical in the future.

Acknowledgments. The authors would like to express their gratitude to Mohammed bin Salman Center for Future Science and Technology for Saudi-Japan Vision 2030 (MbSC2030) for providing financial support.

Disclosure of Interests. The authors have no competing interests to declare that are relevant to the content of this article.

References

1. Lee, C.J., et al.: Bias in peer review, **64**(1), 2–17 (2013)
2. Ginther, D.K., et al.: Race, ethnicity, and NIH research awards **333**(6045), 1015–1019 (2011)
3. Bornmann, L., Mutz, R., Daniel, H.-D.: Gender differences in grant peer review: a meta-analysis, **1**(3), 226–238 (2007)
4. Si, K., et al.: Affiliation bias in peer review and the gender gap, **52**(7), 104797 (2023)
5. Tennant, J.P. et al.: A multi-disciplinary perspective on emergent and future innovations in peer review, **6**, 1151 (2017)
6. Gasparyan, A.Y. et al.: Rewarding peer reviewers: maintaining the integrity of science communication, **30**(4), 360–364 (2015)
7. Al-Khatib, A., Teixeira da Silva, J.A.: Rewarding the quantity of peer review could harm biomedical research, **29**(2), 200–205 (2019)
8. Zaharie, M.A., Seeber, M.: Are non-monetary rewards effective in attracting peer reviewers? A natural experiment, **117**(3), 1587–1609 (2018)
9. Jubb, M.: Peer review: the current landscape and future trends **29**(1), 13–21 (2016)
10. Publons: Publons global state of peer review
11. Tite, L., Schroter, S.: Why do peer reviewers decline to review? A survey, **61**(1), 9–12 (2007)
12. Ellwanger, J.H., Chies, J.A.B.: We need to talk about peer-review-Experienced reviewers are not endangered species, but they need motivation, **125**, 201–205 (2020)
13. Tennant, J.P.: The state of the art in peer review, **365**(19), fny204 (2018)
14. Kelly, J., Sadeghieh, T., Adeli, K.: Peer review in scientific publications: benefits, critiques, & a survival guide, **25**(3), 227 (2014)
15. Weber, S.: The Success of Open Source. Harvard University Press. https://doi.org/10.4159/9780674044999
16. GitHub. https://github.com
17. Lerner, J., Tirole, J.: The open source movement: key research questions, **45**(4), 819–826 (2001)
18. Lerner, J., Tirole, J.: The economics of technology sharing: open source and beyond, **19**(2), 99–120 (2005)
19. Hull, D.L.: Science as a Process: an evolutionary account of the social and conceptual development of science. In: Science as a Process. University of Chicago Press. https://doi.org/10.7208/9780226360492
20. Barabási, A.-L., Albert, R.: Emergence of scaling in random networks, **286**(5439), 509–512 (1999)
21. Sourati, J., Evans, J.A.: Accelerating science with human-aware artificial intelligence, **7**(10), 1682–1696 (2023)
22. Meng, X., Varol, O., Barabási, A.-L.: Hidden citations obscure true impact in science, **3**(5), pgae155 (2024)
23. Bao, H., Teplitskiy, M.: A simulation-based analysis of the impact of rhetorical citations in science, **15**(1), 431 (2024)
24. Tahamtan, I., Bornmann, L.: What do citation counts measure? An updated review of studies on citations in scientific documents published between 2006 and 2018 **121**(3), 1635–1684 (2019)
25. Teplitskiy, M., et al.: How status of research papers affects the way they are read and cited, **51**(4), 104484 (2022)

26. Correlated impact dynamics in science. https://doi.org/10.48550/ARXIV.2303.03646

27. Journal of open source software. https://joss.theoj.org

28. Ghosh, S.S. et al.: Learning from open source software projects to improve scientific review, **6**, 18 (2012)

29. Price, D.J.D.S.: Networks of scientific papers: the pattern of bibliographic references indicates the nature of the scientific research front. **149**(3683), 510–515 (1965)

30. Garfield, E.: Scientography: mapping the tracks of science **7**(45), 5–10 (1994)

31. Morris, S.A. et al.: Time line visualization of research fronts, **54**(5), 413–422 (2003)

32. FPbase: the fluorescent protein database. https://www.fpbase.org/

33. Papers with code. https://paperswithcode.com/

34. Protocols.io. https://www.protocols.io

35. F1000Research | Open access publishing platform | beyond a research journal. https://f1000research.com/

36. Open archives initiative protocol development and implementation. arXiv. https://doi.org/10.48550/arXiv.cs/0101027

37. OpenReview. https://openreview.net/

38. Weissgerber, T., et al.: Automated screening of COVID-19 preprints: can we help authors to improve transparency and reproducibility? **27**(1), 6–7 (2021)

39. Wang, Q., et al.: ReviewRobot: explainable paper review generation based on knowledge synthesis. In: Proceedings of the 13th International Conference on Natural Language Generation, pp. 384–397. Association for Computational Linguistic. https://doi.org/10.18653/v1/2020.inlg-1.44

40. Ivan, O.: Retraction watch. https://retractionwatch.com/

41. Sun, M., Barry Danfa, J., Teplitskiy, M.: Does double-blind peer review reduce bias? Evidence from a top computer science conference, **73**(6), 811–819 (2022)

42. Kikas, R., et al.: Structure and evolution of package dependency networks. In: 2017 IEEE/ACM 14th International Conference on Mining Software Repositories (MSR), pp. 102–112. https://doi.org/10.1109/MSR.2017.55

43. Kapur, P.K.: Software Reliability Assessment with OR Applications. In: Springer Series in Reliability Engineering, Springer, London (2011)

44. Ribeiro, A.C., Sizo, A., Reis, L.P.: Investigating the reviewer assignment problem: a systematic literature review, 01655515231176668 (2023)

45. Yu, Y., et al.: Reviewer recommendation for pull-requests in GitHub: What can we learn from code review and bug assignment? **74**, 204–218 (2016)

46. Bao, L., et al.: A large scale study of long-time contributor prediction for GitHub projects. **47**(6), 1277–1298 (2019)

47. CRediT. https://credit.niso.org/

48. Klein, M. et al.: Comparing published scientific journal articles to their pre-print versions. **20**(4), 335–350 (2019)

49. Horbach, S.P.J.M., Halffman, W.: The ability of different peer review procedures to flag problematic publications. Scientometrics **118**(1), 339–373 (2019)

50. Wang, G. et al.: What have we learned from OpenReview? World Wide Web **26**(2), 683–708 (2023)

51. Schulz, R., et al.: Is the future of peer review automated? **15**(1), 203 (2022)

52. Teixeira da Silva, J.A., Bornemann-Cimenti, H.: Why do some retracted papers continue to be cited?. Scientometrics **110**(1), 365–370 (2017). https://doi.org/10.1007/s11192-016-2178-9

53. XZ Utils backdoor. https://en.wikipedia.org/w/index.php?title=XZ_Utils_backdoor&oldid=1244555273

54. Thung, F. et al.: Network structure of social coding in GitHub. In: 2013 17th European Conference on Software Maintenance and Reengineering, pp. 323–326 (2013). https://doi.org/10.1109/CSMR.2013.41

55. Claxton, L.D.: A review of conflict of interest, competing interest, and bias for toxicologists. Toxicol. Ind. Health **23**(10), 557–571 (2007)

56. Hayati, P. et al.: Definition of spam 2.0: new spamming boom. In: 4th IEEE International Conference on Digital Ecosystems and Technologies, pp. 580–584 (2010). https://doi.org/10.1109/DEST.2010.5610590

57. Dwork, C., Naor, M.: Pricing via processing or combatting junk mail. In: Brickell, E. F. (ed.) Advances in Cryptology - CRYPTO 1992, pp. 139–147. Springer , Heidelberg (1993). https://doi.org/10.1007/3-540-48071-4_10

58. Douceur, J.R.: The sybil attack. In: Druschel, P., Kaashoek, F., Rowstron, A. (eds.) Peer-to-Peer Systems, vol. 2429, pp. 251–260. Springer, Heidelberg. https://doi.org/10.1007/3-540-45748-8_24

59. ORCID. https://orcid.org/

60. Costas, R., Corona, C., Robinson-Garcia, N.: Could ORCID play a key role in meta-research? Discussing new analytical possibilities to study the dynamics of science and scientists. https://doi.org/10.31235/osf.io/sjck6, https://osf.io/sjck6

Towards Website X-Ray for Europe's Municipalities: Unveiling Digital Transformation with Multimodal Embeddings

Jonathan Gerber, Bruno Kreiner, Jasmin Saxer$^{(\boxtimes)}$, and Andreas Weiler

Institute of Computer Science, Zurich University of Applied Sciences,
Technikumstrasse 9, 8401 Winterthur, Switzerland
`Jasminsimona.saxer@zhaw.ch`
`https://www.zhaw.ch/en/engineering/institutes-centres/init/`

Abstract. Local governments are going digital! To track their progress, researchers want to analyze their websites. This study explores finding these websites and understanding their content. Three methods for website discovery were compared, with search engines providing the most results. Different techniques to embed websites were also tested, comparing them by cluster analysis and performance. Homepage2Vec, which analyzes both text and visuals, performed best. This approach seems promising for monitoring European local government websites, but Homepage2Vec's use of visuals needs further exploration.

Keywords: website embedding · cluster analysis · data source evaluation

1 Introduction and Motivation

The World Wide Web is an enormous source of data and modern society is unimaginable without it. Most people rely in many ways on the World Wide Web as an information source, and so do many machine learning models, from Large Language Models (LLMs) such as ChatGPT to automatic stock market trading bots. In this context, website monitoring emerges as another important task that relies on models capable of analyzing dynamic data from the internet. Various applications surround this task (e.g., event detection, price tracking of certain goods, ...). Additionally, it finds its use in the field of political science. Policies concerning websites at a European-wide level have increased in recent years and with that the need to monitor the enforcement of these policies. An example of such policies is the 'Directive (EU) 2016/2102 of the European Parliament and of the Council of October 2016 on the accessibility of websites and mobile applications of public sector bodies' [1]. The first hurdle in monitoring municipality websites is gathering the correct and up-to-date websites. An automated process is needed as website domains change over time and new websites

P. Delir Haghighi et al. (Eds.): iiWAS 2024, LNCS 15342, pp. 125–139, 2025.
https://doi.org/10.1007/978-3-031-78090-5_11

emerge. In this paper, we try to gather websites of municipalities across Europe and discuss this task's challenge. This provides a building block to assess the digital transformation of communities within an interdisciplinary research project Digilog[1] between political and computer science.

There are different methods to determine the digital transformation of a local government. For example, Garcia-Sanchez *et al.* [9] present an analysis of the development of e-governments of 102 Spanish municipalities and Pina *et al.* [22] conduct an empirical study about the effect of e-government on transparency, openness and hence accountability in 15 countries of the EU and a total of 318 government web sites. In this paper, we set the foundation to not only analyze one country or a subset of countries and municipalities but all local authorities in 40 European countries (members of the Council of Europe). The digital transformation assessment itself is not part of this paper.

We evaluate three different data acquisition strategies with the goal of obtaining one URL per municipality, given their name and country. We focus first on quantity and then on quality. We additionally evaluate various pre-trained website embedding models on their capability of building meaningful embeddings for websites. We especially focus on the comparison of local tourism and municipality websites and whether the models are capable of separating them in latent space. A robust embedding is essential for further downstream tasks. Our research has shown that changing domains of municipality websites require periodical crawling to maintain an up to date URL list. Thus, one important task is to be able to flag wrong URLs when periodically crawling for municipality websites. The automation of such a data gathering process can be extended to a completely different domain e.g., monitoring of websites of dementia associations [19].

Finding and analyzing as many web pages as possible is important to derive statistical-driven conclusions on a larger scale. For monitoring the digital transformation of a region it is crucial that the crawled and analyzed URLs genuinely belong to the assumed municipality. Including false URLs could lead to entirely inaccurate evaluations. In this paper however, we focus on the first step of gathering websites from a municipality and clustering them as a binary task without considering whether the municipality searched corresponds to the municipality website found.

2   Related Work

Websites contain mainly unstructured (floating text) or semi-structured (HTML tags) data but rarely any structured data. Thus the analysis of websites relies heavily on (large) language models. However, there are also attempts to analyze websites with numerical features based on manual feature engineering but this is rather a declining branch considering the capabilities of the most recent LLMs. Hashemi [11] provides an extensive overview of the work that has been done in the past years in the field of web page classification. We are going to add some of the most recent papers and also list some work worth mentioning in our context.

---

[1] https://www.digilog-project.org/.

There is recent work on visual based classification [2,8,16]. However, the image-only-based approaches lack the ability of generalization. This is due to the fact that website categories in the used data sets are distinguishable by their appearance rather than by their written content. This difference in appearance might not be the case in other applications (e.g., university homepages vs NGO homepages).

There is a very large amount of related work that has been done in terms of text classification. Surveys from Minaee *et al.* [18] or Kowsari *et al.* [12] present the diversity of approaches. Therefore, we only consider recent work which is related to website classification. Gupta and Bhatia [10] propose an approach that uses several pre-trained BERT base models to learn contextual representations independently and then use a Deep Residual Inception Model Network (DRIMN) for classification tasks of web pages in English. Since the HTML tags are not contained in BERT's word piece vocabulary, the nature of the HTML tags does not have an impact on the classification task. They compare their ensemble model to other models such as k-nearest-neighbor, Support Vector Machine (SVM), Artificial Neural Network, BERT base default, BERT base + Nonlinear layer and BERT Base + convolutional neural network (CNN). The comparisons are made on the data sets DMOZ (13 categories such as business, society, science, ...), WebKB (four categories in the area of education), 20 newsgroups, Conference and Yahoo categories in which their model outperforms all the other models in every data set. Matosevic *et al.* [17] propose a procedure consisting of a combination of expert labeling and machine learning in general to create a model for web page classification. The classification is based on a determination of relevance (low, medium, high) in the context of the other 16 classes (arts, business, computers,...). The classification methods as well as the embedding methods used are not quite state-of-the-art. However, they provide insight into which HTML features are relevant for classification of web pages. This suggests that not only plain text should be considered but also to make use of information of certain HTML tags and select certain content specifically.

Buber and Diri [5] apply a recurrent neural network (RNN) for English web page classification. The training set consists of 887'195 web pages divided into 23 unbalanced distributed categories. Title, description, and keywords of the meta-tags are used as input data. To create the embedding a pre-trained model based on GloVe was used, which is a static word embedding, unlike a BERT model. However, they show that in their case the use of transfer learning does not improve the performance of the model. Nandanwar and Choudhary [20] propose a classification model based on GloVe and a Bidirectional Long Short-term Neural Network (BiLSTM) for categorizing. They test the model on the WebKB data set as well as the DMOZ data set. They further compare their model against the ensemble model of Gupta and Bhatia [10] and an SVM web page classification approach [3]. In most of the cases the proposed model outperforms the other models. Nandanwar and Choudhary [21] propose a fine tuned multilingual contextual embedding-based web page categorization model. They specifically address the problem of polysemy in web page classification. They apply their model on different data sets such as WebKB and DMOZ. Although their model achieves an F1-score of 0.84 they solely focus on textual features and completely ignore visual features and syntactical features of a webpage. Li *et al.* [13] propose MarkupLM, a pre-trained LLM for document understanding tasks, based on the actual text as well as the Markup language. The model is based on a BERT architecture. They add the additional XPath embedding to the embedding layer which is based on different features to identify the target leaf. The pre-training objectives of the models are Masked Markup Language Modeling (prediction of a text token of the DOM tree leaf), Node Relation Prediction (e.g., child, sibling, . . .) and Title-Page Matching. They compare their two models (base and large) with previous models such as FreeDOM-Full [14] and SimpDOM [24] on the SWDE data set considering the F1-score. They also compare their models with BERT base, RoBERTa base and ELECTRA large models from Chen *et al.* [6] on the WebSRC data set. Their large model outperforms every other model in every aspect whereas their proposed base model outperforms the others only in most of the cases. The pre-trained models are only available for the English language.

Bruni and Bianci [4] propose a procedure for website classification based on text features as well as on visual features. They compare different classification algorithms with each other on the task of detecting e-commerce services on a web page. Although the results appear to be not task specific the level of the classification is too sophisticated and assumes the classes to have certain attributes such as e-commerce services. Lungeon *et al.* [15] propose a language agnostic website embedding for classification tasks. With their introduced homepage embedder "Homepage2Vec" they create a multilingual embedding based on word embeddings of the textual content (the first 100 sentences), the metadata tags (title, description, keywords, . . .), and also the visual appearance (screenshot) and other features such as domain name. Those numerical features are reduced used for classifying the homepage into 14 different classes (art, business, computers, games, . . .).

3 Methodology

This section provides insight into our methodology for building our data set of URLs and evaluating different website embedding methods.

3.1 Data Acquisition

To obtain URLs of municipality websites we compared three different data acquisition strategies. The first strategy defines simple rules to 'guess' the URLs of the websites. We denoted this strategy as 'patternwise' data acquisition. The second strategy uses the search engine DuckDuckGo and the third uses the encyclopedia Wikipedia. There are different alternatives to the search engine. We selected DuckDuckGo due to its highest request rate in a free plan. This is especially important when processing a high number of requests.

Patternwise. We guess the URLs of municipality websites by building URLs out of the municipality names. First, we change the municipality names to low-ercase, remove punctuation, delete white spaces and replace it with hyphens, do umlaut normalization (e.g., 'ä' becomes 'ae') and apply the 'Unidecode' library which transforms non-ASCII characters to their closest ASCII representation. The resulting municipality name is then used with various domain extensions to create multiple URLs (e.g., 'www.' + municipality name + domain extension). The first URL that successfully leads to a website is stored. The domain extensions in order of testing are *country code top-level domain, '.gov' + country code top-level domain, '.gov', '.eu', '.gov.eu', '.com'*.

DuckDuckGo. We leverage the DuckDuckGo search engine using the library[2] to gather URLs for each municipality. The search term is the municipality name plus 'official municipality website'. We translate the query 'official municipality website' to the main language of the country. The country's main language was looked up from Wikipedia's 'List of official languages by country and territory', using the first language as the main language. The translation was done using the library translate-python. Since we found that many ambiguous websites lead to Wikipedia or tourism websites, we add '-wikipedia' and '-tourism' which makes DuckDuckGo disregard related websites.

Wikipedia. To access Wikipedia we use the most commonly used Pywikibot[3]. There are other APIs and scrapers that offer a way but in comparison, the Pywikibot performed best for our purposes. Due to the well standardized page structure of the Wikipedia sites, we extracted the website URL from the munic-ipalities from a table of the corresponding page. The page request was done in English which might not necessarily be the official language of the corresponding country. We observed that the HTML layout changes from language to language which means the standardized website extraction is not guaranteed anymore and customized solutions must be created for each language.

3.2   Website Embeddings

As related work shows, there are many different approaches and methods to embed a website, mainly textual, visual and combined approaches. We chose two approaches discussed in Sect. 2 and benchmark them. We selected the models due to their performance as well as the availability of code and a model by the authors. We applied Homepage2Vec [15] as well as MarkupLM [13] on our specific problem to test their ability to generalize and the performance on real world applications. Both models make use of the deeper semantic meaning of a Markup Document. MarkupLM uses the embedding of XPath and the tags as a feature whereas Homepage2Vec uses the visual features as well as the extraction

---

[2] https://pypi.org/project/duckduckgo-search/.
[3] https://github.com/wikimedia/pywikibot.

of certain specific data of a Markup document such as keywords or descriptions in the meta tag section. In addition to that both authors provided a library or a GitHub repository to apply their models. Since the MarkupLM model was not provided in a multilingual version the text components were translated to English and then used for classification.

Homepage2Vec [15] is a pre-trained language-agnostic website embedding and classification model. It is trained on a curated data set from the Curlie Web directory with 92 languages and 14 categories. They excluded the top-level label regional and with that also municipality websites, as it wasn't relevant to their task. The features for embedding the websites are the following: word embeddings (XLM-R) of the textual content (the first 100 sentences), metadata information from title, description, and keywords, domain name, and links; the visual appearance (screenshot) embedded with a pre-trained ResNet-18 model, the top-level domain and 30 most frequent metatags as one-hot encodings. The final feature vector with a dimension of 5'169 is used as input to a fully connected neural network with two hidden layers for reducing the vector and classifying the homepage into 14 different classes. We used the library of Homepage2Vec[4] and its pre-trained models to make embeddings of the websites. We adapted the function to access a website with the library of Homepage2Vec, such that it allows redirects using requests to get the website. Additionally, if it doesn't find a website using requests, we use Selenium with a headless Chrome web driver to access the website. The library offers two different approaches and pre-trained models, one with visual features (screenshot of the main page) and one without. We used the last hidden layer of the respective model as the embedding of the homepage, which has a dimension of 100.

MarkupLM [13] is a pre-trained transformer model for document understanding. It is trained on the text and markup information, such as HTML, of the documents. The pre-trained model is trained on the Common Crawl webpage data set. The encoder part of the model is based on the BERT architecture with a new input for the XPath embeddings. The input features for the model are the following: text embedding, XPath embedding of the markup tag sequence, the 1D position embedding corresponding to the sequence order, and segment embedding for downstream tasks. To apply the MarkupLM model on different languages, we first translated the webpages to English using LibreTranslate with its option to translate HTML files. The language of the HTML was retrieved from the HTML lang tag. If there was no HTML lang tag, German was used as the source language. We used the MarkupLM Base model ('microsoft/markuplm-base'[5]) and feature extraction provided by Hugging Face to get the text and XPath from the HTML. We cut off the number of nodes at 512 as this is the maximum number of nodes that the model can process. Then we applied the

---

[4] https://github.com/epfl-dlab/homepage2vec.
[5] https://huggingface.co/microsoft/markuplm-base.

MarkupLM model to get the embedding for each node. We used the mean over all nodes to get the embedding for the HTML which resulted in an embedding with a dimension of 768.

Basic Embedding. While we don't use the exact same features as Homepage2Vec, we adapted the approach using the same sentence model. Our approach uses the same features as Buber and Diri [5] describe, which are title, description and keywords from the HTML. After using the sentence model 'paraphrase-xlm-r-multilingual-v1' which was also used in Homepage2Vec, we concatenated the three features to get the embedding for the HTML, similar to the feature engineering of Hompage2vec, resulting in a dimension of 2304.

Header Embedding. The website header here refers to the menu usually located at the top of a website. To embed the text in the header of a website, we first located the header section by indications such as the tags nav, menu and header. If no text was found, 'nav', 'menu' and 'header' were searched in the class name or id name. The text from tags and button tags with href was used in the specific found section from before. If less than 2 text elements were found, the span and strong tags were used to find text. When no header section was found accessing the website with requests, selenium was used to get the HTML page source. The cumulated text from the header section was then joined into one string and embedded using the 'paraphrase-xlm-r-multilingual-v1' model, resulting in an embedding with a dimension of 768.

Basic and Header Embedding. We concatenated the basic and header embedding described above after each other to get the basic and header embedding, which resulted in embeddings with a dimension of 3072.

3.3 Embedding Comparison

To assess the effectiveness of the embedding algorithms, we apply a quantitative approach rather than relying purly on visual inspection. While dimensionality reduction techniques like t-SNE or PCA are useful for exploratory analysis, they often result in a loss of high-dimensional information. Thus, we compare the embeddings based on scores which evaluate the statistical and geometric properties of the different cluster groups within the embedding space. The goal is to determine whether a generally trained model or even a model trained on other related specific tasks is capable of separating labeled website embeddings in the vector space accordingly. An encoder model projects the data into the latent space. We use ground-truth labels of the data to create two distinctions: One for municipality websites and another for non-municipality websites. Our cluster analysis focuses on defining the inherent ability of the encoder to organize the latent space so that these two classes are separated without additional fine-tuning.

Silhouette Score. The Silhouette Score first calculates the mean distance of one data point to all other data points in the same cluster ($a(i)$ = average dissimilarity of i to all other objects of A). Then the average distance of the data point to each other cluster is taken. The minimum average distance is selected to find the neighboring cluster. This is denoted as $b(i)$ (= minimum average dissimilarity of i to all other objects of another cluster). If $a(i)$ is smaller than $b(i)$, the silhouette score is $1 - a(i)/b(i)$ which is close to 1 when $a(i)$ is a lot smaller than $b(i)$ i.e. the data point is on average much closer to the points in its own cluster than to the neighboring cluster's points. If $b(i) > a(i)$, the Silhouette Score is $b(i)/a(i) - 1$ which is close to -1 if $a(i)$ is a lot bigger than $b(i)$ i.e. the data point is on average much closer to the points of the neighboring cluster. In the case of $a(i) = b(i)$, the Silhouette Score is set to 0. The Silhouette Score is not robust to outliers [23].

Davies-Bouldin Index. The Davies-Bouldin index assesses clustering quality by comparing the compactness, defined as the average distance of each data point to its centroid within a cluster, with the separation between clusters. Compactness measures how closely data points within a cluster are grouped, while separation measures how distinct clusters are from each other. The calculation are done on each possible cluster pair. Then the sum of their respective compactness is taken and divided by the separation, which is conventionally the distance between the centroids. To get a cluster-specific score, we apply the following formula:

$$R_i = max_{j \neq i} \frac{S_i + S_j}{d(C_i, C_j)} \tag{1}$$

S_i and S_j are the compactness score of cluster i and j and $d(C_i, C_j)$ is the distance between their centroids. The Davies-Bouldin score for the clustering task is the average of the maximum values (R_i) over each cluster pair. While we want to minimize the compactness score, we want to maximize the separation value. Therefore, a smaller Davies-Bouldin index is desirable [7].

Separation Distance General Score. The Separation Distance General Score (SDG score) punishes data structures with blurry clusters which are not easy to separate by whereas it scores data sets higher with easy separable cluster structures. It compares the third Quantile ($Q3$) of the distance of a cluster to its centroid with the first Quantile ($Q1$) of the distance of outside data points of the cluster to its centroid. It rewards clear separations between a cluster and the rest of the data. The score itself is as follows,

$$S_{SDG} = \frac{1}{C} \sum_{c=1}^{C} \frac{Q3(wcd(k))}{Q1(ocd(k))} \tag{2}$$

C is the total number of clusters. The within-cluster distance (wcd) function returns a vector with length J_k of distances of all observations within the k-th cluster to its centroid. The outside cluster distance (ocd) function returns a vector of distances of observations outside the k-th cluster to the centroid of the $k - th$ cluster. The vector has the length $N - J_k$, with N being the number of all observations and J_k the number of observations of the k-th cluster.

4   Case Studies and Results

In this work, we apply different data acquisition methods to get URLs of municipality websites. To determine whether the acquired URLs are official municipality websites in an automated way, we first create numerical representations of the websites. We employ various web embedding techniques and evaluate their effectiveness in distinguishing embeddings of municipality websites from those of other websites, such as tourism websites. For the case study, we used a total of 88232 municipalities in 41 countries of Europe. We made a subset to measure the quality of the embeddings, which we later hand-labeled. The subset consists of 100 random municipalities from Germany, Switzerland, and Austria, with a total of 300 municipalities. We selected German-speaking municipalities for this study because the annotators responsible for labeling the data were all proficient in German.

4.1   Quantity

In a first step, we measured the number of responses from DuckDuckGo, Wikipedia and Pattern as described in Sect. 3.1 for the 88235 municipalities in 41 countries. The response rates per country are shown in Fig. 1b and aggregated in a box plot in Fig. 1a. DuckDuckGo found a response link for over 99.9 % (88196) of the queries, which was to be expected. The pattern algorithm resulted in a response rate of 68.4 % (60312) and Wikipedia with 37.6% (33135). Wikipedia favors Nordic countries which might already be an indication of digital transformation. The pattern-based approach shows some high response rates indicating an apparent convention of URL structure in these Countries. Some of the discrepancies may be a result of the limitations of the Wikipedia scraper. Our implementation of scraping the Wikipedia websites has the following limitations: only English entries were considered, and only the most common English Wikipedia template was considered for scraping the URL. Thus if different templates were used, the scraper may not find the URL. Nevertheless, the results were not unexpected since the database of a search engine is built by crawlers whereas Wikipedia depends on contributions of the Wikipedia community and therefore one might conclude it is not as complete as a search engine. However, the completeness of a database is only one part. Another factor is the capability of matching a user query to the correct database entry. We differentiate these factors of completeness and matching capability by using the smaller hand-labeled subset, described in the next section.

4.2   Quality

To check the quality of the URLs we hand-labeled a subset of the gathered URLs from each data acquisition method into correct and incorrect. We labeled

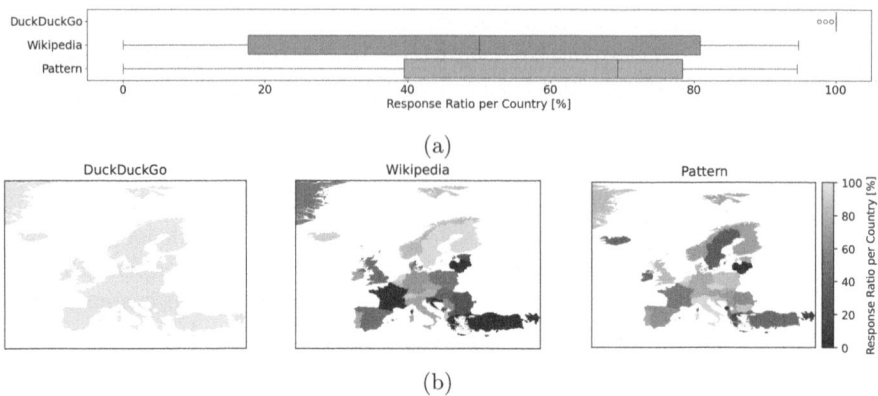

Fig. 1. The distribution of response ratios over all countries and divided into the three data acquisition strategies. The results describe the ratio of how many URLs (not necessarily correct URLs) were found per country.

a URL as "correct" if the corresponding website was a municipality website without considering if it corresponded to the municipality that we searched for. As this would add another complexity to the research question, which is not in the scope of this work. Some of the incorrect URLs were tourism websites, associations websites, or default pages from hosting providers. The quality of the three data acquisition methods is shown in Table 1. DuckDuckGo resulted in the best percentage of correct URLs for the subset, followed by Wikipedia. These results may be explained by the intelligence of the implemented methods. DuckDuckGo with the specified query searches explicitly for municipality websites and returns the most relevant result. Using Wikipedia only the municipality name was looked up, which can lead to results that aren't municipality websites. Furthermore, we observed that in different cases there were outdated URLs provided from former municipality websites. The pattern method is very simplistic and not intelligent, thus it can result in any kind of website that uses a municipality name as its domain.

Table 1. Response rates of the 300 municipality subset. "n found URLs" is the number of URLs the data acquisition method returned. "n correct URLs" is the number of URLs which are municipality websites.

Acquisition	n found URLs	n correct URLs	% correct URLs
DuckDuckGo	**300**	**285**	**95.00**
Pattern	222	164	54.67
Wikipedia	246	221	73.67

Embedding Quality. For applying the different embedding methods, we use the labeled datasets from the previous step of the three data acquisition methods, resulting in 900 data points. To remove duplicate URLs, we selected only unique response URLs from the 900 data points, resulting in 405 URLs (329 municipality URLs, 76 other URLs).

The different embedding methods are not able to embed every website, due to the different drawbacks of each method. Thus we show the rate of successfully embedding the websites in Table 2. The basic and header method shows the best embedding rate, which can be explained by the use of two different embedding methods. The lower embedding rate of the header embedding method can be attributed to the lack of handling websites without a website header (menu located at the top of a website). The scoring of the embedding in Table 2 shows Homepage2Vec with visual embedding to be the best naturally clustering model. This appears to be due to the visual embedding. The version of Homepage2Vec without visual embedding performs otherwise rather badly. The basic embedding performs the worst overall. This model uses 3 raw concatenated features from Homepage2Vec without the additional trained layers that break them down into 100 dimensions. Even though the features used appear to describe the homepage quite distinctively, many webpages lack one or both of the description and keyword tags which both have a strong influence on the embeddings. Thus these homepages with empty values appear to be concentrated around gravitational points, which leads to a wrong clustering, see Fig. 2. There is a similar phenomenon with the embedding of the header. Although clearly distinguishable when looking at a rendered page header. Almost every page follows a different approach to implementing a header which makes it difficult to catch it effectively. A more pragmatic approach like MarkupLM (which uses the first 500 tokens of an HTML document) appears to be more effective in this case.

Table 2. Clustering scores for each embedding method with Homepage2Vec with visual embedding being the clear favorite, Embed Rate showing the rate of successfully embedded Websites from the 405 URLs

Embedding Method	Embed Rate	Silhouette	Davies-Bouldin	SDG
Basic	0.951	0.005	6.691	0.704
Header	0.844	0.169	3.464	0.862
Basic and Header	**0.983**	0.046	5.031	0.828
Homepage2Vec	0.951	0.077	4.069	0.695
Homepage2Vec with visual	0.951	**0.253**	**2.211**	**0.919**
MarkupLM	0.980	0.220	3.651	0.750

4.3 Performance

We measured the performance of the different data acquisition and embedding methods. The mean time in seconds per URL is shown in Table 3. The

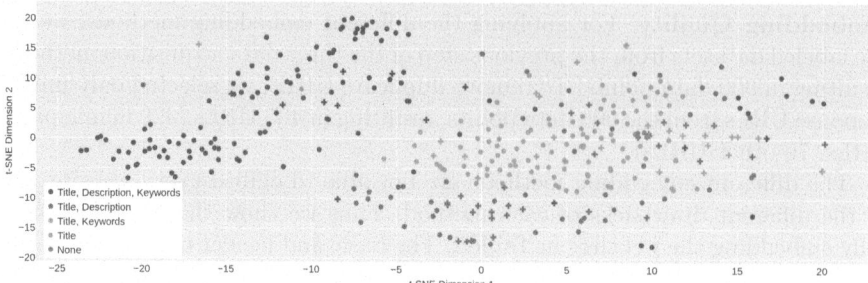

Fig. 2. Basic embedding approach with municipality (circle) and non-municipality (cross) websites. The formation of clusters is due more to missing values than to the type of website.

Table 3. Performance of the methods as the mean time in seconds for one URL.

Data Acq.	Mean Time	Embedding	Mean Time
Wikipedia	0.602	Homepage2Vec with visual	14.944
Pattern	0.195	Homepage2Vec	6.564
DuckDuckGo	1.449	Basic	2.323
		Basic	2.323
		Header	8.313
		MarkupLM	11.942

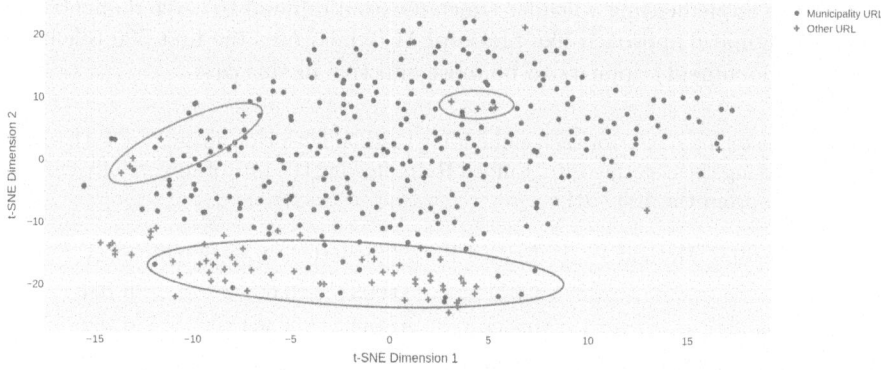

Fig. 3. Homepage2Vec with visual embeddings of unique websites from the different data sources with marked outliers that share similar characteristics. Blue circles depict municipality URLs and red crosses depict other URLs. (Color figure online)

performance was measured using an 11th Gen Intel(R) Core(TM) i9-11950H CPU with 16 cores, 32 GB RAM, and an NVIDIA RTX A2000 Laptop GPU with 4GB dedicated RAM. The time for the embedding includes fetching the HTML and screenshot if needed, followed by the embedding method. For MarkupLM the translation of the HTML to English is also included in the time. The pattern-wise data acquisition was the fastest, followed by Wikipedia. However, the patternwise implementation allowed for multiprocessing (using 8 workers). The DuckDuckGo performance is restricted by the rate limit of the API. The basic embedding method performed the best, followed by Homepage2Vec without visual.

4.4   Cluster Structure Analysis

Since the Homepage2Vec Embedding outperforms the other embeddings, we focus in this section on the results of this embedding shown in Fig. 3. Although there is a clear separation of clusters, there are certain outlier groups. The analysis of those outlier groups shows that they share certain characteristics within these groups. The top left group (circled red in Fig. 3) of non-municipality websites contains websites that are either social/political associations or businesses. The common characteristics are mainly the visual appearance which is also similar to a typical municipality. However, the content is different. The overlapping data of municipality websites below (circled in blue) share both with each other but also with red labeled data a high visual similarity. Most of them have a high proportion of screen area with landscapes, which is characteristic of the analyzed tourism websites. The outlier group on the top right (circled in red) shares a high visual as well as semantic similarity with the surrounding municipality website data points. The sites belong to regional governments which provide certain services the local governments do not. Since they are not local governmental websites, they are classified as non-municipality websites. However, this positioning of the data within the vector space speaks for the model because if the model were able to separate the data from the other cluster the model almost certainly would be overfitted.

5   Conclusions and Future Work

We presented a comparison of three online data sources (search engine, encyclopedia platform, direct URL guess) and evaluated them in terms of quantity as well as quality of the data. We additionally compare different multilingual website embedding methods on their capability to embed German HTML documents with high diversity. We rated the embedding methods with different scores, which reward the capability to separate websites into two predefined (binary) clusters. Only pre-trained models were used to test their performance in unknown tasks. These evaluations were applied to the real-world use case of retrieving homepage URLs of local governments in Europe based on their names. We showed that the approach of using a search engine as a data source appears to be most promising in both quality and quantity. Contrary to what was initially assumed the visual appearance of a website seems to have considerable influence on the embeddings of a website. We found that Homepage2Vec performed best due to its capability to not only analyze the semantics and syntax of a webpage using the HTML-code but also its visual appearance. However, when used without visual features, Homepage2Vec did not perform better than using embeddings of certain metadata in the HTML documents. We also found that embedding with a broader feature selection (header embedding, meta keywords, meta title, screenshot, ...) resulted in a better performance. This was due to the fact that missing data in certain features didn't affect the embedding as much as models with a more focused feature selection. The comparison was performed on German websites. As the models were trained for multilingual purposes and the authors showed their consistency over multiple languages, we thus assume that the findings are consistent over different languages. Future work will focus on developing an efficient website embedder with high performance, that can be used in the continuous monitoring platform. Additionally, we will focus on webpage segmentation and embedding webpage segments with the goal of e-form detection and a more robust website classifier.

Acknowledgments. This work is supported by Grant No. GR 200839 of the Swiss National Science Foundation (SNF) and German Research Foundation (DFG) for the research project "Digital Transformation at the Local Tier of Government in Europe: Dynamics and Effects from a Cross-Countries and Over-Time Comparative Perspective (DIGILOG)".

References

1. Directive (EU) 2016/2102 of the European parliament and of the council of 26 October 2016 on the accessibility of the websites and mobile applications of public sector bodies. In: OJ L 327, pp. 1–15 (2016)
2. Akusok, A., Miche, Y., Karhunen, J., Bjork, K.-M., Nian, R., Lendasse, A.: Arbitrary category classification of websites based on image content. IEEE Comput. Intell. Mag. **10**(2), 30–41 (2015). https://doi.org/10.1109/MCI.2015.2405317
3. Bhalla, V.K., Kumar, N.: An efficient scheme for automatic web pages categorization using the support vector machine. New Rev. Hypermedia Multimedia **22**(3), 223–242 (2016). https://doi.org/10.1080/13614568.2016.1152316
4. Bruni, R., Bianchi, G.: Website categorization: a formal approach and robustness analysis in the case of e-commerce detection. Expert Syst. Appl. **142**, 113001 (2020). https://doi.org/10.1016/j.eswa.2019.113001
5. Buber, E., Diri, B.: Web page classification using RNN. Procedia Comput. Sci. **154**, 62–72 (2019). https://doi.org/10.1016/j.procs.2019.06.011
6. Chen, X., et al.: WebSRC: a dataset for web-based structural reading comprehension. arXiv preprint arXiv:2101.09465 (2021)
7. Davies, D.L., Bouldin, D.W.: A cluster separation measure. IEEE Trans. Pattern Anal. Mach. Intell. (2), 224–227 (1979). publisher: IEEE
8. Espinosa-Leal, L., Akusok, A., Lendasse, A., Björk, K.-M.: Website classification from webpage renders. In: Cao, J., Vong, C.M., Miche, Y., Lendasse, A. (eds.) Proceedings of ELM2019, pp. 41–50. Springer International Publishing, Cham (2021). https://doi.org/10.1007/978-3-030-58989-9_5
9. García-Sánchez, I.M., Rodríguez-Domínguez, L., Frias-Aceituno, J.V.: Evolutions in E-governance: evidence from Spanish local governments. Environ. Policy Govern. **23**(5), 323–340 (2013)

10. Gupta, A., Bhatia, R.: Ensemble approach for web page classification. Multimedia Tools Appl. **80**(16), 25219–25240 (2021). https://doi.org/10.1007/s11042-021-10891-3
11. Hashemi, M.: Web page classification: a survey of perspectives, gaps, and future directions. Multimedia Tools Appl. **79**(17–18), 11921–11945 (2020). https://doi.org/10.1007/s11042-019-08373-8
12. Kowsari, K., Jafari Meimandi, K., Heidarysafa, M., Mendu, S., Barnes, L., Brown, D.: Text classification algorithms: a survey. Information **10**(4), 150 (2019). https://doi.org/10.3390/info10040150
13. Li, J., Xu, Y., Cui, L., Wei, F.: MarkupLM: pre-training of text and markup language for visually-rich document understanding (2022). http://arxiv.org/abs/2110.08518, arXiv:2110.08518 [cs]
14. Lin, B.Y., Sheng, Y., Vo, N., Tata, S.: Freedom: a transferable neural architecture for structured information extraction on web documents. In: Proceedings of the 26th ACM SIGKDD International Conference on Knowledge Discovery & Data Mining, pp. 1092–1102 (2020)
15. Lugeon, S., Piccardi, T., West, R.: Homepage2Vec: language-agnostic website embedding and classification. Proc. Int. AAAI Conf. Web Soc. Media **16**, 1285–1291 (2022). https://doi.org/10.1609/icwsm.v16i1.19380
16. López-Sánchez, D., Corchado, J.M., Arrieta, A.G.: A CBR system for image-based webpage classification: case representation with convolutional neural networks. In: The Thirtieth International Flairs Conference (2017)
17. Matošević, G., Dobša, J., Mladenić, D.: Using machine learning for web page classification in search engine optimization. Future Internet **13**(1), 9 (2021). publisher: MDPI
18. Minaee, S., Kalchbrenner, N., Cambria, E., Nikzad, N., Chenaghlu, M., Gao, J.: Deep learning–based text classification: a comprehensive review. ACM Comput. Surv. **54**(3), 1–40 (2022). https://doi.org/10.1145/3439726
19. Monnet, F., Pivodic, L., Dupont, C., Dröes, R.M., Van den Block, L.: Information on advance care planning on websites of dementia associations in Europe: a content analysis. Aging & Mental Health **27**(9), 1821–1831 (2023). Publisher: Taylor & Francis
20. Nandanwar, A.K., Choudhary, J.: Semantic features with contextual knowledge-based web page categorization using the GloVe model and stacked BiLSTM. Symmetry **13**(10), 1772 (2021). Publisher: MDPI
21. Nandanwar, A.K., Choudhary, J.: Contextual embeddings-based web page categorization using the fine-tune BERT model. Symmetry **15**(2), 395 (2023). https://doi.org/10.3390/sym15020395
22. Pina, V., Torres, L., Royo, S.: Are ICTs improving transparency and accountability in the EU regional and local governments? An empirical study. Public administration **85**(2), 449–472 (2007). Publisher: Wiley Online Library
23. Rousseeuw, P.J.: Silhouettes: a graphical aid to the interpretation and validation of cluster analysis. J. Comput. Appl. Math. **20**, 53–65 (1987). Publisher: Elsevier
24. Zhou, Y., Sheng, Y., Vo, N., Edmonds, N., Tata, S.: Simplified DOM trees for transferable attribute extraction from the web. arXiv preprint arXiv:2101.02415 (2021)

Machine Learning in Healthcare, Climate Change, and Human Behavior

Evolving Applications of Conversational Agents in Healthcare: A Literature Review

Vincenza Carchiolo$^{(\boxtimes)}$ and Michele Malgeri

Dipartimento di Ingegneria Elettrica, Elettronica e Informatica,
Università di Catania, Catania, Italy
vincenza.carchiolo@unict.it

Abstract. The use of conversational agents is becoming increasingly common in various fields, enabling the development of more user-friendly man-machine interfaces. The importance and centrality of employing comfortable user methods for dialogue have become crucial in the medical field. In this context, there has been a significant proliferation of literature in recent years, and this article aims to provide an overview of the most intriguing research topics from both medical and artificial intelligence technique perspectives.

1 Introduction

Conversational agents (CA) represent a significant evolution in the landscape of human-machine interfaces, fitting seamlessly into the trend of change characterizing these interfaces in the modern world. While traditional interfaces based on keyboards, mice, and screens have dominated for decades, there is now an unstoppable rise of more natural and intuitive interfaces capable of interacting with users in a more fluid and engaging manner. The integration of advanced technologies such as artificial intelligence and machine learning allows CAs to adapt to individual needs, personalizing interactions and offering an increasingly refined user experience. This aspect further contributes to the evolution of interfaces, making them more flexible, customizable, and capable of responding to the specific needs of each individual.

This article aims to analyze the applications of conversational agents in the healthcare where they can help patients manage their conditions, schedule appointments, and obtain health information. To construct a comprehensive state-of-the-art study encompassing both technological and application-oriented (health-oriented) aspects, we employed the Scopus and PubMed databases. Scopus [1] is a comprehensive bibliographic database of scientific literature covering a wide range of disciplines, and PubMed [11] is a free resource developed and maintained by the National Center for Biotechnology Information (NCBI) at the U.S. National Library of Medicine (NLM), part of the National Institutes of Health (NIH). The analysis is conducted using quantitative analysis methodologies successfully tested in other fields [9,10].

P. Delir Haghighi et al. (Eds.): iiWAS 2024, LNCS 15342, pp. 143–149, 2025.
https://doi.org/10.1007/978-3-031-78090-5_12

Section 2 describe the dataset used in our analisys and Sect. 3 discusses the methods and presents the results.

2   Exploring the Overlap Between Scopus and PubMed

In this paper, a state-of-the-art review on the use of conversational agents in medicine is conducted through a publication analysis. A dataset is extracted from publications, and a statistical analysis, incorporating NLP elements, is performed. The databases Scopus and PubMed are selected for their relevance in computer science and medicine, respectively.

Scopus is a comprehensive abstract and citation database of peer-reviewed literature launched by Elsevier in 2004, it is widely used by researchers, academic institutions, and other organizations to track and analyze research output across various fields. As of the latest updates, Scopus contains over 82 million records, making it one of the largest databases of its kind. PubMed is a free search engine, primarily accessing the MEDLINE database of references and abstracts on life sciences and biomedical topics. It is maintained by the National Center for Biotechnology Information (NCBI) at the U.S. National Library of Medicine (NLM), which is part of the National Institutes of Health (NIH). As of the latest updates, PubMed includes over 32 million citations and abstracts from more than 5,200 biomedical and life sciences journals.

To ensure that our analysis specifically targeted the intersection of conversational agents and healthcare applications, we employed a keyword selection process focusing our attention on publications having both "Conversational Agent" and "Health" in the title, abstract, or keywords (when provided). While acknowledging the existence of relevant work that might not explicitly use the terms "Conversational Agent" and "Health," this keyword selection strategy offered an efficient and well-defined starting point for our analysis. This selection allowed us to extract 941 papers from Scopus and 1061 papers from PubMed. Figure 1 illustrates the growth in the number of publications over the years for both databases in the field of conversational agents. A discrepancy is highlighted between the

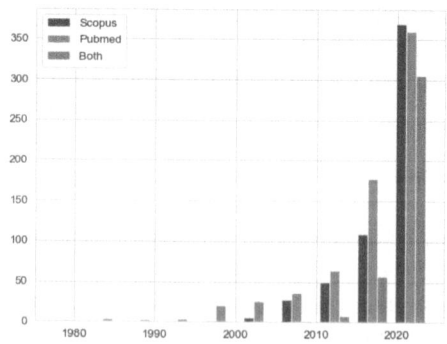

Fig. 1. Summary of publication for year.

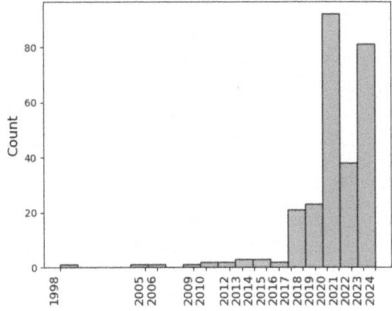

Fig. 2. Number of paper for year on Mixed dataset

datasets: while Scopus reflects trends aligned with recent advancements in NLP and AI, PubMed includes publications from earlier periods, where technology may not have been advanced enough to genuinely address conversational agents. Out of the extracted publications, 371 are found in both databases, with 691 unique to PubMed and 560 unique to Scopus. As shown in Fig. 1, the growth rate of PubMed publications is slower compared to Scopus, but the most significant increase is observed in the number of publications indexed by both databases. In this survey, since our study aimed to primarily capture the interdisciplinarity of the subject, we decided to focus on the 371.

3   Conversational Agents in Scopus and PubMed

As mentioned above, we used a dataset constructed by intersecting data extracted from Scopus and PubMed (called *Mixed*) that contains 371 papers at the time of extraction (April 2024).

Distribution over Time. The initial analysis examines the distribution of publications over the years. Figure 2 shows that significant growth begins in 2018, with the majority of publications concentrated in 2022 and in the first four months of 2024 (data extracted in April 2024). This suggests a potential for further growth in the coming years. Moreover, the figure shows some singularities that are summarized in Table 1. It is noticeable that the publication sources are predominantly medical journals. The main applications are related to patient education and are thus aimed at patients, while some applications are more generally targeted towards social media users. The conversational agents developed/used/evaluated are almost entirely EC, with only one case analyzing a Virtual Assistant based Chatbot.

Geographical Distribution. The second analysis examines the distribution of these articles across different countries, referring to the corresponding authors' affiliations. Figure 3a illustrates the distribution of the articles, demonstrating that the top 10 states account for approximately 75% of the total. Consequently,

Table 1. Oldest paper in the dataset

Paper	Journal	Year	Application	Target	CA kind
[2]	IEEE Transactions on Information Technology in Biomedicine	1998	Aided Computer Vision	Education	EC
[4]	Patient Education and Counseling	2005	Automated health behavior	Patient	EC RBC
[19]	Journal of Biomedical Informatics	2006	Healthy eating dialog	Patient	EC
[15]	Studies in Health Technology and Informatics	2009	Health Promotion	Patient	EC
[5]	Journal of Health Communication	2010	Patient Education	Aged Patient	EC
[3]	Harvard Review of Psychiatry	2010	Psychiatry	Patient	EC
[14]	Journal of Medical Internet Research	2012	Health general	Social	EC
[18]	Cognitive Processing	2012	Eating suggestion	Social	EC
[7]	Journal of the American Geriatrics Society	2013	Active aging	Aged Patient	EC
[6]	Patient Education and Counseling	2013	health counselor	Patient	EC
[12]	Patient Education and Counseling	2013	Mindfulness training	Patient	EC
[16]	Journal of Medical Internet Research	2014	Internet HealthTales Indexer	Healthcare Providers	–
[13]	Journal of the American Board of Family Medicine	2015	Patient Education	Woman/pregnant	
[20]	Hispanic Health Care International	2015	Patient education	Healthcare Providers	EC
[8]	Journal of Medical Internet Research	2016	Internet clinical trials searching	Researcher	EC
[17]	JAMA Internal Medicine	2016	Health information	Social	VA

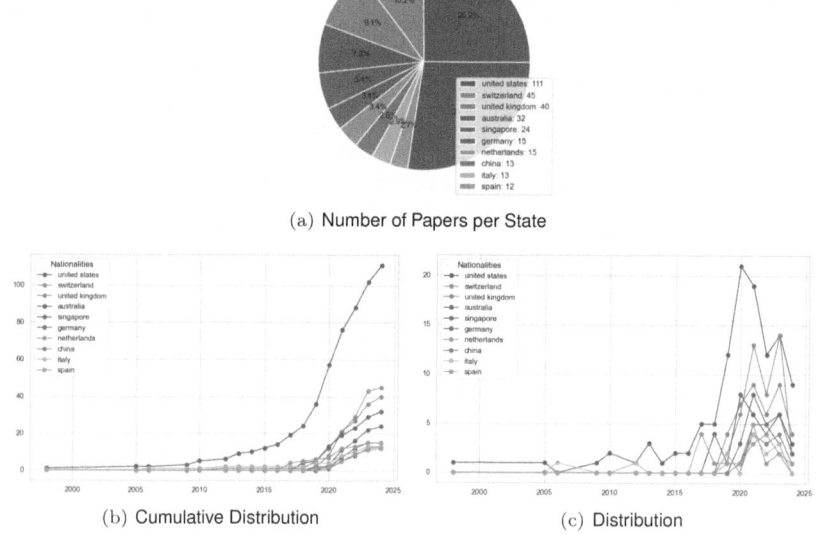

(a) Number of Papers per State

(b) Cumulative Distribution   (c) Distribution

Fig. 3. Publications of countries and their distribution over years.

subsequent figures only present the publication trends by state and year for the top 10 states. Figure 3b presents the cumulative trends of the top 10 states over the years. Notably, the United States emerges as the state with the highest number of papers and the most significant annual increase, in-fact it shows that the United States in particular experienced a peak in 2020 and a slowdown in the number of publications in subsequent years Fig. 3c. Additionally, it is observed that some smaller states have a substantial impact on the overall number of publications.

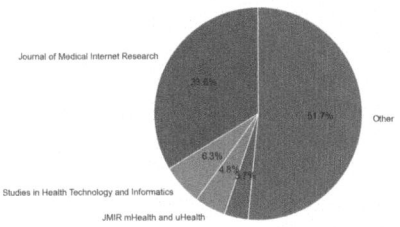

Fig. 4. Distribution of papers over Journal

Source Distribution. We delve into primary sources to understand the distribution of papers across journals. To characterize the journals, we leverage the Scimago classification system, which employs Subject Areas and Categories. Figure 4 depicts the distribution of publications across different journals. A significant portion (33.6%) of the 371 selected publications are concentrated in a single journal, the Journal of Medical Internet Research (JMIR). Notably, JMIR falls under the subject area of Medicine, with Health Informatics as the specific category. The second most prominent journal (6.3%) exhibits a broader classification, encompassing three subject areas: Medicine (Health Informatics category), Engineering (Biomedical Engineering), and Health Professions. The third most frequent journal (4.8%) belongs to the subject area of Medicine with Health Informatics as the category. The fourth journal features publications in both Environmental Science and Medicine subject areas. The remaining journals do not contribute significantly. The above consideration suggests that the majority of publications on CA applications in healthcare are primarily directed towards researchers in the field of medical informatics rather than those specializing in general artificial intelligence.

4   Conclusion

This paper has analyzed a broad set of publications related to CAs, examining how this topic has evolved over the years and how research activity is distributed worldwide. The analysis allows us to notice that the applications are almost always aimed at patients, and the types of CAs used have become increasingly advanced. In older articles, they were mostly of the EC type. Additionally, a very basic analysis of the keywords used by the authors has been presented.

Acknowledgment. The work is partially supported by UDMA project, CUP: G69J18001040007.

References

1. Scopus fact sheet. Accessed Apr 2022
2. Akay, M., Marsic, I., Medl, A., Bu, G.: A system for medical consultation and education using multimodal human/machine communication. IEEE Trans. Inf. Technol. Biomed. **2**(4), 282–291 (1998)
3. Bickmore, T., Gruber, A.: Relational agents in clinical psychiatry. Harvard Rev. Psychiatry **18**(2), 119–130 (2010)
4. Bickmore, T., Gruber, A., Picard, R.: Establishing the computer-patient working alliance in automated health behavior change interventions. Patient Educ. Couns. **59**(1), 21–30 (2005)
5. Bickmore, T.W., et al.: Usability of conversational agents by patients with inadequate health literacy: evidence from two clinical trials. J. Health Commun. **15**(SUPPL. 2), 197–210 (2010)
6. Bickmore, T.W., Schulman, D., Sidner, C.: Automated interventions for multiple health behaviors using conversational agents. Patient Educ. Counsel. **92**(2), 142–148 (2013)
7. Bickmore, T.W., et al.: A randomized controlled trial of an automated exercise coach for older adults. J. Am. Geriatr. Soc. **61**(10), 1676–1683 (2013)
8. Bickmore, T.W., Utami, D., Matsuyama, R., Paasche-Orlow, M.K.: Improving access to online health information with conversational agents: a randomized controlled experiment. J. Med. Internet Res. **18**(1) (2016)
9. Carchiolo, V., Malgeri, M.: Navigating the AI timeline: from 1995 to today. In: Proceedings of the 13th International Conference on Data Science, Technology and Applications - Volume 1: DATA, pp. 577–584. INSTICC, SciTePress (2024)
10. Carchiolo, V., Malgeri, M.: Unlocking the potential of intelligent blockchain: a quantitative analysis. In: Proceedings of Intelligent Computing and Distributed Computing 2024. Springer-Verlag (2024)
11. Health and Human Services (HHS): PubMed National Library of Medicine. https://pubmed.ncbi.nlm.nih.gov
12. Hudlicka, E.: Virtual training and coaching of health behavior: example from mindfulness meditation training. Patient Educ. Counsel. **92**(2), 160–166 (2013)
13. Jack, B., et al.: Reducing preconception risks among African American women with conversational agent technology. J. Am. Board Fam. Med. **28**(4), 441–451 (2015)
14. Kennedy, C.M., Powell, J., Payne, T.H., Ainsworth, J., Boyd, A., Buchan, I.: Active assistance technology for health-related behavior change: an interdisciplinary review. J. Med. Internet Res. **14**(3), E80 (2012)
15. Lisetti, C.: Features for culturally appropriate avatars for behavior-change promotion in at-risk populations. Stud. Health Technol. Inf. **144**, 22–26 (2009)
16. Manuvinakurike, R., Velicer, W.F., Bickmore, T.W.: Automated indexing of internet stories for health behavior change: weight loss attitude pilot study. J. Med. Internet Res. **16**(12) (2014)
17. Miner, A.S., Milstein, A., Schueller, S., Hegde, R., Mangurian, C., Linos, E.: Smartphone-based conversational agents and responses to questions about mental health, interpersonal violence, and physical health. JAMA Internal Med. **176**(5), 619–625 (2016)
18. Novielli, N., Mazzotta, I., De Carolis, B., Pizzutilo, S.: Analysing user's reactions in advice-giving dialogues with a socially intelligent ECA. Cogn. Process. **13**(SUPPL. 2), S487–S497 (2012)

19. Rosis, F.D., Novielli, N., Carofiglio, V., Cavalluzzi, A., De Carolis, B.: User modeling and adaptation in health promotion dialogs with an animated character. J. Biomed. Inf. **39**(5), 514–531 (2006)
20. Wells, K.J., et al.: Acceptability of a virtual patient educator for Hispanic women. Hispanic Health Care Int. **13**(4), 179–185 (2015)

Hybrid Edge-Cloud Federated Learning: The Case of Lightweight Smoking Detection

Amirhossein Douzandeh Zenoozi[1]([envelope]) [ID], Babak Majidi[3] [ID], Lucia Cavallaro[2] [ID], and Antonio Liotta[1] [ID]

[1] Free University of Bozen-Bolzano, Bolzano, Italy
{adouzandehzenoozi,antonio.liotta}@unibz.it
[2] Radboud University, Nijmegen, Netherlands
lucia.cavallaro@ru.nl
[3] Khatam University, Tehran, Iran
b.majidi@khatam.ac.ir

Abstract. The growing demand for real-time data processing on lightweight devices, without compromising data privacy, necessitates innovative approaches to balance these constraints. This study presents a novel hybrid edge-cloud federated learning framework aimed at developing an automated smoking detection system as a case study. Unlike traditional AI solutions that often face scalability and cost challenges due to reliance on high-performance computing resources, our decentralized approach distributes processing tasks across fog-edge layers, significantly reducing the dependence on centralized infrastructure. Additionally, while existing solutions typically focus on object detection (such as cigarettes), our framework specifically targets smoking behavior, enhancing detection accuracy in public, also, we collected a fully balanced dataset for smoking classification. Moreover, we address data privacy concerns by using federated learning, enabling local data processing on edge devices while securely sharing the model with the server. The suggested framework not only represents over 80% accuracy in detecting smoking activities but also addresses architectural challenges in integrating cloud and edge computing. By leveraging federated learning, our solution ensures real-time responsiveness, and operational efficiency, and offers a scalable, accessible method for applying smoke-free zones. This study highlights the potential of combining lightweight devices with federated learning and edge computing to advance public health initiatives and provides a foundation for future research in decentralizing high-performance computing tasks.

Keywords: edge computing · federated learning · smoking detection · human action recognition

P. Delir Haghighi et al. (Eds.): iiWAS 2024, LNCS 15342, pp. 150–159, 2025.
https://doi.org/10.1007/978-3-031-78090-5_13

1   Introduction

Nowadays, the development of reliable edge devices to perform complex detection tasks in real-time is of growing interest [3,9,11,15]. Indeed, developing fast models that preserve also data security is hard to address. In addition, despite the yearly increase of last-generation devices' computing power, it notably lags behind the escalating growth rate of the scale of edge data requiring processing and, thus, communication delays may occur. For those reasons, centralized computing models are shifting to distributed computing models and, more specifically, to a combination of techniques involving both cloud-edge collaborative models and federated learning [4]. Herein, to face those challenges we are addressing the specific use case of smoking detection as it is a task that demands significant computational resources, posing challenges to scalability and financial viability. Unlike existing works that typically focus on object detection (such as cigarettes), we present an architecture that focuses on recognizing the action of smoking, making it more effective in real-world scenarios. This endeavor is pivotal in safeguarding communities against the detrimental impacts of smoking and second-hand smoke exposure [17]. Vulnerable demographics, including children and the elderly, face heightened risks of adverse health outcomes linked to second-hand smoke, encompassing respiratory ailments, asthma, and Sudden Infant Death Syndrome (SIDS). Consequently, deploying automated systems to detect smoking incidents in critical public settings such as schools, hospitals, parks, and recreational areas assumes paramount importance. Beyond mitigating health risks associated with smoking, these systems contribute to cultivating a safer, healthier environment for all societal segments. By vigilant monitoring and enforcing smoke-free directives, automated detection technologies nurture public spaces conducive to well-being, thereby enhancing the overall quality of life for individuals and communities alike.

Traditionally, the adoption of AI-driven smoking detection solutions, particularly those leveraging real-time closed-circuit television (CCTV) footage analysis, has encountered substantial hurdles owing to their heavy reliance on centralized High-Performance Computing (HPC) resources [10]. This reliance has historically constrained the scalability and practical deployment of such systems in CCTV control centers in forbidden areas including hospitals or schools.

Our presented study endeavors to tackle these challenges by proposing an innovative, scalable, and cost-effective framework for autonomous monitoring of smoke-free zones, underpinned by federated learning [8]. Specifically tailored for seamless operation on lightweight devices and edge computing nodes, this approach contrasts with the ones mentioned in Sect. 2 by decentralizing data processing and overcoming the limitations of object detection systems. The framework circumvents the necessity for high-cost, centralized computing power while ensuring data privacy and real-time responsiveness, offering a practical solution for smoke-free zone enforcement.

The rest of this paper is structured as follows. Section 2 shows related works. Section 3 describes the methods and experimental setup used in this study. Finally, in Sect. 4 the results are discussed together with future works.

2   Related Works

Thakur *et al.* [18] introduced a machine-learning framework for real-time smoking activity identification using a wrist-wearable device. By processing sensor data through a sliding window mechanism, the framework extracts relevant features, undergoes hyperparameter tuning, and selects features to optimize models. Achieving up to 98.7% accuracy in multi-class classification, this research pioneers the application of wearable devices for real-time smoking detection. However, it is noteworthy to recall that the implementation of wearable devices in real-world scenarios may incur significant costs, and it does not constitute a feasible solution for deployment in public areas.

Zhang *et al.* [19] proposed a smoking-detection model tailored for real-time monitoring in public places, addressing challenges such as low accuracy and missed detections. Through a single-stage detection approach, the authors introduced a novel smoking detection model incorporating custom attention mechanisms, an improved residual network, and feature fusion techniques. This model enhances overall detection accuracy and contributes to the supervision of smoke-free areas, thereby mitigating fire hazards and safeguarding public health and safety.

The main difference between Zhang *et al.* works and ours is that their proposed smoking-detection model focuses on identifying cigarettes as an object, whereas herein we aim to recognise the action of smoking. In addition, we propose a combined approach that involves federated learning techniques to overcome possible privacy issues and to decentralize data processing, aiming to integrate fog-edge computing architectures to reduce reliance on centralized systems.

Chen *et al.* [5] propose RTVBS, an edge computing solution utilizing CCTV systems and deep learning for smoking detection in high-risk environments. Leveraging *YOLOv3* architecture, RTVBS achieves fast, accurate micro-object detection with low computational requirements, deployable on devices like *NVIDIA JETSON TX2*. Through curated smoking datasets and enhanced training techniques, the model demonstrates exceptional detection performance. RTVBS offers a promising solution to smoking detection challenges in fire-prone environments, providing efficient and accurate detection capabilities. The model was trained using a proprietary dataset consisting of 2,000 images.

The most relevant limitation of the work of Chen *et al.* is that they do not provide any outcomes for real-world scenarios. Herein, to overcome such limitation we considered four real-world scenarios with four different CCTV camera setups (see Sect. 4). Similarly to their approach, we did also use edge computing and deep learning techniques for smoking detection; however, we combined them with federated learning to address scalability limitations.

In summary, despite the interesting outcomes proposed by the authors, the absence of comprehensive details on the dataset used in both the works of Zhang *et al.* [19] and Chen *et al.* [5], and the lack of evaluation metrics compromise the replicability of their findings.

Herein, we conduct a more extensive analysis to highlight the potential for lightweight devices and we provide a more reliable publicly available dataset as detailed in Sect. 3.1. In addition, to solve the data privacy problem in these two works, We provide a face-blurring module. This module can blur the face after the pipeline is finished.

3   Materials and Methods

In this section, the dataset adopted and the framework developed are presented in Sect. 3.1 and Sect. 3.2, respectively.

3.1   Dataset

In this section, we describe and comment on the dataset used.

To the best of our knowledge, there are some unbalances in the available dataset in the state-of-art related to smoking behavior classification. This is why, herein, we made use of a combination of multiple publicly available datasets jointly with some more novel images, as it will be better described later in the section.

Indeed, the 'Cigarette Smoker Detection' dataset proposed by Lee[1] composed of 1,279 non-smoking and 1,996 smoking images, shows a class imbalance. Such imbalances can introduce bias and affect model outcomes. Moreover, the smoking class includes noisy and unrelated images, complicating training. Khan's dataset entitled 'smokingVSnotsmoking'[2] with 1,200 images per class, aims to rectify class imbalance but still exhibits an imbalance within the smoking class. Specifically, fewer images portray smoking individuals compared to cigarettes, potentially impacting classification accuracy. Notably, both datasets lack CCTV footage images.

Another notable dataset that has the potential to contribute to our research is the *Smoke100k* dataset [6]. This dataset encompasses 100,000 synthesized smoke images captured from various locations and angles. However, it is important to note that while this dataset is well-suited for fire detection applications, it may not be the most suitable choice for our specific task of detecting smoking actions in public areas.

To address the datasets' limitations, we employed a comprehensive strategy. We combined multiple datasets and gathered additional images meeting stringent quality criteria from reputable online sources. We aimed to enrich both smoking and non-smoking instances, reducing class imbalance and enhancing overall dataset quality. Our final dataset, named *'Balanced Smoker Detection'* used in our study comprises 5,272 raw images, merging two smoking datasets with manually collected online images and CCTV footage. With 2,636 images representing each category, our dataset facilitates diverse smoking-related cue learning, enabling the model to capture intricate patterns specific to smoking

---

[1] *'Cigarette Smoker Detection'* dataset: https://www.kaggle.com/datasets/vitaminc/cigarette-smoker-detection.

[2] 'smokingVSnotsmoking'   dataset: https://data.mendeley.com/datasets/7b52hhzs3r/1.

behaviors. Thus, with the larger dataset the model's ability to learn intricate patterns specific to smoking behaviors. As a result, our model exhibits improved accuracy and reliability in distinguishing between smoking and non-smoking individuals [2]. To access this dataset, you can send a request on Zenodo, and access will be granted[3]. Table 1 presents the accuracy of our model after training on each dataset and the new dataset.

Table 1. Accuracy post-training comparison on the three datasets under scrutiny.

Dataset Name	Smoking	Non-Smoking
Cigarette Smoker Detection	69.35%	76.00%
smokingVSnotsmoking	72.33%	75.9%
Balanced Smoker Detection	89.24%	82.00%

3.2 Implementation

To conduct our study we made use of federated learning and efficient deep neural networks.

Federated learning is a sub-field of Machine Learning. Its strength relies on the fact that it allows a collaborative training of models across decentralized edge devices, while aggregating results, reducing expenses, and leveraging collective device power [1] still preserving data privacy. Thanks to it, researchers can effectively utilize diverse computing resources concurrently, enhancing the accessibility and affordability of AI technology. We used federated learning to mitigate hardware demands in AI model training and real-time video processing.

This research implements a federated learning model based on McMahan et al. [12], establishing a group of clients with local datasets. Through iterative rounds, a stochastic process selects subsets of clients for computation, facilitated by the server. Resultant updates are transmitted to a smart contract for global state integration, repeating iteratively to optimize model training efficiently. We chose the McMahan learning model (FedAvg) for its ability to handle decentralized, non-IID, and unbalanced data while reducing communication costs and maintaining privacy. The Eq. 1 [12] applies to any finite-sum objective of the form:

$$\min_{w \in \mathbb{R}^d} f(w) \quad \text{where} \quad f(w) \equiv \frac{1}{n} \sum_{i=1}^{n} f_i(w) \tag{1}$$

where, w represents the model parameter, $f_i(w)$ is defined as $\ell(x_i, y_i; w)$, denoting the loss of the prediction on example (x_i, y_i) in a deep learning problem. In the formula, (x_i, y_i) represents a training set where x_i is the input data or

---

[3] https://zenodo.org/records/11197801.

features, and y_i is the corresponding target or label associated with the input data.

Following the training phase of the model, an architectural framework is required for its deployment in large-scale environments. Figure 1 illustrates this topology, where a server-side application is responsible for storing and processing data from video monitoring edge nodes. Also, each node is a cloud-based computational node and they are able to share their data outside their local network, the biggest advantage of this approach is flexibility, and high-speed internet connections can enable us to switch between computational nodes if needed. This infrastructure facilitates secure storage and processing of a multitude of scenes, enabling the server to dedicate additional resources for meticulous processing and timely response during emergencies. Utilizing socket programming, the application minimizes latency, a critical factor for facilitating real-time communication and ensuring optimal system efficiency.

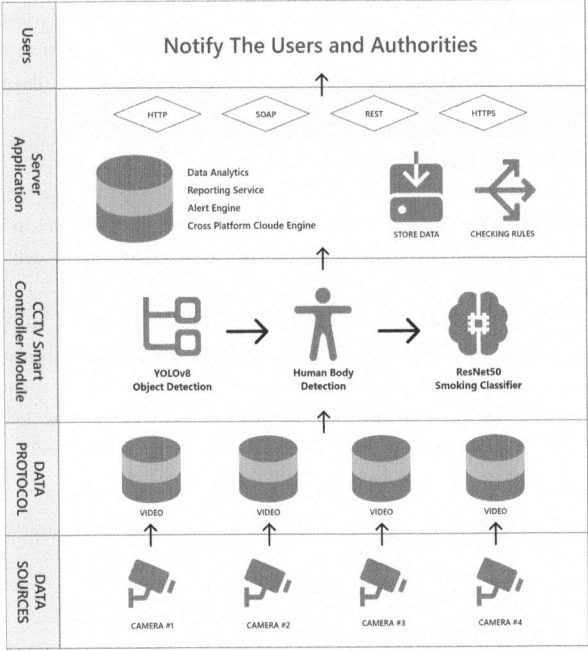

Fig. 1. Smoking detector framework pipeline.

Another relevant task to be considered relies on human body tracking which is a fundamental task within the field of computer vision [7]. Such a task is, however non-trivial to be addressed; hence, the scientific community has made significant contributions by developing their models to address this challenge in recent years. Human tracking in CCTV systems has witnessed significant advancements with the integration of the You Only Look Once (YOLO) model [14], a real-time object detection and image segmentation model based on deep learning.

After conducting extensive experiments and comparative analyses, the selection of YOLOv8[4] was determined to be the most suitable choice for our study. Its superior performance in efficiency and accuracy further justifies its adoption.

To prevent multiple alerts for the same person, a person-tracking mechanism was implemented, ensuring that each individual was tracked consistently throughout the surveillance footage. To focus specifically on the upper body, a segmentation process was applied, enabling a more precise analysis of smoking behavior. Finally, a classification model [13] was employed to distinguish between smoking and non-smoking individuals based on the upper body segments.

To emulate real-world scenarios, our experimental setup entails the utilization of a *Lenovo Legion 5* as a server apparatus for executing federated learning. This server is endowed with an *Nvidia RTX GeForce 3060* graphics processing unit, augmented by 16 GB of RAM. Furthermore, our configuration incorporates four *Nvidia Jetson Nano* units, each designated as an AI Node. The acquisition of the requisite smoking frames, integral to our study, is undertaken through the *Xiaomi Smart Home Camera 2K Pro*. This specialized camera adheres to the rigorous standards of image quality essential for our research objectives.

4   Results and Conclusions

This section presents the outcomes of our proposed classification model specifically designed for smoking detection within the context of real-time CCTV camera streams.

To evaluate the performances of the classification model herein described, we considered F1 score, accuracy, and Matthew's Correlation Coefficient (MCC) [16]. Table 2 shows that, for a total of 100 images, comparable performances in both smoking and non-smoking scenarios were achieved. For comparison purposes, the models were evaluated after a training phase.

Table 2. Comparison of model results with 3 different metrics.

Activity type	Accuracy	F1 Score	MCC
Smoking	82.2435	81.5789	0.636302
Non-Smoking	82.0032	82.0512	0.636302

As mentioned in the previous sections, CCTV cameras were used to add extra images to the dataset in order to balance the ones already available in the literature. Table 3 summarises the types of images collected.

These scenarios were carefully selected to explore the adaptability of our model under diverse environmental conditions. To substantiate the robustness

---

[4] https://github.com/ultralytics/ultralytics

of our model, we deliberately selected four distinct situations for validation purposes. These scenarios are: (i) captured images from a front view, (ii) perspectives from side angles, (iii) black and white streams, which present unique challenges due to the absence of color information; and (iv) instances representative of non-smoking events.

Table 3. Summary image categories collected.

	Entrance	Rooftop	Parking Area	Wall Placement
Front				
Side				
B&W				
Non-Smoking				

Our experiments show that the proposed model achieves noteworthy test accuracy of over 80% in detecting smoking activities. This performance is comparable to, and in some aspects, including considering real-world scenarios and addressing the scalability problem exceeds, the results reported by Zhang *et al.* [19] and Chen *et al.* [5]. Specifically, our model demonstrated robust performance under various conditions, including different angles and lighting, which were not extensively covered in the related works. Moreover, to address the privacy issue of using monitoring systems in public areas, a face-blurring module is implemented as a rapid and cost-effective solution to protect individuals' privacy.

Furthermore, the versatility of our framework extends beyond smoke detection, as it can be applied to other edge solutions for monitoring systems such as face recognition and abnormal activity detection. The integration of the smoking detection model with cloud technologies and edge devices enables real-time monitoring and prompt intervention, reinforcing its potential for broader applications in public safety and security domains.

Continued research and development of the proposed framework will be crucial for its effective and widespread deployment. Further advancements in edge computing technologies and federated learning methods will enhance the scalability, accessibility, and operational efficiency of autonomous monitoring systems, contributing to affordable and scalable AI-based solutions.

Acknowledgments. This work was supported by the PRIN 2020 project COMMON-WEARS (grant number I53C21000210001) and by the STEADIER Project (grant number I55F21001900005). We would like to thank *ArvanCloud Co.* For allowing us to run part of our experiments on-site and providing the necessary resources including the free cloud infrastructure and support to complete this research.

References

1. Alferaidi, A., Yadav, K., Alharbi, Y., Viriyasitavat, W., Kautish, S., Dhiman, G.: Federated learning algorithms to optimize the client and cost selections. Math. Probl. Eng. **2022**, 8514562 (2022). https://doi.org/10.1155/2022/8514562

2. Althnian, A., et al.: Impact of dataset size on classification performance: an empirical evaluation in the medical domain. Appl. Sci. (Basel) **11**(2), 796 (2021)

3. Babu, R., Rajitha, B.: Accident detection through CCTV surveillance. In: 2022 IEEE Students Conference on Engineering and Systems (SCES), pp. 01–06 (2022). https://doi.org/10.1109/SCES55490.2022.9887656

4. Bao, G., Guo, P.: Federated learning in cloud-edge collaborative architecture: key technologies, applications and challenges. J. Cloud Comput. **11**(1), 94 (2022)

5. Chen, R., Zeng, G., Ke Wang, L.L., Cai, Z.: A real time vision-based smoking detection framework on edge. J. Internet Things **2**(2), 55–64 (2020). https://doi.org/10.32604/jiot.2020.09814

6. Cheng, H., Yin, J., Chen, B., Yu, Z.: Smoke 100k: a database for smoke detection. In: IEEE 8th Global Conference on Consumer Electronics (GCCE), pp. 596–597 (2019). https://doi.org/10.1109/GCCE46687.2019.9015309

7. Davies, E.R.: Machine Vision: Theory, Algorithms, Practicalities. Elsevier (2004)

8. Guler, B., Yener, A.: Sustainable federated learning (2021). https://doi.org/10.48550/arXiv.2102.11274

9. Hnoohom, N., Chotivatunyu, P., Maitrichit, N., Sornlertlamvanich, V., Mekruksavanich, S., Jitpattanakul, A.: Weapon detection using faster R-CNN inception-V2 for a CCTV surveillance system. In: 2021 25th International Computer Science and Engineering Conference (ICSEC), pp. 400–405 (2021). https://doi.org/10.1109/ICSEC53205.2021.9684649

10. Lehnert, A., Gawantka, F., During, J., Just, F., Reichenbach, M.: XplAinable: explainable AI smoke detection at the edge. Big Data Cogn. Comput. **8**(5) (2024). https://doi.org/10.3390/bdcc8050050. https://www.mdpi.com/2504-2289/8/5/50

11. Nivedita, M., Pawar, R., Kathuria, H., Siddiqui, I.A.: Real-time CCTV footage violence detection with alarm system using deep learning. In: 2023 6th International Conference on Recent Trends in Advance Computing (ICRTAC), pp. 702–707 (2023). https://doi.org/10.1109/ICRTAC59277.2023.10480789

12. McMahan, B., Moore, E., Ramage, D., Hampson, S., Arcas, B.A.: Communication-efficient learning of deep networks from decentralized data. In: Artificial Intelligence and Statistics, pp. 1273–1282. PMLR (2017)

13. Mehra, N., Gupta, S.: Survey on multiclass classification methods (2013). https://api.semanticscholar.org/CorpusID:550748

14. Redmon, J., Divvala, S., Girshick, R., Farhadi, A.: You only look once: unified, real-time object detection. In: 2016 IEEE Conference on Computer Vision and Pattern Recognition (CVPR), pp. 779–788 (2016). https://doi.org/10.1109/CVPR.2016.91

15. Shi, W., Cao, J., Zhang, Q., Li, Y., Xu, L.: Edge computing: vision and challenges. IEEE Internet Things J. **3**(5), 637–646 (2016). https://doi.org/10.1109/JIOT.2016.2579198

16. Sokolova, M., Japkowicz, N., Szpakowicz, S.: Beyond accuracy, F-score and ROC: a family of discriminant measures for performance evaluation. In: Sattar, A., Kang, B. (eds.) AI 2006. LNCS (LNAI), vol. 4304, pp. 1015–1021. Springer, Heidelberg (2006). https://doi.org/10.1007/11941439_114
17. Tan, G.P.P., Teo, O., van der Eijk, Y.: Residential secondhand smoke in a densely populated urban setting: a qualitative exploration of psychosocial impacts, views and experiences. BMC Public Health **22**(1) (2022). https://doi.org/10.1186/s12889-022-13561-7
18. Thakur, S.S., Poddar, P., Roy, R.B.: Real-time prediction of smoking activity using machine learning based multi-class classification model. Multimedia Tools Appl. **81**(10), 14529–14551 (2022). https://doi.org/10.1007/s11042-022-12349-6
19. Zhang, Z., Chen, H., Xiao, R., Li, Q.: Research on smoking detection based on deep learning. J. Phys. Conf. Ser. **2024**(1), 012042 (2021). https://doi.org/10.1088/1742-6596/2024/1/012042

Anonymization of Unstructured Health Data in Spanish

Sergio Ilarri[1(✉)] , Carlos Tellería[2] , and Marta Morales[3]

[1] I3A, Universidad de Zaragoza, María de Luna 1, Zaragoza, Spain
`silarri@unizar.es`
[2] Instituto Aragonés de Ciencias de la Salud, San Juan Bosco 13, Zaragoza, Spain
`ctelleria@aragon.es`
[3] Universidad de Zaragoza, María de Luna 1, Zaragoza, Spain
`780454@unizar.es`

Abstract. There is an ever-growing availability of health data, which in many occasions are recorded in text documents rather than as structured data. Exploiting those data using data mining techniques to try to extract some useful knowledge can provide substantial benefits, but usually the data analysts should not have access to sensitive data. Therefore, the documents should be anonymized before providing them for data analysis or manual tagging prior to applying machine learning techniques.

In this paper, we present our experience applying anonymization on unstructured health documents written in Spanish. We have developed a prototype that facilitates the anonymization process, which has been adopted by the Aragon Health Sciences Institute (IACS). Our approach is generic and does not require labeled data, which are expensive and difficult to obtain in this context; instead, we mainly rely on regular expressions, dictionaries of named entities, and the categorization of attributes. An experimental evaluation shows the feasibility and performance of the approach.

Keywords: Text anonymization · health textual data · data mining · Spanish documents · supporting tools

1 Introduction

In the context of the project *NEAT-AMBIENCE* (*Next-gEnerATion dAta Management to foster suitable Behaviors and the resilience of cItizens against modErN ChallEnges*) [14], we focus on the design of appropriate data management techniques that can contribute to a better daily life for people and also to foster suitable behaviors in such a way that existing modern challenges that we face as a society (health concerns, environmental challenges, etc.) can be tackled. Within the project, we consider several use case scenarios, including a scenario related to the management of health data, which is a critical issue now in our

P. Delir Haghighi et al. (Eds.): iiWAS 2024, LNCS 15342, pp. 160–175, 2025.
https://doi.org/10.1007/978-3-031-78090-5_14

society, as the COVID-19 pandemic not only had devastating effects for people affected by the coronavirus but also made a profound negative impact on other areas related to the health system, including primary care and other hospital treatments. The final goal is to design solutions based on data mining and/or process mining techniques that can foster suitable behaviors (e.g., for doctors, patients, etc.) that can improve the efficiency and effectiveness of the health system and so lead to a better health service for patients.

In particular, in this work, we focus on the anonymization of the unstructured content of medical documents, as this is usually a key requirement for health data analysis. The use of *Natural Language Processing* techniques [2] applied to clinical documents is a very useful tool to extract relevant information about patients and clinical processes that is not recorded in a structured manner. This is important because, as emphasized in works such as [7], many useful health data are contained in health text documents, rather than as structured data. However, the processing of clinical documents is subject to legal restrictions regarding personal data protection, so data that are considered to be sensitive in a particular usage scenario should be removed before analysis. Moreover, the preparation of clinical documents for training machine learning processes requires the manual tagging of gold standard documents, which requires expertise in the health domain, and this task is usually done by non-clinical persons (with enough domain knowledge) or by clinicians not directly attending the affected patients; therefore, they should access anonymized documents so that the patients' privacy is preserved and data protection regulations are satisfied. Our work intends to ease the process of removing sensitive data from clinical documents while preserving all the useful clinical information for research, and assess the quality of this process. Figure 1 shows a typical workflow using the approach proposed: either the anonymized documents are directly exploited by using text mining techniques or they are manually annotated in order to build Machine Learning (ML) models.

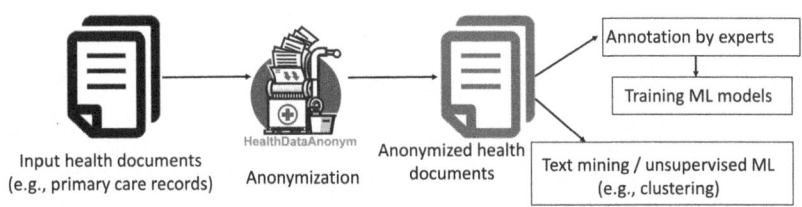

Fig. 1. Workflow showing the use of the tool proposed

Several works have studied the problem of guaranteeing the privacy of health data. For example, the trade-off between anonymization and data utility is pointed out in surveys such as [4,17]. The same trade-off is mentioned in [6], focused on how to improve user privacy and utility, and in [3], which deals with the search of an optimal k-anonymity algorithm with minimization of information loss; these works consider structured datasets of health records composed by specific attributes, rather than unstructured documents as we do in this paper. A software architecture for document anonymization is defined in [16] (not focused on health documents), and a decision-support framework for data anonymization (not in the specific context of health data) is presented in [1]. Most approaches focus on structured health datasets (instead of text documents), and some of them provide supporting tools (such as ARX [12]). As opposed to existing works, we focus on clinical documents written in Spanish and develop a practical solution to be adopted by a specific research health institute. The emphasis of this paper is on the description of the experience and the approach followed (based on regular expressions, dictionaries, and the categorization of attributes), supported by an experimental evaluation that shows the feasibility of the proposal. It should be noticed that the concepts of k-anonymity and differential privacy cannot be applied in our context, since we are not dealing with records of patients but with unstructured health documents; for example, in our scenario, we usually have many documents referring to the same patient and we could also have a single document related with several patients. Despite this, in this context, removing sensitive data (as part of the data preparation process) is still needed to protect the privacy of patients. Instead of focusing on preventing the identification of specific individuals (e.g., by detecting pseudo-identifiers), the goal is to avoid the leakage of personal data that are irrelevant for subsequent data processing.

2   Description of the Approach

In this section, we describe our approach for the anonymization of medical documents and the evaluation of the impact on the subsequent data mining tasks performed. Firstly, in Sect. 2.1, we explain our analysis of medical documents, that led us to consider different categories of attributes and sensitivity labels. Secondly, in Sect. 2.2, we present the procedure followed to anonymize input documents. Finally, in Sect. 2.3, we describe the tool developed.

2.1   Categorization and Labeling of Attributes

First of all, a wide range of text fragments extracted from real medical documents (specifically, primary care reports), provided by the Aragon Health Sciences Institute (IACS) [5], were manually analyzed. These documents contain information about patients with different pathologies. These texts helped us to understand the nature of personal data in actual clinical reports and to identify rules and regular expressions that could detect and delete this sensitive information. These documents frequently contain spelling mistakes, typos, and abbreviations, as clinicians focus their efforts on providing patient care, trying to optimize their time to provide better healthcare services.

With the analysis of these texts, our goal was to detect the types of sensitive data that can be found in health reports. Thus, it is relevant to stress that a patients' identification is not only related to classical direct identifiers (such as the name, family name, ID card or phone numbers); instead, other information contained in clinical records (such as names of relatives, the living place, or the job) can potentially provide enough information to identify a patient, especially when several pieces of information are combined. Particularly, based on our analysis, the personal data that can appear in a medical document can be grouped into four different categories (see Table 1): *personal information, contextual information, lifestyle information,* and *clinical events information.* Each category includes data that characterize one dimension of the patient. The purpose of this categorization is to distinguish among different types of data that may need to be kept (or not) in the documents, during the anonymization process, depending on the analysis that has to be performed later on the data. For example, lifestyle plays a key role in the treatment of problems related with obesity [13]; consequently, that information should be kept if we want to analyze the effectiveness of those treatments. Similarly, geographic data belonging to the category of contextual information (like the city where a patient noticed symptoms for the first time and municipalities that he/she had visited) are particularly relevant if we want to analyze data relative to the spreading of a virus (e.g., see [8]), for example. Thus, this categorization helps with the goal of developing a tool with easy-to-use functionalities to remove, from a set of input documents, all identifying and personal information that is not necessary for the specific use case, while at the same time preserving the information that is necessary. We have not defined a category for diseases, diagnoses or treatments, as these kinds of data are expected to be required for any analysis in the context of health data (and therefore these data should not be removed); nevertheless, our approach could be extended to deal with other types of categories.

Table 1. Categories of sensitive data found in medical documents

Category	Attributes
Personal information (PI)	Name, surname, age, ethnicity, ID number, phone number, address, email, date of birth, date of death, Social Security Number (SSN), professional license number (for doctors), and gender
Contextual information (CI)	Relatives, work, places, countries, cities, and municipalities
Lifestyle information (LS)	Sports and habits
Clinical events information (CE)	Hospitalization, admission date, dates associated to emergencies or other events, and discharge date

Besides categorizing the types of data that we can find in health documents, we have also labeled different types of data according to their *sensitivity* (i.e., risk of patient identification) and *clinical importance* (i.e., potential relevance from the medical perspective). Finally, we have also studied how the simultaneous appearance of several attributes in the same medical document can lead to an increase in the sensitivity of those data. For example, both the age of the patient and the city where he/she lives are considered attributes of medium sensitivity; however, the combination of both values can have a higher sensitivity because the availability of both attributes facilitates the task of patient identification. This *joint sensitivity* is also taken into account during the anonymization process: when several attributes appear at the same time in the document, the tool considers their joint sensitivity instead of their individual sensitivities.

2.2   Anonymization of the Text Documents

In our approach, the input text is analyzed line by line to try to detect sensitive data that need to be anonymized. For that purpose, as usual when applying text mining techniques, before the analysis of the text we first remove the *empty words* [11] (words such as prepositions, articles, and conjunctions, that are usually excluded from the analysis of texts because they are considered to be of little value to understand their content). Then, in the filtered text, sensitive data are detected by matching regular expressions that we have defined based on our previous analysis of medical documents.

Besides, we exploit several dictionaries as a support to detect specific types of entities, as the problem of *Named Entity Recognition (NER)* [10] plays a key role here: a dictionary that contains names and surnames of people residing in the region of Aragón in Spain along with a dictionary with names and abbreviations of hospitals and medical centers belonging to Aragón (as we use and evaluate the developed tool in the context of the health system in the region of Aragón, in Spain), a dictionary containing countries and another one including municipalities that may be of interest in the texts to be processed, and other dictionaries that contain information that can also appear in the input medical documents (alcoholic beverages, demonyms and ethnicities, jobs and professions, neighborhoods in Zaragoza –the capital of Aragón–, sports, and Spanish terms referring to family relations, like "madre", "padre", "abuela", "hijo", "hija", etc.). For the detection of names and last names of patients, when a name or last name within the text is found in the corresponding dictionary, a syntactic analysis of the sentence is also carried out with the aim of ensuring that it actually refers to a person and not a place or illness. This has been done for specific situations that arise when a person has the same surname as a country, a municipality, or even an illness (e.g., some people have a surname that matches the name of the "Cancer" disease, and there are persons named "Borja", which is also the name of an Aragonese municipality).

Even though approaches more sophisticated than the use of regular expressions and dictionaries of named entities could be applied, one of our key goals was to evaluate first whether using those techniques could be enough to provide satisfactory results. More complex approaches, for example based on machine learning, would require a large amount of labeled health documents, which are very difficult to obtain. On the one hand, annotating the documents requires considerable manual human effort. On the other hand, the annotation task is usually performed by people who should not have access to the personal data contained in the documents, due to privacy constraints; notice that, even among health professionals, accessing sensitive data about patients treated by other doctors/colleagues is not allowed. The unavailability of large amounts of annotated health documents for training makes the use of techniques not based on regular expressions very difficult.

The anonymization method used in our current approach is the suppression of the sensitive data detected [9]. Whereas the suppression of data could potentially lead to losing useful data, this strategy is very effective at protecting sensitive information, which is a key issue in the context of health data. As we describe in more detail in Sect. 2.3, the degree of removals to be performed can be configured according to the privacy requirements and the goals of the subsequent data analysis; for example, the user can decide not to remove certain types of data if they are needed in an upcoming data mining process. Therefore, the impact of removing sensitive data can be controlled. Using other strategies, like data perturbation techniques, would modify the documents by adding synthetic data; this would be a significant disadvantage, as in the context of health data it is important to keep reliable and real data. Moreover, the experiments that we have performed (see Sect. 3) show that the approach followed achieves good results, as it effectively eliminates the sensitive data while keeping clinically-relevant terms.

Even if the methods used in our current proposal could be improved, this initial approach provides satisfactory results in the use cases that we have evaluated, and it has led to a tool that has been adopted by the IACS research health institute [5], which is a very relevant health entity in Aragón (Spain). The staff of the IACS is personnel from healthcare and assistance centers in Aragón, including hospitals and primary care centers.

2.3 Supporting Tool Developed

The tool developed focuses on providing support to detect and remove sensitive data from health documents written in Spanish. Table 2 shows a summary of the main requirements considered, which were determined based on the actual needs of health institutes. A key feature of the tool is that it can adapt to the specific existing privacy needs, which may vary depending on the specific use case and purposes. Besides the possibility to request the complete removal of specific categories of data (from those shown in Table 1), the user of our developed tool is also able to indicate the *overall level of anonymization* required (*high, medium, low,* or *don't apply*). Data with higher sensitivity are detected and removed even with the low level of anonymization, since the data with higher sensitivity are the ones that can easily compromise the identity and privacy of the patients; therefore, they have to be removed in any anonymization process, including those applying the lowest level of anonymization. Similarly, the less sensitive data will only be removed if the higher level of anonymization is selected. Finally, if the user selects the *don't apply* option, then no overall anonymization will be performed and only the categories of data explicitly selected by the user will be removed.

Table 2. Main requirements considered for the development of the tool

Requirement	Description
R1	The tool will provide two main functionalities: 1) anonymization of health documents written in Spanish, and 2) evaluation of the impact of the anonymization on a subsequent data mining (classification) task
R2	The user will be able to select specific categories of attributes to remove
R3	The user will be able to select a specific overall anonymization level to apply
R4	The user will be able to require at the same time the removal of certain categories of attributes and the application of a specific overall anonymization level
R5	The user will be able to remove sensitive data from a single document or from a set of documents, executing the tool with a Graphical User Interface (GUI) or in unattended (non-graphical) mode
R6	The user will be able to remove sensitive data in an easy way, without the need of previously-labeled documents (as examples or training data)
R7	To broaden its applicability, the tool will not rely on structure-specific information, which may vary from one health institute to another
R8	Concerning the application of data mining, the user will be able to select a specific algorithm or use them all, obtaining performance metrics

In Fig. 2, we show the different parametrization options of the anonymization tool proposed. Notice that, instead of just removing all personal data, the tool can be configured by the user to have more control over the data that will be removed. Thus, it supports a customization which is important because not all the personal data have the same relevance or imply the same risk of re-identification of a patient. So, depending on the context and specific use case, the user can choose between different *anonymization levels* and/or select different *data categories* to be removed. In this way, it is possible to preserve specific types of personal data that could be relevant for the purposes of the subsequent analysis. For example, in the study of rare diseases or hereditary cancers, the reporting of family background could be very meaningful, so deleting information on relatives would lead to an important information loss; however, for other use cases this information could be safely deleted.

The technologies used for implementation are summarized in Fig. 3. The tool offers two main functionalities. On the one hand, it allows the user to configure the anonymization process that will be carried out (i.e., choose how he/she wants to apply the anonymization, by selecting one or more options that determine the information to be removed from the input documents) and select the file (or set

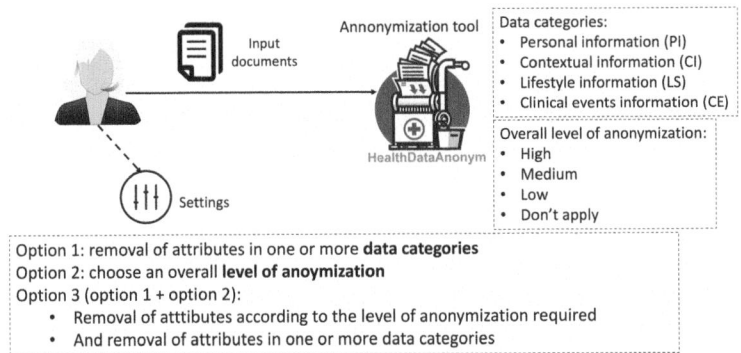

Fig. 2. Parametrization options of the health document anonymization tool proposed

of files) that he/she wants to anonymize. On the other hand, it supports running different text classification algorithms (using k-fold cross-validation), with the aim of comparing the impact of considering as input anonymized versus non-anonymized documents on data mining classification tasks; for this purpose, the user can select both types of input, the number of folds to consider in the evaluation, the attribute that represents the target class for the classification, and the classifier to apply (it is also possible to apply all the available classifiers to compare them). The user can run the desired classification tasks on both the original and the anonymized documents and compare the classification performance achieved. Besides executing the tool with a graphical user interface, it is also possible to execute it in batch mode, to perform unattended tasks that rely on a configuration file that specifies the user preferences. The tool has been adopted by the IACS health institute [5], which shows that the work performed fits the intended purposes; the IACS is currently using and fine-tuning the tool. The tool's website is [15].

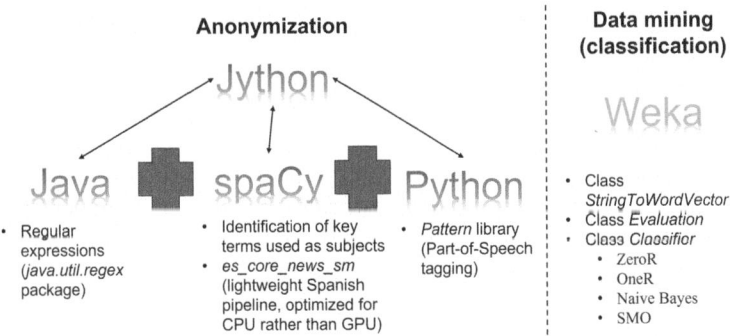

Fig. 3. Technologies used for the implementation of the anonymization tool

3   Experimental Evaluation

In this section, we describe the experiments performed to assess the proposal. In Sect. 3.1, we focus on the performance of the anonymization, and in Sect. 3.2 we show an example of how to evaluate the impact on a data mining task.

3.1   Performance of the Anonymization

For the first set of experiments that we carried out, we used as input a dataset of medical records provided by the Aragon Health Sciences Institute (IACS), concerning primary care reports of patients who reside or receive health care in the region of Aragon in Spain. To comply with privacy regulations, the IACS compiled for us all the clinical documents in a single large text file (containing more than four million lines) and the lines were re-ordered randomly so that the original individual clinical documents cannot be directly inferred. As we cannot know which lines go together in the original clinical documents (we did not have access to the individual clinical records, only to their combined contents), we finally generated synthetic clinical reports by partitioning that single input text file in several files. These reports, which contain real text lines from clinical documents, will be used to evaluate the capability of our tool to remove the sensitive data required.

In these experiments, we applied different combinations of anonymization tasks, supported by the tool, and evaluated their quality. As performance metrics, we measured the *True Positives* (*TP*), *False Positives* (*FP*), and *False Negatives* (*FN*) for each of the anonymized files generated with different anonymization input parameters selected. According to the usual terminology used in information retrieval, TP refers to those attributes that have been eliminated and should have been eliminated, FP are those attributes that have been eliminated and should not have been removed (i.e., they represent loss of information that could have been avoided), and FN are those attributes that remain in the text despite the fact that they should have been eliminated (i.e., they are sensitive data that the anonymization process did not detect, and therefore represent a privacy risk). For the sake of privacy, FP are always preferred to FN, as false negatives are terms that could potentially help an attacker to identify a patient. True negatives (TN), that represent not deleted information that should not be deleted, have not been measured. The reason for not considering TN is that the vast majority of the terms and words used in a clinical record are actually TN. Therefore, using the value of accuracy (i.e., the capability to correctly identify the TP and TN) or just the TN as a performance measurement would distort our results: the number of TN is very high, but this is expected, even for a "do nothing" algorithm, rather than a merit of the anonymization approach. We also computed the *recall* (calculated as the ratio between the TP and the sum of TP and FN) and the overall *quality* of the anonymization algorithm (calculated as the ratio between the TP and the sum of FP and FN).

Quality for an Overall Level of Anonymization. Firstly, we evaluated the quality of the anonymization when the user selects an overall level of anonymization (see Table 3). In our experiment, the *Low level* and the *Medium level* modes eliminated all the sensitive data according to those levels, which led to a recall of 1, whereas the *High level* provided a high (but not perfect) recall. All levels of anonymization detected the sensitive information they had to eliminate and deleted it. However, *the value of the quality of the algorithm as a whole* was not greater than 1 in the case of the *Low level* mode, which implies that the number of terms that it eliminated or maintained incorrectly (FP and FN, respectively) was higher than the number of sensitive terms correctly identified (TP). This was due to the FP (i.e., eliminated words that should have not been removed); however, we did not detect non-sensitive clinically-relevant words removed by the algorithm, so unnecessary removals did not have a negative impact.

Table 3. Performance for different overall anonymization levels

	TP	FP	FN	Recall	Quality
Low level	18	25	0	1	0.72
Medium level	31	19	0	1	1.63
High level	33	14	1	0.97	2.2

Quality for Category Removal. Secondly, we evaluated the quality of the anonymization when the user wants to remove one or more specific categories of data (*Personal information*, *Context information*, *Lifestyle*, and/or *Clinical events*, as explained in Sect. 2.1). We performed 15 different tests, each representing a different combination of categories to remove for the anonymization. From the perspective of clinical information, the FP could reduce the amount of information that can be analyzed. However, after conducting the tests, we observed that the majority of the FP are data that lack meaning in the text and, even when they are eliminated when they should not, they did not cause the text to lose its meaning; the fact that FP are data with no clinical meaning is a direct perception, and a way to assess it quantitatively could be defined. Besides, the tests performed when removing specific categories of attributes yield a recall higher than 66% in all cases, with an average recall over all the possible combinations of categories of 79.7%; this has been considered a quite good value for the purposes of a first-level anonymization process, as the tool developed is currently used. Moreover, it should be stressed that much higher recall values are obtained when the user uses the anonymization tool without requiring specific categories of data to be removed (as in the first experiment), which shows that identifying the category of personal data is more challenging than just detecting that some data are personal data. Regarding the overall quality, as shown in Fig. 4, all values obtained are equal or greater than 1, which means that the anonymization algorithm detects correctly a higher number of sensitive data than those that it eliminates or maintains by mistake.

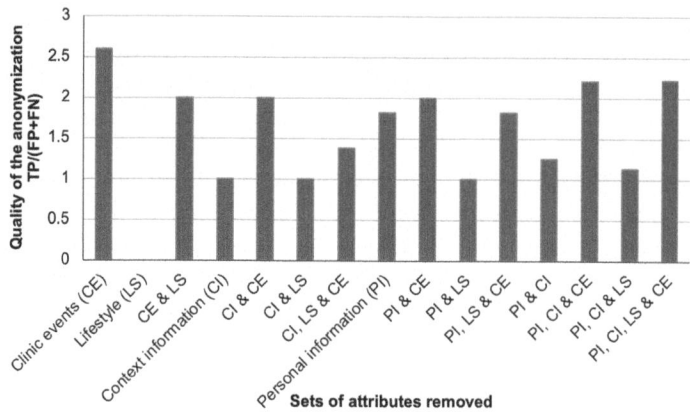

Fig. 4. Quality of the anonymization when removing specific categories of attributes

Quality for Joint Category Removal and Level of Anonymization.
Thirdly, we evaluated the quality of the anonymization when both types of
options were combined. From all the possible combinations, we did not consider
the tests with the *High level* anonymization option, since it already eliminates all
sensitive information independently of whether specific categories of attributes
are selected for removal or not. As an example, we show in Fig. 5 the quality of
the anonymization in a total of 15 tests, representing different combinations of
input parameters, carried out by considering a *Low level* anonymization. In these
tests, we observed that most FN values were very small (smaller than 5 in all
the tests). Moreover, given that in the tests related to the anonymization level
this value was practically 0 (see Table 3), it can be concluded that the FN failures mainly occurred when specific sets of attributes were selected for removal.
Regarding the FP, we can observe something similar to what happened in the
tests related to the anonymization level: the data values that are eliminated
did not affect the clinical content of the text. Finally, regarding the quality of
the algorithm as a whole, the values obtained in the tests usually exceeded 1,
which implies that more sensitive attributes were detected and eliminated correctly than those eliminated or maintained by mistake. However, there are some
cases, when the option to remove *Personal information* is not marked, where the
value of this metric is lower than 1; since the *Low level* anonymization option
was selected in these tests, the conclusion is that this level of anonymization
eliminates more data of the *Personal information* category than it should.

Summary and Time Performance. As a conclusion, we can say that the
quality of the anonymization process can be considered acceptable. Besides, the
anonymization errors detected during the evaluation can be exploited to refine
the tool and further improve its anonymization capabilities. Finally, if a very
high quality could be required in a specific use case, an expert user could further
revise the output of the tool; even in this supervised use case, the tool would
have saved him/her a huge amount of time by avoiding a manual anonymization.

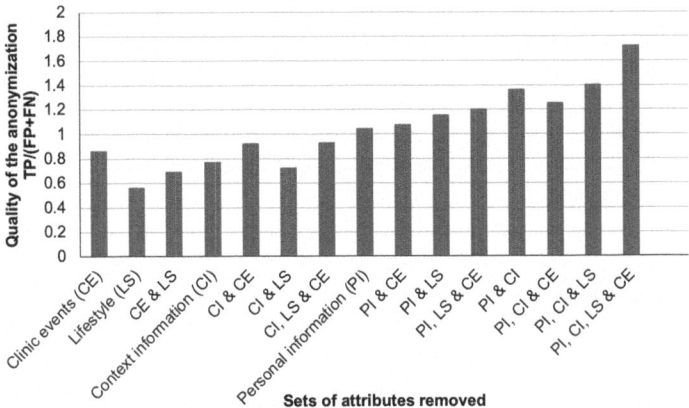

Fig. 5. Quality of the anonymization when removing specific categories of attributes and also selecting a *Low level* anonymization option

We also evaluated the amount of time required to perform the anonymization process. The tests were performed on a computer with an Intel Core i7 processor, 16 GB of RAM, and a 512 GB SSD. It should be noted that the content of the documents being anonymized is highly influential on the time needed to execute the algorithm: if the file is long, it may take longer; however, if the file does not contain much sensitive information, even if it is long, it will likely take less time than shorter files containing a lot of sensitive information to remove. Some of the most relevant experimental results obtained concerning the latency of the anonymization process are shown in Fig. 6. These results show that the execution time increases as the number of attributes to be removed increases, which was expected. When only one anonymization option was selected, the execution time ranged between 1 and 5 min. This also depends on the set of attributes to be removed and the amount of sensitive data in the document being processed. In this case, anonymization processes that included the removal of data in the *Personal information* category took longer than other combinations of input parameters that did not involve that category. This may be due to the fact that this category includes many attributes (see Table 1). The tests that needed the longest amount of time to execute were those that combined the anonymization level with a set of attributes to be removed, as they required more analysis than when only one of them was selected. The longest test took 9 min, which may seem a bit high, but suitable for the needs of IACS, as the anonymization is performed prior to providing the data to the data analysts and the time needed for anonymizing is not critical. So far we did not try to optimize the tool. Nevertheless, these execution times may not be suitable when processing very large datasets, as it is common in big-data population wide observational studies, so large computing infrastructures or software optimization techniques may be needed to use our approach in those contexts.

3.2   Impact of the Anonymization Process on a Classification Task

In this experiment, the goal was to illustrate a use case scenario where we assess whether a data mining classification task is affected when its input documents are anonymized first, as this type of evaluation is supported by the tool developed. Specifically, we considered two datasets of documents related to cerebral strokes and other diseases, respectively, provided by the IACS. The first dataset was thus composed by documents that contain information related to cerebral strokes, while the second one contained information related to other types of diseases. We have 307 documents of each type and a typical report contains around 700–800 words. This test aimed to evaluate the quality of non-loss of relevant information when anonymizing the documents, from the perspective of the data mining task to be applied. That is, the goal was to see if the classifier behaves similarly despite applying anonymization, which would reveal that there is no significant loss of useful information for that classification, while protecting sensitive information.

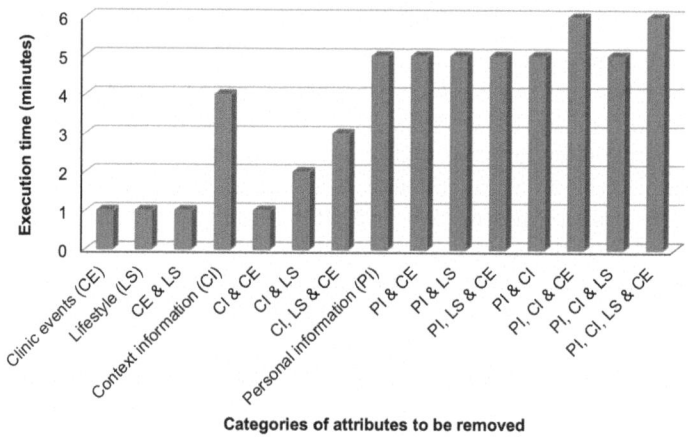

Fig. 6. Execution time depending on the categories of attributes to be removed

The anonymization applied was the removal of attributes in the categories *Personal information* and *Clinical events*. Ideally, we expect the results of the classification with anonymized and non-anonymized documents to be as similar as possible. Overall, the classifier that obtained the best results was SMO: both with the original and the anonymized documents, it obtained 99% of precision and recall; such high values are probably due to the fact that the documents can be easily classified in the two expected target classes, independently of whether a previous anonymization has been performed or not. Moreover, the results obtained with the original documents varied only in a 0.05% compared to those obtained with the anonymized documents. While these results are linked to the classification task considered and the features of the input documents, this experiment shows that the anonymization process ensures the non-loss of relevant information in this context. Besides, it represents an example scenario where our developed tool can be use to evaluate the impact of the anonymization in a subsequent data mining task. Thus, this experiment complements previous experiments focused on assessing the ability of the tool to remove only the data that are considered sensitive, which is a key issue in the health domain.

4   Conclusions and Future Work

A significant amount of relevant data is embedded in unstructured medical documents. Whereas it would be useful to analyze those documents using text mining techniques, to extract useful knowledge, those documents usually contain sensitive data that need to be kept away from the data analysts. Motivated by this, in this paper, we have described an approach and experience developing a tool for the anonymization of medical documents in Spanish. Most related works focus on documents written in English, so we believe that reporting this experience can be useful for the research community, as it contributes to the scarce existing literature that considers the Spanish language (despite its popularity around the world). Moreover, in this work, we have focused on a practical real-world problem, which we have addressed satisfactorily. The prototype tool developed has been adopted by the IACS (which is linked to the public health system in the region of Aragon in Spain), which has validated the tool in the field and it is further extending and improving it, so our work could be considered a successful research transfer case. Although in the development of the prototype we have analyzed unstructured data provided by a specific health institute, it can be applied in any other context where Spanish clinical documents are handled, since our approach does not rely on institute-specific aspects of the documents or their structure (it just considers the plain natural language expressions used in the documents); therefore, it can provide potential benefits to research in the health area in general. Furthermore, we have released the prototype, so it can be extended and fine-tuned, if necessary, and used in various contexts.

As future work, several improvements could be considered. For example, additional evaluations could be performed (e.g., systematizing the collection and analysis of user feedback, building upon our initial informal considerations of user comments). Besides, an in-depth analysis of the real casuistry in clinical reports, not only from primary care reports (as it was the case in the present work) but also from emergency room discharge reports or medical images, would allow to enhance the rules for personal information detection. Finally, the use of deep neural networks or other ML algorithms could improve the accuracy and latency, but would require large amounts of tagged texts, which are usually very difficult to obtain in real scenarios; nevertheless, the analysis of the actual casuistry may help to create synthetic reports as input for training.

Acknowledgments. This publication belongs to the following project: PID2020-113037RB-I00, funded by MICIU/AEI/10.13039/501100011033. We also acknowledge the Government of Aragon (COSMOS research group; last group reference: T64_23R) and the Aragon Health Sciences Institute (IACS).

References

1. Caruccio, L., Desiato, D., Polese, G., Tortora, G., Zannone, N.: A decision-support framework for data anonymization with application to machine learning processes. Inf. Sci. **613**, 1–32 (2022). https://doi.org/10.1016/j.ins.2022.09.004
2. Chowdhary, K.R.: Natural language processing. In: Fundamentals of Artificial Intelligence, pp. 603–649. Springer, New Delhi (2020). https://doi.org/10.1007/978-81-322-3972-7_19
3. Emam, K.E., et al.: A globally optimal k-anonymity method for the de-identification of health data. J. Am. Med. Inform. Assoc. **16**(5), 670–682 (2009). https://doi.org/10.1197/jamia.m3144
4. Eze, B., Peyton, L.: Systematic literature review on the anonymization of high dimensional streaming datasets for health data sharing. Procedia Comput. Sci. **63**, 348–355 (2015). https://doi.org/10.1016/j.procs.2015.08.353
5. Gobierno de Aragón.: Aragon Health Sciences Institute (IACS, Instituto Aragonés de Ciencias de la Salud). https://www.iacs.es (2017–2023). Accessed 13 Sept 2024
6. Majeed, A.: Attribute-centric anonymization scheme for improving user privacy and utility of publishing e-health data. J. King Saud Univ. Comput. Inf. Sci. **31**(4), 426–435 (2019). https://doi.org/10.1016/j.jksuci.2018.03.014
7. Malmasi, S., Hosomura, N., Chang, L.S., Brown, C.J., Skentzos, S., Turchin, A.: Extracting healthcare quality information from unstructured data. In: AMIA Annual Symposium Proceedings, pp. 1243–1252. American Medical Informatics Association (AMIA), April 2018
8. McMahon, T., Chan, A., Havlin, S., Gallos, L.K.: Spatial correlations in geographical spreading of COVID-19 in the United States. Sci. Rep. **12**(1) (2022). https://doi.org/10.1038/s41598-021-04653-2
9. Murthy, S., Bakar, A.A., Rahim, F.A., Ramli, R.: A comparative study of data anonymization techniques. In: Fifth IEEE International Conference on High Performance and Smart Computing (HPSC 2019), pp. 306–309. IEEE, May 2019. https://doi.org/10.1109/bigdatasecurity-hpsc-ids.2019.00063
10. Nasar, Z., Jaffry, S.W., Malik, M.K.: Named entity recognition and relation extraction. ACM Comput. Surv. **54**(1), 1–39 (2021). https://doi.org/10.1145/3445965
11. Nayak, A.S., Kanive, A.P.: Survey on pre-processing techniques for text mining. Int. J. Eng. Comput. Sci. **5**(6), 16875–16879 (2016). https://doi.org/10.18535/ijecs/v5i6.25
12. Prasser, F., Kohlmayer, F., Lautenschläger, R., Kuhn, K.A.: ARX – a comprehensive tool for anonymizing biomedical data. In: AMIA Annual Symposium, pp. 984–993. American Medical Informatics Association (AMIA), November 2014
13. Sassi, F., Cecchini, M., Lauer, J., Chisholm, D.: Improving lifestyles, tackling obesity: the health and economic impact of prevention strategies. In: OECD Health Working Papers, pp. 1–107. Organisation for Economic Co-Operation and Development (OECD) Publishing, November 2009. https://doi.org/10.1787/220087432153
14. Ilarri, S.: Universidad de Zaragoza: NEAT-AMBIENCE Project. http://webdiis.unizar.es/~silarri/NEAT-AMBIENCE/ (2021–2025). PID2020-113037RB-I00, funded by MICIU/AEI/10.13039/501100011033. Accessed 13 Sept 2024
15. Universidad de Zaragoza: HealthDataAnonym – website of the tool developed. http://webdiis.unizar.es/~silarri/prot/HealthDataAnonym/ (2023–2024). Accessed 13 Sept 2024

16. Vico, H., Calegari, D.: Software architecture for document anonymization. Electron. Notes Theor. Comput. Sci. **314**, 83–100 (2015). https://doi.org/10.1016/j.entcs.2015.05.006
17. Zuo, Z., Watson, M., Budgen, D., Hall, R., Kennelly, C., Moubayed, N.A.: Data anonymization for pervasive health care: systematic literature mapping study. JMIR Med. Inf. **9**(10) (2021). https://doi.org/10.2196/29871

When Good Enough is the Best Option: Use of Digital Sufficiency to Fight Climate Change

Nicolas Tirel[1,2](✉) [ID], Sergio Ilarri[1] [ID], Philippe Roose[2] [ID], Adel Noureddine[2] [ID], and Olivie Le Goaër[2] [ID]

[1] Instituto de Investigación en Ingeniería de Aragón (I3A), Universidad de Zaragoza, Mariano Esquillor s/n, 50018 Zaragoza, Spain
`silarri@unizar.es`
[2] Laboratoire Informatique Université de Pau et des Pays de l'Adour (LIUPPA), 2, Allée du Parc de Montaury, 64600, Anglet, France Avenue de l'Université, 64000 Pau, France
{`ntirel,roose,adel.noureddine,olegoaer`}`@univ-pau.fr`

Abstract. The ICT sector has seen many improvements in productivity and efficiency in the past decades. However, its total energy consumed, as well as its carbon emissions, has never decreased. This is mostly due to a systemic phenomenon called the rebound effect: although each process consumes less energy, the global increase in process usage results in an unexpected growth in carbon emissions. In this paper, we present energy-efficient techniques and we argue why it is necessary to combine efficiency with a new approach. This novel approach is digital sufficiency, involving users and developers to reduce the demand in addition to efficiency improvements.

Keywords: Climate change · Digital sufficiency · Sustainable computing

1 Introduction

Anthropogenic climate change fueled by the emissions of greenhouse gases such as carbon dioxide is a threat to human well-being and planetary health [5]. A recent report shared that there is a 50% likelihood to reach a 1.5 °C increase above the 1850–1900 average if we emit at least 200 Gigatonnes of CO_2 (Gt CO_2) after 2024 [2]. It will be achieved by 2029 at the current emission level.

The Information and Communication Technology (ICT) sector plays a major role in carbon emission, as we burn fossil fuels and emit carbon dioxide throughout the whole lifecycle of digital equipment and services, in addition to being a driving force behind human activities. New digital services (Artificial Intelligence, blockchain, IoT, etc.) are likely to boost the demand and increase carbon emissions in the next few years. In this paper, we argue in favor of sufficiency techniques, which aim to reduce this demand. An example of a digital sufficiency approach is approximate computing, where energy consumption can be reduced with a 'good enough' solution [9]. Our purpose is to provide an overview of the following points:

- Limitations of energy efficiency techniques to reduce carbon emissions.
- Challenges to apply digital sufficiency.
- Opportunities of digital sufficiency.

2 Limitations in Energy Efficiency Improvements

Many improvements in energy efficiency have been achieved in the past decades. At the software level, we can mention the use of virtualization, workload balancing through consolidation and placement of virtual machines, data management strategies to optimize data placement, etc. At the hardware level, we can consider the use of low-power processors, dedicated energy-saving architectures such as Field-programmable Gate Arrays, accelerators such as Graphic Process Units, Dynamic Voltage and Frequency Scaling (that adjusts power and speed settings of resources to maximize power savings), the adoption of eco-labels to promote efficient energy use, etc. At the data center level, we can consider the adoption of cooling methods to reduce the heat generated by devices with air-conditioning, free cooling, liquid cooling, overhead, and underfloor air delivery technologies [1].

These combined techniques have certainly helped to limit the increase in electricity consumption, but there is no evidence that this trend will continue or accelerate to reduce carbon emissions. According to Freitag et al. [3], carbon emissions from the ICT sector have always increased to reach 1.8–3.9% of global carbon emissions in 2021. This can be explained by the explosion of demand, faster than improvements per-device, which is called a rebound effect [8]. Rebound effects explain the increase in global energy consumed by the global increase in users and use. For instance, data centers are more efficient, and the energy used to compute a workload is lower, but as the Internet traffic and workloads to compute have grown faster, the overall energy consumption has increased.

In Fig. 1, we illustrate both efficiency improvements and the consequences of increasing demand using four key measures. We depicted the evolution of the average Power Usage Effectiveness (PUE) of industries over the last few years, which represents the energy consumption of their IT equipment on the global infrastructure, the decrease in energy consumption per computing instance between 2010 and 2018, the increase in total internet traffic worldwide over the last few years, and finally the evolution of the energy consumed to power data centers worldwide. We elaborated these graphs considering data provided by [3] and other related reports.

We believe that it is necessary to apply new techniques to reduce the overall demand for current and future digital services. These new techniques are called sobriety or sufficiency techniques. This global concept was presented in the latest Intergovernmental Panel on Climate Change (IPCC) reports [5], and then

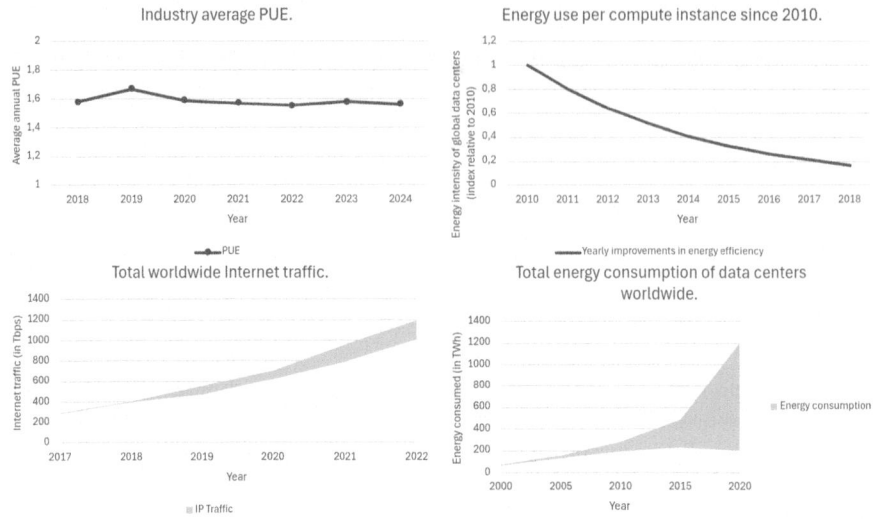

Fig. 1. Trends in energy efficiency of ICT and Internet traffic worldwide.

adapted by Santarius et al. in the ICT sector as digital sufficiency [11]. Santarius et al. defined digital sufficiency as 'any strategy aimed at directly or indirectly decreasing the absolute level of resource and energy demand from the production or application of ICT'. Digital sufficiency is also used by the French community, such as the association 'The Shift Project' with their work on lean ICT, and by the French Environment and Energy Management Agency to present policy recommendations to businesses, local governments, and the general public.

3 Challenges

To reduce demand, we identified three main challenges. We need systematic assessments of the coming demand if we want to be able to act at this level. In addition, we need to be able to share with end-users, and/or developers, carbon emissions assessments to propose an alternative to encourage action. Finally, we must try to involve as many actors as possible, as this is a global problem, it is necessary to deploy it at the largest scale as possible.

3.1 Challenge 1: Reducing the Demand

Nowadays, most people are not necessarily aware of carbon emissions linked to the use of their IT devices, nor of the world's remaining carbon budget or the climate targets we are committed to achieving. This information is however necessary to act on the right scale. Santarius et al. identified in [11] that many of the current studies on sustainability do not include a proposal to reduce direct or indirect rebound effects.

In addition, improving the efficiency of the services solutions share a narrative that technology will be sufficient to reduce carbon emissions, without the need to reduce the demand [3]. Including the rebound effects assessment is a complex task, and often involves many actors, but we argue that it is a necessity to reduce effectively carbon emissions.

3.2   Challenge 2: Assess Carbon Emissions

To assess carbon emissions of the ICT sector, the current usual solution is to use life cycle assessments (LCA), protocols (e.g., the Greenhouse Gas protocol), and measurement tools (with event counters or sensors like Intel RAPL, or with power meters). The challenges associated with assessing carbon emissions are the choice of method, the access to data from companies and users, and the heterogeneity of collected data. The margin of error is significant, depending on the scope of the assessment. Freitag et al. described this difficulty in their review with the example of 'truncation error': the partial exclusion of supply chain pathways leads to underestimation of the carbon footprint of ICT [3].

Monitoring and collecting accurate energy data in real time is also difficult with today's devices and their various hardware architectures. Not all equipment includes sensors for collecting energy data or models for estimating usage. Kanso et al. show the possibilities of generating power models for appliances and equipment and the advantages of having an accurate power model for smart and non-smart appliances [6]. Due to this high variability and complexity, current assessments vary considerably [3]. The lack of reporting by researchers or companies increases the difficulty of providing accurate results and limits the reproducibility of experiments [7].

3.3   Challenge 3: Involve the User to Apply User Sufficiency

The current limitation to raising awareness of good behavior is to share good information with the user and suggest alternatives. When we give the user an estimate of carbon emissions, one has to bear in mind that this is only an estimate of CO_2 emissions, as we can only provide a forecast of the cost of a specific digital service [4]. This is a concern because users will never know the real impact of their use, and this might push them to act when it is not necessary. The feedback to users must also be accompanied by solutions which are not always available. End-users can be discouraged if they cannot change their behavior because of that, and might also resist change with high workload or when energy consumption is perceived as low, as analyzed in the study of Noureddine et al. [10].

4   Opportunities

Implementing sufficiency techniques offers many opportunities. These techniques are already available and they do not require revolutionary technology. Furthermore, ICT is currently not sustainable if we consider the limits of extracting non-renewable resources such as coal, fuel, rare metals, etc., to build devices, networks, and data centers. The application of sufficiency techniques is also a solution for increasing ICT sustainability beyond carbon emissions.

To implement sufficiency techniques, it is possible to set constraints on carbon emissions when developing efficiency techniques [12]. With this approach, the sector is more likely to reduce its emissions year after year, which will encourage demand reduction when energy efficiency improvements are insufficient. An example of sufficiency techniques is workload shifting in space and time. This concept includes a set of solutions to deploy digital services where and when there is available renewable energy, with a negligible impact on the quality of service provided to the users. For example, Wiesner et al. have estimated a 20% saving in carbon emissions in most regions of the world by shifting part of the workload to weekends [13]. Another example is the approximate computing paradigm, which accepts a good enough solution to save resources and energy [9].

To involve users in changing their behavior, Noureddine et al. [10] proposed three techniques inspired by the building sector: social interactions (comparing users' energy consumption), gamification (involving people emotionally with interactive games), and eco-feedback (providing energy consumption indicators to users). Labels such as energy scores are also good examples of feedback to influence users' choices towards energy-efficient products. Guyon et al. proposed their own ecolabel 'GLENDA' (Green Label towards Energy proportioNality for IaaS DAta centers), combining Power Usage Effectiveness (PUE) and Green Energy Coefficient (GEC) to push cloud providers to do more for greener data centers and helping energy-conscious users to choose among cloud providers [4].

5   Conclusion

We argue the urgent need to adopt a 'sufficiency' attitude with actions and policies to reduce carbon emissions. We reviewed some of the energy efficiency solutions implemented over the last few decades and their limitations in terms of reducing carbon emissions. In particular, we have identified the need to implement sufficiency techniques aimed at reducing demand to limit rebound effects. Implementing digital sufficiency techniques faces several challenges: the complexity of assessing the carbon footprint of digital services, the lack of consideration for rebound effects in current literature, and an absence of coordinated action in favor of reducing demand in ICT. To enable the use of sufficiency techniques, we support the need to develop and use monitoring tools with understandable metrics to raise awareness of end-users and developers, and to involve users with positive feedback. Suitable data management techniques are needed to help people to take decisions. As this decade is crucial for tackling climate change, sufficiency techniques represent a good opportunity, as they are already available and will contribute to increasing the sustainability of ICT.

Acknowledgements. This publication is part of the project PID2020-113037RB-I00, funded by MICIU/AEI/10.13039/501100011033. Besides the NEAT-AMBIENCE project, we also thank the support of the Departamento de Ciencia, Universidad y Sociedad del Conocimiento del Gobierno de Aragón (Government of Aragon: Group Reference T64_23R, COSMOS research group).

References

1. Alkrush, A.A., Salem, M.S., Abdelrehim, O., Hegazi, A.A.: Data centers cooling: a critical review of techniques, challenges, and energy saving solutions. Int. J. Refrig **160**, 246–262 (2024). https://doi.org/10.1016/j.ijrefrig.2024.02.007
2. Forster, P.M., al.: Indicators of global climate change 2023: annual update of key indicators of the state of the climate system and human influence. Earth Syst. Sci. Data **16**(6), 2625–2658 (2024). https://doi.org/10.5194/essd-16-2625-2024
3. Freitag, C., al.: The real climate and transformative impact of ICT: a critique of estimates, trends, and regulations. Patterns **2**(9) (2021). https://doi.org/10.1016/j.patter.2021.100340
4. Guyon, D., Orgerie, A.C., Morin, C.: GLENDA: green label towards energy pro-portioNality for IaaS DAta centers. In: Eighth International Conference on Future Energy Systems (E-Energy), pp. 302–308. Association for Computing Machinery, New York, NY, USA (2017). https://doi.org/10.1145/3077839.3084028
5. IPCC: Technical summary. In: Intergovernmental Panel On Climate Change (IPCC) (ed.) Climate Change 2022 - Mitigation of Climate Change, pp. 51–148. Cambridge University Press, 1 edn. (2023). https://doi.org/10.1017/9781009157926.002
6. Kanso, H., Noureddine, A., Exposito, E.: Automated power modeling of computing devices: implementation and use case for Raspberry PIS. Sustain. Comput. Inf. Syst. **37**, 100837 (2023). https://doi.org/10.1016/j.suscom.2022.100837
7. Kennes, T.: Measuring IT carbon footprint: what is the current status actually? (2023). https://doi.org/10.48550/arXiv.2306.10049
8. Lange, S., Kern, F., Peuckert, J., Santarius, T.: The Jevons paradox unravelled: a multi-level typology of rebound effects and mechanisms. Energy Res. Soc. Sci. **74**, 101982 (2021). https://doi.org/10.1016/j.erss.2021.101982
9. Mittal, S.: A survey of techniques for approximate computing. ACM Comput. Surv. **48**(4), 62:1–62:33 (2016). https://doi.org/10.1145/2893356
10. Noureddine, A., Lodeiro, M.D., Bru, N., Chbeir, R.: The impact of green feedback on users' software usage. IEEE Trans. Sustain. Comput. **8**(2), 280–292 (2023). https://doi.org/10.1109/TSUSC.2022.3222631
11. Santarius, T., et al.: Digital sufficiency: conceptual considerations for ICTs on a finite planet. Ann. Telecommun. **78**(5), 277–295 (2023). https://doi.org/10.1007/s12243-022-00914-x
12. Widdicks, K., et al.: Systems thinking and efficiency under emissions constraints: addressing rebound effects in digital innovation and policy. Patterns **4**(2), 100679 (2023). https://doi.org/10.1016/j.patter.2023.100679
13. Wiesner, P., Behnke, I., Scheinert, D., Gontarska, K., Thamsen, L.: Let's wait awhile: how temporal workload shifting can reduce carbon emissions in the cloud. In: Proceedings of the 22nd International Middleware Conference, pp. 260–272 (2021). https://doi.org/10.1145/3464298.3493399

Multi-target Feature Selection Method for Predicting User-Level Psychological Status from Text

Danmeng Cai[ID], Kei Wakabayashi[✉][ID], and Shaoyu Ye[ID]

University of Tsukuba, Tsukuba, Japan
s2226089@s.tsukuba.ac.jp, {kwakaba,shaoyu}@slis.tsukuba.ac.jp

Abstract. Estimating psychological status from linguistic information is essential for understanding human actions across various domains. Conventional machine learning methods often face overfitting issues due to the tendency of linguistic features outnumbering data entries, which need to be collected by questionnaire survey. Our study addresses this issue by employing a multi-target feature selection (MTFS) method, which selects linguistic features relevant to multiple psychological variables to enhance the generalization ability of the prediction model. We tested MTFS against single-target feature selection (STFS) methods using several machine learning algorithms on two datasets. The results show that the MTFS method improves prediction performance, which suggests that implications from the field of social psychology can enhance the selection of relevant linguistic features.

Keywords: Psychological Status Prediction · Multi-Target Feature Selection · Machine Learning

1 Introduction

Predicting psychological conditions is crucial because it enhances our understanding of human actions, which is valuable across various domains. For example, in the public health domain, understanding personality traits can help in predicting behaviors and designing effective interventions to improve overall well-being [26]. One method researchers use to infer psychological status involves the analysis of language, as it can reflect an individual's social and mental states, and thereby provide a quantifiable means to study psychological phenomena [15,18]. By using linguistic features such as word frequencies, numerous studies have tried to predict the psychological status of sample populations [5,13,17,21].

One challenge in developing the models for these studies is overfitting, as the number of linguistic features often exceeds the number of entries available for analysis [10]. To address this challenge, researchers typically apply feature selection methods that use only the selected influential features when constructing prediction models. The feature selection processes in these studies typically focus on relevance to only one target variable. However, evidence suggests that

P. Delir Haghighi et al. (Eds.): iiWAS 2024, LNCS 15342, pp. 182–197, 2025.
https://doi.org/10.1007/978-3-031-78090-5_16

socioeconomic and psychological factors have a multifaceted influence on psychological variables such as stress, subjective well-being (SWB), and level of worry [1,3,7,12,23]. These findings highlight the association between an individual's psychological status and its associated factors, suggesting the potential effectiveness of using the linguistic features relevant to multiple psychological variables as independent features in prediction models.

No previous studies have tried to mitigate overfitting by selecting linguistic features that are influential to multiple psychological variables. In addressing this research gap, our study uses a multi-target feature selection (MTFS) method to select linguistic features that are informative to multiple psychological variables. Previous studies in non-psychological domains have shown that model performance in multi-target prediction tasks can be improved when features are selected by using MTFS methods [8,9,22]. In this study, we hypothesize that the MTFS method that considers multiple related psychological variables can enhance model performance even in a single-target prediction task for the primary target variable (e.g., SWB or level of worry). To test this hypothesis, we conducted two empirical studies (Study A and B[1]). The use of the MTFS method demonstrates promising results across various prediction models in both studies.

This research makes two contributions: 1) we show that the MTFS approach can be applied to the task of predicting a writer's psychological status from text data to mitigate overfitting issues even when a single variable is the target to be predicted. 2) through two empirical studies, we demonstrate that the MTFS method performs better than traditional single-target feature selection (STFS) in psychological status prediction tasks. The paper also details differences in the features identified by MTFS from those identified by STFS.

2   Related Work

2.1   Overfitting Challenges in Using Linguistic Information to Predict Psychological Status

The significance of analyzing language use in psychological research had been recognized since the early 20th century [19,24]. Recently, a vast amount of text data can now be collected, particularly from social media platforms, offering an opportunity to analyze psychological statuses of larger populations using text data [13,21]. One challenge in developing models for predicting psychological status is overfitting. This issue is particularly prevalent in tasks involving linguistic features, where the number of features often exceeds the number of entries available for analysis [10]. To mitigate overfitting when using linguistic features to predict psychological variables, a common strategy is to first select features

---

[1] The dataset used in Study B is identical to the one collected in Ye et al. [27] (See Sect. 4.2). While the study [27] investigates the statistical relationships between personality traits, patterns of social media and mental health, this paper studies the effect of the MTFS method in machine learning prediction by using the dataset for evaluations.

that are influential to the target outcome and then use only the selected features when constructing prediction models [16,17].

Despite differences in the prediction models and targeted psychological variables, previous studies have consistently focused on linguistic features that are relevant to only one specific target psychological variable. Psychological status, however, can be affected by a complex interplay of various factors. For example, research has shown that indicators of psychological strengths are positively associated with SWB [3], whereas experiences of depression are negatively associated with SWB [12]. Furthermore, studies have found that lower levels of emotion regulation correlate with increased worry in young and older adults [7,14]. These studies underscore the importance of a range of factors when analyzing psychological status. In this paper, we consider multiple factors in the linguistic feature selection in psychological status prediction and examine the effectiveness of this approach in mitigating overfitting issues.

2.2 MTFS Approach to Multi-target Prediction Tasks

MTFS involves identifying and selecting the most relevant features from a dataset, where features are evaluated on the basis of their influence across multiple targets. For example, Sechidis et al. [22] proposed a joint mutual information (JMI) scoring method to select features that accounts for dependencies among target variables in multi-target prediction tasks. Hashemi et al. [8] utilized cosine similarity to assess correlations between features and target variables, by applying a multi-criteria decision making (MCDM) method for feature ranking and selection. These studies indicate that leveraging features that are informative across multiple target variables could enhance the prediction performance of a model.

However, no previous study has taken an MTFS approach to predict psychological status with linguistic features. Given its potential superiority in model performance to traditional STFS approaches, we chose to use MTFS to select linguistic features that would be informative to both the primary and related psychological variables. We hypothesized that the MTFS approach could select features with less noise and broader coverage, and thereby enhance the predictive model's performance.

3   MTFS Method for Selecting Linguistic Features

In this section, we propose an MTFS method that aggregates feature importance scores across multiple target variables, thus identifying the most relevant linguistic features to the entire set of targets. We hypothesize that linguistic features contributing to multiple psychological variables can enhance the model's predictive power for the primary target variable. Following the MTFS phase, the predictive model is trained for predicting the designated primary target variable, by utilizing only the selected linguistic features.

Let us assume that we have a set $D = \{d^{(1)}, d^{(2)}, \ldots, d^{(n)}\}$ of documents as the training data, which are written by the participants of a survey. Let $T = \{t_1, t_2, \ldots, t_m\}$ be the set of target variables, which represent the psychological status of a participant measured in the survey. Each document $d^{(l)}$ is associated with m target variables $y^{(l)} = \{y_1^{(l)}, y_2^{(l)}, \ldots, y_m^{(l)}\}$, where each $y_j^{(l)}$ represents the value of variable t_j for the writer of $d^{(l)}$. In our task setting, there is one target variable $t_{primary} \in T$ that we are interested in predicting. Given a new document $d^{(new)}$, the goal is to predict the target variables $y_{primary}^{(new)}$ for the writer of $d^{(new)}$.

Since the amount of training data based on surveys is generally limited, the trained model tends to overfit and perform worse on unseen test data. To address this issue, we consider the use of feature selection methods to improve the generalization performance of the model.

Here, we will focus on the word frequency features as the linguistic features. Let $X = \{x_1, x_2, \ldots, x_p\}$ be the set of word frequency features extracted from the document set D. The goal of feature selection is to select a subset of features $X^* \subset X$ that maximizes the generalization performance of the model predicting the target variable $t_{primary}$. That is, given a number of features $|X^*| = k$, we select the k features with the highest scores $S_\phi(x)$, where $S_\phi(x)$ is an importance score of feature x defined by a feature selection method ϕ.

3.1   Single-Target Feature Selection (STFS)

In single-target feature selection, we select the features that are most relevant to the target variable $t_{primary}$. Here, we used an ANOVA-F value scoring function to evaluate the importance of each linguistic feature. ANOVA-F is a score that is used to determine if there are significant differences between the means of two or more groups. In the context of feature selection for machine learning, the ANOVA-F value evaluates the importance of each feature with respect to the target variable. A higher F-value indicates that the variance between groups is significantly larger than the variance within groups, suggesting that the feature is important for predicting the target variable.

Let $F(x, t)$ be the ANOVA-F value for a linguistic feature x and target t, which measures the importance of x with respect to t. The feature importance score of x in the STFS method $S_{STFS}(x)$ is defined as

$$S_{STFS}(x) = F(x, t_{primary}).$$

3.2   Multi-target Feature Selection (MTFS)

The STFS method selects features on the basis of their relevance to the target variable $t_{primary}$. However, given that the target variable $t_{primary}$ is affected by other psychological variables, features that are relevant to the other variables might also be helpful in predicting $t_{primary}$, particularly when the training data is limited, which is often the case in psychological studies. Given this motivation, we propose a MTFS method that considers the relevance of features to multiple target variables.

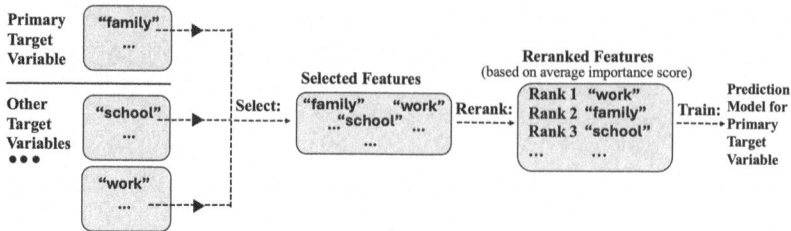

Fig. 1. Illustration of Proposed MTFS Method

Figure 1 illustrates the overall process of the proposed method. First, the linguistic features are selected using a scoring function (ANOVA-F value) to evaluate the importance of each feature for each target variable specified (**Select**). The selected features are then reranked on the basis of the average importance score across all target variables (**Rerank**). Finally, models are trained exclusively on the designated primary target by utilizing only the reranked features (**Train**).

Let $F(x, t_j)$ be the ANOVA-F value for linguistic feature x with respect to each target variable t_j (primary and associated included) The feature importance score of x in the MTFS method $S_{MTFS}(x)$ is defined as:

$$S_{MTFS}(x) = \frac{1}{m} \sum_{j=1}^{m} F(x, t_j)$$

where m is the total number of target variables (primary and associated included) in T.

3.3   Model Training and Evaluation

After determining the importance scores $S_\phi(x)$ for each feature x, we select the top k features that exhibit the highest averaged importance scores. With the selected features in hand X^*, the next step is to train the predictive model on t_{primary}. The training process involves fitting a model M by using data restricted to the features in X^* and t_{primary}. This step can involve using various machine learning algorithms, depending on the nature of the data and the specific requirements of the study.

Once the model is trained, it is crucial to evaluate its performance by using appropriate metrics. For classification tasks, accuracy, precision, recall, and F1-score are common metrics. In situations with unbalanced datasets, PR AUC can be considered. PR AUC provides a single value that summarizes the performance of a classifier across all possible levels of precision and recall, which is useful when the positive class is much less prevalent than the negative class.

4   Experiment

4.1   Datasets

Study A: We utilized the Real World Worry Waves Dataset (RW3D), a multi-modal dataset designed to examine the psychological impacts of the COVID-19 pandemic on individuals in the UK. Integrating survey responses about emotions with free-text narratives, this dataset encompasses individual emotional experiences related to the pandemic, collected over three consecutive years (2020–2022). RW3D captures a wide range of psychological dimensions, including emotional responses, coping styles, and specific concerns during the pandemic [25].

Emotion Data. Participants were required to rate their level of worry about the COVID-19 situation on a 9-point scale (1 = not worried at all; 9 = very worried). Additionally, participants assessed their current emotions regarding the COVID-19 situation by rating how strongly they felt each of the following eight emotions on a 9-point scale (1 = none at all; 9 = very much): anger, disgust, fear, anxiety, sadness, happiness, relaxation, and desire.

Text Data. Participants were asked to provide written responses in two formats: long texts (more than 500 characters) and short texts (fewer than 280 characters) to express their feelings about the COVID-19 situation.

Binary Transformation of Target Variables. A binary transformation was applied to all target variables (eight emotion variables and one level of worry variable) to facilitate classification. A high-level threshold was established at the 75th percentile, assigning a class number "1" to indicate higher-level outcomes. A low-level threshold was set at the 50th percentile, where a class number "0" indicates lower-level outcomes.

Text Data Manipulation. For the purposes of this study, both short and long texts were combined into a single text category, and texts from the same participant across different years were treated as separate entries. After removing all punctuation marks, the texts were lowercased and tokenized into words. Following tokenization, common English stop words were removed by using the stop word list from the Natural Language Toolkit (NLTK) [2]², supplemented with the words "le", "nh", and "lm". Each token was then tagged with its part-of-speech, and only nouns were retained. Finally, words appearing in less than 1% of the entries were eliminated from the analysis to exclude uncommon words.

---

² https://github.com/nltk/nltk_data/blob/gh-pages/packages/corpora/stopwords.
  zip, accessed May 25, 2024.

Study B: We collected demographic information as well as psychological conditions through two online surveys in 2021 and 2022. The first time was on May 10–22, 2021, and the second time was on May 9–23, 2022[3]. The participants were mainly university students in the Kanto region of Japan, as some participants continued to answer the survey after their graduation. The completed responses numbered 1,681 and 1,292, respectively, and both surveys measured participants' levels of SWB, self-presentation desire, social support received from others, and depression tendency. Among the measures, SWB and self-presentation desire used a 5-point Likert scale, while social support used a 7-point Likert scale, and depression tendency was evaluated by "yes" (=1) or "no" (=0). Previous research has shown that these variables are significantly associated with SWB [27,28].

Posts Collection. Participants in the two surveys were also asked to provide up to three X accounts that they use, which allowed us to conduct log data analysis. For each account, we collected public posts made during the one-year period leading up to each survey (from May 22, 2020 to May 22, 2021 and from May 23, 2021 to May 23, 2022) by using the Twitter API. Each X account used during different period was treated as a separate entity. We aggregated all posts made from a single participant for each specific period and paired these compiled posts with the user's corresponding SWB score for that corresponding survey. In total, 1,091 samples were collected (550 collected from May 22, 2020 to May 22, 2021; 541 collected from May 23, 2021 to May 23, 2022).

Binary Transformation of Target Variables. We applied a binary transformation to SWB and its related variables. A low-level threshold is set at the 25th percentile, where the class number (1 for SWB and 0 for others) indicates a lower level or less favorable outcome. A high-level threshold is set at the 50th percentile, where the class number (0 for SWB and 1 for others) indicates a higher level or more favorable outcome.

Text Data Manipulation. Mentions, URLs, emojis, punctuation, special characters, and numbers were removed from the posts. Then, we extracted Japanese nouns as words for analysis. Low-frequency words, used in less than 20% of the samples, were regarded as uncommon words and removed from the analysis. Among the common words, words that have an extreme frequency were also removed: First, we calculated the total word frequency for each word in common words. Then, the first quartile (Q1), third quartile (Q3), and interquartile range (IQR) for the distribution of the total word frequency were computed. The extreme frequency is defined as 1.5 times of the IQR beyond Q1 or Q3.

---

[3] The dataset including the collected posts is identical to one collected in Ye et al. [27].

4.2 Prediction Models

Previous research has demonstrated that the capacity for emotion regulation is associated with the level of worry [7,14]. On the basis of these findings, for Study A, our prediction model identified the level of worry as the primary target variable, along with eight associated emotion levels as associated targets.

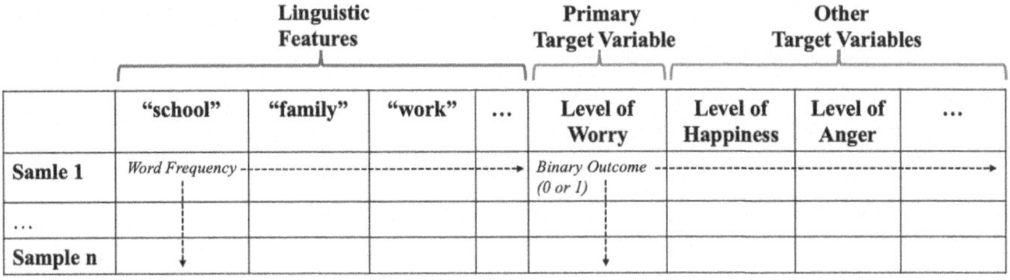

	Linguistic Features				Primary Target Variable	Other Target Variables		
	"school"	"family"	"work"	...	Level of Worry	Level of Happiness	Level of Anger	...
Samle 1	*Word Frequency* - →				*Binary Outcome* - → *(0 or 1)*			
...								
Sample n	↓				↓			

Fig. 2. Illustration of Preprocessed Dataset for Study A

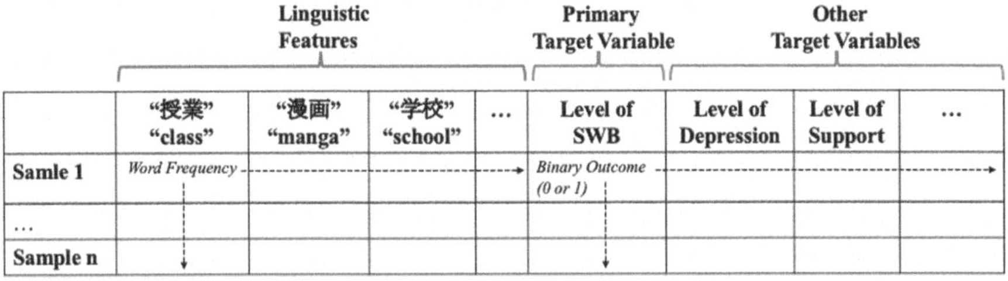

	Linguistic Features				Primary Target Variable	Other Target Variables		
	"授業" "class"	"漫画" "manga"	"学校" "school"	...	Level of SWB	Level of Depression	Level of Support	...
Samle 1	*Word Frequency* - →				*Binary Outcome* - → *(0 or 1)*			
...								
Sample n	↓				↓			

Fig. 3. Illustration of Preprocessed Dataset for Study B

Research utilizing multivariate stepwise regression has identified significant personal traits impacting SWB, such as self-presentation desire, depression tendency, and the amount of support received [28]. On the basis of these findings, in Study B, our prediction model identified the level of SWB as the primary target variable, along with the level of praise acquisition factor (a factor of self-presentation desire that is significantly linked to SWB), tendency to experience depression, and amount of support received as the associated target variables.

In both studies, we utilized the frequency of commonly used nouns as the independent variables. Figure 2 and Fig. 3 illustrate the two datasets used to build the prediction models. For comparison, we also formulated an STFS prediction model using the same independent features but focusing only on the primary target variable. Three models were used with hyperparameters optimized by using the grid search, as detailed below. The number of selected features k, one of the hyperparameters, was varied among 10, 30, and 50 in each grid

Table 1. Percentage (%) of Level of Outcomes across Target Variables

	Worry	Anger	Disgust	Fear	Anxiety	Sadness	Happiness	Relaxation	Desire
Class "1"	30.8	26.4	24.4	28.7	27.3	30.5	43.0	47.7	33.3
Class "0"	69.2	73.6	75.6	71.3	72.7	69.5	57.0	52.3	66.7

search. These three models were chosen to examine the effects of the proposed method on models with different principles: separating hyperplain, bagging, and boosting.

Support Vector Machines (SVMs) are robust machine learning algorithms, recognized for their ability to handle linear and non-linear classification through the use of kernel methods [20]. In the grid search for hyperparameter optimization, we tested different values for the penalty parameter c of the error term, specifically 0.01, 0.1, 1, and 10. Additionally, we used two types of kernels in the model: linear and radial basis function (rbf).

Random Forest (RF) is an ensemble model that constructs multiple decision trees during training and outputs the mode of the classes of the trees [11]. In the grid search, the number of trees in the forest was varied among 10, 50, and 100. The maximum depth of the trees was tested with values of 3, 6, and 9.

Extreme Gradient Boosting (XGBoost) is a gradient boosting model that is improved by introducing several advanced features [4]. In the grid search, the number of trees in the model was varied among 10, 50, and 100. The maximum depth of the trees was tested with values 3, 6, and 9. The learning rate was also adjusted, with values of 0.01, 0.1, and 0.2 being tested.

4.3   Performance Evaluation

Identifying linguistic features in digital texts that can predict psychological status is crucial, particularly for detecting individuals with poor mental health conditions. The PR AUC was chosen as an evaluation metric for this research because it focuses on the minority class. The PR AUC ranges from 0 to 1. When identifying individuals with low psychological conditions, a higher PR AUC indicates that the model effectively identifies most individuals with the condition (high recall) while maintaining a low rate of misclassifying those with normal conditions as having poor conditions (high precision) [6].

To test the predictive power of models using the proposed MTFS method, we took a ten-by-ten nested cross-validation approach. For each model, the optimal combination of hyperparameters was determined through a grid search in the ten-fold inner cross-validation, and the performance of the model with this optimal combination was assessed using 10-fold outer cross-validation. The ten-fold outer cross-validation yielded ten PR AUC scores. The ten-by-ten nested cross-validation was conducted five times. This approach yielded a total of 50 PR AUC scores for each model, which were then used in statistical test.

Table 2. Average PR AUC Scores - STFS and MTFS Comparison in Study A

Model	Avg with STFS Method	Avg with MTFS Method	T-statistic	P-value
SVMs	0.4494	0.5357	−6.1282	2.06×10^{-8}
RF	0.4698	0.5349	−4.1847	6.23×10^{-5}
XGBoost	0.4682	0.4382	2.070	4.10×10^{-2}

Table 3. Percentage (%) of Level of Outcomes across Target Variables for Study B

	SWB	Support	Praise	Depression
Class "1"	33.4	66.1	69.5	54.1
Class "0"	66.6	33.9	30.5	45.9

5 Results

5.1 Study A Direct Responses to COVID-19

After the binary transformation of target variables and manipulation of the text data, our dataset comprised 1,369 entries. It included nine target variables and 332 linguistic features serving as independent variables.

Table 1 shows the skewness towards Class "0" for most of the emotional and worry states in our dataset. PR AUC is suitable for evaluating such imbalanced datasets, as it specifically focuses on the ability of the classifier to correctly predict the minority class (high-level outcomes) while distinguishing it from the majority class (low-level outcomes). The statistical analysis was performed using Welch's t-tests to compare the average of 50 PR AUC scores of three different machine learning models-SVMs, RF, and XGBoost. Table 2 shows the average PR AUC scores. These results indicate significant improvements in performance when the proposed MTFS method was applied to both SVM and RF models.

However, the XGBoost model did not show a statistically significant change. The performance slightly decreased when the proposed MTFS method was applied from 0.4682 to 0.4382. These findings suggest that while the proposed method significantly enhanced the performance of the SVM and RF, it did not yield the same outcome for the XGBoost under the conditions tested.

5.2 Study B Social Media Usage and SWB During COVID-19

After the binary transformation of target variables and manipulation of text data, our dataset comprised 407 entries. It included four target variables and 2,390 linguistic features serving as independent variables.

As shown in Table 3, skewness towards Class "0" was observed. The statistical analysis was performed using Welch's t-tests to compare the average 50 PR AUC scores of three different machine learning models-SVMs, RF, and XGBoost. According to Table 4, the XGBoost model showed a highly significant improvement in performance with the MTFS method. This suggests that while the SVM and RF models' performance remained largely unaffected by the choice of feature selection method, the XGBoost model benefited substantially from the MTFS method, highlighting its potential for improving more complex models.

6 Discussion

6.1 Mitigating Data Sparseness in the Feature Selection Process with the MTFS Method

Given the feature space is much larger than the number of data points when making predictions using linguistic features, the features selected from the training dataset by the traditional STFS method might be statistically unreliable and may not represent the underlying patterns. This unreliability can lead to inconsistent model performance, undermining the predictive power of the models.

Table 4. Average PR AUC Scores - STFS and MTFS Comparison for Study B

Model	Avg with STFS Method	Avg with MTFS Method	T-statistic	P-value
SVMs	0.4153	0.3793	1.3318	0.186
RF	0.4098	0.4122	−0.1028	0.918
XGBoost	0.3977	0.5441	−6.8025	8.22×10^{-10}

To explain the improved prediction performance when using our MTFS method compared, we applied both methods to the entire dataset to identify the top-50 linguistic features selected by each method in both Study A (Table 5) and Study B (Table 6). Table 5 presents the linguistic features extracted from direct responses to the COVID-19 pandemic. The MTFS method selected context-relevant features such as "vaccine", "travel", "risk", "die", and "delivery". In contrast, the STFS method selected features that were less relevant, including "cant", "let", "thing", and "point". Table 6 shows the linguistic features extracted from public tweets collected one year before the survey. The STFS method tended to select features limited to certain topics, such as "問題 (problem)", "計算 (calculation)", "関数 (function)", and "プログラミング (programming)". On the other hand, the MTFS method selected a diverse range of linguistic features relevant to various psychological aspects such as the level of support received, level of depression, and level of praise received, as shown in Table 7.

From these results, we assume that due to data sparseness, the STFS method tends to select linguistic features that are narrowly focused and potentially less informative. In contrast, the MTFS method, by considering multiple psychological variables, captures a broader and more relevant set of linguistic features, which enhances overall prediction performance. By integrating knowledge from social psychology, MTFS mitigates overfitting and improves the robustness of the predictive models. The results of the experiments demonstrate the benefits of leveraging statistical insights from socio-psychological studies when constructing prediction models with linguistic features.

6.2 Differences in Best Models Yielding Optimal Performance Between Study A and Study B

We observed significant improvements in the performance of the SVMs and RF using the proposed MTFS method in Study A. In contrast, the performance of

Table 5. Features Selected by STFS and MTFS Methods in Study A

Both STFS and MTFS	family, covid, restriction, worker, flu, anxiety, home, house, booster, corona, mask, jab, year, normality, summer, job, health, friend, uncertainty, continue, life, partner, government, cold, group, stay, parent, daughter, cope, glad, advice, wait, please, line
Only STFS	war, symptom, move, member, population, cant, health, let, guideline, pandemic, country, thing, staff, distance, point
Only MTFS	people, case, food, vaccine, travel, risk, dad, husband, vaccination, sense, die, cause, minister, number, delivery

Table 6. Features Selected by STFS and MTFS Methods in Study B

Both STFS and MTFS	おじ (uncle), かわ (cute), この世 (this world), ころ (around), すべて (everything), そもそも (first place), つもり (intention), とき (time), ほんま (really), もん (thing), やつ (guy), 事実 (fact), 二 (two), 体 (body), 作家 (writer), 効率 (efficiency), 反省 (reflection), 呼吸 (breath), 地獄 (hell), 壁 (wall), 概念 (concept), 理論 (theory), 異常 (abnormal), 禁止 (prohibition), 穴 (hole), 紙 (paper), すき (like), へん (strange)
Only STFS	事故 (accident), 印刷 (printing), 問題 (problem), 展開 (development) 計算 (calculation), 途中 (on the way), 関数 (function), 食料 (food), 首 (neck), アイコン (icon), エラー (error), ダーク (dark), テキスト (text), デ (de), バグ (bug), パーティー (party), ファイル (file), プログラミング (programming), マスター (master), モチベ (motivation), モノ (thing), 物 (thing)
Only MTFS	ねこ (cat), 中身 (content), 主人 (master), 人格 (personality), 仮面 (mask), 作品 (work), 出身 (origin), 労働 (labor), 原因 (cause), 否定 (denial), 回収 (collection), 土曜 (Saturday), 場合 (case), 白 (white), 破壊 (destruction), 福岡 (Fukuoka), 筑波 (Tsukuba), 範囲 (range), 系 (system), 絵柄 (design), 絶望 (despair), 耳 (ear)

Table 7. Features Selected by Only MTFS Method Highlighted in <u>Blue</u>

Top features for Level of Support Received

紙 (paper), かわ (cute), つもり (intention), <u>原因 (cause)</u>, へん (strange),
異常 (abnormal), 界隈 (vicinity), <u>仮面 (mask)</u>, 紫 (purple), 身 (body),
白 (white), ほんま (really), <u>系 (system)</u>, <u>福岡 (Fukuoka)</u>, 事情 (circumstances),
生誕 (birth), <u>ねこ (cat)</u>, 確定 (confirmation), <u>人格 (personality)</u>, <u>絵柄 (design)</u>,
穴 (hole), 落書き (graffiti), <u>労働 (labor)</u>, 訳 (reason),
勘違い (misunderstanding), 虚無 (nothingness)

Top features for Level of Depression

とき (time), セリフ (line/serif), あと (after), <u>場合 (case)</u>, 空間 (space),
中身 (content), 登場 (appearance), 画像 (image), <u>耳 (ear)</u>, 全体 (whole),
便利 (convenience), 事実 (fact), 出席 (attendance), <u>作品 (work)</u>, 以下 (below),
範囲 (range), <u>破壊 (destruction)</u>, 博士 (doctor), 七 (seven), <u>土曜 (Saturday)</u>

Top features for Level of Amount of Praise Received

地獄(hell), 絵柄(design), 出身(origin), 一致(match), 筑波(Tsukuba), 習慣(habit),
回収 (collect), 出場 (appearance), 解釈 (interpretation), 相互 (mutual), 白 (white),
供給(supply), 二人(two people), 今朝(this morning), 語彙(vocabulary), <u>作品(work)</u>

---

the XGBoost showed notable improvement with the MTFS method in Study B. These differences in model performance between Study A and Study B might be attributed to the nature of the text data collected in each study.

In Study A, the dataset comprised participants' direct responses to the COVID-19 pandemic and their self-evaluated emotional levels. As a result, the linguistic features extracted in Study A were more specific to the COVID-19 context. On the other hand, Study B utilized a dataset of the participants' previous public tweets. Consequently, the linguistic features extracted in Study B were broader and covered a wider range of contexts.

The context-specific nature of the data in Study A likely contributed to the effectiveness of the SVM and RF models, as these models can utilize specific features related to the pandemic. However, when the data is context-specific, the extracted linguistic features tend to be thematically similar (e.g., "dad", "husband", "family", "daughter" as shown in Table. 5). XGBoost builds trees sequentially, with each tree attempting to correct the errors made by the previous trees. This similarity can lead XGBoost to treat some features as redundant, thereby limiting the model's ability to fully utilize these features in making predictions. In contrast, the broader context in Study B favored the use of XGBoost, which is well-suited for handling diverse and complex feature sets. The sequential building process allows XGBoost to learn from the complex patterns within the data, making it particularly powerful for datasets with a broader range of linguistic features, as in Study B.

There may be other reasons for the difference in performance. For example, the results may be partly due to the social language environment (English vs. Japanese), which needs further examination in the future.

These observations underscore the importance of considering the nature of the dataset when selecting and optimizing machine learning models. Understanding the data collection context and the inherent characteristics of the models can guide the selection of the most appropriate models to achieve optimal performance with our MTFS method.

7   Conclusion

In this study, we conducted psychological status prediction by using an MTFS method to identify linguistic features relevant to both primary and related psychological variables. Our analysis demonstrates that the MTFS method is capable of mitigating the data sparseness problem in feature selection, resulting in a more stable and reliable set of features. Our findings indicate that in psychological status prediction tasks, such as assessing SWB or levels of worry, leveraging implications from fields such as social psychology significantly enhances the selection of relevant linguistic features, thereby improving prediction performance. To the best of our knowledge, this study represents the first empirical demonstration of the effectiveness of integrating social psychology insights into linguistic feature selection for psychological status prediction.

Furthermore, our research underscores the significant potential of leveraging associations among related psychological variables for linguistic feature selection. In the current study, we employed a straightforward approach of averaging feature importance scores (ANOVA-F values) to determine overall feature significance. The effectiveness of this straightforward technique suggests that there is substantial room for further improvement with more sophisticated MTFS methods [8,9,22]. Subsequent studies could explore the intricate relationships among related psychological variables and develop more nuanced mathematical models to reflect these relationships in feature importance assessment.

Acknowledgments. This study was supported by JSPS KAKENHI Grant Number 23K21842 (21H03770). The authors would like to thank those who helped answer the surveys.

Disclosure of Interests. The authors have no competing interests to declare that are relevant to the content of this article.

References

1. Adler, N.E., Epel, E.S., Castellazzo, G., Ickovics, J.R.: Relationship of subjective and objective social status with psychological and physiological functioning: preliminary data in healthy, white women. Health Psychol. **19**(6), 586 (2000)

2. Bird, S., Klein, E., Loper, E.: Natural language processing with Python: analyzing text with the natural language toolkit. " O'Reilly Media, Inc." (2009)
3. Campbell, F., et al.: Factors that influence mental health of university and college students in the UK: a systematic review. BMC Public Health **22**(1), 1778 (2022)
4. Chen, T., Guestrin, C.: XGBoost: a scalable tree boosting system. In: Proceedings of the 22nd ACM SIGKDD International Conference on Knowledge Discovery and Data Mining, pp. 785–794 (2016)
5. Cook, B.L., Progovac, A.M., Chen, P., Mullin, B., Hou, S., Baca-Garcia, E., et al.: Novel use of natural language processing (NLP) to predict suicidal ideation and psychiatric symptoms in a text-based mental health intervention in Madrid. Comput. Math. Methods Med. **2016**, 8708434 (2016)
6. Davis, J., Goadrich, M.: The relationship between precision-recall and roc curves. In: Proceedings of the 23rd International Conference on Machine Learning, pp. 233–240 (2006)
7. Gould, C.E., Edelstein, B.A.: Worry, emotion control, and anxiety control in older and young adults. J. Anxiety Disord. **24**(7), 759–766 (2010)
8. Hashemi, A., Dowlatshahi, M.B., Nezamabadi-pour, H.: VMFS: a VIKOR-based multi-target feature selection. Expert Syst. Appl. **182**, 115224 (2021)
9. He, D., Sun, S., Xie, L.: Multi-target feature selection with subspace learning and manifold regularization. Neurocomputing **582**, 127533 (2024)
10. Kern, M.L., et al.: Gaining insights from social media language: methodologies and challenges. Psychol. Methods **21**(4), 507 (2016)
11. Liaw, A., Wiener, M., et al.: Classification and regression by randomforest. R News **2**(3), 18–22 (2002)
12. Malone, C., Wachholtz, A.: The relationship of anxiety and depression to subjective well-being in a mainland Chinese sample. J. Relig. Health **57**, 266–278 (2018)
13. Mehta, Y., Fatehi, S., Kazameini, A., Stachl, C., Cambria, E., Eetemadi, S.: Bottom-up and top-down: predicting personality with psycholinguistic and language model features. In: 2020 IEEE International Conference on Data Mining (ICDM), pp. 1184–1189. IEEE (2020)
14. Mennin, D.S., Heimberg, R.G., Turk, C.L., Fresco, D.M.: Applying an emotion regulation framework to integrative approaches to generalized anxiety disorder. Clin. Psychol. Sci. Pract. **9**(1), 85–90 (2002)
15. Miller, G.A.: The place of language in a scientific psychology. Psychol. Sci. **1**(1), 7–14 (1990)
16. Panicheva, P., Mararitsa, L., Sorokin, S., Koltsova, O., Rosso, P.: Predicting subjective well-being in a high-risk sample of Russian mental health app users. EPJ Data Sci. **11**(1), 21 (2022)
17. Park, G., et al.: Automatic personality assessment through social media language. J. Pers. Soc. Psychol. **108**(6), 934 (2015)
18. Pennebaker, J.W., Mehl, M.R., Niederhoffer, K.G.: Psychological aspects of natural language use: our words, our selves. Annu. Rev. Psychol. **54**(1), 547–577 (2003)
19. Ramsay, R.W.: Speech patterns and personality. Lang. Speech **11**(1), 54–63 (1968)
20. Schölkopf, B., Smola, A.J.: Learning with Kernels: Support Vector Machines, Regularization, Optimization, and Beyond. MIT press (2002)
21. Schwartz, H.A., et al.: Predicting individual well-being through the language of social media. In: Biocomputing 2016: Proceedings of the Pacific Symposium, pp. 516–527. World Scientific (2016)
22. Sechidis, K., Spyromitros-Xioufis, E., Vlahavas, I.: Information theoretic multi-target feature selection via output space quantization. Entropy **21**(9), 855 (2019)

23. Sydenham, M., Beardwood, J., Rimes, K.A.: Beliefs about emotions, depression, anxiety and fatigue: a mediational analysis. Behav. Cogn. Psychother. **45**(1), 73–78 (2017)
24. Vane, J.R.: The thematic apperception test: A review. Clin. Psychol. Rev. **1**(3), 319–336 (1981)
25. van der Vegt, I., Kleinberg, B.: A multi-modal panel dataset to understand the psychological impact of the pandemic. Sci. Data **10**(1), 537 (2023)
26. Williams, J.E., et al.: Cross-cultural variation in the importance of psychological characteristics: a seven-country study. Int. J. Psychol. **30**(5), 529–550 (1995)
27. Ye, S.Y., Ho, K.W.K., Wakabayashi, K., Kato, Y.: Relationship between university students' emotional expression on tweets and subjective well-being: considering the effects of their self-presentation and online communication skills. BMC Public Health **23**, 594 (2023). https://doi.org/10.1186/s12889-023-15485-2
28. Ye, S.Y., Ho, K.W.K.: Social media use and subjective well-being among university students in Japan during the COVID-19 pandemic. Library Hi Tech (2024)

FIEAP: A Machine Learning Approach for Fair and Interpretable Employee Attrition Prediction

Ginel Dorleon[(✉)] [iD]

SogetiLabs, Capgemini, Toulouse, France
ginel.dorleon@sogeti.com

Abstract. In the current competitive job market, industries are confronting significant hurdles with employee attrition and notable turnover rates. To address these pressing concerns, organizations are progressively leveraging artificial intelligence (AI) to forecast employee attrition and deploy efficient retention strategies. Many existing machine learning approaches have tried to predict employee attrition rate across diverse organizations. However, we notice that they have limited ability to deal with fairness and interpretability while predicting employee attrition rate.

To address this disparity, we present FIEAP in this paper, an interpretable machine learning method designed for fair prediction of employee attrition. Our approach employs ensemble learning with a stacking strategy, incorporating four distinct machine learning algorithms. To ensure fairness and enhance interpretability, we integrate LIME (Local Interpretable Model-Agnostic Explanations).

We evaluate the proposed approach using a real-life dataset from CPC HR Employee Analytic and report on its performance in terms of prediction accuracy, fairness metrics, and feature importance. The results demonstrate the potential of our approach to provide clear explanations while maintaining fairness in attrition prediction.

Keywords: Machine Learning · Fairness · Explainable AI · Ensemble Learning · Employee Attrition

1 Introduction

Employee attrition, the departure of employees from an organization, presents a significant challenge for modern workforce management, organizational productivity, and overall performance [7,28]. As businesses strive to maintain a stable and engaged workforce, the ability to predict attrition accurately has become paramount. However, the mere accuracy of predictions is no longer sufficient. To address this multifaceted issue effectively, predictive models must be transparent, interpretable, and, most importantly, fair [6,13].

The problem of employee attrition is not merely an operational concern but also has profound societal implications. Discriminatory attrition predictions can perpetuate existing biases and inequalities, potentially exacerbating disparities

P. Delir Haghighi et al. (Eds.): iiWAS 2024, LNCS 15342, pp. 198–211, 2025.
https://doi.org/10.1007/978-3-031-78090-5_17

in the workforce [1, 20]. Therefore, the need for interpretable and fair employee attrition prediction models is not just a technical challenge but also an ethical imperative.

In light of the aforementioned considerations, this research addresses the pressing need for interpretable and fair employee attrition prediction models. We develop a predictive model that not only accurately forecasts attrition but also offers clear explanations for its predictions, ensuring transparency in the decision-making process. We base our explanations on the use of LIME [22], which is popular and effective technique for interpreting machine learning models. LIME (Local Interpretable Model-agnostic Explanations) is another method for explaining the predictions of machine learning models, particularly focusing on local interpretability [25]. Furthermore, the proposed approach is designed to uphold fairness, thereby avoiding any adverse impacts on demographic groups [3, 30].

The significance of fairness in employee attrition prediction cannot be overstated. Predictive models that are not inherently fair can inadvertently perpetuate biases in hiring, promotion, and retention decisions, leading to detrimental consequences for employees and organizations alike [5]. Fairness in attrition prediction empowers organizations to make informed decisions that are equitable, respectful of diversity, and foster a more inclusive work environment [26]. Our research introduces a significant contribution to the field of employee attrition prediction, promoting not only the accuracy of predictions but also the ethical considerations of transparency and fairness in workforce management. Ultimately, we seek to provide organizations with a tool that facilitates more equitable and responsible decision-making in managing their human resources.

The contributions on this study can be summarized as follow:

- We propose a fair machine learning approach for employee attrition, leveraging state-of-the-art techniques while prioritizing interpretability.
- The transparency of our proposed approach is demonstrated through the integration of Local Interpretable Model-agnostic Explanations (LIME).
- Our proposed approach ensures fairness among different groups defined by sensitive features such as gender or age, thereby mitigating disparities.

The rest of this paper is organized as follow: in Sect. 2 we provide an overview of existing machine learning algorithms on employee attrition and fairness. In Sect. 3, we give details of our proposed approach, Sect. 4 we present results of our experiments and conclude in Sect. 5.

2   Related Work

Different authors have conducted studies on predicting employee attrition using machine learning techniques.

In a comparative study conducted by [21], the accuracy and memory utilization of various algorithms for predicting employee turnover were investigated. They applied several classification algorithms including (XGBoost), logistic regression, Naïve Bayesian, RF, and KNN. The study revealed that XGBoost demonstrated superior performance in terms of accuracy and memory utilization.

Authors in [14] conducted another research utilizing XGBoost to predict turnover rates. Their findings indicated that age, gender, marital status, years at the company, job satisfaction, and distance from home were the most significant attributes affecting turnover in the dataset.

In a study by [31], the authors sought to identify the key factors contributing to employee turnover. They discovered a significant correlation between the department and work and found that gender had a significant impact on turnover. Logistic regression was employed to predict turnover with an accuracy of 87.2%.

Sisodia D. et al. [23] have investigated the causes of employee turnover by constructing models using machine learning algorithms. They found that time spent with the company, workload, and promotion were the primary reasons for high employee turnover rates. The models were built using decision tree, support vector machine, Naïve Bayesian, KNN, and RF algorithms.

While the above methods have used classic machine learning to build their models, none of them has addressed the issues of fairness in their predictive models. Transparency and fairness are fundamental principles in employee attrition prediction. While predictive models offer valuable insights into attrition risk, understanding the reasons behind these predictions is vital for building trust and making informed decisions. Recent research by [17] on interpretable machine learning has highlighted the importance of providing explanations for complex model predictions.

Other researchers have previously addressed the notion of fairness in machine learning with a focus on sensitive features [8] that might impact model decisions. According to [8,12], a sensitive feature is a feature that is of particular importance either for social, ethical or legal reasons when making decision. We notice two groups of work around fairness studies.

The first group has revolved around the mathematical elucidation and validation of fairness. Within this trajectory, alternative metrics like statistical parity, divergent impact, and individual equity have been generated as outlined in [4]. Kleinberg Jon et al. have [15] proposed the inclusion of "sensitive" attributes in algorithms as a means to enhance both the fairness and efficiency of models. Additionally, they highlight that currently popular fairness metrics suffer from problematic statistical constraints, potentially leading to adverse consequences for the very groups researchers aim to safeguard.

The other group has focused on the development of algorithms tailored to attain fairness. In the context of divergent impact, Chierichetti Flavio et al. have [4] introduced the concept of sensitive features, a concept that will be instrumental in our paper. The concept of divergent impact has permeated various machine learning problems. For instances of alternative applications, the authors in [29] construct equitable classifiers that strike a balance between maximizing accuracy while adhering to fairness constraints, thereby guaranteeing disparate treatment and divergent impact.

All the above techniques have shown promise for fairness in various domains, including healthcare [2] and other social decisions problems [12]. However, their application to predicting employee attrition remains a relatively unexplored area. Thus, this unexplored area forms the foundation of our study. In the section below, we introduce our proposed approach.

3   FIEAP: Fair and Interpretable Approach

In this section we present our novel strategy of achieving fair and interpretable machine learning predictive model in employee attrition prediction. In the Fig. 1 below, we introduce the different steps (Data Processing and Feature Selection, Bias and Imbalanced Data Mitigation, Model Implementation, and XAI) of our approach to achieve fair and interpretable results. Below, we describe each of these steps.

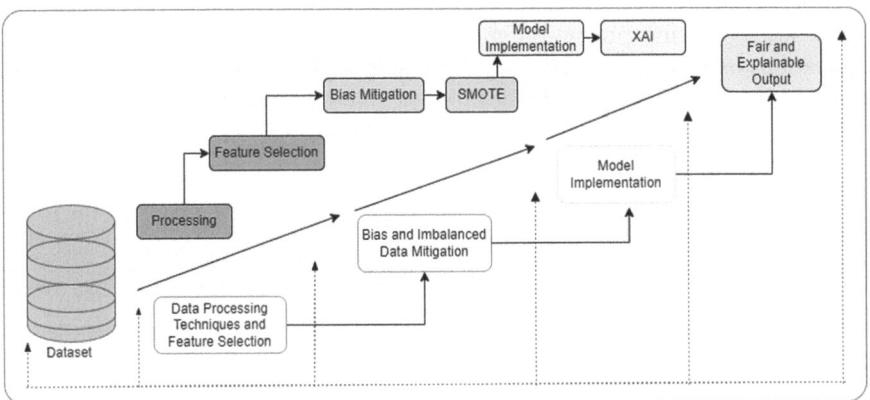

Fig. 1. Different Steps of the Proposed Approach

3.1   Data Processing and Feature Selection

This step involves cleaning, transforming, and organizing our data into a suitable format for subsequent analysis. It addresses challenges such as handling missing values, identifying outliers, and reducing noise within the dataset we are working with. Additionally, in this step, we employ a fair feature selection strategy proposed by Dorleon et al. [9] where sensitive attributes such as gender and age are treated fairly before any algorithm implementation. In their proposed approach, the authors have employed a strategy to ensure that all highly correlated features with the sensitive feature are removed.

3.2 Bias and Imbalanced Data Mitigation - Ensuring Fairness

To mitigate possible bias and imbalanced data in the dataset, we have used the proposed by authors in [10]. In this approach, a fairness-aware strategy based on the use of balanced and stable clusters is used. SMOTE is used to balance the clusters. The strategy involves dividing the input data into K stable clusters, followed by ensuring balance regarding the sensitive feature within each cluster. In cases of imbalance, SMOTE oversampling technique is applied. Once all clusters are balanced, they compute a fairness score. If the fairness score falls within the acceptable range, namely between 0.8 and 1, authors retain the related balanced clusters as they ensure a level of fairness. These balanced clusters are then used to fit the ensemble learning strategy and obtain a meta model.

3.3 Model Implementation

In this step, we employ a stacking strategy [16] for ensemble learning. We adhere to the standard machine learning strategy by dividing our data into training, testing, and validation sets for the model training phase. Initially, we utilize this technique to create a meta-model, which is subsequently employed to generate predictions. Following prediction generation, we provide both local and global explanations using LIME [27] and SHAP [19] thereby enhancing our understanding of the model's decision-making process. Below, we break down the process of the stacking strategy utilized in the model implementation step.

Ensemble Learning - Stacking Strategy: Stacking [16] is an ensemble learning technique that combines multiple meta models to enhance predictive performance.

In our study, we integrate four machine learning algorithms as illustrated in Fig. 2 below: Random Forest, SVM, XGBoost, and Logistic Regression, each producing a model denoted as M. Thus, we have four base algorithms: $M1, M2, M3, M4$.

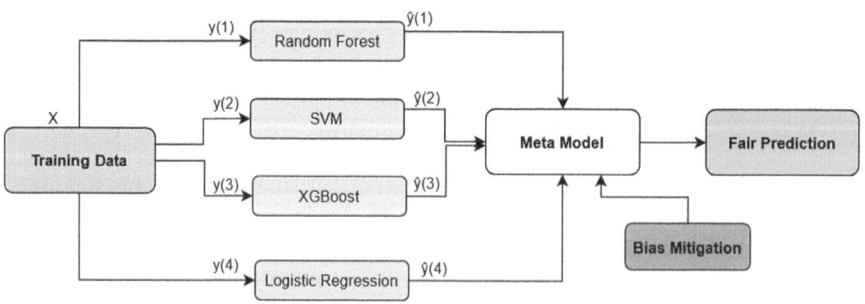

Fig. 2. Ensemble Learning with Stacking Strategy

1. **Training Phase:**
   - We train each meta model on the training data, denoted as X (features) and y (labels). Let's denote the predictions of each meta model as $y^{(1)}, y^{(2)}, y^{(3)}, y^{(4)}$, respectively.
   - Once trained, we obtain predictions from each meta model on the validation set using cross-validation, denoted as X_{val}. The predicted outputs are denoted as $\hat{y}^{(1)}, \hat{y}^{(2)}, \hat{y}^{(3)}, \hat{y}^{(4)}$.
2. **Meta-model Training Phase:**
   - Now, we combine these predictions from the meta models and use them as features for training a meta-model.
   - Let's denote the combined feature matrix from the meta models as X_{meta}, where each row corresponds to a sample in the validation set, and each column corresponds to a meta model's prediction.
   - We also have the true labels y_{val} corresponding to the validation set.
   - We train the meta-model using X_{meta} and y_{val}.
3. **Prediction Phase:**
   - For prediction, we first obtain predictions from each meta model on the test data (unseen data), denoted as $\hat{y}_{\text{test}}^{(1)}, \hat{y}_{\text{test}}^{(2)}, \hat{y}_{\text{test}}^{(3)}, \hat{y}_{\text{test}}^{(4)}$.
   - Similar to the training phase, we combine these predictions to form the feature matrix $X_{\text{test\_meta}}$.
   - We then use this feature matrix as input to the trained meta-model to obtain the final predictions for the test data.

Mathematically, let's represent:
   - $X_{\text{val}} = \{x_{\text{val},i}\}_{i=1}^{N_{\text{val}}}$ as the validation set with N_{val} samples.
   - $y_{\text{val}} = \{y_{\text{val},i}\}_{i=1}^{N_{\text{val}}}$ as the true labels for the validation set.
   - $X_{\text{test}} = \{x_{\text{test},i}\}_{i=1}^{N_{\text{test}}}$ as the test set with N_{test} samples.

Then,
   - For each meta model M_j, $j = 1, 2, 3, 4$: During training:

$$y_{\text{val}}^{(j)} = M_j(X_{\text{val}}) \tag{1}$$

During testing:

$$\hat{y}_{\text{test}}^{(j)} = M_j(X_{\text{test}}) \tag{2}$$

   - Combine predictions for the meta-model:

$$X_{\text{meta}} = \left[\hat{y}^{(1)}, \hat{y}^{(2)}, \hat{y}^{(3)}, \hat{y}^{(4)}\right] \tag{3}$$

$$X_{\text{test\_meta}} = \left[\hat{y}_{\text{test}}^{(1)}, \hat{y}_{\text{test}}^{(2)}, \hat{y}_{\text{test}}^{(3)}, \hat{y}_{\text{test}}^{(4)}\right] \tag{4}$$

   - Train the meta-model:

$$\text{Meta-model: } f_{\text{meta}}(X_{\text{meta}}) = y_{\text{val}}$$

   - Final prediction:

$$\text{During testing: } \hat{y}_{\text{test}} = f_{\text{meta}}(X_{\text{test\_meta}})$$

This process allows our meta-model to learn how to best combine the predictions of the base models to make final predictions on unseen data for our attrition prediction task.

3.4   Model Intepretability

Over the years, algorithms have predominantly focused on exploratory data analysis to aid decision-making processes. While data acquisition and analysis often suffice for informed decisions, there are instances where the need to substantiate decisions based on discernible patterns arises. This is where the significance of Artificial Intelligence (AI) becomes pronounced. Historically, machine learning algorithms have prioritized achieving high precision in results, increasingly relying on black-box algorithms. Consequently, the interpretability of these algorithms, crucial for decision-making, has been limited. This underscores the necessity for the emergence of interpretable algorithms [11]. Thus, in the following sections, we delve into two methods employed for enhancing the interpretability of our models. The choice of employing Local Interpretable Model-agnostic Explanations (LIME) stems from its effectiveness in providing actionable insights into the decision-making process, thereby enhancing the overall interpretability of the models.

LIME for Local Interpretations: LIME is used to provide local explanations for individual predictions made by the meta model. It creates interpretable models (typically linear models) that approximate the behavior of the meta model in the vicinity of a specific instance of interest. Essentially, the explanations rely on local surrogate models. Surrogate models are interpretable models that learn about the predictions of the original model. However, instead of attempting to fit a global surrogate model, LIME focuses on fitting local surrogate models to explain individual predictions [27]. In our approach, the process of using LIME is as follows:

- Choose the instance for which an explanation of the predictions is desired.
- Perturb the dataset and obtain predictions for the new points resulting from the perturbation.
- Weight new samples by their proximity to the instance of interest.
- Fit a weighted and interpretable model (surrogate) on the dataset with the variations.
- Explain the prediction by interpreting the met model.

Mathematically, LIME approximates the behavior of our meta model as follows: Let:

- f_{MM} be the meta model.
- f_{approx} be the linear model created by LIME for local explanation.
- X_{instance} be the instance (employee) for which we want an explanation.
- $w_0, w_1, w_2, ..., w_p$ be the weights of the linear model.
- X_{neighbor} be a perturbed version of the instance X_{instance} with small changes.

LIME constructs the linear model f_{approx} by solving the following optimization problem:

$$\min_{f_{\text{approx}}} L(f_{\text{approx}}, X_{\text{neighbor}}, f_{MM}) + \Omega(f_{\text{approx}}) \tag{5}$$

where:

- $L(f_{\text{approx}}, X_{\text{neighbor}}, f_{MM})$ is a loss function that measures the dissimilarity between $f_{\text{approx}}(X_{\text{neighbor}})$ and $f_{MM}(X_{\text{neighbor}})$.
- $\Omega(f_{\text{approx}})$ is a regularization term to keep the linear model simple.

The optimized linear model f_{approx} provides insights into the local behavior of our meta model near the instance X_{instance}.

4 Experiment

In this section, we present the experiments conducted to predict employee attrition using a real dataset from CPC HR Analytics Employee [18]. Fifteen features including *JobSatisfaction*, *YearsofExperience*, *Degree*, *MaritalStatus*, *Gender*, etc. were used.

We begin by training a meta model and subsequently enhance transparency, interpretability, and fairness through the application of LIME and SHAP. Below we detail on our goal, the dataset used, the experimental approach, and results.

4.1 Goal

We conducted an experimental approach aimed at predicting employee attrition while ensuring fairness and interpretability. Specifically, for the first objective, we employed four machine learning algorithms within an ensemble learning framework utilizing a stacking strategy. For our second objective, we utilized LIME and SHAP techniques to offer explanations for the model outputs, thereby enhancing transparency and interpretability. We recall here that the model was trained on stable, fair, and balanced clusters, as detailed in Sect. 3.2.

4.2 Dataset

Similar to IBM HR Dataset [24], the CPC HR dataset encompasses a range of interesting features to understanding and analyzing various aspects of employee engagement, performance, and retention within the organization. These features as shown on Table 1 include both categorical and numerical variables, offering insights into demographic composition, job roles, work-related behaviors, and compensation structures. Attrition represents the target variable, where 'Yes' indicates that the employee has left the company, and 'No' indicates that they are still with the company. Feature like gender shows a distribution of 52% males and 48% females in the dataset. Since this dataset is from an internal data collection process, there were no missing values. In terms of data points, we have observed three thousands rows in the dataset.

Table 1. CPC HR Dataset - Features List

Features		
Age	Marital Status	Monthly Income
Attrition	Business Travel	Monthly Rate
Daily Rate	Number of Companies Worked	Department
Distance from Home	Over Time	Percent Salary Hike
Education	Performance Rating	Education Field
Employee Count	Standard Hours	Stock Option
Environment Satisfaction	Total Working Years	Gender
Hourly Rate	Year Since Last Promotion	Work Life Balance
Job Involvement	Years at Company	Job Level
Job Role	Years in Current Role	Job Satisfaction
Job Satisfaction	Years with Current Manager	

4.3   Predicting Employee Attrition

As discussed in Sect. 3.3 above, we have used an ensemble learning with fours ML base models in a stacking strategy. A primary evaluation of these ML algorithms is being conducted, and results are presented in Table 2. Each base model was assessed through a cross-validation process (K-fold), evaluating metrics such as receiver operating characteristic (ROC), area under the curve (AUC), and mean accuracy were used. This approach provides an initial insight into determining the meta model that will be used for the explanation of the main results.

Table 2. Base Algorithms ML after bias and imbalanced data mitigation

Algorithm	ROC AUC Mean	Accuracy Mean
XGBoost	79.23	85.91
Random Forest	79.20	85.81
SVM	80.78	83.87
Logistic Regression	81.20	75.90
Meta Model	80.35	84.96

In the Table 2 above, we present the results obtained with the base models and our meta model. In Table 3a, we present the results for the meta-model before implementing bias mitigation techniques, while Table 3b displays the outcomes after the application of mitigation strategies. Furthermore, in Fig. 3, we provide the Receiver Operating Characteristic/Area Under the Curve (ROC/AUC) scores for the meta-model employed in predicting attrition.

As observed above, the improvement in recall for the 'Attrition = Yes' category is noteworthy, rising significantly from 0.25 to 0.65. However, there is a slight

Table 3. Comparison of results before and after bias mitigation

(a) Results before bias and imbalanced mitigation			(b) Results after bias and imbalanced mitigation		
Attrition	Precision	Recall	Attrition	Precision	Recall
Yes	0.86	0.25	Yes	0.47	0.65
No	0.87	0.99	No	0.93	0.86

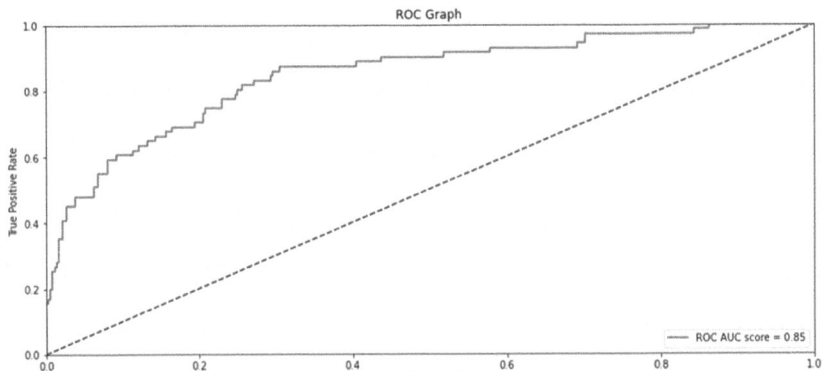

Fig. 3. Meta Model ROC/AUC after bias and imbalance data mitigation

decline in the recall value for the 'Attrition = No' category, decreasing from 0.99 to 0.86. Our primary focus is on accurately predicting employee attrition, prioritizing the identification of those who are likely to leave, even at the expense of occasionally misclassifying employees who ultimately remain. Notably, the ROC/AUC value has increased from 79.23 (as shown in Table 6) to 0.85 (84.96), indicating enhanced predictive performance specifically for 'Attrition = Yes'. This improvement reflects a substantial enhancement in the model's ability to identify employees likely to leave the company. The subsequent step involves conducting an interpretability analysis, recognizing that XGBoost, being a black-box algorithm, requires further examination to elucidate its decision-making process.

4.4   Model Explainability

Below, we provide a practical application of the models detailed in Sect. 3.4.

Interpretability with LIME: It generates locally faithful explanations by selecting a data point and constructing a dataset of similar yet slightly perturbed instances. It then utilizes a simpler and interpretable surrogate model, such as linear regression, to elucidate the predictions of the complex model within the vicinity of the chosen data point. This technique proves valuable for comprehending the factors influencing specific predictions.

For example, in Fig. 4, the forecast for an employee remaining with the company (attrition = 'No') achieves 100% certainty for the chosen subject in

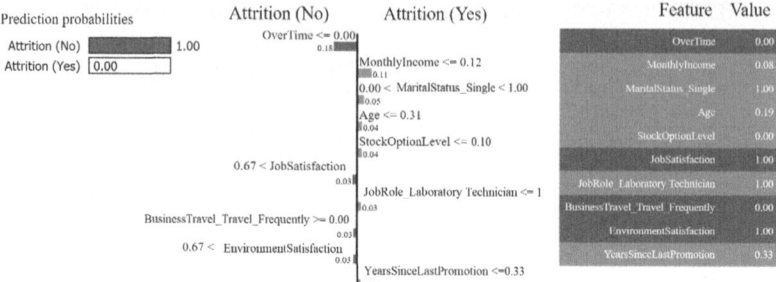

Fig. 4. Local Attrition Prediction for 'No'

the sample, while in Fig. 5, the estimation for an employee departing the company (attrition = 'Yes') is approximately 77%, aligning with the departure of an employee who indeed left the company. LIME provides local interpretable model-agnostic explanations by analyzing the most relevant features determining employee attrition ('Yes' or 'No').

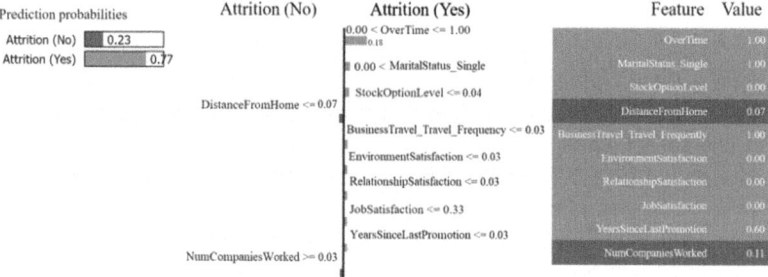

Fig. 5. Local Attrition Prediction for 'Yes'

4.5   Discussion

The proposed approach, FIEAP, sheds light on the importance of integrating AI into business environments, especially those focusing on personnel management. Indeed, the ability to interpret predictions facilitates the prompt identification of risk factors associated with attrition and enables proactive mitigation measures. The use of LIME enhances transparency by offering local insights into how the model generates predictions. Understanding the model's behavior allows us to identify and address fairness concerns, ensuring that attrition predictions are fair and free from gender bias. To our knowledge, this is the first study to employ a machine learning approach to tackle fairness issues in attrition prediction studies.

In our research, we introduce several novel contributions:

- Our study presents a comprehensive framework tailored specifically for integrating interpretability into the machine learning pipeline within the human resources domain. This framework includes a fairness strategy that addresses bias and imbalanced data.
- Our approach represents an advancement in decision-making in HR by leveraging machine learning models, fairness, and interpretability techniques to inform decisions regarding employee attrition. Understanding the influential factors contributing to attrition can guide HR strategies, ultimately improving the retention of valuable employees and fostering a more productive work environment.
- Our study underscores the significance of identifying key factors linked to employee attrition. Through developed models and interpretability, we highlight variables that significantly influence attrition, enabling organizations to proactively design targeted retention and recruitment strategies.

5 Conclusion

In conclusion, this paper introduces FIEAP, a machine learning approach aimed at addressing the critical issue of employee attrition prediction while emphasizing fairness and interpretability. Our approach utilizes an ensemble learning model with a stacking strategy, enhancing transparency and fairness through the use of LIME (Local Interpretable Model-Agnostic Explanations). We evaluated FIEAP using a real-life HR Employee Analytics dataset, assessing its performance in terms of prediction accuracy, fairness metrics, and feature importance.

The results of our study demonstrate the potential of FIEAP to provide clear and understandable explanations while ensuring fairness in attrition predictions. By leveraging LIME, we gain valuable insights into how the model considers critical features in both individual predictions and overall feature importance. This approach enables us to identify and address biases in attrition predictions, ensuring that our model produces equitable results.

Moreover, to enhance transparency and reproducibility in our research, we have made both the dataset and the code for FIEAP available on GitHub. We believe that open access to these resources will facilitate collaboration, further research, and practical applications that prioritize fairness and transparency in predictive analytics.

References

1. Barocas, S., Hardt, M., Narayanan, A.: Fairness and machine learning (2019). http://fairmlbook.org/
2. Caruana, R., et al.: Intelligible models for healthcare: predicting pneumonia risk and hospital 30-day readmission. In: Proceedings of the 21st ACM SIGKDD International Conference on Knowledge Discovery and Data Mining (2015)

3. Chen, J., Song, L., Wainwright, M.J., Jordan, M.I.: Learning to explain: an information-theoretic perspective on model interpretation. In: Proceedings of the 35th International Conference on Machine Learning (2018)

4. Chierichetti, F., Kumar, R., Lattanzi, S., Vassilvitskii, S.: Fair clustering through fairlets. In: Advances in Neural Information Processing Systems (NeurIPS), pp. 5029–5037 (2017)

5. Chouldechova, A.: Fair prediction with disparate impact: a study of bias in recidivism prediction instruments. Big Data 5(2), 153–163 (2017)

6. Datta, A., Sen, S., Zick, Y.: Algorithmic transparency via quantitative input influence: theory and experiments with learning systems. In: Proceedings of the 2016 IEEE Symposium on Security and Privacy (2016)

7. Deb, S.: Employee attrition prediction using machine learning: a review and analysis. In: 2019 IEEE/WIC/ACM International Conference on Web Intelligence (WI) (2019)

8. Dorleon, G.: Mitigation of Data Bias through Fair Features Selection Methods. Ph.D. thesis, Paul Sabatier. Université Toulouse III-Paul Sabatier (UPS), Toulouse, FRA. (2023)

9. Dorleon, G., Megdiche, I., Bricon-Souf, N., Teste, O.: Feature selection under fairness and performance constraints. In: Wrembel, R., Gamper, J., Kotsis, G., Tjoa, A.M., Khalil, I. (eds) International Conference on Big Data Analytics and Knowledge Discovery, pp. 125–130. Springer, Cham(2022). https://doi.org/10.1007/978-3-031-12670-3_11

10. Dorleon, G., Megdiche, I., Bricon-Souf, N., Teste, O.: FAPFID: a fairness-aware approach for protected features and imbalanced data. In: Hameurlain, A., Tjoa, A.M. (eds) Transactions on Large-Scale Data-and Knowledge-Centered Systems LIII, pp. 107–125. Springer, Berlin, Heidelberg (2023). https://doi.org/10.1007/978-3-662-66863-4_5

11. Dwivedi, R., et al.: Explainable AI (XAI): core ideas, techniques, and solutions. ACM Comput. Surv. 55(9), 1–33 (2023)

12. Fang, B., Jiang, M., Cheng, P.y., Shen, J., Fang, Y.: Achieving outcome fairness in machine learning models for social decision problems. In: IJCAI, pp. 444–450 (2020)

13. Hardt, M., Price, E., Srebro, N.: Equality of opportunity in supervised learning. In: Advances in Neural Information Processing Systems, vol. 29 (2016)

14. Jain, R., Nayyar, A.: Predicting employee attrition using XGBoost machine learning approach. In: Proceedings of the International Conference on System Modeling & Advancement in Research Trends, pp. 113–120 (2018)

15. Kleinberg, J., Mullainathan, S., Raghavan, M.: Inherent trade-offs in the fair determination of risk scores. arXiv preprint arXiv:1609.05807 (2016)

16. Koopialipoor, M., Asteris, P.G., Mohammed, A.S., Alexakis, D.E., Mamou, A., Armaghani, D.J.: Introducing stacking machine learning approaches for the prediction of rock deformation. Transp. Geotech. 34, 100756 (2022)

17. Lundberg, S.M., et al.: From local explanations to global understanding with explainable AI for trees. In: Advances in Neural Information Processing Systems (2020)

18. Ajmal, M.S., Deshpande, T., Data Scientists, I.: IBM HR analytics employee attrition & performance (2023). https://doi.org/10.21227/2m1g-6v47

19. Mangalathu, S., Hwang, S.H., Jeon, J.S.: Failure mode and effects analysis of RC members based on machine-learning-based Shapley additive explanations (SHAP) approach. Eng. Struct. 219, 110927 (2020)

20. Obermeyer, Z., Powers, B., Vogeli, C., Mullainathan, S.: Dissecting racial bias in an algorithm used to manage the health of populations. Science **366**(6464), 447–453 (2019)
21. Punnoose, R., Ajit, P.: Prediction of employee turnover in organizations using machine learning algorithm. Int. J. Adv. Res. Artif. Intell. **5**(9), 22–26 (2016)
22. Sangroya, A., Rastogi, M., Anantaram, C., Vig, L.: Guided-LIME: structured sampling based hybrid approach towards explaining BlackBox machine learning models. In: CIKM (Workshops) (2020)
23. Sisodia, D., Vishwakarma, S., Pujahari, A.: Evaluation of machine learning models for employee churn prediction. In: Proceedings of International Conference on Inventive Computing and Informatics, pp. 1016–1020. Coimbatore, India (2017)
24. Subhash, P.: IBM HR analytics employee. https://www.kaggle.com/pavansub hasht/ibm-hr-analytics-attrition-dataset
25. Tan, Z., Tian, Y., Li, J.: GLIME: general, stable and local lime explanation. In: Advances in Neural Information Processing Systems, vol. 36 (2024)
26. Verma, S., Rubin, J.: Fairness definitions explained. In: Proceedings of the 2018 ACM Conference on Fairness, Accountability, and Transparency (2018)
27. Visani, G., Bagli, E., Chesani, F., Poluzzi, A., Capuzzo, D.: Statistical stability indices for lime: obtaining reliable explanations for machine learning models. J. Oper. Res. Soc. **73**(1), 91–101 (2022)
28. Yasin, M., Aris, H., Romli, R.: Predicting employee attrition with machine learning approach: a case study in manufacturing company. In: 2018 International Conference on Information and Communication Technology for the Muslim World (ICT4M) (2018)
29. Zafar, M.B., Valera, I., Rodriguez, M.G., Gummadi, K.P.: Fairness constraints: mechanisms for fair classification. arXiv preprint arXiv:1507.05259 (2015)
30. Zemel, R., Wu, Y., Swersky, K., Pitassi, T., Dwork, C., et al.: Learning fair representations. In: Proceedings of the 30th International Conference on Machine Learning (ICML-13) (2013)
31. Zhang, H., Xu, L., Cheng, X., Chao, K., Zhao, X.: Analysis and prediction of employee turnover characteristics based on machine learning. In: Proceedings of the 18th International Symposium on Communications and Information Technologies, pp. 371–376. Bangkok, Thailand (2018)

HOCON34k: A Corpus of Hate Speech in Online Comments from German Newspapers

Max-Emanuel Keller[1(✉)] ⓘ, Maximilian Auch[1] ⓘ, Alexander Döschl[1] ⓘ,
Fabian Vlk[2], Julian Quernheim[2] ⓘ, Mike Hartmann[3], Peter Mandl[1] ⓘ,
Alexander Kaul[2], and Markus Franz[3]

[1] HM Hochschule München University of Applied Sciences, Munich, Germany
{Max-Emanuel.Keller,Maximilian.Auch,Alexander.Doschl,Peter.Mandl}@hm.edu
[2] BIVAL GmbH, Ingolstadt, Germany
{Fabian.Vlk,Julian.Quernheim,Alexander.Kaul}@bival.de
[3] Ippen Digital GmbH & Co. KG, Munich, Germany
{Mike.Hartmann,Markus.Franz}@ippen-digital.de

Abstract. We present a dataset of 34,223 comments in German,
authored by users of online platforms associated with public discourse in
German newspapers. Each comment was annotated for hate speech and
the adequacy of contextual information by 29 volunteers using a binary
annotation scheme. The inter-rater reliability for hate speech, measured
by Fleiss' Kappa, is 0.4428 across all annotators, improving to 0.6078
when focusing on an optimized subset of 12 annotators. Additionally,
we provide a baseline text classification using BERT, which achieved an
MCC-score of up to 0.32 and an F_2-score of up to 0.64 in initial experiments with this corpus. The dataset, named HOCON34k, comprising
German hate speech comments from newspapers, is publicly available
for research purposes.

Keywords: Hate speech · BERT · corpus · dataset · German
newspaper

1 Introduction

Online news portals are key platforms for public discourse. Ensuring civility
and preventing hate speech is essential to fostering constructive dialogue and
encouraging the exchange of diverse viewpoints-both of which are fundamental
to a pluralistic society. Additionally, the recognition and removal of hate speech
is critical for complying with legal frameworks that govern online content.

In Germany, the Network Enforcement Act (NEA) mandates that social
media platforms with more than 2 million users remove *clearly criminal content*
within 24 h of receiving a complaint. Although the General Equal Treatment
Act (AGG) primarily addresses discrimination, it complements hate speech regulations by establishing guidelines to combat discriminatory practices in various

P. Delir Haghighi et al. (Eds.): iiWAS 2024, LNCS 15342, pp. 212–226, 2025.
https://doi.org/10.1007/978-3-031-78090-5_18

sectors, including online communication. Furthermore, Sect. 130 of the German Criminal Code criminalizes incitement to hatred and insults that violate human dignity based on racial, national, religious, or ethnic origins. It also includes provisions against Holocaust denial and Neo-Nazi propaganda. These legal measures underscore Germanys commitment to balancing freedom of expression with the protection of individuals and groups from hate speech, thus supporting a pluralistic and democratic society.

Given the legal requirements, the automatic detection of hate speech is vital for online discussion platforms to meet both the goals of open discourse and regulatory compliance. With the Digital Services Act (DSA) [5] now in effect, online platforms face even greater responsibility for content moderation, necessitating the use of advanced intelligent systems.

To evaluate comments from online newspaper platforms for hate speech, annotated texts are required as a training resource that categorize each comment as either hate speech or not. Unfortunately, there are limited German-language corpora that feature newspaper comments annotated for hate speech [1,10,14,18]. To address this gap, we created a new corpus, **H**ate speech in **O**nline **C**omments from German **N**ewspapers of around 34,000 comments (HOCON34k). The comments, written in German, were sourced from seven online platforms. The annotation process was carried out by 29 volunteers who assessed each comment for both hate speech and the presence of enough context for a fairly confident rating of hate speech. The HOCON34k dataset supports the training of classifiers to detect hate speech in new texts. Our goal is to develop a robust framework for identifying hate speech in user comments on newspaper platforms. Additionally, the corpus has broader potential for applications in natural language processing (NLP) and text classification. For this reason, we have made the dataset publicly available to the scientific community.

In this paper, we make the following contributions:

- We position our research within the context of related work in Sect. 2.
- We provide our definition of hate speech (Sect. 3) and describe the characteristics of our dataset (Sect. 4).
- We detail our methodology and the hate speech annotation process in Sect. 5.
- We discuss the optimization of inter-rater reliability in Sect. 6.
- We present a baseline text classification of hate speech using a fine-tuned BERT model in Sect. 7 and review the results in Sect. 8.
- Finally, we release the dataset to the scientific community in Sect. 9.

2   Related Work

Creating corpora is essential for detecting hate speech. These corpora serve as training and evaluation data for machine learning models designed to identify hate speech and also act as benchmarks for comparing different studies. Consequently, there are numerous related works in the field of hate speech classification that utilize data from various sources (e.g., social media) and in multiple languages. A comprehensive review [24] analyzed a total of 63 hate speech datasets, which are cataloged on hatespeechdata.com. They discovered that 25 datasets include English texts, while only four include German texts. On average, these datasets contain about 8,000 texts, with approximately 36.7 % classified as abusive. We focus on datasets relevant to the two main aspects of our work: hateful texts in German and comment sections of newspapers as a source.

The dataset presented by [17] consists of 469 anti-refugee hate posts in German from Twitter during the European refugee crisis. Another dataset by [2] includes around 6,000 German Facebook posts featuring anti-foreigner comments, annotated for the strength and target of the statements, with about 11 % classified as abusive. For the GermEval 2018 task focused on identifying offensive statements, [25] provided a dataset comprising 8,500 German posts from Twitter, annotated for the presence (binary) and intensity of offensive statements, with roughly 34 % of the texts deemed abusive. In GermEval 2019, [22] published a dataset with 8,541 German posts from Twitter that cover various political orientations and topics, with 33.81 % classified as abusive. In GermEval 2021, [16] published over 4,188 Facebook user comments from a German political talk show, with about 36 % identified as toxic. Additionally, [13] contributed a dataset containing about 4,500 German posts from Twitter and Facebook, annotated for the presence and severity of hate speech or offensive content, with approximately 24 % being abusive. [4] supplied a dataset of 10,000 German posts from Twitter, annotated for hate speech, sentiment, and various other categories, with around 10.85 % of the posts classified as abusive. [8] provide a dataset with 10,996 German texts, with 42.4 % labeled as hate speech. Another dataset by [7] includes 7,061 German posts from Twitter and Facebook, with 22.29 % classified as abusive and 6.51 % as misogynistic.

To the best of our knowledge, there are only a few datasets specifically focused on detecting hate speech in German newspaper comments. Three of them originate from the Austrian newspaper DerStandard. The One Million Post Corpus [18] is a collection of one million comments, with 11,773 of them classified into seven categories. The second dataset [10] contains 8,000 comments labeled on sexism and misogyny. A third one [14] consists of 4,562 user comments annotated for offensiveness. Additionally, [1] provided a dataset of 85,000 German posts from the newspaper Rheinische Post, annotated for the presence and type of offensive language, with about 8.4 % of the posts classified as abusive. There are similar efforts to detect abusive language in newspaper comments in other languages, including Croatian [19,20], Danish [21], Estonian [19] and Latvian [15]. This highlights the widespread issue of hate in newspaper comments across different languages and countries, underscoring the importance and relevance of efforts like ours to detect and eliminate hate speech in this setting.

3   Hate Speech Definition

Our definition of hate speech is based on the hate-related guidelines outlined in the *Netiquette* [23], a publisher-wide usage policy that governs interactions within the comment sections of IPPEN newspapers. In brief, any comment is classified as hate speech if it contains:

- Racist and xenophobic content (e.g., religious hatred, antisemitism, or other misanthropic statements),
- Sexism or homophobia (hostility towards women, men, or queer individuals),
- Anti-constitutional or extremist content,
- Profanity or vulgar, obscene, and offensive language,
- Insults, or
- Threats and harassment.

When assessing comments, we also considered the target of the criticism. For example, vulgar language directed at organizations or legal entities such as companies or associations was judged less harshly than language aimed at individuals or groups of private persons.

Annotating hate speech requires a careful, nuanced, and context-aware approach. Despite strict annotation guidelines, many newspaper comments defied clear categorization. Below, we present examples from our dataset to illustrate the challenges annotators faced and how difficult it can be to annotate borderline cases.

A lack of context often complicates the annotation of certain texts. For instance, the comments shown in Table 1 could be interpreted either as insults or as neutral questions. While the annotator of post 617690717 could not be certain the question wasnt serious, the annotator of post 3819334885 believed the question about sexual orientation was used offensively.

Table 1. Missing context

Post id	Label	Text (original)	Text (translated)
617690717	Not Hate speech (not enough context)	Inzest??	Incest??
3819334885	Hate speech (not enough context)	Sind Sie auch transsexuell?	Are you also transsexual?

Subjective perceptions of speech and expression vary significantly, influencing how texts are interpreted. What one person might find offensive or hateful, another may perceive as harmless or even humorous. The two comments in

Table 2. Subjective perception of speech

Post id	Label	Text (original)	Text (translated)
1744989649	Not Hate speech (enough context)	Umbennen könnte er den Song auch mit 'I've been looking for strong liquor' ...	He could also rename the song I've been looking for strong liquor ...
2288235147	Hate speech (enough context)	Grad der alte Hässler. Der taugt doch nur zum Wasserträger vom Michael Skibbe😀😀😀	Especially old Hässler. He's only good as Michael Skibbe's water carrier😀😀😀

Table 2, for example, could be seen as humorous or as cheeky football jargon, but they could just as easily be interpreted as discriminatory towards people struggling with alcoholism or older individuals.

German migration policy is a frequently discussed topic within our dataset, and it can be difficult to distinguish between fringe political opinions and harmful, racist statements (see Table 3). This challenge is partly due to the frequent lack of context, but also because xenophobia is often cleverly paraphrased, making it harder to identify through specific wording. Ultimately, the annotators personal political and moral perspective plays a significant role in the classification of such comments.

Table 3. Hidden xenophobia

Post id	Label	Text (original)	Text (translated)
2415423662	Not Hate speech (enough context)	So werden eben Probleme in anderen Ländern gelöst ...	This is how problems are solved in other countries ...
949223179	Hate speech (enough context)	Asylbewerber, ist das das neue Wort für Wirtschaftsflüchtlinge?	Asylum seekers, is that the new word for economic migrants?

4 Dataset

The dataset comprises comments written in German by readers of newspapers, sourced from seven online platforms in Germany. These platforms include TZ, fr-online.de, DA-imNetz, Kreiszeitung, come-on.de, BGLand24.de and Rosenheim24.de. Initially, we selected 60,077 comments for annotation. Given that a random selection would likely contain only a small proportion of actual hate comments, this would have resulted in a significant annotation effort. To create a more balanced dataset with a higher proportion of hate speech, we applied a combination of targeted selection criteria.

A preliminary analysis of the sample revealed that the comments still visible on the websites contained very little hate speech, as expected. However, among the comments deleted by community managers, hate speech accounted for roughly 36 % of the total, along with other violations such as spam and advertising. Based on this observation, we selected 90 % of the deleted comments and 10 % of the undeleted ones. We also ensured that the number of comments selected from each newspaper was proportional to the overall volume of comments from all sources.

To minimize the reading effort, only comments with a length of 500 characters or less were included. Each comment consists of an ID and its corresponding text. Before annotation, the text was preprocessed for future classification tasks: HTML elements were removed, special characters were converted to ASCII, and URLs were enclosed in parentheses e.g., "(https://www.google.de)", while emoticons and emojis were retained. To ensure anonymity, all user references were replaced with "[user]".

5 Annotation

A total of 29 volunteers from the three institutions involved in this work assisted in the annotation process, which was conducted over four months (January to April 2023). The annotation was carried out in three consecutive phases, following a procedure that has proven reliable in previous studies [7,9] before. Volunteers evaluated two aspects of each comment: the presence of hate speech and the presence of enough context for a fairly confident rating of hate speech. This allowed the volunteers to assign one of the following four labels to each comment: *Hate speech (enough context), Not Hate speech (enough context), Hate speech (not enough context), Not Hate speech (not enough context)*.

During Phase 1, the volunteers met to discuss and review 19 comments. For each comment, they read the text and assigned labels based on the availability of hate speech and context. If there were disagreements on how to assess either aspect, the group discussed the issue until a consensus was reached. This approach helped establish a shared understanding of how to apply the annotation criteria.

Phase 2 aimed to determine whether the volunteers were consistently applying the same standards. To validate this, each volunteer independently annotated the same randomly selected set of 52 comments, using the rules established in Phase 1. The results were then analyzed to assess the uniformity of the annotations, with Fleiss Kappa [6] used to measure inter-rater reliability. The agreement for all volunteers was $\kappa = 0.4428$ for hate speech, representing a moderate [11] agreement, and $\kappa = 0.0917$ for the context, which indicated only slight agreement.

In the final Phase 3, the 29 volunteers annotated additional 34,223 randomly selected comments. Due to the solid inter-rater reliability, each comment was annotated by only one volunteer, without the need for multiple evaluations.

Table 4 summarizes the details of the annotation process across the three phases, including the total number of annotations, the number of unique comments, and the average number of annotations per volunteer. A total 34,294 comments were labeled during the entire process. Of these, 71 unique comments were used in Phases 1 and 2 to train the volunteers and calculate inter-rater reliability, so their annotations are not guaranteed to be of high quality. Phase 3, in contrast, involved the annotation of 34,223 additional comments, which form the core of the dataset due to the quality of their labels.

Table 4. Phases of the annotation process

		Number of annotations	
Phase	Comments	Total	Per volunteer
1	19	19	-
2	52	1,508	52
3	34,223	34,223	∅ 1,556

Table 5 shows the distribution of comments across the different classes. The majority of comments, 84.7 %, were labeled as not hate speech. The criterion for determining whether there was enough context for the evaluation of hate speech depended significantly on the hate speech rating itself. For non-hate speech comments, sufficient context was identified in 83.0 % of cases, whereas for hate speech comments, sufficient context was identified only 63.1 % of the time. This suggests that the presence of sufficient context is more often considered critical when classifying hate speech, whereas it is less frequently a concern for non-hate speech comments, where it is almost always assumed to be sufficient.

Table 5. Number of comments per class in 34,223 comments

	Comments	Percent
Not hate speech	28,992	84.7%
- Not enough context	4,922	17.0%
- Enough context	24,070	83.0%
Hate speech	5,231	15.3%
- Not enough context	1,932	36.9%
- Enough context	3,299	63.1%
Not enough context	6,854	20.0%
Enough context	27,369	80.0%

6   Inter-rater Reliability Optimization

The inter-rater reliability observed in Phase 2 underscores the difficulty of achieving a consistent understanding of hate speech across a large group of annotators. We found that the Fleiss Kappa score can be improved by reducing the size of the annotator group. The main challenge lies in identifying the annotators whose interpretations of hate speech are most aligned with the desired understanding. To address this, we compared the annotation behavior of all annotators with the assessments made by a lead expert. This expert, with extensive experience in the field and a rigorous evaluation process, served as the benchmark. In our case, the lead expert was a community manager from a large publishing group, who regularly screens and moderates a high volume of user comments.

We used the results from Phase 2 to compare the annotators' understanding of hate speech with the expert's judgments. For each annotator, we calculated their pairwise inter-rater reliability with the expert. A threshold was then applied, where only the annotations from those achieving a $\kappa \geq 0.61$ with the lead expert were retained. This threshold was met by twelve annotators. As a result, the overall Fleiss Kappa score for the group increased from $\kappa = 0.4428$ (moderate agreement) to $\kappa = 0.6078$ (substantial agreement) as shown in Fig. 1a. While this method improved inter-rater reliability, it also reduced the amount of annotated data. However, previous tests indicated that models trained on this filtered dataset benefited from the increased agreement rate. The final dataset, comprising 15,358 comments (see Fig. 1b), strikes an effective balance between data quality and quantity for our application.

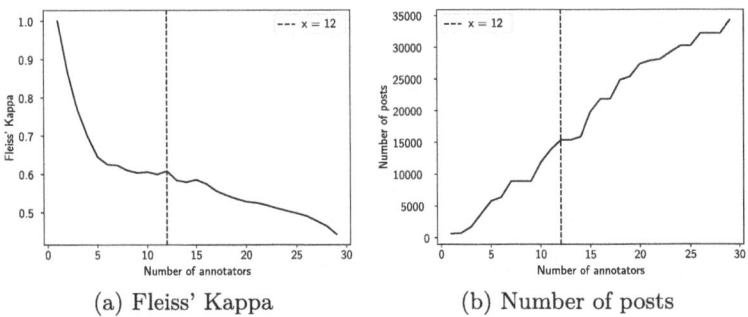

(a) Fleiss' Kappa   (b) Number of posts

Fig. 1. Annotator group size for inter-rater reliability optimization

7   Experiments

Based on the 34,223 annotated comments, we trained and evaluated first baseline models that classify new texts according to our definition of hate speech. It is a binary classification characterized by the fact that each comment is assigned to one out of two classes, which in our case represent *hate speech* and *not hate speech*. The second criterion *context* only serves as a filter. If we are interested in comments that the annotator felt confident about, we can limit the selection to those with *enough context*. Otherwise, we can also include the ones with *not enough context*. We do not filter by context in the following, as preliminary classification results did not differ significantly between including and excluding comments with *not enough context*.

As features of the classification, only the text of the comments was used, while other attributes of the comment, such as the author, online platform of the newspaper and time of publication were not taken into account. We used a pre-trained BERT model [3] with a classification layer on top and fine-tuned it with our training dataset. The process was conducted with a learning-rate of 3×10^{-3}, a batch size of 64 and the AdamW optimizer [12].

For the evaluation of the models, the corpus of 34,223 comments was split by 0.8 into a training set and by 0.1 each into a validation and test set. Since the dataset is imbalanced, we applied a random oversampling to the training set. This training set was then used to train the classifier while tuning the hyperparameter by testing the fine-tuned models against the validation set. Finally the classifier was evaluated with the test set. In order to further explore the generalizability of the classifier, we extended the test set with additional comments from another dataset on German hate speech [7].

The results of the baseline classification are given in Table 6. The results include standard metrics such as Precision, Recall, F_1, F_2, MCC, as well as a custom score S, on which we optimized the threshold to during the validation. The custom score addresses the goals of our project, which aims to automate the comparison and selection of proven machine learning (ML) models using a champion-challenger approach. This approach makes it possible to benchmark a current leading model - called the champion - against new models - called the challengers - in order to continuously identify and deploy the best performing model. To this end, we have developed the custom score that is as robust as possible and tailored to the use case. This score serves as a benchmark for objectively comparing the performance of the models, in order to ensure a reliable and transparent selection process. For the moderation of online newspapers, as a specific use case of our work, it is crucial to identify hate speech in comments with a high degree of certainty in order to be able to eliminate it shortly after publication. Actual hate speech, which the model correctly classifies as such, represents a true positive case. We prefer to filter strictly, which might result in False Positives, i.e. comments that are not hate speech are falsely classified as hate speech. This deviates from the often used F_1-score, which is a balanced measure combining recall and precision with equal weighting. Since recall is more important in our case, as it measures the degree to which actual hate speech texts are correctly recognized (true positives), it is weighted more significantly. Hence, the F_2-score in Equation (1) is more suitable because it weights the recall above the precision.

$$F_2 = \frac{(1+2)^2 \cdot TP}{(1+2)^2 \cdot TP + FP + 2^2 \cdot FN} \tag{1}$$

For binary classifiers, the Matthews Correlation Coefficient (MCC) can also be used, which reflects a balanced picture of the overall performance of a classifier. In order to reduce the bias in our champion-challenger procedure, we use a composite metric S shown in Equation (2), that combines the F_2-score, calculated in a binary fashion, and MCC.

$$S = \frac{M^{norm} + F_2^{binary}}{2} \tag{2}$$

Possible values of our metric S lie in the value range $[0; 1]$, whereby a higher value indicates better quality. The values of both input metrics must also lie within this interval. While F_2-score is already in the interval $[0; 1]$, the MCC falls within the interval $[-1; 1]$, which requires normalization of MCC as M^{norm}, as shown in Equation (3).

$$M^{norm} = \frac{MCC - (-1)}{1 - (-1)} = \frac{MCC + 1}{2} \tag{3}$$

As part of our champion-challenger approach, it must be ensured that allegedly improved models are not automatically taken productive if the performance of their classification shows strong deviations between the metrics F_2 and MCC. This a situation might occur, for example, if the model tends extremely in the direction of hate speech and thus achieves a good recall, which in turn leads to an increased F_2-score. The MCC is typically worse in such a case, but does not always fully compensate for the increased F_2-score. In such a case, the calculated score S can be misleading. Therefore, we recommend a conservative approach that follows the conditions of Equation (4). It states that a challenger model b is only suggested over the current champion model a if its value S_b is greater than that of the champion model S_a. In addition, both the normalized MCC (M_b^{norm}) and the F_2-score ($F_{2,b}$) must be at least equal to or better than that of the champion model.

$$V(S_a, S_b) = \begin{cases} S_b, & \text{if } S_b > S_a \text{ and } M_b^{norm} \geq M_a^{norm} \text{ and } F_{2,b} \geq F_{2,a} \\ S_a, & \text{else} \end{cases} \tag{4}$$

Since this custom score S is an important part of the given use case, this metric was used during training to select the best model out of all epochs. Additionally, this metric was used to optimize the threshold against the validation set. Table 6 provides the optimized threshold for each fine-tuned BERT model as well as the evaluation results on the test dataset for both. To get further insights, the confusion matrix of each model on the test dataset is provided in Fig. 2. Both matrizes show that an optimization of the threshold against the custom score leads to a larger amount of false negatives. Because of the proposed custom score it is an expected result.

Table 6. Results of the baseline classification (29 experts vs. 12 experts)

Model	Samples					Metrics (Test)					
	Total	Train.	Valid.	Test	Thresh.	Prec.	Rec.	F_1	F_2	MCC	S
BERT model (29 experts)	34,223	27,378	3,422	3,423	0.513	0.269	0.792	0.401	0.570	0.291	0.608
BERT model (12 experts)	15,358	12,275	1,491	1,592	0.523	0.327	0.851	0.472	0.644	0.320	0.652

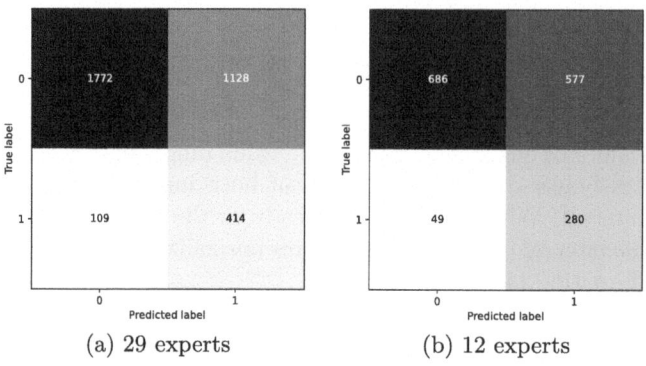

(a) 29 experts   (b) 12 experts

Fig. 2. Confusion matrizes of both models

Furthermore, the ROC curves in Fig. 3 show the comparison of the true positive rates (sensitivity or recall) on the y-axis against the false positive rate (1-specificity) on the x-axis at various threshold settings for each model. The closer the ROC curve is to the top-left corner, the higher the true positive rate and the lower the false positive rate, indicating better performance. Both curves approach the top-left corner, indicating balance of sensitivity and specificity.

8   Discussion and Limitations

A major challenge in annotating hate speech comments is the role of context. While some comments can be clearly annotated in isolation, others require context for accurate interpretation, particularly when sarcasm, irony, or controversial topics are involved, as discussed in Sect. 3. To address this, we plan to include the associated article text in future annotations and classification tasks to provide more context.

In Sect. 6, we described how filtering the annotated data improved inter-rater reliability. By comparing individual annotators' reliability with that of a lead expert, we removed all annotations from annotators whose kappa value fell below a certain threshold. This approach significantly increased inter-rater reliability while moderately reducing the dataset size. We assumed that the lead experts interpretation of hate speech was definitive, which may have introduced some potential bias.

The annotation process was completed over a short period of four months, ensuring that the annotations reflect current social norms and ethics, which

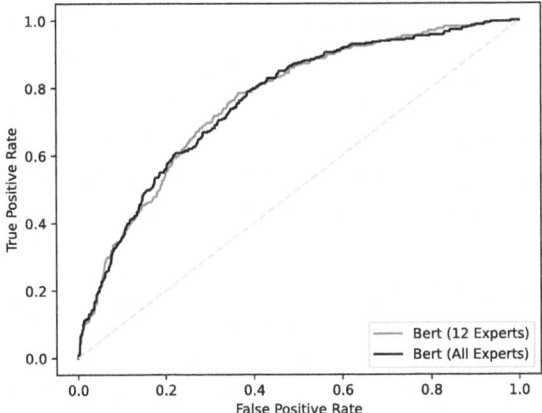

Fig. 3. ROC curve for both BERT models in comparison

inevitably influence the interpretation of hate speech. However, as language evolves, perceptions of hate speech may shift over time. To address this, we plan to continuously annotate additional data to re-train our model and keep it aligned with these changes.

We observed that hate speech comments account for a relatively small proportion of the overall dataset, consistent with the distribution seen on the online platforms from which the data was sourced. In our dataset, 15.3 % of the comments are labeled as hate speech, creating a slightly imbalanced dataset. To assess the impact of this imbalance on model performance and avoid bias, we trained two models: one using the true distribution of the data and another using random oversampling.

We utilized a pre-trained BERT model with an additional classification layer, fine-tuning it on our training data. Hyperparameters were optimized by testing the fine-tuned models against the validation set. Future research should focus on exploring a more extensive model selection process, detailing the pros and cons of various model configurations and hyperparameters in relation to class imbalance, temporal data drift, and optimizing Fleiss' Kappa.

9   How to Use the Corpus?

We are making the corpus presented in this paper, along with its comments and annotations, available to the scientific community for research purposes through a dedicated website website (https://ccwi.github.io/corpus-hocon34k) and on Zenodo (https://doi.org/10.5281/zenodo.12665947).

10   Conclusion and Future Work

In this work, we presented a corpus of 34,223 German-language comments from seven online newspaper platforms in Germany. The comments were annotated by volunteers for both hate speech and context, achieving a solid degree of agreement with inter-rater reliability scores of 0.4428 for hate speech and 0.0917 for context, as measured by Fleiss' Kappa. To evaluate data quality, we provided a baseline text classification that predicted hate speech based on the comment text. In order to facilitate future applications in natural language processing (NLP) and classification, we provide our dataset on **H**ate speech in **O**nline **C**omments from German **N**ewspapers of around 34,000 comments (HOCON34k) to the scientific community.

Acknowledgments. Our special thanks goes to the volunteers who contributed to the annotation of the corpus. The presented work was conducted as part of a project funded by *Forschungs- und Entwicklungsprogramm Informations- und Kommunikationstechnik des Freistaates Bayern*. Funding reference number: DIK-2104-0033// DIK0278/01, DIK0278/02, DIK0278/03.

References

1. Assenmacher, D., et al.: RP-Mod & RP-crowd: moderator- and crowd-annotated german news comment datasets. In: Vanschoren, J., Yeung, S. (eds.) Proceedings of the Neural Information Processing Systems Track on Datasets and Benchmarks, vol. 1. Curran (2021)
2. Bretschneider, U., Peters, R.: Detecting offensive statements towards foreigners in social media. In: Proceedings of the 50th Hawaii International Conference on System Sciences (2017). Proceedings of the Annual Hawaii International Conference on System Sciences, Hawaii International Conference on System Sciences (2017). https://doi.org/10.24251/HICSS.2017.268
3. Chan, B., Schweter, S., Möller, T.: German's next language model (2020). http://arxiv.org/abs/2010.10906, arXiv:2010.10906
4. Demus, C., Pitz, J., Schütz, M., Probol, N., Siegel, M., Labudde, D.: A comprehensive dataset for German offensive language and conversation analysis. In: Proceedings of the Sixth Workshop on Online Abuse and Harms (WOAH), pp. 143–153. Association for Computational Linguistics, Seattle, Washington (Hybrid) (2022). https://doi.org/10.18653/v1/2022.woah-1.14, https://aclanthology.org/2022.woah-1.14
5. European Union: EUR-Lex - 02022R2065-20221027 - EN - EUR-Lex. https://eur-lex.europa.eu/eli/reg/2022/2065/2022-10-27, doc ID: 02022R2065-20221027 Doc Sector: 0 Doc Title: Règlement (UE) 2022/2065 du Parlement européen et du Conseil du 19 octobre 2022 relatif à un marché unique des services numériques et modifiant la directive 2000/31/CE (règlement sur les services numériques) (Texte présentant de l'intérêt pour l'EEE)Texte présentant de l'intérêt pour l'EEE Doc Type: R Usr_lan: en
6. Fleiss, J.L.: Measuring nominal scale agreement among many raters. Psychol. Bull. **76**(5), 378–382 (1971). https://doi.org/10.1037/h0031619
7. Glasebach, J., Keller, M.E., Döschl, A., Mandl, P.: GMHP7k: a corpus of german misogynistic HateSpeech posts. In: Proceedings of the International AAAI Conference on Web and Social Media **18**, 1946–1957 (2024). https://doi.org/10.1609/icwsm.v18i1.31438

8. Goldzycher, J., Röttger, P., Schneider, G.: Improving adversarial data collection by supporting annotators: lessons from GAHD, a German hate speech dataset (2024). http://arxiv.org/abs/2403.19559, arXiv:2403.19559

9. Keller, M.E., Forster, J., Mandl, P., Aich, F., Althaller, J.: A German corpus on topic classification and success of social media posts. In: Proceedings of the 25th Conference of Open Innovations Association FRUCT. FRUCT 2025, FRUCT Oy, Helsinki, Finland (2019)

10. Krenn, B., Petrak, J., Kubina, M., Burger, C.: GERMS-AT: A sexism/misogyny dataset of forum comments from an austrian online newspaper. In: Calzolari, N., Kan, M.Y., Hoste, V., Lenci, A., Sakti, S., Xue, N. (eds.) Proceedings of the 2024 Joint International Conference on Computational Linguistics, Language Resources and Evaluation (LREC-COLING 2024), pp. 7728–7739. ELRA and ICCL, Torino, Italia (2024). https://aclanthology.org/2024.lrec-main.683

11. Landis, J.R., Koch, G.G.: The measurement of observer agreement for categorical data. Biometrics **33**(1), 159 (1977). https://doi.org/10.2307/2529310

12. Loshchilov, I., Hutter, F.: Decoupled weight decay regularization (2019). http://arxiv.org/abs/1711.05101, arXiv:1711.05101

13. Mandl, T., et al: Overview of the HASOC track at FIRE 2019: hate speech and offensive content identification in Indo-European languages. In: Proceedings of the 11th Forum for Information Retrieval Evaluation, pp. 14–17. ACM, Kolkata India (2019). https://doi.org/10.1145/3368567.3368584

14. Pachinger, P., Goldzycher, J., Planitzer, A.M., Kusa, W., Hanbury, A., Neidhardt, J.: AustroTox: a dataset for target-based austrian german offensive language detection (2024). http://arxiv.org/abs/2406.08080, arXiv:2406.08080

15. Pollak, S., et al.: EMBEDDIA tools, datasets and challenges: resources and hackathon contributions. In: Toivonen, H., Boggia, M. (eds.) Proceedings of the EACL Hackashop on News Media Content Analysis and Automated Report Generation, pp. 99–109. Association for Computational Linguistics, Online (2021). https://aclanthology.org/2021.hackashop-1.14

16. Risch, J., Stoll, A., Wilms, L., Wiegand, M.: Overview of the GermEval 2021 shared task on the identification of toxic, engaging, and fact-claiming comments. In: Risch, J., Stoll, A., Wilms, L., Wiegand, M. (eds.) Proceedings of the GermEval 2021 Shared Task on the Identification of Toxic, Engaging, and Fact-Claiming Comments, pp. 1–12. Association for Computational Linguistics, Duesseldorf, Germany (2021). https://aclanthology.org/2021.germeval-1.1

17. Ross, B., Rist, M., Carbonell, G., Cabrera, B., Kurowsky, N., Wojatzki, M.: Measuring the reliability of hate speech annotations: the case of the european refugee crisis (2016). https://doi.org/10.17185/duepublico/42132, http://arxiv.org/abs/1701.08118, arXiv:1701.08118 [cs]

18. Schabus, D., Skowron, M., Trapp, M.: One million posts. In: Kando, N., Sakai, T., Joho, H., Li, H., de Vries, A.P., White, R.W. (eds.) Proceedings of the 40th International ACM SIGIR Conference on Research and Development in Information Retrieval - SIGIR 2017. pp. 1241–1244. ACM Press (2017). https://doi.org/10.1145/3077136.3080711

19. Shekhar, R., Karan, M., Purver, M.: CoRAL: a context-aware croatian abusive language dataset. In: He, Y., Ji, H., Li, S., Liu, Y., Chang, C.H. (eds.) Findings of the Association for Computational Linguistics: AACL-IJCNLP 2022, pp. 217–225. Association for Computational Linguistics, Online only (2022). https://aclanthology.org/2022.findings-aacl.21

20. Shekhar, R., Pranjić, M., Pollak, S., Pelicon, A., Purver, M.: automating news comment moderation with limited resources: benchmarking in croatian and estonian. J. Lang. Technol. Comput. Linguist. **34**(1), 49–79 (2020). https://doi.org/10.21248/jlcl.34.2020.224, https://jlcl.org/article/view/224

21. Sigurbergsson, G.I., Derczynski, L.: Offensive Language and Hate Speech Detection for Danish. In: Calzolari, N., et al. (eds.) Proceedings of the Twelfth Language Resources and Evaluation Conference, pp. 3498–3508. European Language Resources Association, Marseille, France (2020). https://aclanthology.org/2020.lrec-1.430

22. Struß, J.M., Siegel, M., Ruppenhofer, J., Wiegand, M., Klenner, M.: Overview of GermEval Task 2, 2019 shared task on the identification of offensive language. In: Proceedings of the 15th Conference on Natural Language Processing (KONVENS 2019), pp. 354–365. German Society for Computational Linguistics & Language Technology, Erlangen, Germany (2019)

23. Team von tz.de: Netiquette von tz.de (2019). https://www.tz.de/ueber-uns/netiquette-tz-online-1184194.html

24. Vidgen, B., Derczynski, L.: Directions in abusive language training data, a systematic review: garbage in, garbage out. PLoS ONE **15**(12), e0243300 (2020). https://doi.org/10.1371/journal.pone.0243300

25. Wiegand, M., Siegel, M., Ruppenhofer, J.: Overview of the GermEval 2018 shared task on the identification of offensive language. In: Ruppenhofer, J., Siegel, M., Wiegand, M. (eds.) Proceedings of GermEval 2018, 14th Conference on Natural Language Processing (KONVENS 2018), Vienna, Austria - September 21, 2018, pp. 1 – 10. Austrian Academy of Sciences, Vienna, Austria (2019). https://nbn-resolving.org/urn:nbn:de:bsz:mh39-84935

Sequence and Similarity Search Techniques

SISIS : Sequence Indexing for SImilarity Search

Sara Jarrad$^{(\boxtimes)}$ ⓘ, Hubert Naacke ⓘ, and Stéphane Gançarski ⓘ

LIP6, Sorbonne University, Paris, France
{sara.jarrad,hubert.naacke,stephane.gancarski}@lip6.fr

Abstract. Similarity search is a well-studied task aimed at identifying data with
common elements. As data size grows, this process becomes increasingly complex and computationally demanding. In this work, we focus on finding sequences
similar to a user-provided sequence query. Most approaches rely on applying
a similarity function to each sequence, which becomes inefficient with large
datasets. To overcome this, we introduce SISIS, a method that leverages sequence
indexing for faster retrieval of sequences with matching elements in the same
order. Furthermore, to provide similar sequences even when their points do not
exactly match but are contextually close, we introduce SISIS*, a variant of SISIS
based on points embeddings. This variant yields more comprehensive results than
the exact SISIS method. Our extensive experimental validations demonstrate that
the proposed approach significantly outperforms a baseline method based on the
well-known LCSS (Longest Common SubSequence).

Keywords: Sequence · Similarity search · Sequence indexing

1 Introduction and Motivation

The similarity search between sequences is a crucial task for retrieving sequences that
are closely similar to a given query q (q being a sequence of points). Numerous studies
have focused on measuring the similarity between two sequences using well-established
methods. However, these methods often suffer from high computational costs, particularly when applied to large datasets. One such method is the Longest Common Subsequence (LCSS) [5], which computes the length of the longest subsequence common
to both sequences, considering two points as matching only if they are identical. In
our study, we use the LCSS length to quantify the similarity between sequences. However, this method becomes computationally expensive when applied to large collections
of sequences. In a straightforward approach to finding sequences similar to a query q,
the LCSS is calculated between q and every other sequence, leading to inefficiency.
This computational inefficiency is the first challenge we address in our work. Another
limitation of the exact matching approach is that it can be overly restrictive, yielding
few or no results. In many cases, points that are contextually close but not identical
to those in the query should also be considered. To address these challenges, we propose SISIS (Sequence Indexing for Similarity Search), an efficient method that uses
sequence indexing to accelerate the search for similar sequences. SISIS achieves the
same results as LCSS but at a significantly faster rate, allowing users to set a similarity

P. Delir Haghighi et al. (Eds.): iiWAS 2024, LNCS 15342, pp. 229–235, 2025.
https://doi.org/10.1007/978-3-031-78090-5_19

threshold based on the number of points shared with the query. Additionally, we introduce SISIS*, a variant that leverages point embeddings generated from the Word2Vec model [7]. This approach increases the number of results by considering contextually similar points, thus providing a more flexible and effective similarity search.

2   Problem Statement

Let $T = (t_1, \cdots, t_n)$ be a set of sequences, and let $q, t \in T$ with $LCSS(q, t)$ denoting the size of the Longest Common Subsequence (LCSS) between q and t. A sequence t is considered similar to q given a similarity threshold $S \in [0, 1]$ if the LCSS contains at least $p = \lceil |q| \times S \rceil$ points. In other words, the ratio of the sizes of q and $LCSS(q, t)$ must be greater than S. This similarity property is represented as:

$$q \approx_S t \equiv \frac{LCSS(q, t)}{|q|} \geq S$$

A user submits a query consisting of an input sequence q and a similarity threshold S, aiming to retrieve the set $T'(q)$ of sequences in T that are sufficiently similar to q. The naive approach involves calculating the LCSS between q and every other sequence, which is time-consuming. This LCSS-based approach serves as our baseline, and our goal is to improve its efficiency.

3   Related Work

Several studies have addressed the problem of finding similar sequences. For instance, [6] categorizes different similarity measures, discussing their respective advantages and disadvantages. Common measures such as Euclidean, Hausdorff, Fréchet, DTW, EDR, and ERP are widely used, but they are not robust to noise. In [6], LCSS is identified as one of the most robust measures, as it handles most transformations better than other methods. LCSS is also employed in biological applications, such as DNA alignment. Other methods with similar goals include local alignment [10], global alignment [8], multiple alignment [9], and BLAST [1]. However, these approaches do not address the computational cost problem. While effective for small datasets, they become costly and time-consuming when scaled to larger datasets. More recent works, such as [2,4], propose approximating LCSS in linear time with respect to sequence size, reducing computation time. However, these methods trade accuracy for speed, providing only approximate results based on probabilistic estimates. Unlike these works, which focus on finding the LCSS regardless of its size, we address a different problem where the user specifies the minimum size of the sub-sequence to retrieve.

4   Exact Sequence Indexing

Let $T = (t_1, \cdots, t_n)$ be a set of sequences, and $T'(t)$ the set of sequences in T that are sufficiently similar to sequence t. Our approach leverages on sequence indexing to efficiently identify $T'(t)$ by reducing the number of candidate sequences.

4.1   Sequence Index Definition

Definition 1 (Single Point Index). The sequence index $IP : p_i \mapsto \bar{p}_i$ maps each point p_i to the set $\bar{p}_i$ of sequences passing through p_i. This index is structured as a dictionary associating each POI with its corresponding sequences, defined as:

$$\bar{p}_i = \{t \in T \mid p_i \in t\}$$

4.2   Index-Based Similarity Search

Given the similarity threshold S, the user expects sequences that share at least p points with q. We generate all sub-sequences of q of size p. For each sub-sequence, candidate sequences are obtained by intersecting the corresponding sets $\bar{p}_i$. Finally, we verify if the points in the sub-sequence appear in the correct order within the candidate sequence. If not, the candidate is discarded. The implementation of our solution is available to readers at[1]. A long version of this paper, including additional algorithmic explanations, can be found at[2].

5   Sequence Indexing Based on Point Embeddings

Both the LCSS-based baseline and SISIS effectively find similar sequences but rely on exact point matching, which can be overly restrictive. To address this, we propose a method using point embeddings generated by Word2Vec (W2V) [7]. W2V assumes that words occurring in similar contexts have similar vector representations. Similarly, we treat points as words and sequences as sentences, allowing sequences to be similar based on contextually similar points, not just exact matches. We introduce SISIS*, an embedding-based variant of SISIS, which incorporates a user-defined relaxation threshold. This method compares sequences based on contextual similarity, yielding more results than SISIS by identifying sequences that, while not matching the exact query points, are close in the embedding space, reflecting contextual proximity.

5.1   Contextual Similarity and Sequence Index

Let p_i and p_j two points, and p'_i and p'_j their respective embedding obtained by Word2Vec.

Definition 2 (Point ϵ-Similarity). We say that p_i and p_j are ϵ-similar if the cosine between p'_i and p'_j is above a similarity threshold ϵ given by the user. We define sim_ϵ as

$$sim_\epsilon(p_i, p_j) \equiv cosine(p'_i, p'_j) >= \epsilon$$

Considering a contextual version of LCSS, denoted $LCSS(q, t, sim_\epsilon)$, where two points match if they are ϵ-similar, we can generalize the definition of the index.

---

[1] https://gitlab.lip6.fr/jarrad/tisis/-/tree/main.

[2] http://arxiv.org/abs/2409.11301.

Definition 3 (Contextual Sequence Index). The contextual sequence index *CTI* : $p_i \mapsto \bar{\bar{p}}_i$ associates each point p_i with the set $\bar{\bar{p}}_i$ of sequences that pass through a point p_j ϵ-similar to p_i and defined by

$$\bar{\bar{p}}_i = \{t \in T | \exists p_j \in t, \ s.t. \ sim_\epsilon(p_i, p_j)\}$$

5.2 Sequence Search Based on Point Embeddings

We train the W2V model using the input sequences to generate point embeddings, which are then used to construct the contextual sequence index $\bar{\bar{p}}_i$ and identify similar sequences. On line 3, we create combinations of p points from the query q. On line 7, the point order check takes into account ϵ-similarity point matching. Note that the size of $\bar{\bar{p}}_i$ set depends on the ϵ similarity threshold. We study the impact of ϵ on the number of additional sequences in our experiments.

Algorithm 1. Find similar sequences

Require: q: query sequence, S: threshold

1: **function** SIMILAR_SEQUENCES(q, S)
2:     $result \leftarrow \emptyset, \quad p \leftarrow \lceil |q| \times S \rceil$
3:     $C_{|q|,p} \leftarrow$ the set of $C_p^{|q|}$ combinations of size p in q
4:     **for** $combi \in C_{|q|,p}$ **do**
5:         $candidates \leftarrow \bigcap\limits_{i \in combi} \bar{\bar{p}}_i$
6:         **for** $c \in candidates$ **do**
7:             **if** $c \notin result$ and $same\_order(c, combi, sim_\epsilon)$ **then**
8:                 $result \leftarrow result \cup \{c\}$
9:             **end if**
10:         **end for**
11:     **end for**
12:     **return** $result$
13: **end function**

---

6   Experimental Validation

We apply our experiments to three datasets: Foursquare [12] and Gowalla [3] on New York city, and YFCC [11] on France. We use 10,087 sequences from Foursquare, 23,698 from YFCC, and 5,186 from Gowalla.

6.1   Exact Sequence Indexing: Experimental Methodology

In our experiments, we use three datasets and compare our solution with the LCSS-based baseline. We use dataset sequences as queries, retrieving similar ones to each query. We investigate the worst case, setting the similarity threshold to 0.5. We focus on the impact of query size on response time and report average times for each size.

6.2 Sequence Indexing Based on Points Embeddings: Experimental Methodology

In this section, we use the Foursquare dataset to compare the performance of SISIS* (embedding-based) with SISIS (exact method). The goal is to show that SISIS* produces better results due to contextual similarity. We trained W2V with a vector size of 10, 5 epochs, and a window size of 5, keeping other parameters at default. The user threshold S remains at 0.5, with ϵ values ranging from 0.65 to 1.

6.3 Results

Exact Indexing with 1 Point Results

Average computing time as a function of query size on Foursquare dataset, with a threshold of 0.5. In this section, we analyse the average execution time based on user-defined query size. The threshold is set to 0.5, as this represents the worst case for SISIS. The results are displayed in Figs. 1 and 2.

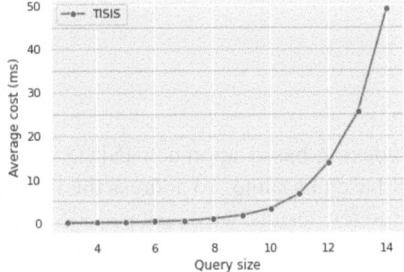

Fig. 1. *SISIS response time*

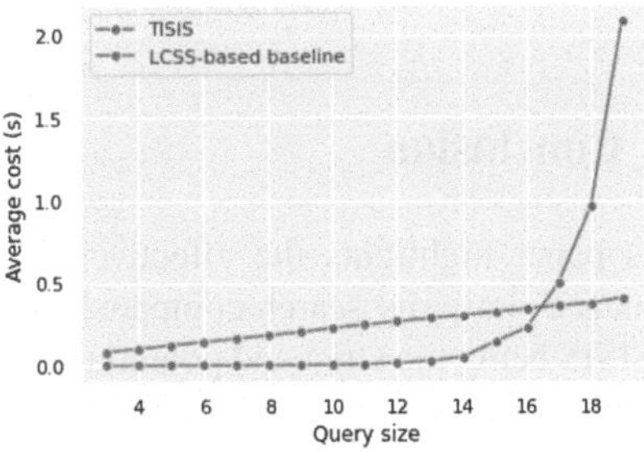

Fig. 2. *Average time as a function of query size*

We observe on Fig. 1 that SISIS responds in under 1 ms for query sizes less than 8, meeting user expectations. As shown on Fig. 2, SISIS is faster than the LCSS-based baseline for sequences with fewer than 17 points, but becomes slower for larger queries. However, queries with more than 17 points are unrealistic in practical scenarios. Thus, SISIS significantly outperforms the LCSS-based baseline for most realistic queries. We conducted the same experiment on the Gowalla and YFCC datasets to demonstrate that SISIS performs well across different datasets. The results are comparable to those from Foursquare. Notably, for average sequence sizes (6 for Gowalla and 5 for YFCC), SISIS is 330x and 2200x faster than the baseline, respectively.

Embedding-Enhanced Indexing-Based Results. We report the number of sequences in relation to varying ϵ values. The y-axis on Fig. 3 shows the average percentage of extra sequences returned by queries. For example, $\epsilon = 0.72$ results in twice as many sequences, as the number of neighbors increases with ϵ : 14 neighbors for $\epsilon = 0.72$ versus only 1 for $\epsilon \geq 0.9$. Moreover, the cost remains close to that of exact SISIS: less than 0.7 s for $\epsilon > 0.72$, making our approach efficient. However, for $\epsilon < 0.72$, the cost rises significantly (up to 1.4 s for $\epsilon = 0.65$), but this range is impractical as it returns too many sequences compared to exact SISIS.

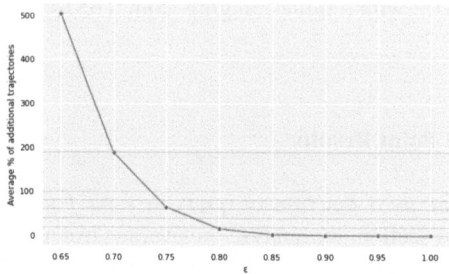

Fig. 3. Effect of ϵ on the average percentage of additional sequences

7 Conclusion

This paper highlights the effectiveness of an indexing-based approach (SISIS) for sequence similarity search compared to the LCSS-based baseline. To address the issue of SISIS being too strict and potentially returning too few results, we developed SISIS*, a variant that incorporates point embeddings and a user-defined relaxation threshold. This variant yields more results (twice as many with a threshold of 0.72) while maintaining computational efficiency. Our experiments on three real-world datasets demonstrate that SISIS and SISIS* outperform the LCSS-based baseline and are applicable to various datasets.

References

1. Altschul, S.F., Gish, W., Miller, W., Myers, E.W., Lipman, D.J.: Basic local alignment search tool. J. Mol. Biol. **215**(3), 403–410 (1990)
2. Bringmann, K., Cohen-Addad, V., Das, D.: A linear-time n0.4-approximation for longest common subsequence. ACM Trans. Algorithms **19**(1), 1–24 (2023)
3. Cho, E., Myers, S.A., Leskovec, J.: Friendship and mobility: user movement in location-based social networks. In: ACM SIGKDD, pp. 1082–1090 (2011)
4. Hajiaghayi, M., Seddighin, M., Seddighin, S., Sun, X.: Approximating LCS in linear time: Beating the $\sqrt{n}$ barrier. In: ACM-SIAM, pp. 1181–1200 (2019)
5. Hirschberg, D.S.: A linear space algorithm for computing maximal common subsequences. Commun. ACM **18**(6), 341–343 (1975)
6. Magdy, N., Sakr, M., Abdelkader, T., Elbahnasy, K.: Review on trajectory similarity measures. In: ICICIS, pp. 613–619 (2015)

7. Mikolov, T., Chen, K., Corrado, G., Dean, J.: Efficient estimation of word representations in vector space. In: ICLR (2013)
8. Needleman, S.B., Wunsch, C.D.: A general method applicable to the search for similarities in the amino acid sequence of two proteins. J. Mol. Biol. **48**(3), 443–453 (1970)
9. Notredame, C., Higgins, D.G., Heringa, J.: T-Coffee: a novel method for fast and accurate multiple sequence alignment. J. Mol. Biol. **302**(1), 205–217 (2000)
10. Smith, T.F., Waterman, M.S., et al.: Identification of common molecular subsequences. J. Mol. Biol. **147**(1), 195–197 (1981)
11. Thomee, B., et al.: YFCC100M: the new data in multimedia research. Communu. ACM **59**(2), 64–73 (2016)
12. Yang, D., Zhang, D., Zheng, V.W., Yu, Z.: Modeling user activity preference by leveraging user spatial temporal characteristics in LBSNS. IEEE Trans. Syst. Man Cybern. Syst. **45**(1), 129–142 (2015)

Top-k on Sequences: A New Approach to Enhanced Similarity Search

Sara Jarrad$^{(\boxtimes)}$ [ID], Hubert Naacke [ID], and Stéphane Gançarski [ID]

LIP6, Sorbonne University, Paris, France
{sara.jarrad,hubert.naacke,stephane.gancarski}@lip6.fr

Abstract. Performing efficient top-k similarity search on massive data sets is challenging due to the increasing complexity with data scale, and many existing methods are computationally expensive. In this context, top-k sequence similarity search, which aims to identify the k most relevant sequences to a query sequence using a scoring function, becomes a critical task. We argue that the similarity between two sequences should not be based only on their longest common subsequence, but should consider all common subsequences. This approach allows for a more comprehensive similarity score, recognising as more similar sequences that share many subsequences and thus providing a more meaningful ranking. Our study addresses these challenges by proposing: (1) a novel scoring function that assigns higher scores to candidates that share more subsequences with a query sequence, and (2) an efficient method that factorises the computation while computing all sequence scores simultaneously. Our contributions include a detailed analysis of existing techniques and the proposal of an efficient method for top-k similarity search. We validate our approach through extensive experimental evaluations and demonstrate its efficiency compared to a baseline method. Our results provide a promising solution for sequence similarity search that significantly improves the speed of top-k sequence retrieval in large mobility datasets.

Keywords: Top-k similarity search · sequence ranking · scoring function · common subsequences

1 Introduction and Motivation

In the era of big data, an important challenge is the top-k similarity search, in particular for sequence data. An example of a sequence is user's mobility data, which describes their movement through the order of visited points. In this study, we focus on retrieving similar sequences to a query sequence q, and ranking the top-k most similar ones using a novel scoring function. This task is fundamental in applications such as sequence classification/recommendation, among others.

Efficiently performing top-k similarity searches in massive datasets is non-trivial and becomes increasingly complex as the size of the data increases. It

© The Author(s), under exclusive license to Springer Nature Switzerland AG 2025
P. Delir Haghighi et al. (Eds.): iiWAS 2024, LNCS 15342, pp. 236–251, 2025.
https://doi.org/10.1007/978-3-031-78090-5_20

therefore requires advanced computational techniques to ensure timely and accurate results.

Many existing studies have focused on sequence similarity search methods such as DTW, LCSS, ERP, EDR [1–3,7,8,16]. Among them, LCSS (Longest Common Subsequences) is considered the most effective measure due to its robustness against various transformations that can be applied to sequences [14,18,19].

We argue that the similarity between two sequences should not be based solely on their LCSS but should instead consider *all common subsequences*. This allows for a more complete similarity score, recognizing as more similar sequences that share numerous subsequences and thus providing a more precise ranking.

To this end, we propose a novel scoring function that assigns higher scores to candidates that share more subsequences with a query sequence. It discriminates between sequences with identical LCSS similarity. We also propose an efficient method that factorizes computation while computing all sequence scores simultaneously. We validate our approach through extensive experimental evaluations, comparing our method with a baseline approach. The results demonstrate the efficiency and effectiveness of our proposed solution, which significantly improves top-k sequence retrieval in large sequence datasets. Our contributions offer a promising solution to the challenges of top-k similarity search, providing a robust and scalable method for dealing with the increasing complexity of massive datasets.

We define a new scoring function in Sect. 2 and present related work in Sect. 3. Then, we present a first method to search for similar sequences in Sect. 4. In Sect. 5 we propose an efficient and accurate method for top-k similarity search. We experimentally validate our approach in Sect. 6 and conclude in Sect. 7.

2   Scoring

We propose a scoring function to rank the top-k most similar sequences to a given query sequence. This function should not only be based on the longest common subsequence as LCSS does, but must consider all common subsequences. This method allows for a more thorough similarity score, identifying sequences with many common subsequences as more similar and thus providing a more detailed and reliable ranking. The definition of our proposed score function is given below. The notations frequently used throughout this paper are summarised in Table 1.

Definition 1. (Subsequence) Let s_1 and s_2 be two sequences of elements. The fact that s_1 is a subsequence of s_2 is denoted $s_1 \sqsubset_o s_2$.

Definition 2. (Set of subsequences) Let q be a sequence and $i \leq |q|$, we define $C_{q,i}$ as the set of all subsequences of q of size i. We define $E(q)$ to be the set of all subsequences of q of any size: $E(q) = \bigcup_{i=1}^{|q|} C_{q,i}$. Note that $C_{q,i}$ contains $C_{|q|}^i$ subsequences, and $E()$ is the powerset of q minus the emptyset.

Definition 3. (Order preserving intersection) Let s_1 and s_2 be two sequences of elements. We define $s_1 \cap_o s_2$ as the intersection operation between s_1 and s_2 such that it preserves the order of elements in sequence s_1.

Note that in general $\cap_o$ is not commutative *i.e.* $s_1 \cap_o s_2 \neq s_2 \cap_o s_1$. For example, $ABC \cap_o DBA = AB$ whereas $DBA \cap_o ABC = BA$.

Given a query q and a list of sequences, we assign a similarity score to each of them.

Definition 4. (Score) The similarity score between two sequences, s_1 and s_2, is defined as the number of common subsequences between the two sequences. Formally, it can be expressed as the size of the intersection between $E(s_1)$ and $E(s_2)$ defined above. We define the $score(s_1, s_2)$ function as :

$$score(s_1, s_2) = |E(s_1) \cap E(s_2)|$$

Table 1. Notations used for scoring sequences and similarity search

Notation	Description
q	A query sequence
$E(q)$	Set of all subsequences of q of any size
$\cap_o$	Order preserving intersection operator
Cq, i	Set of all subsequences of q of size i
s_1, s_2	Sequences
e, e_i, e_j	elements of a sequence
I_1	An index that associates each element with the sequences that contain it
I_2	An index that associates each pair of elements with the sequences that contain it
D_p	Set of sequences in D dataset that contain a sequence p
L_i	A layer that contains all patterns of q of size i

There are simpler and more intuitive ways to score similar sequences, but they fall short for our needs. For example, counting the number of common points between the query and the similar sequences and ranking them in descending order. Although this method is easy to implement, it does not preserve the sequence order. A more appropriate approach would be to use methods such as LCSS, which preserve the order of points. However, as mentioned above, LCSS only considers the longest common subsequence, whereas our goal is to consider all common subsequences to achieve a more accurate ranking.

Here is an application of our function to a sequence example. Consider a query $q = [A, B, C, D, E, F, G, H]$, and two sequences $t_1 = [A, B, C, D, E]$ and $t_2 = [A, B, C, H, G, F, E, D]$. For these, $LCSS(q, t_1) = 5$, and $LCSS(q, t_2) = 4$.

Using our defined score function, we have $score(q, t_1) = 31$ (consisting of 5 common subsequences of size 1, 10 of size 2, 10 of size 3, 5 of size 4, and 1 subsequence of size 5) and $score(q, t_2) = 47$ (8 subsequences of size 1, 18 of size 2, 16 of size 3, and 5 of size 4).

Note that although $LCSS(q, t_1) > LCSS(q, t_2)$, $score(q, t_2) > score(q, t_1)$. This discrepancy arises because our approach considers all common subsequences, not just the longest one, illustrating the relevance of our method.

3 Related Work

Ribeiro *et al.* present in [15] an operator of the StreamPref query language that allows to obtain a top-k closest sequences to the user's temporal preferences. A sequence is considered as a set of tuples $s = < t_1, t_1, ..., t_n >$. Each tuple consists of attributes describing the movement and direction of a given user in a given environment. The objective of their approach is comparable to ours, as both aim to identify the top-k sequences most aligned with user preferences. However, their definition of sequence similarity (based on user preferences) differs from ours. In their method, two sequences s and s' are considered similar if they match up to a certain position i. At this position, s is preferred if it contains a preferred value at i compared to s', according to a set of logical rules for inferring preferred attribute values. In contrast, our approach allows the user to express preferences by providing a query sequence. The top-k most similar sequences to this query are those with the highest number of common subsequences. Nonetheless, we adopt the same evaluation strategy as they do, measuring the solution's effectiveness by comparing its cost against a naive baseline method.

Xuan *et al.* present in [21] a top-k LCSS search problem. Given n sequences as input, they search for the k sequences that are closest to each other in terms of LCSS using a divide-and-conquer algorithm, whereas we search for the k sequences that are closest to a query sequence given as input.

Ma *et al.* introduce in [13] a novel p-distance measure for measuring dissimilarity between trajectories, defined as sequences of visited locations. Using this measure, the goal is to identify the top-k trajectories that are most similar to a given query trajectory (KSQ). The authors achieve this by ranking trajectories based on the p-distances between them and the query, selecting the k trajectories with the smallest p-distances. While their goal is similar to ours, a key difference is that they apply their solution to uncertain trajectories, where the data may be noisy and the positions may not be exact, and are described by a probability distribution function over the possible positions. Their approach also includes a UTgrids structure for indexing uncertain trajectories. However, this structure is not applicable to our work because we assume that the sequences are deterministic and the positions are exact.

A number of studies have been carried out on probabilistic data to find the top-k similar sequences/objects. These works include [5,9,13,17,23]

Cormode *et al.* propose in [5] a method for ranking a top-k based on the scores of tuples and introduces the properties required for constructing a top-k (exact-k, containment, unique-ranking, value-invariance, stability). In this case, the tuples are not sequences but objects, with each tuple consisting of a set of score values and associated probabilities, which reflects their assumption of data uncertainty, similar to [13]. The scores of each tuple are known in advance, and the authors aim to construct a top-k from this information. However, since each score value is paired with a probability, they generate multiple possible worlds corresponding to different score values for each tuple in order to rank them. In contrast, our study focuses on defining a top-k of the most similar sequences, for which we must compute a score for each sequence, information that, unlike in [5], is not available beforehand. Furthermore, as mentioned in [13], we assume our data is certain. Therefore, their solution is not applicable to our case. For deterministic data, other works such as [6,10–12,20] have proposed methods for identifying the top-k tuples with the highest scores. [6] ranks top-k objects, where these objects can be strings, images, videos, etc. According to their approach, each object is described by multiple attributes, with each attribute assigned a score. To adapt their idea to our problem, we can consider the object as a sequence of points, with the sole attribute being its similarity to the input query. In this case, the score corresponds to the similarity score. However, in contrast to our task, where we compute similarity scores, they assume the attribute scores of each object are given as input. Their focus is on combining these individual scores to obtain an overall score that represents the object, which is then used to rank the top-k objects.

The article [11] has the same goal as [6] in terms of finding the top-k objects with the highest scores, so the scores are also known in advance. They also provide an overview of the different top-k processing techniques (query modelling, data certainty, data access, implementation level, ranking function) and describe the different types of each of these techniques. For ranking functions, they present the 3 types of functions which are monotonic, generic or untyped.

We note that all these works are related to the top-k similarity search problem. However, they are all far from our work, either in terms of the methods used or the assumptions made (uncertain data, different definition of similarity, objects instead of sequences, previously known score). Consequently, their solutions are not suitable for our problem.

4   Sequence Similarity Search: A Baseline Approach

We introduce a baseline approach in which scores are computed separately for each sequence (according to the score definition presented in Sect. 2). Then the sequences are ranked by score keeping only the first top-k sequences with the highest score values.

4.1   Baseline Sequence Similarity Search Algorithm

We detail Algorithm 1 which scores sequences according to their similarity to a given query. It takes as input the query q, a set of sequences T, and a number k of sequences. It returns the top-k most similar sequences to q.

Algorithm 1. Baseline sequence similarity search

Input: q: query sequence, S: set of all sequences, k: number of sequences
Output: top_seq_list : top-k similar sequences

```
 1: function SCORING_SEQUENCES(q, S, k)
 2:     s_score_list ← ∅
 3:     for s ∈ S do
 4:         E(q*) ← ∅,    E(s*) ← ∅
 5:         q* ← q ∩ₒ s,    s* ← s ∩ₒ q*
 6:         for i ← 1 to |q*| do
 7:             // add into E(q*) the set C_{q*,i} of combinations of size i in q*
 8:             E(q*) ← E(q*) ∪ C_{q*,i}
 9:         end for
10:         for j ← 1 to |s*| do
11:             // add into E(s*) the set C_{s*,j} of combinations of size j in s*
12:             E(s*) ← E(s*) ∪ C_{s*,j}
13:         end for
14:         score = |E(q*) ∩ E(s*)|    // scoring function defined in Section 2
15:         s_score_list ← s_score_list ∪ {(s, score)}
16:     end for
17:     OT ← s_score_list ordered by descending score
18:     top_seq_list ← first k sequences s in OT
19:     return top_seq_list
20: end function
```

First, for each candidate sequence s (line 3), we compute in line 5, the intersections q^* and s^* between q and s, preserving the order in q and s, respectively. Then, in lines 6–9, we compute $E(q^*)$ the set of all subsequences of size between 1 and $|q^*|$ (see Definition 4). We similarly compute $E(s^*)$ in lines 10–13.

This allows us to consider only subsequences containing points shared by both q and s, since $E(q) \cap E(s) = E(q^*) \cap E(s^*)$, thus saving computation.

Subsequently, in lines 14–15, the score of s with respect to q is calculated. Finally, the sequences are ordered in descending order of score value in lines 17–19, and the top-k results are returned.

We run this algorithm on the following example: We consider q and s such as $q = $ [A, B , C, D, E] and $s = $ [A, E, D, C, B]. From q and s we compute q^* and s^* : $q^* = $ [A, B, C, D, E] and $s^* = $ [A, E, D, C, B].

We have $E(s^*) = $ [*A, E, D, C, B, AE, AD, AC, AB, ED, EC, EB, DC, DB, CB, AED, AEC, AEB, ADC, ADB, ACB, EDC, EDB, DCB, ECB, AEDC, AEDB, AECB, ADCB, EDCB, AEDCB*].

The same method is used to compute $E(q^*)$. From $E(s^*)$ and $E(q^*)$, we obtain :

$$E(q^*) \cap E(s^*) = [A, B, C, D, E, AB, AC, AD, AE]$$

The score value between q and s is then calculated as follows :

$$score(q, s) = |E(q^*) \cap E(s^*)| = 9$$

4.2   Limitation

The baseline method has 2 important limitations.

- When assigning scores to sequences in the dataset, the baseline method compares the query to each sequence in the dataset individually, which becomes costly with large-scale datasets.
- When comparing the query q and a sequence s, the baseline method considers all subsequences of $s*$, even if the order is different from that of q. However, if a subsequence ss of $s*$ is not in the same order as in $q*$, then any sequence containing ss will also be in the wrong order. This implication is not used to reduce unnecessary comparisons.

We use this method as a baseline for comparison purposes. Our goal is to introduce a more efficient approach to achieve the same result, which is to identify the top K highest score sequences.

5   Efficient and Accurate Top-k Similarity Search

We propose an efficient method for top-k similarity search, that overcomes the limitations of the baseline approach presented in Sect. 4. The idea is to adopt a collection-oriented approach that allows efficient manipulation of sets of sequences. We make use of efficient intersection operations between sets of sequences in order to identify those that contain a given sub-sequence. Unlike the baseline, which computes the score of each sequence independently, our approach determines the subsequences contained in sequences, and the sequence scores, for all sequences simultaneously. By enumerating subsequences in increasing order of size, we aim to significantly reduce unnecessary computation, since a subsequence p of the query that does not exist in any other sequence can be discarded as well as all sequences containing p. We first define a subset of a dataset filtered by sequence.

Definition 5. (pattern-based selection of sequences) Let D be a dataset of sequences and a sequence p which we call a pattern. The selection of D on p, denoted D_p, is the set of the sequences in D that contain p. It is formally defined as follows (using the $\subset_o$ operator for subsequence assertion): $D_p = \{s \in D | p \subset_o s\}$

Then, we define an index I_1 to efficiently access sequences that contain a given element, and an index I_2 to capture precedence information between elements in a sequence.

Definition 6. (Sequence indexes) The index $I_1 : e \mapsto D_{(e)}$ is an inverted list that associates an element e with the sequences it contains. The index $I_2 : (e_i, e_j) \mapsto D_{(e_i, e_j)}$ associates a pair of elements (e_i, e_j) with the set of sequences that contains e_i then e_j (i.e. e_i precedes e_j).

The index data structures are implemented as hashtable for efficient access (in $O(1)$) to sets of sequences. The bottom-up approach for enumerating the subsequences is described in detail below, creating the layers, and computing the scores.

5.1   Enumerating Subsequences

The main principle of the algorithm is to incrementally merge the precedence information expressed in subsequences. We follow a bottom-up approach by first considering small subsequences and then gradually extending them. We consider the subsequences of query a q by increasing order or size from the shortest ones to the largest one which is the query itself.

Definition 7. (Layers) Let q be a query sequence, a size-based partition of subsequences of q is defined, where the patterns of a given size i define a **layer**, denoted L_n. The layer L_n contains all patterns p of q of size n that are also subsequences of at least one sequence of D. It is formally defined as follows:

$$L_n = \{p|p \sqsubset_o q \wedge |p| = n \wedge \exists s \in D, p \sqsubset_o s\}$$

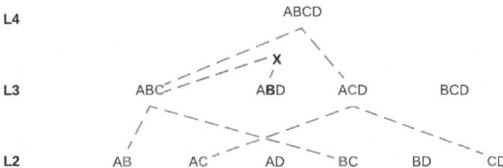

Fig. 1. Example of layers from L_2 to L_4 for a query $q = [A, B, C, D]$

We consider the series of L_n layers of increasing sequence size, from L_1 to $L_{|q|}$. We build each layer L_n in turn, and attach to each pattern p in that layer its corresponding set of dataset sequences D_p, creating the corresponding LD_n, which is a list of (p, D_p) pairs.

5.2   Creating Layers L_1 and L_2

For layer L_1, the list LD_1 is instantiated with all the elements of the query sequence. The index I_1 (see Definition 6) is probed to get the corresponding D_p sets:

$$LD_1 = \{(e, I_1(e)) \mid e \in q \ \wedge \ I_1(e) \neq \emptyset\}$$

For layer L_2, the creation of LD_2 is detailed in Algorithm 2 which takes a query q as input and returns a list of (p, D_p) pairs as output. LD_2 is instantiated with all the subsequences of size 2 of q (line 3). As for the previous level, the index I_2 is probed to get the corresponding D_p sets (line 4). In line 6, the LD_2 list is sorted in ascending order of the size of D_p before being returned, the aim being to speed up the building of the next layer by giving priority to smaller sizes of D_p.

Algorithm 2. Creation of LD_2

Input : q : query sequence
Output : LD_2 : list of (p, D_p) couples

```
1: function BUILD_L2(q)
2:     LD₂ ← ∅
3:     for eᵢeⱼ ∈ C|q|,2 do    // for all subsequences of size 2 in q
4:         if I₂(eᵢeⱼ) ≠ ∅ then
5:             LD₂ ← LD₂ ∪ (p : eᵢeⱼ, Dₚ : I₂(eᵢeⱼ))
6:         end if
7:     end for
8:     return sort(LD₂, sortkey = |Dₚ|)    // sort by ascending size of Dₚ sets
9: end function
```

5.3 Creating Upper Layers

For $n \in [2, |q| - 1]$, the layer L_{n+1} is instantiated based on the previous layer L_n. The Algorithm 3 is used to construct LD_{n+1} from LD_n. Starting in line 10, each pair (p_i, p_j) of patterns from L_n is checked for compatibility in order to be extended. This is done by the EXTEND function (lines 1–7), which returns a sequence of size $|p| + 1$ from two sequences p and r of size $|p|$, provided that r can *extend* p by adding only one precedence information from the last element of p to a new element not in p. This new element should be the last element of r. Note that r must not contain any other precedence information that is not already in p.

The conditions for two sequences p and r to be compatible for extension are formally stated as:

- r minus its last element must be a subsequence of p.
- the second-to-last (*i.e.* penultimate) element of r must be the same as the last element of p.

For example (see Fig. 1) the sequences ABC and BCD are compatible for extension, and EXTEND(ABC, BCD) is equal to $ABCD$, as is EXTEND(ABC, ACD), whereas ABC and ABD cannot be extended together, because the precedence between C and D is missing.

In lines 12–13, if p_i and p_j are compatible for extension, then p_i is merged with p_j (preserving the order) to get a new p' pattern of size $|p_i| + 1$. Then, in line 14, to get the corresponding $D_{p'}$, the intersection between D_{p_i} and D_{p_j} is computed and only patterns associated with non empty $D_{p'}$ sets are kept (line 17). For better performance, the (p, D_p) pairs are sorted in ascending order of the size of D_p, then returned (line 22).

Algorithm 3 is applied repeatedly up to the construction of the uppermost layer $L_{|q|}$. To sum up, the layers act as an index dedicated to a given query q. The layers are built bottom-up, from the smallest pattern to the largest. This allows us to use information from previous layers and avoid redundant computations by reusing D_p sets.

Algorithm 3. Creating an upper layer

  Input : LD : List of $\left((p_1, D_{p_1}), \cdots (p_n, D_{p_n})\right)$ at layer $L_{|p|}$
  Output : $upperLD$: List of $(p', D_{p'})$ at layer $L_{|p+1|}$

 1: **function** EXTEND(p, r) // p: $(p_1, \cdots, p_{|p|})$ pattern, r: $(r_1, \cdots, r_{|r|})$ pattern
 2: **if** $\left(p_{|p|} = r_{|r|-1} \wedge (r_1, \cdots, r_{|r|-1}) \subset_o p\right)$ $\vee$
 3: $\left(r_{|r|} = p_{|p|-1} \wedge (p_1, \cdots, p_{|p|-1}) \subset_o r\right)$ **then**
 4: **return** $p \cup_o r$
 5: **else return** $\emptyset$
 6: **end if**
 7: **end function**
 8: **function** BUILD_UPPER_LAYER(LD)
 9: $upperLD \leftarrow \emptyset$, $L \leftarrow \emptyset$
10: **for** $(p_i, D_{p_i}) \in LD$ **do**
11: **for** $(p_j, D_{p_j}) \in \left((p_{i+1}, D_{p_{i+1}}), \cdots (p_n, D_{p_n})\right)$ **do**
12:   $p' \leftarrow$ EXTEND(p_i, p_j)
13:   **if** $p' \neq \emptyset \wedge p' \notin L$ **then**
14:    $D_{p'} \leftarrow D_{p_i} \cap D_{p_j}$
15:    **if** $|D_{p'}| \neq \emptyset$ **then**
16:     $L \leftarrow L \cup \{p'\}$
17:     $upperLD \leftarrow upperLD \cup \{(p', D_{p'})\}$
18:    **end if**
19:   **end if**
20: **end for**
21: **end for**
22: **return** $sort(upperLD, sortkey = |D_{p'}|)$ // sort by ascending size of $D_{p'}$ sets
23: **end function**

5.4 Computing Sequence Scores

Once the query patterns p have been identified at each layer, and the D_p sets of sequences have been associated with each pattern, the score of each sequence is computed considering all the D_p from all patterns in all layers as follows:

$$score(s) = |\{p | \forall i \in [1, |q|], \ \forall l \in L_i, \ \forall p \in l, s \in D_p\}|$$

The Algorithm 4 gives details of the procedure for scoring the sequences and returning the k highest scoring sequences. We provide the readers with the code used to implement the solution, which is available on[1].

6 Experimental Validation

In this section, we present the experiments conducted with our proposed approach and compare its performance with the baseline.

---

[1] https://gitlab.lip6.fr/jarrad/topK-similarity-search.

Algorithm 4. Sequence scoring

Input : q: query, L: the set of $\{L_1, \cdots, L_{|q|}\}$ layers, k: number
Output : the top-k sequences with the highest score

1: **function** SEQUENCE_SCORING(q, L, k)
2:     $score \leftarrow \{\}$ // empty dictionary, the default value is 0 for any non existing key.
3:     **for** $l \in L$ **do**   // for each layer
4:         **for** $p \in l$ **do**   // for each pattern in a layer
5:             **for** $s \in D_p$ **do**   // for each sequence that contains p
6:                 $score[s] \leftarrow score[s] + 1$
7:             **end for**
8:         **end for**
9:     **end for**
10:     $ordered\_traj = sort(score.items(), key = -score)$ /* sort items by descending score */
11:     **return** $\{ordered\_traj_1, \cdots, ordered\_traj_k\}$
12: **end function**

First, we outline the various datasets used and the experimental methodology applied to our solution. We then analyse and discuss the results obtained.

It is important to note that all subsequent experiments were performed on a Dell PowerEdge R440 Linux server equipped with 370 GB of RAM, and the programming language used was Python.

6.1   Data Preparation

We conduct our experiments using two datasets: Foursquare [22] and Gowalla [4] for New York City. These two datasets contain mobility data, so the constructed sequences are sequences of points (visits) representing user movements in chronological order. Our goal is to show that our method achieves good performance on different datasets.

This study focuses exclusively on points with more than 15 visits. We aim to build sequences of frequently visited points in order to identify a reasonable number of neighbors for each sequence, containing common subsequences of points.

We then construct user sequences on a daily basis (from 12:00 am to 11:59 pm). We only keep sequences of a realistic size, i.e., between 3 and 13 points. This results in 9,761 sequences from Foursquare, and 5,040 from Gowalla.

6.2   Experimental Methodology

To evaluate our method, we perform a comparative analysis between the baseline approach and the proposed solution for two different datasets. Note that for all experiments, the value of k, corresponding to the top sequences most similar to the query given by the user, is set to 10. We focus on the average cost relative to the query size and the data size (number of sequences in the dataset).

We hypothesise that the cost increases proportionally with the values of these parameters. Our goal is to show that the average cost of the baseline approach consistently exceeds that of the proposed solution. In terms of accuracy, note that our solution is 100% accurate and provides the same top-k as the baseline, as they are both based on the same score function.

6.3   Results

We ran our experiments on the Foursquare and Gowalla datasets. We report the results in the figures below; the corresponding tables with numerical values are available on our companion website[2].

Average Cost as a Function of Query Size. We analyse the average cost, measured in seconds, as a function of the query size specified by the user. We calculate the average query response time for each query size from 3 to 13 elements.

Foursquare dataset: We observe on Fig. 2 that the average cost of the top-k similarity search using our approach is less than 1 s for all query sizes. Therefore, our solution meets users' expectations regarding response time. On Fig. 3 we observe that our approach (in blue) is faster than the baseline (in red) for all query sizes.

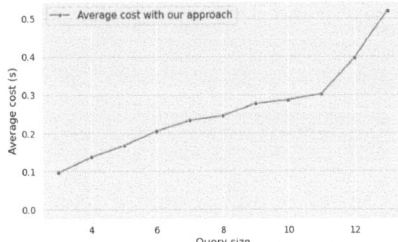

Fig. 2. *Average cost as a function of query size using our approach on Foursquare*

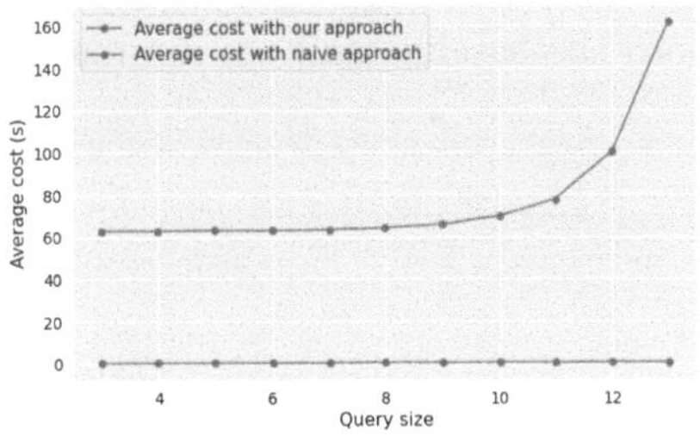

Fig. 3. *Benefit of our approach vs baseline on Foursquare dataset*

We emphasize the benefit of our method for queries with an average sequence size of 5: our method is 376 times faster than the baseline.

Gowalla dataset: To assess the applicability of our method, we performed an identical experiment on the Gowalla dataset. The performance results are reported on Figs. 4 and 5.

---

[2] https://gitlab.lip6.fr/jarrad/topK-similarity-search.

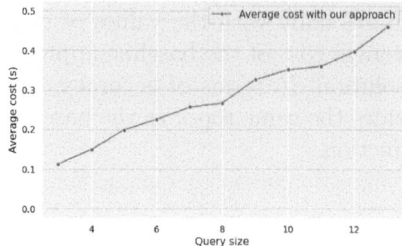

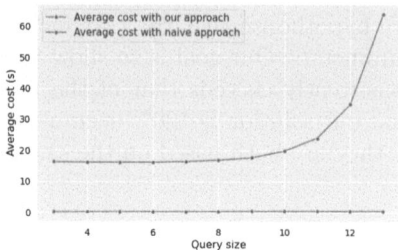

Fig. 4. *Average cost as a function of query size using our approach on Gowalla dataset*

Fig. 5. *Benefit of our approach vs baseline on Gowalla*

We highlight the benefit of our method for queries with an average sequence size of 6: our approach is 71 times faster than the baseline. We note that the results are similar to those obtained on the Foursquare dataset, confirming that our approach outperforms the baseline on different datasets.

Effect of the Dataset Size on the Performance. We aim to measure the average cost for various dataset sizes. To this end, we create smaller datasets from the Foursquare dataset, with sizes ranging from 1,000 to 9,761 sequences. For these datasets, we use queries of size 5 (corresponding to the average sequence size). We compute the average response time of queries for each dataset size. The curves in Figs. 6 and 7 show that as the dataset size increases, the cost of both the baseline and our approach increases.

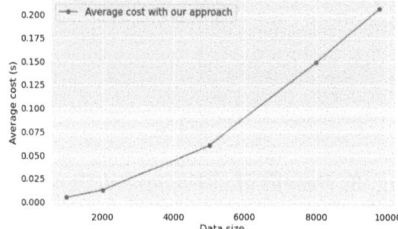

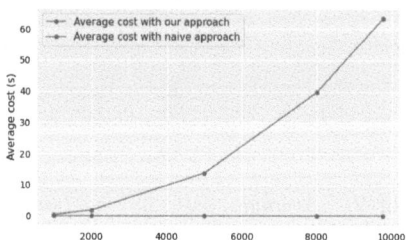

Fig. 6. *Average time as a function of data size using our approach*

Fig. 7. *accurate top-k similarity search approach vs. baseline approach*

However, our solution tends to evolve less quickly than the baseline. As the dataset size is increases from 1000 to 8000, the cost becomes 31x higher, whereas it is 94x higher for the baseline. Thus our proposed approach performs better than the baseline.

Discussion. Through the experiments conducted, we can confirm that our approach provides identical results (top-k) to the baseline, while achieving significantly better performance for different datasets and data sizes. Let q be a query of size n. Theoretically, there are $2^n - 1$ subsequences generated from q. This suggests that the cost should be exponential to n. However, in practice (see Fig. 2 and 4), we only keep a subsequence if it is found in at least one sequence in the dataset. The actual number of generated subsequences is then less than $2^n - 1$. On Figs. 9 and 8, we report the average number of subsequences for various query sizes, for the Foursquare dataset.

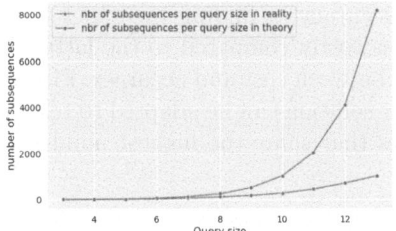

Fig. 8. *number of generated subsequences in reality vs. theory*

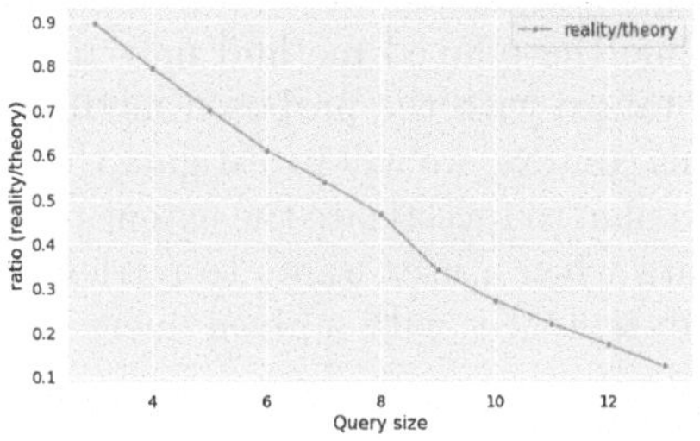

Fig. 9. *#subsequences in theory divided by #subsequences in reality*

We observe on Fig. 8 that the actual number of created subsequences (in blue) is less than the theoretical one (in red) for query sizes between 3 and 13. In Fig. 9, the ratio between the theoretical and actual number of subsequences ranges from 0 to 1. The larger the query size, the lower the ratio will be.

Finally, we compared our approach with a simple method that retrieves the top-k sequences with the highest LCSS with the query. We found that such a method does not retrieve the k expected sequences, but only $0.72 \times k$ on average, thus lacking precision.

7   Conclusion

We addressed the problem of top-k similarity search in a dataset of sequences, and the challenge of defining a meaningful similarity measure between two sequences that is not only based on the well-known LCSS, but also takes into account *all common subsequences*. We propose a new similarity measure for sequences that is more accurate than LCSS, recognises sequences that share many sub-sequences as more similar and thus provides a more meaningful ranking.

We also propose an efficient algorithm for computing top-k queries on sequences. We apply it to trajectories which are sequences of visited points. We overcome the performance limitation of a naive search method (baseline) which computes the score of each sequence independently, by proposing an approach that allows efficient manipulation of sets of sequences, to determine the sequence scores, for all sequences simultaneously. This significantly reduces unnecessary computation. We conducted experiments on two real-world datasets and show that the proposed approach consistently matches the baseline results while largely outperforming it, and can be applied to different datasets.

Our future research directions include working on optimising the proposed method, by adding more pruning techniques, and more efficient intersection operations to identify sequences containing a given sub-sequence. This will thereby further reduce unnecessary computation. To further reduce the cost, we intend to relax the top-k similarity search method by skipping the creation of top layers while still having enough information to rank the sequences. We estimate that while the relaxed method may reduce the accuracy of finding the exact top-k obtained with the proposed method, it is less costly compared to the latter. In this context, we will investigate the trade-off between cost and accuracy. Finally, we plan to investigate the extent to which our solution can be adapted to textual data when a user wants to retrieve sentences that share the highest number of sub-sentences with a given query sentence.

References

1. Berndt, D.J., Clifford, J.: Using dynamic time warping to find patterns in time series. In: KDD, pp. 359–370 (1994)
2. Chen, L., Ng, R.: On the marriage of Lp-norms and edit distance. VLDB **30**, 792–803 (2004)
3. Chen, L., Tamer Özsu, M., Oria, V.: Robust and fast similarity search for moving object trajectories. In: ACM SIGMOD, pp. 491–502 (2005)
4. Cho, E., Myers, S.A., Leskovec, J.: Friendship and mobility: user movement in location-based social networks. In: ACM SIGKDD, pp. 1082–1090 (2011)
5. Cormode, G., Li, F., Yi, K.: Semantics of ranking queries for probabilistic data and expected ranks. In: ICDE, pp. 305–316 (2009)
6. Fagin, R., Lotem, A., Naor, M.: Optimal aggregation algorithms for middleware. In: ACM PODS (2001)
7. Hirschberg, D.S.: A linear space algorithm for computing maximal common subsequences. Commun. ACM **18**(6), 341–343 (1975)
8. Hirschberg, D.S.: Algorithms for the longest common subsequence problem. J. ACM **24**(4), 664–675 (1977)
9. Hua, M., Pei, J., Zhang, W., Lin, X.: Ranking queries on uncertain data: a probabilistic threshold approach. In: ACM SIGMOD, pp. 673–686 (2008)
10. Ilyas, I.F., Aref, W.G., Elmagarmid, A.K., Elmongui, H.G., Shah, R., Vitter, J.S.: Adaptive rank-aware query optimization in relational databases. ACM TODS **31**(4), 1257–1304 (2006)
11. Ilyas, I.F., Beskales, G., Soliman, M.A.: A survey of top-k query processing techniques in relational database systems. ACM Comput. Surv. **40**(4), 11:1–11:58 (2008)
12. Li, C., Chang, K.C.-C., Ilyas, I.F., Song, S.: RankSQL: query algebra and optimization for relational top-k queries. In: ACM SIGMOD, pp. 131–142 (2005)
13. Ma, C., Hua, L., Shou, L., Chen, G.: KSQ: top-(k) similarity query on uncertain trajectories. IEEE TKDE **25**(9), 2049–2062 (2013)

14. Magdy, N., Sakr, M.A., Mostafa, T., El-Bahnasy, K.: Review on trajectory similarity measures. In: ICICIS, pp. 613–619 (2015)
15. Ribeiro, M.R., Barioni, M.C.N., de Amo, S., Roncancio, C., Labbé, C.: Finding top-k sequences over data streams according to temporal conditional preferences. In: SBBD, pp. 73–84 (2018)
16. Sellers, P.H.: An algorithm for the distance between two finite sequences. J. Combinatorial Theory **16**(2), 253–258 (1974)
17. Soliman, M.A., Ilyas, I.F., Chang, K.C.-C.: Top-k query processing in uncertain databases. In: ICDE (2007)
18. Han, S., Liu, S., Zheng, B., Zhou, X., Zheng, K.: A survey of trajectory distance measures and performance evaluation. VLDB J. **29**(1), 3–32 (2020)
19. Wang, H., Su, H., Zheng, K., Sadiq, S., Zhou, X.: An effectiveness study on trajectory similarity measures. Australasian Database Conf., 13–22 (2013)
20. Xin, D., Han, J., Chang, K.C.-C.: Progressive and selective merge: computing top-k with ad-hoc ranking functions. In: ACM SIGMOD, pp. 103–114 (2007)
21. Xuan, W., Chen, Z., Zhai, L.: An improved divide-and-conquer algorithm for finding top-k longest common subsequence. In: NLPIR, pp. 200–204 (2020)
22. Yang, D., Zhang, D., Zheng, V.W., Yu, Z.: Modeling user activity preference by leveraging user spatial temporal characteristics in LBSNs. IEEE Trans. Syst. Man Cybern. Syst. **45**(1), 129–142 (2015)
23. Zhang, X., Chomicki, J.: On the semantics and evaluation of top-k queries in probabilistic databases. In: ICDE, pp. 556–563 (2008)

Exploratory Data Analysis of Time Series Using Pre-segmented Clustering

Vineeta Jain[1]([📧]) [iD], Zihao Huang[2], Anna Richter[1], Ulf Wetzker[1],
and Andreas Frotzscher[1]

[1] Fraunhofer Institute for Integrated Circuits, Division Engineering of Adaptive
Systems EAS, Dresden, Germany
vineeta.jain@eas.iis.fraunhofer.de
[2] Technische Universität Dresden, Dresden, Germany

Abstract. Time series clustering is an unsupervised method of organizing homogeneous time series in groups based on certain similarity criteria. As a result, it can be an essential step in Exploratory Data Analysis (EDA), especially for complex time series data. This applies specifically to industrial datasets for applications like predictive maintenance, energy consumption, etc., due to the heterogeneity and peculiarity of collected data sets. Understanding the underlying trends and patterns in such datasets could help strategize advanced analysis methods such as forecasting, regression testing, etc. In this paper, we present a case study on a real-world energy consumption dataset of 4G cells, where we perform a pre-segmented clustering based EDA to uncover hidden insights about the data. The empirical study demonstrates that performing pre-segmented clustering based EDA enhances data interpretation by revealing prevalent and infrequent patterns, empowering users to refine analyses such as prediction more precisely, leading to performance improvement.

Keywords: Exploratory Data Analysis · Times series · Clustering

1 Introduction

In traditional time series clustering, time series data are typically clustered as whole entities, i.e., a time series dataset T consisting of p time series $\langle Y_1, Y_2...Y_p \rangle$ are clustered into R clusters based on certain criteria. However, when dealing with long time series data, for instance, the ones spanning different seasons, this approach often fails to yield meaningful results as their behavior can vary significantly over time. Alternatively, dividing a long time series $Y = \langle y_1, y_2...y_h \rangle$ into smaller, meaningful and equal N segments $\{\langle X_1, X_2, ..X_N \rangle | X_1 \cup X_2.. \cup X_N = Y\}$ and clustering these segments into k clusters can reveal different patterns and trends present in one single time series. For instance, clustering a time series representing the electricity consumption of a customer could reveal differences in his consumption behavior on weekdays, weekends, summer/winter holidays, special events, etc., that could be used for tasks like customer profiling, maintenance scheduling, etc. Hence, this approach of pre-segmentation clustering could potentially offer a comprehensive view of the time series data.

For clustering real-world time series datasets that contain a lot of variations and noise, an algorithm is required that can effectively handle data with non-linearity, homogeneity, and outliers. The most common approach is Hierarchical Density-Based Spatial Clustering of Applications with Noise (HDBSCAN) [4]. Unlike k-means and agglomerative clustering, HDBSCAN can detect clusters of varying shapes, and unlike DBSCAN, it can detect clusters of varying densities, making it a suitable choice for practical applications. However, HDBSCAN detects many outliers[1] due to its sensitivity to low-density regions [5]. Not all points are true outliers; some are just falsely labeled due to local density fluctuations and the inherent complexity of the data [5]. This diminishes the interpretability and quality of resulting clusters. In this paper, we integrated an outlier reduction step known as Centroid Proximity Outlier Reduction (CPOR) in HDBSCAN, which, after clustering, performs a post-processing of outliers to reduce mislabeling, making the clusters more representative of the intrinsic data patterns.

The objective of this paper is to demonstrate the usefulness of pre-segmented clustering during the exploration phase of intricate and heterogeneous datasets. We perform a case study on a real-world energy consumption time series dataset, where we have data available for several months. For better visualization, the detected clusters are mapped on a monthly calendar using different colors. We discuss the significance of each cluster and the impact it has on advanced analyses to reflect the utility of pre-segmented clustering in comprehending the data and polishing the follow-up analysis.

2   Background

This section explains the pre-segmented clustering method used for performing exploratory data analysis of the time series dataset. It includes three steps:

Pre-segmentation: We define pre-segmentation as the human-assisted process of dividing a time series into smaller segments. Given a time series X containing n data points $X = \{x_1, x_2, ...x_n\}$ and L as a segment length $(n \gg L)$, X can be divided into $m = \frac{n}{L}$ segments, where each segment d_i consists of L consecutive data points: $d_i = \{x_{(i-1)L+(1)}, x_{(i-1)L+(2)}, ...x_{(i-1)L+(L-2)}, x_{(i-1)L+(L-1)}, x_{(iL)}\}$, where $i = 1, 2.....m$. A new dataset $D = \{d_1, d_2,...,d_m\}$ is created such that $\{d_1 \cup d_2....\cup d_m = X\}$.

Clustering: We use HDBSCAN to perform clustering. It has one crucial hyperparameter - minimum number of points necessary to form a cluster ($MinPts$),

---

[1] In this paper, terms noise and outlier(s) are used interchangeably.

to be specified while clustering. Since tuning of $MinPts$ is ambiguous, we implement a grid-search function $gridS(D, MinPts_{min}, MinPts_{max}) \rightarrow MinPts_{best}$, such that:

$$MinPts_{best} = \underset{MinPts_{min} \leq MinPts \leq MinPts_{max}}{\text{argmax}} \{SC(HDBSCAN(D, MinPts)\} \quad (1)$$

where,

- $[MinPts_{min}, MinPts_{max}]$ is the range for $MinPts$ to search over,
- HDBSCAN(D,$MinPts$) represents the HDBSCAN clustering performed on D using $MinPts$ as hyperparameter,
- SC represents the silhouette coefficient for the predicted clusters.

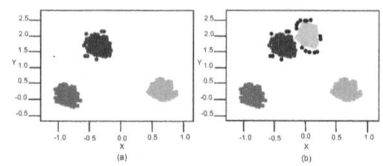

Fig. 1. An example of mislabeling of data points as outliers by HDBSCAN. Here, the points labeled as black in (b) are mislabeled as outliers due to the close proximity of two dense clusters.

In simple words, the $MinPts$ value, which generates the clusters that gives the maximum SC is selected for the final clustering. SC is defined as the ratio of intra-cluster distance to inter-cluster distance and lies in the range of $[-1, 1]$ [6]. The higher the value of SC, the better the clustering is [6]. Since silhouette coefficient represents the tightness of a cluster and works well for density based clustering methods [2], we use SC as an objective function for choosing $MinPts_{best}$[2]. After obtaining $MinPts_{best}$, for a given dataset D, HDBSCAN(D, $MinPts_{best}$) generates k clusters $C = \{C_{-1}, C_1, C_2....C_{k-1}\}$, where C_{-1} contains the outliers, i.e., points which are not clustered by HDBSCAN in any cluster $C_{i|i \in [1,k-1]}$.

Post-processing: When two dense clusters are detected very close to each other, some points near those clusters are mislabeled as outliers by HDBSCAN. Figure 1 represents an example. To handle such outliers, we implement a Centroid Proximity Outlier Reduction (CPOR) algorithm detailed in Algorithm 1. The fundamental idea of CPOR is to represent each cluster by a centroid and assign an outlier to the cluster whose centroid is closest to the outlier in the feature space. However, not every outlier is a mislabeling. To prevent such outliers from getting assigned to clusters, we measure the relative proximity of the outlier to the clusters (Line 8 in Algorithm 1). By comparing the minimum centroid distance of an outlier (L_{min}) against the normalized centroid distances, we ensure that the outlier is reassigned only if it is relatively close to the clusters, taking into account inherent variability in cluster spreads and overall cluster distribution.

3 Application on Industrial Dataset - A Case Study

We used the presented approach to conduct the EDA of a real-world energy consumption dataset collected for the CANOPY project [1]. It is a project that

---

[2] For more details about silhouette coefficient, please refer to [6].

Algorithm 1.. Centroid Proximity Outlier Reduction (CPOR)

Require: Clusters $C = \{C_{-1}, C_1, C_2, \ldots, C_{k-1}\}$
Ensure: Reassigned outliers
1: Calculate centroids CC_i for each cluster C_i, where $i \in [1, k-1]$
2: **for** each pair of clusters (C_i, C_j), $1 \le i, j < k$ and $i \ne j$ **do**
3:      Compute centroid distances $CD_{i,j} = \|CC_i - CC_j\|$
4: **for** each outlier $O \in C_{-1}$ **do**
5:      **for** each cluster C_i, $i \in [1, k-1]$ **do**
6:          Compute Euclidean distance $L_i = \|O - CC_i\|$
7:      Find the minimum distance $L_{min} = \min\{L_i \mid i \in [1, k-1]\}$
8:      **if** $L_{min} > \underset{i,j \in [1, k-1] \wedge i \ne j}{\forall} \frac{CD_{i,j}}{max\{CD_{u,v} \mid 1 \le u,v < k\}}$ **then**
9:          $C^O = -1$ ▷ O remains in C_{-1} as an outlier
10:     **else**
11:        $C^O = \underset{1 \le i < k}{\operatorname{argmin}} [\|O - CC_i\|]$ ▷ O is assigned to the nearest cluster

---

focuses on the optimization of 4G/5G mobile communication networks. The dataset contains hourly values for energy management counters that provide a comprehensive overview of energy consumed by all cells within a designated site. The dataset encompasses a total of 22 urban sites for which geographical locations are also available and spans over seven months, from October 2022 to April 2023 (5088 h). We perform univariate clustering[3] by using the power consumption of 4G cells, which is equal to the sum of power consumption of the boards and RF (Radio frequency) modules working in LTE (Long-Term Evolution) mode. We segment the time series of a cell into days such that every day (24 h) is a separate time series and then cluster similar days together by using the approach explained in Sect. 2. Table 1 shows the parameters used for clustering. To enhance explainability, we plot the clusters on a calendar.

Figure 2(b) shows the clusters generated for the time series shown in Fig. 2(a), where the x-axis represents time and the y-axis represents scaled values of the counter 'VS.EnergyCons.BTS.Adding' for a cell located in a university. Due to the semester exams in January, the energy consumption of the cellular network during the holidays and weekends this month

Table 1. Values used for clustering

Param	Value
m	$\frac{n}{L} = \frac{5088}{24} = 212$
$MinPts_{min}$	2
$MinPts_{max}$	7(no. of months)

is more than the rest of the months. This indicates a strong correlation between student activity and network usage. For cellular network providers who plan to optimize resources by shutting down cells or baseband processors during periods of low traffic, such events can be helpful as they need to consider periods of high activity to ensure consistent and efficient service. Similarly, Fig. 3(a) shows the behavior of a cell located near a hospital that is functional 24X7. One could clearly observe the reduced network traffic during Christmas vacations in hospitals, probably due to fewer staff and patients. This underscores the importance of considering human activity patterns in network management.

---

[3] If the clustering is performed on a time series containing a single value for every time interval, i.e., only one counter is used, it is known as univariate clustering.

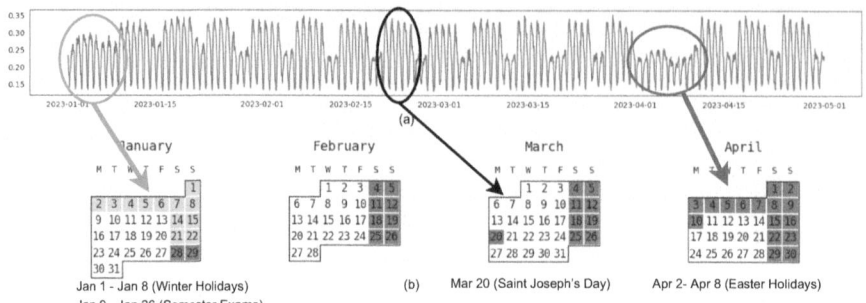

Fig. 2. (a) Time series of a cell located in a University. (b) Detected clusters marked on a calendar using different colors. (Color figure online)

Figure 3(b) shows clusters identified for a cell located near a stadium. On 6th and 7th April, a game was played in the stadium, so the energy consumption for the mobile network was higher in the area. This is an infrequent event. If the time series is explored by traditional EDA methods like visual representation, one could miss this event. However, with our approach, this event gets highlighted. Also, all such events when the game was played in the stadium could be easily extracted using this EDA step, and then this information can be used to forecast future consumption patterns in case of such events. Thus, including this EDA step can be a useful tool for analyzing and understanding the data better.

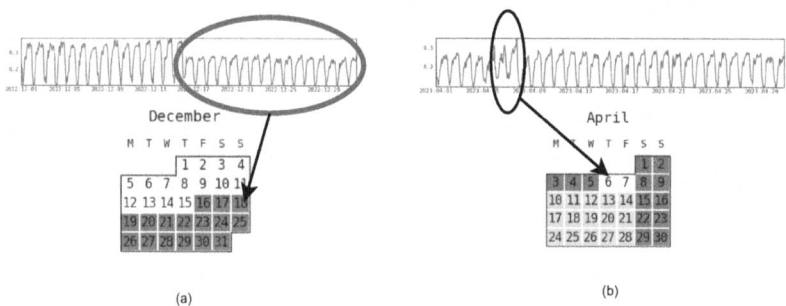

Fig. 3. Time series and clusters detected for cells located near (a) hospital, (b) stadium.

3.1   A Study on Sensitivity of CPOR

In this section, we assess the accuracy and robustness of CPOR in relation to assigning outliers near dense and sparse clusters using two benchmark datasets. The first dataset [7] is a time series dataset from the UCI Machine Learning repository. Figure 4(a) shows the clusters detected by HDBSCAN for this dataset

(SC = 0.28). Due to the sensitivity of HDBSCAN to sparse regions, outliers are detected (plotted in red color in Fig. 4(a)). Applying CPOR reassigned these outliers (Fig. 4(b)), improving the SC to 0.54, indicating better cluster quality. However, for the second dataset [3], CPOR wrongly labeled some outliers, marked by an arrow in Fig. 4(d). This issue arises when clusters are more dispersed, causing outliers near the border to be incorrectly assigned to smaller, nearby clusters, as CPOR only measures the minimum distance to the centroid (Line 11 of Algorithm 1) for determining the suitable cluster for an outlier. In the future, we plan to work towards refining CPOR with adaptive thresholds or alternative distance metrics to improve its accuracy further in handling outliers in various clustering scenarios.

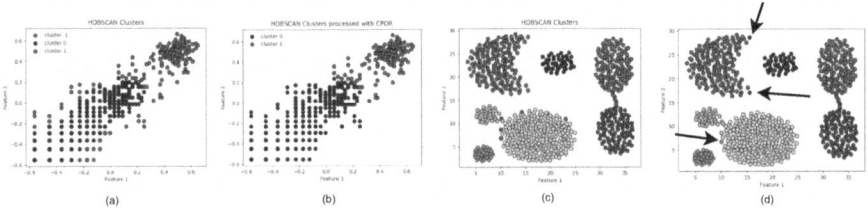

Fig. 4. Clusters generated for benchmark datasets from HDBSCAN and post processed via CPOR

4   Conclusions

By conducting a case study on a real-world dataset, we showed that pre-segmented clustering based EDA provides deep insights into time series data by highlighting not only recurring patterns, but also and rare, uncommon and anomalous cases. Moreover, the clusters could be additional information for further analysis. This can result in significant improvement compared to an equal form analysis where a single non-optimal method is applied over the whole time series. This can be useful for professionals working with time series data related to predictive maintenance, energy consumption, network planning, etc., for optimizing allocation of resources. As stated, "The goal is to turn data into information, and information into insight." We believe this EDA step greatly aids in achieving it.

Acknowledgments. This work is supported by Federal Ministry for Economic Affairs and Climate Action of the Federal Republic of Germany (BMWK) within the CELTIC-NEXT project "CANOPY" (https://www.celticnext.eu/project-canopy/) under Funding Label 01MJ22013A.

References

1. Cognitive and automated network operations for present and beyond (2023). https://www.celticnext.eu/project-canopy/. Accessed 01 Jan 2024
2. Dockhorn, A., Braune, C., Kruse, R.: An alternating optimization approach based on hierarchical adaptations of DBSCAN. In: 2015 IEEE Symposium Series on Computational Intelligence, pp. 749–755. IEEE (2015)
3. Fränti, P., Sieranoja, S.: K-means properties on six clustering benchmark datasets (2018). http://cs.uef.fi/sipu/datasets/
4. Kurki, S., Halla-Aho, V., Haussmann, M., Lähdesmäki, H., Leinonen, J.V., Koskinen, M.: A comparative study of clinical trial and real-world data in patients with diabetic kidney disease. Sci. Rep. **14**(1), 1731 (2024)
5. Peng, J., Chen, Y.: Density-based clustering with boundary samples verification. Appl. Soft Comput., 111685 (2024)
6. Shutaywi, M., Kachouie, N.: Silhouette analysis for performance evaluation in machine learning with applications to clustering. Entropy **23**(6), 759 (2021)
7. Tan, J.: Sales Transactions Weekly. UCI Machine Learning Repository (2017). https://doi.org/10.24432/C5XS4Q

A Data Science Approach for Predicting Soccer Passes Using Positional Data

Sebastian Eigenrauch[1], Jonas Bischofberger[2] (ID), Arnold Baca[2] (ID),
and Erich Schikuta[1]([✉]) (ID)

[1] Research Group Workflow Systems and Technology, Faculty of Computer Science,
University of Vienna, Vienna, Austria
sebastian.eigenrauch@gmx.de, erich.schikuta@univie.ac.at
[2] Centre for Sport Science and University Sports,
University of Vienna, Vienna, Austria
{jonas.bischofberger,arnold.baca}@univie.ac.at

Abstract. Data-driven approaches for evaluating tactical team behavior in soccer are nowadays a widespread method in sport analytics. The large amount of data collections enables experts to generate a deep tactical understanding and extract valuable measurements out of team-performances. However, these approaches are often limited in their comprehensibility and applicability for domain experts. Additionally, defensive behaviour in soccer is notoriously difficult to measure and has been receiving less attention in research and practice compared to measuring offensive performance. The motivation of this research is the design, implementation and validation of data science algorithms, that predict tactical motion of defending players after an occurring event of a pass, one of the most common events in soccer matches. The focus is the establishment and validation of different sets of rules, which simulate the movement behavior of the defending team, based on domain knowledge. The approach provides a high level of applicability for domain experts, in order to use and combine variable predefined rules for prediction, simulation and evaluation of different tactical approaches of defensive behavior.

Keywords: Data Science Model · Sport Analytics · Soccer
Simulation · Pass Prediction

1 Introduction

The application of tracking technology, in order to measure the tactical match performance of a team, is nowadays a commonly used feature in professional soccer. A large amount of data, which provides the possibility to gain valuable insights into tactical team-performances, has been collected over the years. Data-driven approaches enable the extraction of representative measurements, which researchers, as well as domain experts can use, in order to gain a deeper understanding and insights into tactical soccer projections. In soccer, a team's

P. Delir Haghighi et al. (Eds.): iiWAS 2024, LNCS 15342, pp. 259–274, 2025.
https://doi.org/10.1007/978-3-031-78090-5_22

tactical behavior is an important component for a successful winning strategy, whereby the application of data-driven approaches for evaluation and analysis is a widespread method [6]. One of the most frequently occurring events during a soccer match are passes. Every pass of the attacking team results in a reaction of the defending team, in most cases through an adaptation of the positions of the defending players [9].

In this research, we focus on the design, implementation and validation of data science algorithms, that predict tactical motion of defending players, based on the occurring event of a pass. Thus, we follow the approach of Rule-based Systems [12]. We concentrate on the establishment and validation of different sets of rules, which simulate the movement behavior of the defending team. These sets of rules follow common defending tactics in modern soccer, which we use to predict and evaluate defending player motion after a played pass. We focus on the establishment of a framework, that is applicable for domain experts. Thus, we aim to enable soccer experts to use and combine variable predefined rules, in order to predict, simulate and evaluate different tactical approaches for defensive behavior.

The paper is structured as follows: In the next Sect. 2 the related work is presented. In Sect. 3 we describe the problem in focus and the used theoretical models. The justification and evaluation of our approach is detailed in Sect. 4, which is followed by the lessons learned and limitations of our findings in Sect. 5. The paper closes with the summary and an outlook onto future work.

2   State of the Art

By large data sets, experts are capable of using the underlying data in order to extract information and establish valuable predictions. In soccer, positional data sets help researchers to simulate, how hypothetical actions or events influence the tactical team performance and player positioning of the participating actors [3]. In general, we distinguish between the approaches of Rule-based Systems and Machine Learning, where the methods of Machine Learning can be further divided into Supervised Learning (SL), Unsupervised Learning (UL) and Reinforcement Learning (RL):

Unsupervised Learning algorithms enable the extraction of rules from data without any human intervention. Occurring patterns and conclusions are found by the model through the provided unlabeled data. Thus, the model does not require any learning instructions, as it discovers solutions by itself [5]. UL is applicable to large data sets and a commonly used approach for the evaluation of tactical team sport behavior. For instance, an Unsupervised Learning approach is applied by [20], where tactical soccer patterns based on match logs are automatically identified through the UL method of principal component analysis (PCA). The study applies PCA, in order to reduce redundant data, by mapping similar types of player to one role. These roles serve as representatives for a general tactical team evaluation. [4] applies the UL method of hierarchical clustering to detect tactics out of soccer matches. Thus, different clusters of the phases of a match are established, where one team is in possession of the ball. Frequently occurring patterns are then identified and evaluated [4].

Supervised Learning approaches are rather applicable for training algorithms to classify data or predict specific outcomes. Since these algorithms are defined by labeled data sets, they differ from an Unsupervised Learning approach [8]. The method usually develops models from data sets, using previously known input and output values [1]. Thus, models are fed with input data, where they adjust their weights until they have been fitted appropriately [8]. An SL approach in team sport is applied in [15], using neural networks to classify offensive strategies in NBA basketball games, based on players tracking data. A similar approach is performed by [18]. The research focuses on artificial neural networks and decision trees, to forecast game results in basketball, while similar methods are being applied to soccer [7].

In Reinforcment Learning, an agent learns a policy independently through specific actions in order to maximize cumulative rewards. Thus, the model uses a trial and error approach, where a sequence of successful outputs is further reinforced to develop the best recommendation or policy for a given problem [17]. A model's reward function can be estimated from observed data through statistical learning techniques. Besides, explicit assumptions for an optimal criteria of player motion can be made with predefined reward functions such as the score in soccer [5]. A RL approach in team sport is used in [19]. This method establishes a mapping between player and the decision to double team. This mapping is compared to a cumulative reward of blocked shots. Thus, a policy can be established, where the actions that maximize the expected reward are selected [19]. Another projection to be mentioned is conducted by [10]. This method follows an approach called *Deep Imitation Learning*, where a model automatically learns from expert behavior instead of a predefined reward function. The motion of defending soccer players can therefore be predicted, by comparing the movement of the league average or a specific team with the actual defending team [10].

Many different models exist, in order to forecast player motion in soccer, with a focus on rule-based approaches [2]. These Rule-based Systems are usually defined as a set of rules, in order to apply and evaluate data. Thus, they use the knowledge of domain experts, to establish hypotheses and extract representative values from data [12]. RBS are a commonly used approach in different sports sectors, where experts define theories, based on the characteristical behavior of multi-agents, such as individual players in soccer [5]. Representative values through RBS in soccer are applied in [11], in order to analyze a team's goal scoring probability. The implemented rules define an increasing goal scoring probability, within a decreasing distance to the opponent's goal and an increasing centrality of the ball position. A rule based approach with a rather focus on predicting specific values, is applied in [16]. Thus, the approach predicts the scoring opportunity of players, that are not in possession of the ball. Hypotheses are defined, with regard to an attacking team's ball control, the likelihood of a successful pass and the goal scoring probability. These prerequisites are used to provide a future indicator of a team's probability to score [16].

3   Prediction Framework

3.1   Problem Description

In modern soccer, tactical defending behavior is an essential ability and decisive for the success of a team. Since various tactical approaches exist, the behavior of defending players differs, based on the underlying tactical inputs and leads to different movements of the defenders. As mentioned in the previous sections, literature provides different projections, in order to predict player motion in soccer. Even though, many of them enable a highly accurate prediction and a detailed match analysis such as [10], evaluations based on a team's underlying tactical background are rather rare. Without this information, prediction models tend to be difficult to understand for domain experts and might complicate their applicability [5].

With our framework, we follow the approach of establishing predefined rules, in order to forecast and evaluate the movement of defending players of different matches and game constellations. We decide to establish prediction models, that use the knowledge of domain experts. While the previously described RBS approaches rather focus on the extraction of representative values in soccer, e.g. the evaluation of a team's goal scoring probability [11], our focal point is the establishment of different sets of rules, in order to predict and evaluate the movement of defending players. Thus, we use domain knowledge, in order to deploy different prediction models with a common tactical soccer approach as basement. We define rules for describing different projections of defending behavior in soccer, such as e.g. zone defense or man marking defending. Besides, the set up of our framework is designed, that it can easily be used by soccer experts, in order to combine different rules and build new models.

3.2   Data Sets

For the evaluation and establishment of our prediction models, we use the public data set provided by Metrica Sports [14], which includes three independent and anonymous soccer games. The data has been collected through video tracking systems at a frequency of 25 Hz. To enhance data evaluation, the collected data is subdivided into different Game Events such as e.g. passes or dribblings. Passes are defined as the change of possession of the ball, between two players of the same team. As our prediction models are based on a pass event, we filtered out the events relevant for our models. This results in a total amount of 1074 passes for Game 1, 1191 passes for Game 2 and 1434 passes for Game 3.

3.3   Single-Rule Models

To accurately predict the defending players' positions on the field, we implemented three single-rule models. These models, each based on a specific rule, employ basic tactical approaches to provide baseline references for predicting player movement. They demonstrate fundamental team behaviors and can be integrated with more complex prediction models.

No Movement Model (NMM). The No Movement Model (NMM) assumes that defenders maintain their current positions following a pass. This model serves as a baseline for comparison with other predictive models.

Rule: The predicted positions of the defenders are identical to their positions before the pass.

Each defender's velocity is set to zero. The model predicts defenders' positions based on their initial coordinates without movement. This baseline is crucial for validating other models; if the NMM outperforms other models, it indicates potential inaccuracies in those models.

Move Towards Ball Model (MTBM). The Move Towards Ball Model (MTBM) posits that defenders move towards the ball's position after a pass. This model is relevant in scenarios like corner kicks, where defenders focus on the ball to prevent shots or clear it.

Rule: Defenders move towards the ball's new position.

The distance covered by each defender is calculated based on their velocity and the time duration of the pass. Using Bayesian optimization, we determine each player's velocity. The movement direction is calculated using the angle between the player's position and the ball's new position, forming a right-angled triangle. This model provides insight into ball-oriented defending and can be expanded by combining it with other rules.

Pass Angle Model (PAM). The Pass Angle Model (PAM) assumes defenders move in the same direction as the pass, maintaining their formation. This model is suitable for scenarios where the ball is in a neutral area and the defending team retains its shape.

Rule: Defenders move in the direction of the ball's movement.

The distance covered by each defender is calculated similarly to the MTBM. The passing angle is determined using the ball's positions before and after the pass, forming a right-angled triangle. This angle is applied to each defender's movement direction. Although the model is based on a single rule, it predicts specific game constellations and can be integrated with other rules for more complex tactical models.

3.4 Complex-Rule Models

Predicting soccer players' positions involves numerous factors, such as physical condition and individual decision-making. Despite this complexity, professional players adhere to fundamental defensive rules to optimize their performance. Our approach utilizes these principles, creating rulesets for position prediction and training models based on various tactical behaviors.

Complex-rule models rely on domain expertise to formulate hypotheses and extract representative values for robust evaluations. The rules employed are based on current tactical behaviors and have been validated by two independent experts (see Sect. 4.1). Due to the complexity and variability of player movements, our models are designed for high flexibility and adaptability, allowing easy modification of rulesets by adding or removing rules.

Man Marking. Our initial prediction model is based on man marking, where each defender is assigned to an opponent. Unlike strict man marking, which maintains fixed assignments, our Man Marking Model (MMM) employs a loose man marking approach, allowing dynamic reassignment based on the attackers' movements. The MMM ruleset includes:

– Player Marking: Defenders mark the nearest unmarked opponent, starting with the most defensive player.
– Go Towards Ball: The closest defender moves towards the ball, overriding other assignments.
– Direct Opponent: If a defender's closest opponent is within two meters, the defender moves towards them.
– Do Not Move: Goalkeepers remain stationary after a pass.

Figure 1 visualizes how defenders adjust positions post-pass, with the closest defender moving towards the ball and others marking their nearest unmarked opponents. This model can be expanded with additional rules, offering a robust tool for simulating and predicting defensive behaviors.

Zone Defending. Our Zone Defending Model (ZDM) employs a zone defense strategy, where defenders cover specific areas rather than marking individual opponents. This involves establishing defending lines that move cohesively based on ball position and player spacing. The ZDM divides defenders into lines corresponding to their initial formation, with an orientation player leading the movement. Key features of the ZDM include:

– Line Establishment: Defenders form lines according to their formation (e.g., 4-4-2).
– Ball-Oriented Movement: Lines shift as a unit based on the ball's position.
– Optimization: Player distances within lines are optimized using Bayesian Optimization, typically ranging from 5 to 15 m.
– Ball Pursuit: The closest defender moves towards the ball, regardless of line position.
– Goalkeeper: Goalkeepers remain stationary.

Figure 2 illustrates how defenders adjust positions within their lines, maintaining structured defense while dynamically responding to the ball.

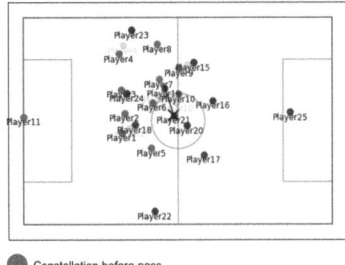

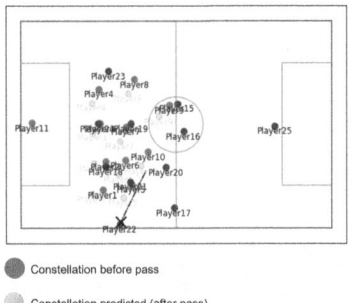

Fig. 1. Constellation plot of the *Man Marking Model* for the defending team (red figures). The transparent figures forecast, where the player of the defending team will move, after a pass has been played. The filled figures simulate the current game constellation and the actual position of the defenders. The black line visualises the pass that has been played, with the filled X as the ball position after the pass has been played. (Color figure online)

Fig. 2. Constellation plot of the *Zone Defending Model* for the defending team (red figures). The transparent figures forecast, where the player of the defending team will move, after a pass has been played. The filled figures simulate the current game constellation and the actual position of the defenders. The black line visualises the pass that has been played, with the filled X as the ball position after the pass has been played. (Color figure online)

Combination Model. Modern soccer tactics often require blending different defensive approaches based on game context. Our Combination Model (CM) integrates multiple rulesets within a single framework, adapting to specific game situations. This meta-ruleset approach applies different rulesets to different pitch zones (Attacking Zone, Midfield Zone, and Defending Zone). The CM uses Bayesian Optimization to define zone boundaries, applying appropriate rulesets accordingly. For example, the ZDM might govern neutral zones, while the MMM is used near the goal. Figures 3 and Fig. 4 demonstrate dynamic switching between rulesets based on the ball's position, providing a nuanced and realistic prediction model for defender movements.

Overall, the Combination Model enhances predictive accuracy and flexibility, offering a valuable tool for analyzing and planning defensive tactics in soccer.

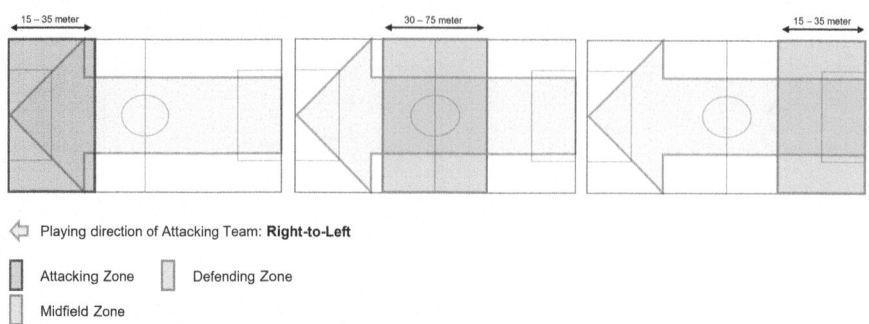

Playing direction of Attacking Team: **Right-to-Left**

Attacking Zone   Defending Zone

Midfield Zone

Fig. 3. Visualisation of the three different zones for our Metaruleset.

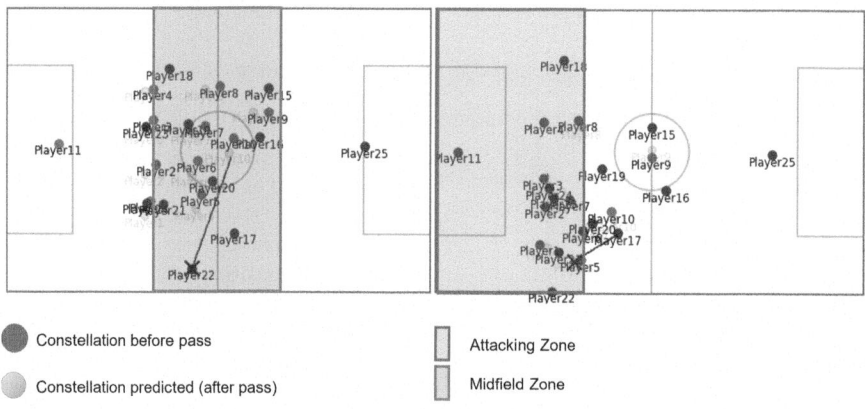

Constellation before pass   Attacking Zone

Constellation predicted (after pass)   Midfield Zone

Fig. 4. Visualisation of our *Combination Model*. On the left-hand side, the current ball position is located in the Midfield Zone, whereby the ZDM is applied. On the right-hand side, the ball enters the Attacking Zone, why defenders change their defending behavior according to the MMM.

4   Justification and Evaluation of Approach

In this section, we employ predictive modeling to anticipate the movements of defending players, followed by an evaluation of the results. To establish a reliable benchmark for comparison, we introduce a prediction error (Θ) for each model, serving as a measure of prediction accuracy. We describe the optimization of variable parameters in our models and provide justification from independent domain experts to ensure the credibility of our approach. Subsequently, we evaluate each prediction model, analyzing prediction errors and identifying recurring defending patterns. Comparative analysis of our prediction models is conducted to generate insights into tactical defending approaches in soccer.

4.1   Justification

To ensure the realism of our models and the alignment of established rules with real-world tactical strategies, we sought validation from two independent domain experts. Through interviews, we elucidated the behavior of our models and their tactical underpinnings. Both experts affirmed the realism and applicability of our models in real-world scenarios. In particular, ball-oriented defending, man-marking, and zone-based defending are considered to be relevant tactical concepts that are well suited for modelling the defensive behaviour of players.

The first expert consulted was X[1], who served as the Head Coach of a University soccer for over 20 years. X led the University soccer team to multiple appearances in the Bavarian University Championship and participated in international matches, including contests against the Student National Team of other countries and various partner universities.

The second expert, Y[3], currently serves as the Head Coach of the Under 15 youth team at a German Bundesliga club. Y began his career as a player for German Bundesliga teams, playing under renowned coaches. Following his playing career, Y transitioned into coaching, eventually assuming the role of Head Coach for the Under 15 youth team.

Both experts possess extensive coaching experience at a high level, validating the tactical foundation of our models against contemporary soccer strategies. Leveraging their expertise, we developed robust prediction models capable of forecasting and evaluating various game scenarios based on diverse tactical approaches.

4.2   Validation Model

We outline our validation model to accurately measure the performance of the deployed prediction models. The prediction error (Θ)) is computed by comparing the predicted and actual motions of defending players using the Euclidean distance formula 1.

$$\boldsymbol{\theta}_{(c)} = \frac{\sum_d^{11} \sqrt{(x_{d(pr)} - x_{d(a)})^2 + (y_{d(pr)} - y_{d(a)})^2}}{\frac{\sum_d^{11} P_d}{\lambda_c}} \tag{1}$$

Our defined *prediction error* (Θ) is computed for a given game constellation *(c)*. To compare predicted with actual positions, we calculate the distance for each defender *(d)*, between his predicted and his actual position. Thus, we apply the Pythagorean Theorem [13] with the x-coordinates (y-coordinates) of the predicted player positions $x_{d(pr)}$ respectively $y_{d(pr)}$ and the actual positions $x_{d(a)}$ respectively $y_{d(a)}$. In order to form the weighted average, we divide the quantum of the distances between predicted and actual position for each defender, through the total amount of defending players P_d, also taking into consideration the *time frame* (λ) of the played pass. We involve the duration of a pass, as shorter passes

---

might implicate lower prediction errors than a longer passes, due to a shorter movement time for each defender and therefore resultant a shorter deviation of the predicted and actual positions.

This error is calculated for each defender in a given game scenario, considering the duration of the pass. Our validation approach ensures equitable weighting of prediction errors across different passes, enabling meaningful comparisons between prediction models.

4.3 Evaluation

In this section, we assess the accuracy of our established models by examining the prediction error. We conduct a detailed analysis of three separate matches, scrutinizing individual game outcomes as well as calculating a cumulative prediction error for the entire dataset according to Eq. 1. Recognizing the diverse tactical approaches employed by soccer teams, we evaluate the performance of our models for both home and away teams, enabling us to discern any model suitability biases towards specific teams or their tactical strategies. Additionally, we compute predictions for both teams collectively to offer general insights into the effectiveness of the prediction model. Subsequently, we compare the prediction results of various models to ascertain which approach yields the lowest prediction error.

To mitigate the effects of parameter optimization on prediction error (denoted as Θ), we adjust the parameters within the Bayesian Optimization (BO) process to include 125 iterations and 75 initial points. This adjustment aims to minimize the deviation of Θ in each run of our prediction models. Furthermore, for consistency in the evaluation process, we employ a fixed seed number generator to ensure identical samples for every model run, thereby maintaining consistent prediction errors across individual models.

In our analysis of model applicability across different field areas, we identify the optimal prediction scores for each game. This involves establishing a threshold for acceptable prediction errors, below which each pass is evaluated. We illustrate these *best passes* by visualizing the ball's position after each pass. Given the convention of visualizing the defending team's playing direction from right-to-left, passes with a left-to-right direction are reversed to maintain consistency in visualization. Through the spatial distribution of ball positions, we discern patterns on the field to determine where each model demonstrates the highest accuracy.

Single-Rule Models. Now, we conduct an evaluation of our single-rule and complex-rule models, assessing their predictive performance and comparing them against our baseline model, the No Movement Model (NMM). We begin with the evaluation of the single-rule models, namely the No Movement Model (NMM), Move Towards Ball Model (MTBM), and Pass Angle Model (PAM), followed by an analysis of the complex-rule models, the Man Marking Model (MMM) and the Zone Defending Model (ZDM).

No Movement Model (NMM). The No Movement Model serves as our baseline, where defenders maintain their positions without movement after a pass. We observe the prediction errors (Θ) for each game and team, as summarized in Fig. 5. Notably, the away team generally exhibits lower prediction errors compared to the home team, suggesting potential differences in tactical approaches. Visualizations of the distribution of *best passes* for each game reveal patterns primarily along the wings and center of the field, with fewer defensive movements in non-threatening areas.

Move Towards Ball Model (MTBM). The Move Towards Ball Model emphasizes a ball-oriented defending approach. Figure 6 illustrates the prediction errors for each game, showing an overall lower error compared to the NMM. The away team consistently demonstrates lower prediction errors, indicating a more ball-oriented defensive strategy. Visual patterns of *best passes* reveal a focus on central midfield areas and offensive wings, suggesting a tendency towards ball-pressing movements and defensive positioning.

Pass Angle Model (PAM). The Pass Angle Model combines a ball-oriented approach with zone defense considerations. Evaluation results in Fig. 7 show a reduced overall prediction error compared to the NMM. Interestingly, the away team consistently exhibits lower prediction errors across games. Visualizations of *best passes* indicate a preference for attacking half positions, with notable patterns around the halfway line and wings, suggesting a zone-oriented defending behavior.

Complex-Rule Models

Man Marking Model (MMM). The Man Marking Model employs a player-oriented defending approach. Results in Fig. 8 indicate a lower overall prediction error compared to the NMM, with variations between home and away teams across games. Visual patterns of *best passes* reveal instances of man-marking behavior, particularly around the halfway line, indicating potential effectiveness in certain scenarios.

Zone Defending Model (ZDM). The Zone Defending Model implements a modern zone defense strategy. Evaluation results in Fig. 9 show a reduced overall prediction error compared to the NMM and MMM. Patterns of *best passes* suggest a focus on the midfield area and wings, indicating suitability for predicting defensive behavior in neutral field zones.

In summary, our models demonstrate varying degrees of accuracy in predicting defensive behavior, with complex-rule models generally outperforming single-rule models. The evaluation highlights the importance of considering tactical approaches in soccer for accurate defensive motion prediction.

Combination Model. The Combination Model (CM) seems to be a sophisticated approach to predicting defending player motion in soccer. Let break down the key points and findings from our analysis: The CM is built upon a Metarule-set framework that enables the combination and application of several rulesets. It combines two complex-rule based models: the Man Marking Model (MMM) and the Zone Defending Model (ZDM). ZDM is assigned to the attacking and midfield zones for a more zone-based defensive strategy, while MMM is applied in the defending zone for a man-oriented defensive behavior. Prediction errors Θ are used to evaluate the CM's performance, compared to individual models and a baseline model (No Movement Model). The total prediction error Θ for both teams is lower than the error for MMM and ZDM individually. This indicates that combining different tactical approaches results in higher prediction accuracy. There are similarities in prediction errors between home and away teams, with slightly lower errors for the away team. The prediction errors for the Combination Model are summarized in Fig. 10. A comparison of different models reveals that all established models provide better prediction accuracy than the baseline No Movement Model. The Man-to-Ball Model (MTBM) shows the highest accuracy, indicating that movement for defenders strongly depends on the ball's position on the field. The ZDM shows a slightly higher prediction error, possibly due to its rudimentary zone-defending behavior, which could be enhanced with additional rules focusing on a ball-oriented approach. Analysis of the *best passes* patterns suggests that zone-oriented defending is more common when passes are played towards the touchline, while a more man-oriented defense is needed for passes played in the center around the halfway line. The Combination Model (CM) demonstrates a higher prediction accuracy than individual models and the baseline No Movement Model. Understanding different tactical defending behaviors helps in predicting player motion more accurately, especially when considering the ball's position on the field. Overall, the Combination Model appears to be a promising approach for predicting defending player motion in soccer, offering insights into the effectiveness of different defensive strategies across various game scenarios.

5   Findings and Limitations

We developed models based on real-world soccer tactics, extracting fundamental soccer rules to build our prediction models. These models can predict various game scenarios using their tactical foundations. By comparing our models to a baseline where players remain stationary after a pass, we confirmed that our models provide predictions for real-world soccer.

Our framework predicts defending players' movements after a pass with above-baseline accuracy. Evaluations revealed that ball-oriented defending approaches are most effective for forecasting defending behavior. Defenders tend to follow certain rules that define their tactical movements, with a strong dependency on the ball's position. Our MTBM and PAM models, which rely heavily on ball movement, showed the highest prediction accuracy. We also identified

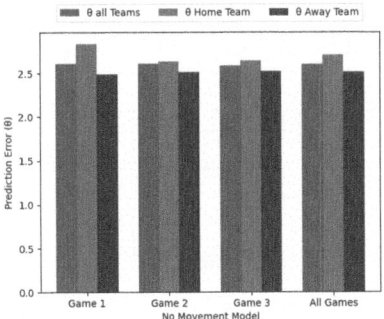

Fig. 5. Pred. errors for NMM

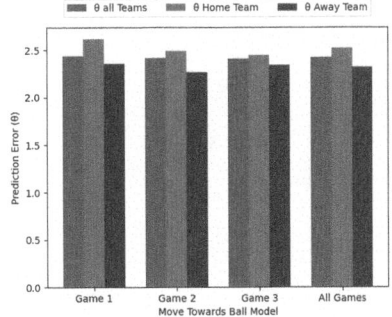

Fig. 6. Pred. errors for MTBM

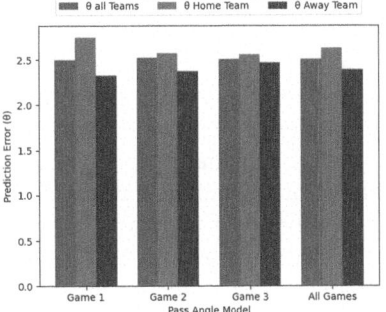

Fig. 7. Pred. errors for PAM

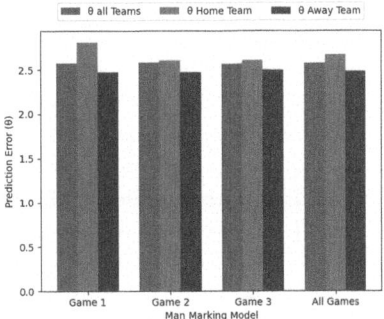

Fig. 8. Pred. errors for MMM

recurring defending patterns, finding that ball- and zone-oriented approaches are most accurate around the halfway line, while man-oriented approaches are effective around the penalty area. Overall, a significant forecasting error remains in all models, hinting at the inherent complexity of the mechanisms underlying defensive behaviour.

Comparing man-marking and zone defense approaches, we found that zone defense is more adaptable to in-game situations, with the ZDM outperforming the MMM in prediction accuracy. Enhancing our Zone Defending Model with more focus on ball-oriented movement could reduce prediction errors. Teams likely use a mix of tactics during a game, with defending behavior varying according to in-game situations.

Our findings suggest that ball-oriented defending is most promising, while strict man-marking seems outdated. Our framework, comprising Rules, Rulesets, and Metarulesets, allows for easy reconstruction and adjustment by adding new rules. This high reproducibility enables domain experts to refine our models, focusing on ball-oriented defending, and create new models to analyze game situations from different tactical perspectives.

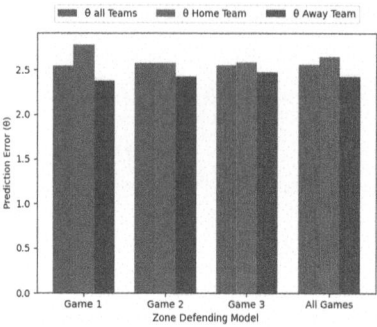

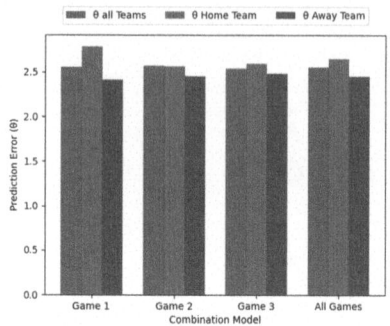

Fig. 9. Pred. errors for ZDM

Fig. 10. Pred. errors for CM

Despite the value of our prediction framework, it faces limitations. Accurate player motion prediction in soccer is complex, influenced by various factors. Our models rely on the tactical knowledge of domain experts, limiting their scope to the experts' insights. However, our framework's structure allows for easy rule adjustments and enhancements. Our evaluation was limited to three games; analyzing more matches could provide better tactical understanding and different results, as well as insights into the relation between tactical approach and match success. Not knowing the teams in the evaluated games complicates prediction analysis, as different teams have different tactical approaches. Our models also don't account for changes in match score or external factors like players' physical conditions.

6 Conclusion

We introduced a new method for predicting and evaluating player movement in soccer, focusing on defending players. Our framework, based on Rule-based Systems (RBS), uses defined rules as the core of our prediction models. This structure allows domain experts to easily create new models or adjust existing ones, enhancing the approach's applicability and flexibility.

Our evaluation showed that ball-oriented defending behavior yields the highest prediction accuracy and is most useful for analyzing specific game situations. All our models outperform the benchmark of no player movement, providing valuable forecasts for defending player motions. We also identified recurring defending patterns indicating where each model is most applicable. Man-oriented defending is effective around the penalty area and halfway line, while zone- and ball-oriented defending approaches perform best around the halfway line. This suggests that zone- and ball-oriented strategies are more relevant for modern soccer tactics than man-marking.

For future work, we plan to enhance our models by incorporating more rules focused on ball-oriented defending behavior, leveraging deeper domain knowledge to improve tactical complexity. Additionally, we see potential in integrating

Machine Learning algorithms, such as Imitation Learning, to replicate domain experts' behavior, which could further refine our approach.

References

1. Baladram, M.S., Koike, A., Yamada, K.D.: Introduction to supervised machine learning for data science. Interdisc. Inf. Sci. **26**(1), 87–121 (2020)
2. Bischofberger, J., Baca, A., Schikuta, E.: Event detection in football: improving the reliability of match analysis. PLoS ONE **19**(4), 1–17 (2024). https://doi.org/10.1371/journal.pone.0298107
3. Cichy, R.M., Kaiser, D.: Deep neural networks as scientific models. Trends Cogn. Sci. **23**(4), 305–317 (2019)
4. Decroos, T., Van Haaren, J., Davis, J.: Automatic discovery of tactics in spatio-temporal soccer match data. In: Proceedings of the 24th ACM SIGKDD International Conference on Knowledge Discovery & Data Mining, pp. 223–232 (2018)
5. Fujii, K.: Data-driven analysis for understanding team sports behaviors. J. Rob. Mechatron. **33**(3), 505–514 (2021)
6. Goes, F.R., Kempe, M., Meerhoff, L.A., Lemmink, K.A.: Not every pass can be an assist: a data-driven model to measure pass effectiveness in professional soccer matches. Big Data **7**(1), 57–70 (2019)
7. Hucaljuk, J., Rakipović, A.: Predicting football scores using machine learning techniques. In: 2011 Proceedings of the 34th International Convention MIPRO, pp. 1623–1627 (2011)
8. Jiang, H.: Machine Learning Fundamentals: A Concise Introduction. Cambridge University Press (2021)
9. Kempe, M., Vogelbein, M., Nopp, S.: The cream of the crop: analysing FIFA world cup 2014 and Germany's title run (2016)
10. Le, H., Carr, P., Yue, Y., Lucey, P.: Data-driven ghosting using deep imitation learning. In: MIT Sloan Sports Analytics Conference (2017)
11. Link, D., Lang, S., Seidenschwarz, P.: Real time quantification of dangerousity in soccer using spatiotemporal tracking data. In: International Association of Computer Science in Sport (IACSS) Conference, p. 12 (2016)
12. Liu, H., Gegov, A., Stahl, F.: Categorization and construction of rule based systems. In: Mladenov, V., Jayne, C., Iliadis, L. (eds.) EANN 2014. CCIS, vol. 459, pp. 183–194. Springer, Cham (2014). https://doi.org/10.1007/978-3-319-11071-4_18
13. Mathwarehouse.com: Pythagorean Theorem. https://www.mathwarehouse.com/geometry/triangles/how-to-use-the-pythagorean-theorem.php. Accessed 16 May 2023
14. Metrica-Sports: Metrica sports sample data (2021). https://github.com/metrica-sports/sample-data/commit/e706dd506b360d69d9d123d5b8026e7294b13996. Accessed 18 May 2023
15. Shah, R., Romijnders, R.: Applying deep learning to basketball trajectories. arXiv preprint arXiv:1608.03793 (2016)
16. Spearman, W.: Beyond expected goals. In: Proceedings of the 12th MIT Sloan Sports Analytics Conference, pp. 1–17 (2018)
17. Sutton, R.S., Barto, A.G.: Reinforcement Learning: An Introduction. MIT Press (2018)
18. Thabtah, F., Zhang, L., Abdelhamid, N.: NBA game result prediction using feature analysis and machine learning. Ann. Data Sci. **6**(1), 103–116 (2019)

19. Wang, J., Fox, I., Skaza, J., Linck, N., Singh, S., Wiens, J.: The advantage of doubling: a deep reinforcement learning approach to studying the double team in the NBA. arXiv preprint arXiv:1803.02940 (2018)
20. Wang, Q., Zhu, H., Hu, W., Shen, Z., Yao, Y.: Discerning tactical patterns for professional soccer teams: an enhanced topic model with applications. In: Proceedings of the 21th ACM SIGKDD International Conference on Knowledge Discovery and Data Mining, pp. 2197–2206 (2015)

Knowledge Graphs, Databases, and Ontologies

A Method for Integrating Heterogeneous Data into a Knowledge Graph

Christoph Göpfert$^{(\boxtimes)}$ ⓘ, Sheeba Samuel ⓘ, and Martin Gaedke ⓘ

Technische Universität Chemnitz, 09111 Chemnitz, Germany
{christoph.goepfert,sheeba.samuel,
martin.gaedke}@informatik.tu-chemnitz.de

Abstract. Knowledge graphs have gained popularity in many areas as a means of representing knowledge in a structured format. A large number of approaches for knowledge graph construction have been developed based on unstructured, semi-structured, or structured data sources. Many approaches focus on narrowly defined application areas or specific data source formats. In this paper, we describe a systematic method for knowledge graph construction from sources with heterogeneous data formats. The method comprises steps from ontology development to data acquisition and integration, mapping, and data refinement as well as the evolution of the constructed knowledge graph. We evaluate our approach using the case study of TUCgraph, a knowledge graph covering entities from the academic environment. This knowledge graph is actively being used within a research information system, demonstrating the practical applicability and effectiveness of our method.

Keywords: Knowledge Graph Development · Knowledge Graph Construction · Data Integration · Data Mapping · Data Evolution

1 Introduction

Knowledge graphs (KG) are a powerful tool to represent knowledge in a structured manner. As such, KGs have been increasingly adopted across various areas [1–3]. A common challenge in KG construction (KGC) is the integration of heterogeneous data from distributed sources. Integration of these data into a uniform structure plays a vital role in comprehensive data analysis, knowledge discovery, and decision-making [1].

The integration of heterogeneous data poses several challenges: diversity in data formats, structures, and multiplicity of sources complicate data extraction, cleaning, and harmonization processes [4]. Failure to address these may result in incorrect representations in the KG. Therefore, there is a strong need for a robust, systematic approach to overcoming these challenges. While the need to update a KG when source data changes is considered by some KGC approaches, it is often limited to KG maintenance and one-directional updates [4], disregarding that changes may have occurred in the KG itself.

© The Author(s), under exclusive license to Springer Nature Switzerland AG 2025
P. Delir Haghighi et al. (Eds.): iiWAS 2024, LNCS 15342, pp. 277–282, 2025.
https://doi.org/10.1007/978-3-031-78090-5_23

In this paper, we propose a six-step method for integrating heterogeneous data into a KG. We go beyond the sole consideration of maintenance aspects and address the evolution of data source(s) as well as the KG. In our case study, we demonstrate how the method was applied to construct a KG, which currently serves as the primary data source for a research information system.

2 Related Work

The development of ontologies, which provide the basis for KGs, is usually strongly dependent on the knowledge domain and format of the data source(s). Al-Zaidy and Giles [5] present a KGC approach to automatically extract entities and relations from scientific documents. Yet et al. [6] provide a survey that distinguishes generative KGC approaches, most of which assume unstructured text as source data. Kommineni et al. [7] illustrate an approach leveraging LLMs to support KGC tasks. However, a downside of automated approaches is that incorrect data may be generated, necessitating a subsequent review and refinement step. In addition, approaches to systematize KGC have been proposed. Asprino et al. [8] suggest an approach to transform heterogeneous data directly into the Resource Description Framework (RDF). However, their approach requires connectors dedicated to every source format. Tamašauskaitė and Groth [4] provide a literature review on KGC and propose a systematic six-step approach.

We present a systematic method that can be used to generate a KG from unstructured, semi-structured, or structured data sources. The method pays particular attention to the evolution of the KG and its data sources, an aspect that previous methods either neglected or only considered to a limited extent.

3 Method Description

Our method includes the steps: 1) ontology development, 2) data acquisition, 3) extraction and integration, 4) mapping, 5) refinement, and 6) update and evolution, which are based on previous methods such as [4]. However, we consider the ontology underlying the KG as a fundamental basis which should be in place in the data acquisition step. We also emphasize that a KG may be subject to change, i.e. evolving. Consequently, we extend the final step, which in previous approaches commonly involves only maintenance tasks, to account for the evolution of data source(s) and the KG itself.

3.1 Ontology Development

First, the underlying ontology of the KG must be developed. Entities and their relationships need to be described. This typically involves steps such as requirements specification, ontology design, construction, and evaluation [9]. For all identified entities, attributes and relations that are relevant to the selected domain or use case need to be identified. Next, the ontology can be modeled, manually or using an ontology editor. Based on the given entities, attributes and relationships, classes and properties are derived. Before defining new classes and properties, it should be checked if existing ontologies describe them and can be reused. Before defining new classes and properties, it should be checked if suitable ontologies exist that can be reused. Reusing ontologies reduces development effort and may enhance interoperability with established standards [8]. Once the ontology has been constructed, it should be evaluated based on the initially defined competency questions (cf. [9]). In addition, its quality should be evaluated. Should the evaluation yield unsatisfactory results, then the ontology should be improved, and the evaluation repeated, until a satisfactory result is achieved.

3.2 Data Acquisition

Data acquisition involves the identification and retrieval of data from one or multiple data sources. First, relevant data sources must be identified. Common techniques to obtain data include the utilization of APIs, which facilitate programmatic access to data provided by many online services and databases. To extract data from web pages, a popular method is web scraping. Another common data source is data dumps, which usually provide data in semi-structured formats, providing a convenient way to acquire a large amount of data at once. Once data sources have been identified and the data acquisition methods have been determined, the necessary infrastructure to collect and store data can be setup. Depending on the data volume and update frequency, this may include data pipelines, storage systems, and processing frameworks [10].

3.3 Extraction and Integration

Next, the acquired, raw data is converted into a structured format for integration. This step aims to ensure that the data is cleaned and curated, to enable an accurate mapping to the ontology in the next step. Extraction begins with identifying and isolating relevant entities, attributes, and relationships from the acquired data. Rule-based, dictionary-based, template-based approaches [11] may be used to automate this process fully or partially. In addition to entities, their describing attributes must also be extracted, as well as relations between entities. For this purpose, pattern-based or deep learning-based relation extraction approaches [12] can be utilized. The suitability of tools and techniques for extraction depends heavily on the format of the source data.

Once data is extracted, it needs to be cleaned. Data cleaning involves the correction or removal of incorrect, duplicate or incomplete data. This aims to recognize inconsistencies and errors in the data and, ideally, to correct them to improve data quality.

This is followed by data integration, in which data from multiple sources is harmonized and merged to create a unified data set. This may involve several challenges: different data sources may use different identifiers for one and the same entity, requiring a reconciliation of these identifiers to ensure consistency. In case of multiple data sources providing conflicting information about an entity, a conflict resolution strategy needs to be established. Finally, the result of this step is a unified dataset.

3.4 Mapping

The unified data must be aligned with the structure defined by the ontology. Entities must be assigned to appropriate classes; attributes, and relationships to corresponding data and object properties. For data type properties with a restricted value range, value type conversion is needed to ensure data integrity and consistency. This can be realized using the two-stage mapping process proposed by Asprino et al. [8]. First, mappings are defined to adhere to the structure of the ontology. Then, the mappings are processed to generate RDF data. This is repeated – editing mappings and evaluating the generated RDF data against the input data to identify errors – until a satisfactory result is achieved.

3.5 Refinement

Refinement involves evaluating the accuracy, consistency, completeness and adherence to defined constraints, i.e. on data types, cardinality, properties, or further constraints set through additional rules, e.g. using SHACL [13]. In addition, a reasoning engine should be used to infer based on the rules defined in the ontology. Doing so may enrich the data by inference [12] and identify any violated constraints. For further approaches to KG refinement, we refer to the survey of Paulheim [14].

3.6 Update and Evolution

Changes in source data should be reflected in the KG to keep it up to date. This may be realized by subscribing to data update events (active update techniques), or by periodically checking each data source for changes [15]. Active updates are not always realizable, as it requires an event feed of recent changes. In such cases, an update frequency predictor can be employed [16]. To distinguish older from new data and to ensure only the latest information is used, a versioning system can be employed [4]. More complex situations may require merging changes from multiple sources, analogous as described in Sect. 3.3. If the KG itself is subject to being modified, the update process becomes yet more complex, as data co-evolution (term as defined by Faisal et al. [17]) must be taken into account to integrate the updates to the data source(s) and the KG seamlessly.

Synchronization processes may also lead to errors, e.g. data inconsistencies, failed data updates, or incorrect merges. Therefore, the automation of synchronization with data sources requires careful monitoring and validation to detect errors. Automated processes must be able to handle situations where changes occur to a data source's schema that might disrupt data extraction and integration pipelines. Regular validation and plausibility checks may contribute to the early detection of such changes so that adjustments can be made to the extraction and mapping processes. Furthermore, over time it may be necessary to modify the ontology, refining or extending the ontology. This may require the migration of existing data in the KG to meet the requirements of the updated ontology. Consequently, assumptions made in the previous steps of extraction, processing, mapping, and validation steps may need to be reconsidered as well.

4   Case Study: TUCgraph

We applied the proposed method to construct TUCgraph, a KG currently used by the research information system (RIS) of Chemnitz University of Technology as the primary data source. At present (July 2024), TUCgraph contains 1,050,821 triples, aggregating and aligning data from multiple data sources. It entails entities such as university staff, organizational units, research projects, lab devices, events, and facilities.

Ontology Development. TUCgraph is employed by a RIS based on the open-source platform VIVO [18]. As VIVO requires a predefined set of ontologies, these were (re-) used as the basis of TUCgraph to satisfy the requirement.

Data Acquisition. The selected data sources include both internal university data sources and external API endpoints and websites. Whenever available, API endpoints were utilized. People and project data were enriched with data from external databases and websites of funding organizations. Data was partially obtained via web scraping due to the lack of a public API.

Extraction and Integration. For each source format, a Python script was developed to acquire, validate and integrate data into an aligned structure. To disambiguate entities referred to by differing names, we used the entity linking approach of Zhao et al. [11]. The remaining ambiguities were addressed through manual review, however, some remained unresolvable due to missing contextual information.

Mapping. The mapping step involved translating the aligned data onto the KG. In the case of TUCgraph, the target model is RDF. In this regard, entities and properties were mapped. Entities were mapped to their corresponding classes in the ontology and attributes and relations were mapped to their corresponding properties. We constructed SPARQL INSERT queries to insert the data directly into the KG.

Refinement. We used a reasoner to find inconsistencies and datatype violations in the KG. The reasoner enriched the KG by inferring additional types of individuals, based on the rules of the ontology. In case of type violations, we either manually corrected the value, or, in case of uncorrectable, faulty data, removed it.

Update and Evolution. We use a Python script for periodic updates of the KG. The script automates data acquisition, extraction, processing and integration, and mapping to generate SPARQL queries. As the KG is used by a RIS and can be modified by RIS users, a conflict resolution strategy is in place to prevent source data overwriting more recent user input. So far, a complex merge strategy was not needed in our case.

Despite its successful application, our method has limitations. The quality of source data in particular impacts the required effort, especially in step three where corrective measures are performed. Furthermore, in some cases, missing data could not be reliably inferred. This made data mapping impossible, effectively leading to data loss.

5 Conclusion

In this paper, we present a novel approach that considers KGC as a continuous process, addressing challenges from the co-evolution of source data and the KG, that were previously unaddressed. Our method fills this gap and offers guidance to KG engineers, contributing a practical solution for integrating multiple sources in heterogeneous formats into a unified KG. We demonstrate our method's applicability through TUCgraph, a KG developed in an academic setting. TUCgraph integrates a wide range of entities related to university operations. TUCgraph serves as the primary data source for a research information system, highlighting its utility.

Acknowledgments. This work was funded by German Research Foundation (DFG), TRR-386, TP INF, project number 514664767.

Disclosure of Interests.   The authors have no competing interests to declare that are relevant to this work.

References

1. Li, L., et al.: Real-world data medical knowledge graph: construction and applications. Artif. Intell. Med. **103**, 101817 (2020)
2. Wang, C., et al.: Information extraction and knowledge graph construction from geoscience literature. Comput. Geosci. **112**, 112–120 (2018)
3. Nayak, A., et al.: Knowledge graph based automated generation of test cases in software engineering. In: Proceedings of the 7th ACM IKDD CoDS and 25th COMAD. pp. 289–295. ACM, New York, NY, USA (2020)
4. Tamašauskaitė, G., Groth, P.: Defining a knowledge graph development process through a systematic review. ACM Trans. Softw. Eng. Methodol. **32**, 27:1–27:40 (2023)
5. Al-Zaidy, R.A., Giles, C.L.: Automatic knowledge base construction from scholarly documents. In: Proceedings of the 2017 ACM Symposium on Document Engineering. pp. 149–152. Association for Computing Machinery, New York, NY, USA (2017)
6. Ye, H. et al.: Generative knowledge graph construction: a review (2023)
7. Kommineni, V.K., et al.: From human experts to machines: an LLM supported approach to ontology and knowledge graph construction (2024)
8. Asprino, L., et al.: Knowledge graph construction with a façade: a unified method to access heterogeneous data sources on the web. ACM Trans Internet Technol. **23** (2023)
9. Bravo, M. et al.: Methodology for ontology design and construction. Contad. Adm. (2019)
10. Lin, Z.-Q., et al.: Intelligent development environment and software knowledge graph. J. Comput. Sci. Technol. **32**, 242–249 (2017)
11. Zhao, Z., et al.: Architecture of knowledge graph construction techniques. IJPAM **118**, 1869–1883 (2018)
12. Yan, J., et al.: A retrospective of knowledge graphs. Front. Comput. Sci. **12**, 55–74 (2018)
13. Kontokostas, D., Knublauch, H.: Shapes Constraint Language (SHACL) (2017)
14. Paulheim, H.: Knowledge graph refinement: a survey of approaches and evaluation methods. Semantic Web. **8**, 489–508 (2016)
15. Wu, T., et al.: A survey of techniques for constructing chinese knowledge graphs and their applications. Sustainability. **10**, 3245 (2018). https://doi.org/10.3390/su10093245
16. Liang, J., et al.: How to keep a knowledge base synchronized with its encyclopedia source. In: Proceedings of the Twenty-Sixth International Joint Conference on Artificial Intelligence. pp. 3749–3755. Melbourne, Australia (2017)
17. Faisal, S., et al.: Co-evolution of RDF datasets. In: Bozzon, A., et al. (eds.) Web Engineering, pp. 225–243. Springer International Publishing, Cham (2016)
18. Conlon, M., et al.: VIVO: a system for research discovery. J. Open Source Softw. **4** (2019)

Predicting Knowledge Graph Updates from Edit Histories

Maiki Okura[1] and Toshiyuki Amagasa[2(✉)] ⓘ

[1] Graduate School of Systems and Information Engineering, University of Tsukuba, Tsukuba, Japan
okura@kde.cs.tsukuba.ac.jp
[2] Center for Computational Science, University of Tsukuba, Tsukuba, Ibaraki, Japan
amagasa@cs.tsukuba.ac.jp

Abstract. Knowledge graphs (KGs) are inherently incomplete and require continuous maintenance to keep up with the latest status of the target domain. Various studies have been conducted to automate this maintenance, but it still relies heavily on human labor. To alleviate such a burden, predicting updates in KGs is useful for maintaining KGs. In this study, we focus on predicting which entities to be updated in KGs containing many entities. Our basic idea is to exploit the KG's structural information and the edit history, making it possible to predict entities likely to be updated in the next time interval. We have constructed a dataset including edit history based on Wikidata, a general-purpose knowledge graph, and developed a method to predict entities that will be updated based on link relations and edit history, and confirmed their usefulness through experiments.

Keywords: Knowledge graph · Update prediction · Edit history

1 Introduction

Recently, there has been a growing demand for knowledge graphs (KGs), representing general knowledge about entities and their relationships in terms of a set of triple consisting of a head entity, relation, a tail entity. They are used in various applications; e.g., many companies use KGs to accumulate information about their business and exploit them for different tasks, including data integration, customer relationship management, question answering, etc. Besides, KGs are a useful source of information in various machine learning tasks from which training data are derived.

While KGs have been gaining growing popularity, they exhibit several drawbacks. One such problem is that they are always imperfect; i.e., they need continuous maintenance to keep up with the change in the target domain. Specifically, they require adding, deleting, and updating information according to real-world facts. Besides, missing relations may have to be completed using relation prediction because of the imperfectness of the input.

To address these problems, various studies have been conducted. As for the research on automation of adding new information to KGs, OpenIE [7] extracts new triples from public and unstructured data such as web documents. Entity recognition [15] performs

P. Delir Haghighi et al. (Eds.): iiWAS 2024, LNCS 15342, pp. 283–297, 2025.
https://doi.org/10.1007/978-3-031-78090-5_24

entity identity determination that help us to identify the related entity for a given piece of information. As for completing missing triples, there has been a lot of research on KG completion whereby we can predict a missing element in a triple from the rest [3, 11, 14]. Although these techniques have been proposed, the maintenance of KGs still heavily relies on human intervention – the human maintainers use them to facilitate their maintenance work. Since a KG may contain millions of entities, it is hard for the maintainers to perform their maintenance perfectly even with (semi-)automated support of KG completion.

Note here that, in many cases, updates in real-world entities are not independent and are correlated with each other. We can exploit such correlations to predict the entities in a KG that need updates. For example, if the prime minister in a country has been changed, the cabinet member should also be changed. If we detect a cabinet member in a KG unchanged, we can predict that he/she needs to be updated. Such predictions can be performed by carefully investigating the edit history of a KG.

From these observations, in this paper, we propose a method for predicting entities that need to be updated in a KG using the edit history. Our basic idea is an edit in an entity propagates further updates in the same or related entities along with the relationships in the KG. We also conducted evaluation experiments to compare the performance of the proposed method with baseline methods using entity link relationships and edit history, and verify the effectiveness of the proposed method.

2   Related Work

2.1   Detecting State Change of Entities in KGs

Wijaya et al. proposed a method for detecting entities in a KG that are in the status where new factual information is added. To this end, they introduced *contextual temporal profiles (CTPs)* [13], which is the profile of entities in each age group that is estimated from the corpus of documents that appeared in that period. To generate CTPs, they map the words or phrases around the entity mentions in the domain. Then, for each age, they compute the difference between the profile vectors, detecting the transition state of the entity in the domain. Finally, they construct the profile vector of the new entity of the domain and compare it with the pre-obtained profile vectors and transition state vector of the domain for estimating the age of the entity's change. This approach has a limitation in that the user has to select seed entities that represent the target domain manually. In addition, the source for modeling relies on the corpus containing long-term data.

2.2   Link Prediction in KGs

The link prediction methods for KGs, which allow us to predict missing links in a KG, have been actively studied for the last decade. They are regarded as a part of *knowledge graph completion* methods and can effectively be used to maintain KGs.

Recent trends in this area are to use embeddings where entities (and other elements in KGs) are embedded in a vector space, allowing us to perform subsequent tasks in terms of operations over vectors. For given triples $\{(h, r, t)\}$ in a KG, TransE [3] by

Bordes et al. is a method for learning 1) vector representations of entities e_i and 2) those for relations l_j between a couple of entities so that $e_h + l_r = e_t$ is satisfied. By using this method, we can obtain the candidate entities that can be tail of triple $(h, r, ?)$ by finding the vector e_t that is highly associated with the vector $e_h + l_r$.

TransE has been extended in many ways for improving accuracy and application [11, 14]. Among them, Leblay et al. proposed a method for knowledge graph completion with temporal information. By computing the embedded by taking time information into account, they made it possible to predict the time when facts occurred and the missing element in a triple.

Note here that, to our knowledge, none of the existing work addressed the problem of predicting such entities that are likely to be updated according to the past edit history of a KG.

2.3 Update Analysis in KGs

In the context of the management of KGs, the evolution trends in KGs have been discussed in [9]. Such trends could provide hints about the entities and the types of updates in KGs. Besides, [4,5,10] surveyed the completeness, quality, and error detection in KGs. Understanding those different aspects of KG updates helps improve the effectiveness of the proposed approaches. Exploitation of such high-level information is a part of our future work.

3 Proposed Method

3.1 Base Idea

Our basic idea is to exploit the observation that a change in the real world is, in many cases, propagated to a KG as a series of correlated edit operations, i.e., if an entity is updated, then it is likely that its neighboring entities are likely to be updated shortly. Let us consider that Fumio Kishida became the prime minister of Japan. The update in a KG corresponding to this real-world update can be represented as an addition of a relation *prime minister* between entities *Fumio Kishida* and *Japan*. At this moment, updated entity *Fumio Kishida* is likely to be updated in the future because various changes in his properties and updates on his neighboring entities will be made, which, in turn, will cause additional updates; e.g., the year of this change (2021) will be added, the members of the cabinet will be changed, etc.

Let us take a closer look at the propagation of changes along the relation (link) between entities. There are different types of relations, and different relation types exhibit different likelihoods of propagating changes. For example, the change of *prime minister* (or *president* of an organization) will cause further updates on the cabinet members (or board members) while adding *friend* or *follow* relation does not usually cause such changes. Note that becoming a cabinet (board) member causes further changes in his/her properties and neighboring entities (e.g., the addition of a secretary, etc.). The past edit history of a KG can be used to estimate the likelihood of propagating changes.

We should also notice the different types of entities in a KG. Specifically, conceptual entities, such as *thing*, *human*, etc., tend to be less updated compared with instance entities, such as **Fumio Machida**. The former only happens when there is systematic maintenance, e.g., version renewal of ontology. In contrast, the latter happens according to the updates in real-world entities, e.g., promotion to the prime minister. Note also that conceptual entities tend to get more references than instance entities because instance entities are usually typed by being associated with conceptual entities. In this case, the type links do not cascade changes in either conceptual entire is or instance entities to the other end.

3.2   Method Details

According to the idea mentioned above, we propose our method. Specifically, we use an extended version of PageRank, a well-known method for quantifying the importance of a node in a graph, called *personalized PageRank (PPR)* [6]. Given a query node in a graph, PPR is a method to calculate the similarity nodes against the query node by repeating a random walk with restart from the query node with the probability α.

Let the number of nodes in the graph be N, the query vector where element i represents the query probability of a node be $b \in \mathbb{N}$, the adjacency matrix where each column is a vector of the transition probabilities of a node to its neighbors be A, and final existence probabilities of the random surfer on each node be $v \in \mathbb{N}$. v in the steady-state can be obtained by recursively computing the following equation:

$$v = (1 - \alpha)Av + \alpha b$$

We modify the basic PPR to incorporate the above idea and consider editing history to the KG. Specifically, we attempt to characterize the tendency of edits for an entity as *non-stationary*, meaning that entities with high non-stationary value tend to be edited by real-world events compared to those with low values. To this end, we partition the edit history by different time slots, called *periods*, according to their timestamps.

Then, we define an edit non-stationarity of an entity, and based on this score, we introduce the following change and constraint to the adjacency matrix A and query node b, respectively.

Non-stationarity Score for Edits to the Entity. We design score $escore(e_i)$ to represent the non-stationarity of edits to entity e_i to capture the tendency of edits against the entity according to real-world events in an unpredictable way.

1. **Ratio of #edits to entity between the previous and current period**. This captures the existence of non-stationary edits to the entity. The choice of the current and the previous periods is a key (and user-defined) parameter that affects the performance and depends on the dataset. In this work, we set the current period as one week from the present time and the previous period as one month from the current period.

2. **Number of links to entity**. Suppose an entity has many relations by which it can be associated with other entities or literals. In that case, we can assume that it tends to be edited more frequently than the ones with fewer links because the probability of being edited increases by the links. Therefore, we normalize the ratio of the number of edits against an entity by the number of links.

Based on these observations, we define an entity's non-stationarity score of edits as follows:

$$escore(e_i) = \frac{D_w(e_i)}{N_{out}(e_i)D_{lm}(e_i)}$$

where $N_{out}(e_i)$ is the number of outer links of entity e_i; $D_w(e_i)$ is the number of edits against entity e_i in the current period; and $D_{lm}(e_i)$ is the number of edits against entity e_i in the previous period.

Adjacency Matrix. For relation r_j in a KG, we define score $rscore(r_j)$ representing the total number of edits of the entities at both ends:

$$rscore(r_j) = \frac{1}{|E_{(e_h,r_j)}|} \sum_{e_i \in E_{edited}} \frac{N_{in}(e_i)}{N_{in}(e_j)} \sum_{e_k \in E_{(e_i,r_j)}} escore(e_k)$$

where E_{edited} is the set of entities that are edited in the current period; $E_{(e_i,r_j)}$ is the set of entities that are linked from entity e_i by relation r_j and is edited during the previous week of the current period; and $N_{in}(e_i)$ is the number of incoming links.

Based on $rscore$, we compute the weight value of each element in adjacency matrix $W_{(e_i,e_j)}$ representing the weight of the link between entities e_i and e_j:

$$s(r_i) = rscore(r_i) + \min\{rscore(r) \mid \exists r \in R, rscore(r) \neq 0\} \tag{1}$$

$$W_{(e_i,e_j)} = \frac{\frac{N_{in}(e_i)}{N_{in}(e_j)} \sum_{r_l \in R_{(e_i,e_j)}} s(r_l)}{\sum_{e_k \in E} \frac{N_{in}(e_i)}{N_{in}(e_k)} \sum_{r_m \in R_{(e_i,e_k)}} s(r_m)} \tag{2}$$

In Eq. (2), E is the set of all entities in a knowledge graph; E_{e_i} is the set of entities linked to entity e_i; R is the set of all relations; and $R_{(e_i,e_j)}$ is the set of all relations between entities e_i and e_j.

Query Vector. We designed a query vector to give a higher probability to such entities with many edits and edited more recently. Figure 1 depicts the basic idea of query vector computation. Let t_{base} be the current (or base) timestamp, $t(d)$ be the time of edit d, and H_{e_i} be the set of edit histories of entity e_i in the current period. Then, we compute each element in the query vector b of entities e_i, b_{e_i} as follows:

$$b_{e_i} = \sum_{d \in D_{e_i}} \frac{1}{t_{base} - t(d) + 1}$$

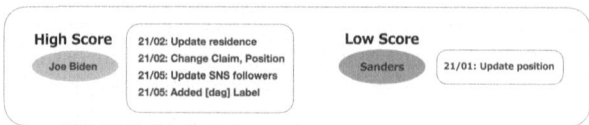

Fig. 1. Base idea for query vector computation. Higher score are given to entities that have been edited more recently and more frequently.

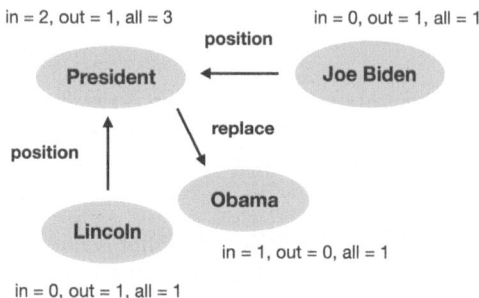

Fig. 2. Example of counting links of an entity

4   Experiments

We conducted a set of experiments to evaluate the proposed method.

4.1   Baseline Methods

We compare the performance of the proposed method with the following baseline methods.

 # Links of Entity. This is based on an intuition that an entity is more likely to be edited because it has many associated entities and literal values and an edit on an entity propagates via the link as discussed above. Thus, we consider the number of links of an entity as a score representing its tendency to be edited. We assume that an edit to an entity will occur when the number of links exceeds a predefined threshold, and we use the following three variations: # of outgoing links (nlink-out), # of incoming links (nlink-in), and the sum of incoming and outgoing links (nlink-all). Figure 2 shows an example of counting the number of links of an entity. The entity *President* has two incoming links *position* and one outgoing link *replace*. Consequently, $in = 2$, $out = 1$, and $all = 3$.

# of Recent Edits of Entity. In reality, updates to an entity concentrates on a short period of time, i.e., multiple edits happen to an entity and its neighbooring entities, and there is a long blank time for the following edits. To consider such a nature in reality, we adopted a method (nedit) that predicts an entity to be edited if the number of recent edits exceeds a predefined threshold.

PageRank Score. It is natural to consider that essential entities that attract attention are more likely to be edited. There are many ways to estimate the importance of an entity in a KG. From a graph point of view, the degree centrality is one such measurement, and the baseline using the number of links can be regarded as one such approach. Besides, PageRank [8] is a more sophisticated method to estimate the importance of a node in a graph, which has been applied to a wide variety of graph-based problems. Besides, there are several variants, such as T-Rank [2], we used PageRank as one of the baseline methods. PageRank value $PR(A)$ for a node A in a graph is calculated by Eq. (4.1), where $T_i(1 \sim n)$ for the nodes linked to node A, $C(T_i)$ for the total number of nodes linked to node Ti, and d is a hyperparameter called dumping factor, usually set to 0.85

$$PR(A) = (1 - d) + d \sum_{i=1}^{n} \frac{PR(T_i)}{C(T_i)}$$

In this work, we calculate the PageRank score of each entity with a consideration that a KG to be a directed graph and predict that the entity whose score exceeds the threshold will be updated.

Ablated Methods w/query Vector or Adjacency Matrix. To assess the effect of the query vector and adjacency matrix in the proposed method, we tested two variations where either the query vector or the adjacency matrix is ablated from the proposed method, respectively abbreviated as adjacency matrix only (proposed-w) and query vector only (proposed-qv).

4.2 Dataset

To evaluate the proposed methods, we have created our dataset. The dataset has to fulfill the following requirements: 1) not only the KD but also its edit history are publicly available, 2) the edit history contains the edits on entities in such a way that each edit is timestamped. To this end, we employed Wikidata [12][1] which is one of the most popular publicly available and collaboratively edited large-scale KG. Wikidata provides a dump of the entire graph every week[2], and each entity's edit history can be retrieved from its detail page.

We constructed the dataset in the following steps.

1. Get the dump of Wikidata for 2021/05/24 and 2021/05/31 from download page.
2. Pick up the first 100 entities in the data from the graph in 2021/05/24.

---

[1] https://www.wikidata.org.
[2] https://dumps.wikimedia.org/wikidatawiki/entities/.

3. Using the initial 100 entities as a starting point, we use as a dataset the entities that appear up to 4 hops away and the triples that have them as heads.
4. Scrape the edit histories of all the entities from the detail page of each entity.

Table 1 summarizes the detailed statistics about the dataset.

Table 1. Statistics of the dataset extracted from Wikidata.

	2021/05/24	2021/05/31
number of triples	8,487,493	8,495,281
Edited entities	62751 (5/25 ∼ 5/31)	48379 (6/1 ∼ 6/7)
number of entities	995,012	
number of relations	5,782	

4.3   Prediction of Entities to Be Edited

In general, a KG may contain massive entities. So, it is useful for a maintainer of the KG to predict entities that are likely to be edited in the near future. For this reason, in this experiment, we assess the accuracy of the proposed method in predicting entities to be edited.

Experimental Setting. We computed for each entity e_i the value $escore(e_i)$ and detected it as to be edited if the value is greater than the threshold value. The evaluation measurement is the average $escore$, precision, and recall. Given the set of entities predicted to be edited, the precision is the fraction of true edited entities in the predicted entities. At the same time, the recall is the fraction of predicted entities in the entire edited entity.

The precise step is as follows:

1. For the dataset on 2021/05/24, we predicted entities to be edited between 2021/05/25 and 2021/05/31. We obtained the optimal threshold maximizing the average $escore$, precision, and recall using the hyperparameter optimization framework, Optuna [1]. As the edit history, we use the history from 2021/05/17 to 2021/05/24 for method nedit and the period from 2021/05/10-2021/05/17 and the period from 2021/05/17-2021/05/24 for the proposed method.
2. For the dataset on 2021/05/31, we predict the entities to be edited between 2021/06/01 and 2021/06/07 using the threshold values obtained in the previous step and evaluated the performance of each method. As a past editing history of entities, we use the period from 2021/05/24 to 2021/05/31 for nedit, and the period from 2021/05/17 to 2021/05/24 and the period from 2021/05/24 to 2021/05/31 for proposed method.

Table 2. Result (For thresholds where Recall is the maximum).

	Top 100	Precision	Recall	mean escore[*]
nlink-in	38	29.4%	0.467%	0.19
nlink-out	38	15.9%	**8.13%**	0.0868
nlink-all	38	27.7%	0.961%	0.185
nedit	43	17.4%	2.15%	0.173
pagerank	**49**	**47.3%**	0.104%	0.224
proposed-w	21	8.62%	0.885%	0.0833
proposed-qv	39	42.9%	0.105%	**4.98**
proposed	25	30.1%	0.875%	2.08

[*] When all edits are predicted accurately, the mean escore is 1.24.

Table 3. Result (For thresholds where mean escore is the maximum).

	Top 100	Precision	Recall	mean escore[*]
nlink-in	38	66.7%	0.0239%	0.72
nlink-out	38	31.8%	**0.653%**	0.259
nlink-all	38	66.7%	0.0239%	0.72
nedit	43	47.8%	0.0145%	1.35
pagerank	**49**	64.3%	0.0153%	0.721
proposed-w	21	16.7%	0.00251%	0.333
proposed-qv	39	**70.6%**	0.0301%	8.95
proposed	25	36.4%	0.01%	**15.0**

[*] When all edits are predicted accurately, the mean escore is 1.24.

Result. Tables 2 and 3 show the results.

If we look at the result in Table 2, we can see that the recall is the highest for the nlink-out, and the mean escore is the highest for the proposed method.

Next, looking at the result in Table 3, we can see that the proposed method outperformed w.r.t. the mean escore. Thus, we can say that the method using outgoing links is better if the number of updates detected is important, and the proposed method is better if the detection of updates to non-stationary entities is important.

Also, comparing the proposed method with proposed-w and proposed-qv, it can be seen that the proposed method is better in terms of recall but worse in terms of precision, etc., and better than proposed-w in most aspects. The reason for this result may be that proposed-qv predicts edits that have occurred more recently and more frequently. Hence, it is more accurate in capturing edit trends, while using only the adjacency matrix, which only considers relations, predicts edits to minor entities that have not been edited in the prediction period and are linked to entities of higher concepts with larger orders. However, the proposed method, which combines proposed-qv with proposed-w, increases Recall, indicating that it can capture edits that cannot be predicted by simply assigning a high score to edit that has been made.

Next, looking at the change in accuracy to the number of detections and the non-stationary of the detected edits for each method. Figure 3 shows the transition of precision w.r.t. the change in recall, and Fig. 4 shows the transition of mean escore with respect to the change in the recall. Looking at each result, in the range where the recall is small, the nlink method is better in precision, while the proposed method is better in terms of mean escore. However, looking at the whole range, we cannot see a significant difference. In addition, PageRank and the proposed method do not have a threshold where Recall is about the middle of the range, so it is difficult to detect many entities to be edited. The reason for this result may be that many of the edits made to Wikidata is difficult to predict based on the information in the graph alone, and in cases where the recall exceeds a certain level, the success or failure of the prediction is almost random.

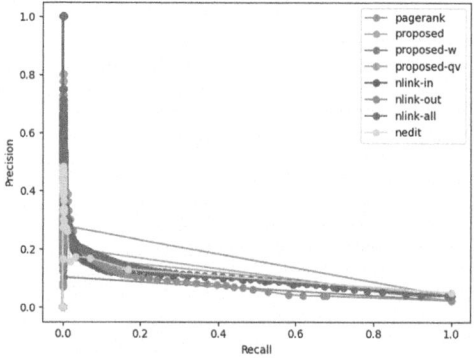

Fig. 3. Precision and recall comparing.

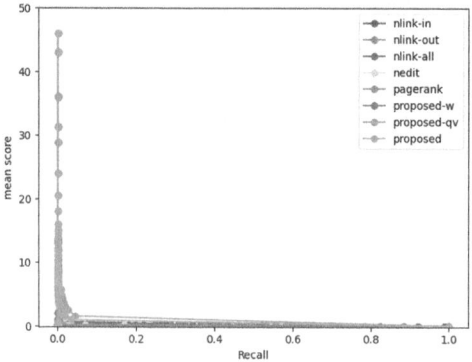

Fig. 4. Mean escore and recall comparison.

4.4   Analysis of Prediction Result for Each Method

Examples of High-Score Entities. To see trends in the prediction results of each method, we picked up high-score entities. Table 4 shows the top five entities for each method. Looking at the table, we can observe that nlink, PageRank, proposed-w, and proposed-qv show similar results in that highly-scored entities exhibit many links, i.e.,

Table 4. High-scored entities.

nlink-in		nlink-out		nlink-all		nedit	
ID	Label	ID	Label	ID	Label	ID	Label
Q5	human	Q21014429	The Complete Encyclopedia of World Aircraft	Q5	human	Q1154115	Pratt & Whitney F100
Q4167836	Wikimedia category	Q525	Sol	Q4167836	Wikimedia category	Q29251	McDonnell Douglas F-15 Eagle
Q148	People's Republic of China	Q23558762	2017 German presidential election	Q148	People's Republic of China	Q844500	McDonnell Douglas F-15E Strike Eagle
Q6985	UTC+08:00	Q451110	1999 German presidential election	Q6985	UTC+08:00	Q4653390	AN/APQ-181
Q6581097	male	Q707063	2010 German presidential election	Q6581097	male	Q4652819	AN/APQ-153
pagerank		proposed-w		proposed-qv		proposed	
ID	Label	ID	Label	ID	Label	ID	Label
Q4167836	Wikimedia category	Q6985	UTC+08:00	Q4167836	Wikimedia category	Q20909	The Cage
Q5	human	Q13406463	Wikimedia list article	Q5	human	Q244157	Igbo people
Q148	People's Republic of China	Q382617	mayor of a place in France	Q148	People's Republic of China	Q6985	UTC+08:00
Q6985	UTC+08:00	Q4167836	Wikimedia category	Q6985	UTC+08:00	Q6781336	Maryland Center for History and Culture
Q13100073	village-level division in China	Q101352	family name	Q13100073	village-level division in China	Q13406463	Wikimedia list article

Table 5. For entities detected by each method, list the number of non-overlaps with those detected by another method.

comp src \ comp dst	nlink-in	nlink-out	nlink-all	nedit	pagerank	proposed-w	proposed-qv	proposed
nlink-in	0 (0.0%)	47 (58.8%)	1 (1.25%)	80 (100%)	17 (21.2%)	56 (70.0%)	24 (30.0%)	71 (88.8%)
nlink-out	84 (71.8%)	0 (0.0%)	83 (70.9%)	115 (98.3%)	83 (70.9%)	94 (80.3%)	84 (71.8%)	113 (96.6%)
nlink-all	1 (1.25%)	46 (57.5%)	0 (0.0%)	80 (100%)	17 (21.2%)	57 (71.2%)	23 (28.7%)	71 (88.8%)
nedit	105 (100%)	103 (98.1%)	105 (100%)	0 (0.0%)	105 (100%)	105 (100%)	98 (93.3%)	92 (87.6%)
pagerank	17 (21.2%)	46 (57.5%)	17 (21.2%)	80 (100%)	0 (0.0%)	48 (60.0%)	15 (18.8%)	68 (85.0%)
proposed-w	84 (77.8%)	85 (78.7%)	85 (78.7%)	108 (100%)	76 (70.4%)	0 (0.0%)	82 (75.9%)	99 (91.7%)
proposed-qv	43 (43.4%)	66 (66.7%)	42 (42.4%)	92 (92.9%)	34 (34.3%)	73 (73.7%)	0 (0.0%)	53 (53.5%)
proposed	71 (88.8%)	76 (95.0%)	71 (88.8%)	67 (83.8%)	68 (85.0%)	71 (88.8%)	34 (42.5%)	0 (0.0%)

high-level conceptual entities. On the other hand, nedit gave high score to aircraft. So, we can guess it reflects the editorial trend.

Finally, the scores of the proposed method tended to be significantly influenced by the most recent edit history, and on top of that, the number of references and other factors were taken into account. Therefore, it is considered that nlink and pagerank should be used to find the most influential entities in the knowledge graph, nedit should be used to present entities based on the most recent edit trend, and the proposed method should be used to consider both of them.

Number of Overlaps Among Different Methods. The above results show that the proposed method and baselines exhibit different characteristics in detected entities. Therefore, it is possible to detect more entities more updated entities can be detected by combining methods having fewer overlaps in the results. To assess the possibility of this ensemble approach, we verified how many entities were not overlapped.

The values in Table 5 represent the number of entities detected by the method indicated by the label in the left column that was not detected by the method in each column. Looking at the result, entities detected by nlink-out, nedit, proposed-w, proposed method have little overlap with those detected by the other methods. In particular, nedit and the proposed method have less than 15% overlap with ogher methods. Therefore, it is practical to use it in combination with other methods.

4.5 Recommending Entities by Cascades of Edit

When an update is made to an entity in the knowledge graph, recommending entities with high relevance and likely to be highly edited in the neighborhood is considered helpful in real applications. Therefore, we tested whether it is possible to recommend entities to be edited, which is in the neighborhood of the edited entities by ordering the candidates by the proposed score.

Experimental Setting. The experiment is conducted as following steps.

1. Calculate the score of each method using the dataset on 2021/05/24 and the edit history from 2021/05/25 to 2021/05/31.
2. In the dataset on 2021/05/31, we ordered the entities neighboring to the entity Q6279 (Joe Biden) and Q1490 (Tokyo) which were edited between 202106/01 and 2021/06/07 by the score and confirm their usefulness.

Result. Table 6 shows the result for the entity Q6279 (Joe Biden), and Table 7 shows the result for the entity Q1490 (Tokyo). First, looking at the result for entity Q6279 (Joe Biden), nlink and PageRank tend to give higher scores to high-level concepts about the residence and a political party, and nedit and proposed method scores entities related to a person and relatives, which are concepts of the same level as Joe Biden and editing propagation will occur. Also, comparing proposed-w, proposed-qv, and the proposed method, the results of the proposed method are similar to those of proposed-qv, and

Table 6. Entities highly scored by each method which are adjacent of the entity Q6279 (Joe Biden)

nlink-in		nlink-out		nlink-all		nedit	
relation	tail	relation	tail	relation	tail	relation	tail
work location	Washington, D.C.	different from	Joe Biden	different from	Joe Biden	significant event	Joe Biden presidential campaign
different from	Joe Biden	depicted by	Joe Biden	depicted by	Joe Biden	sibling	Francis Biden
residence	Claymont	notable work	Promises to Keep	notable work	Promises to Keep	child	Naomi Biden
member of political party	Democratic Party	spouse	Jill Biden	spouse	Jill Biden	child	Ashley Biden
topic's main category	Category: Joe Biden	candidacy in election	2020 U.S. presidential election	candidacy in election	2020 U.S. presidential election	sibling	Valerie Biden Owens
pagerank		**proposed-w**		**proposed-qv**		**proposed**	
relation	tail	relation	tail	relation	tail	relation	tail
significant event	Joe Biden presidential campaign, 1988	topic's main category	Category: Joe Biden	child	Beau Biden	child	Beau Biden
place of birth	St. Mary's Hospital	significant event	Joe Biden presidential campaign, 1988	significant event	Joe Biden presidential campaign, 2020	significant event	Joe Biden presidential campaign, 2020
residence	Arden	topic's main template	Template: Joe Biden	sibling	Francis Biden	member of sports team	Delaware Fightin' Blue Hens football
residence	Claymont	member of sports team	Delaware Fightin' Blue Hens football	award received	Grand Cross of the Order of Boyacá	child	Naomi Biden
notable work	Promises to Keep	notable work	Promises to Keep	child	Naomi Biden	sibling	Valerie Biden Owens

Table 7. Entities highly scored by each method which are adjacent of the entity Q1490 (Tokyo)

nlink-in		nlink-out		nlink-all		nedit	
relation	tail	relation	tail	relation	tail	relation	tail
named after	capital	head of government	Shunichi Suzuki	head of government	Shunichi Suzuki	contains administrative territory	Utsuki
contains administrative territory	Chūō-ku	head of government	Ryokichi Minobe	head of government	Ryokichi Minobe	public holiday	Tokyo Citizen's Day
↓	Musashino	flag	flag of Tokyo	flag	flag of Tokyo	contains administrative territory	Ōkagō
↓	Shinjuku-ku	head of government	Ryotaro Azuma	head of government	Ryotaro Azuma	↓	Itsukaichi
shares border with	Chiba Prefecture	↓	Seiichirō Yasui	↓	Seiichirō Yasui	↓	Hōya
pagerank		**proposed-w**		**proposed-qv**		**proposed**	
relation	tail	relation	tail	relation	tail	relation	tail
anthem	Tokyo Metropolitan Song	topic's main Wikimedia portal	Portal: Tokyo	public holiday	Tokyo Citizen's Day	public holiday	Tokyo Citizen's Day
public holiday	Tokyo Citizen's Day	public holiday	Tokyo Citizen's Day	headquarter location	Tokyo Metropolitan Government Complex	headquarter location	Tokyo Metropolitan Government Complex
category of people buried here	Catégorie: Personnalité inhumée à Tokyo	highest point	Mount Kumotori	archives at	Tokyo Metropolitan Archives	archives at	Tokyo Metropolitan Archives
flag	flag of Tokyo	economy of topic	economy of Tokyo	contains administrative territory	Utsuki	contains administrative territory	Utsuki
category for the view of the item	Category: Views of Tokyo	seal description	Symbols of Tokyo	history of topic	timeline of Tokyo	history of topic	timeline of Tokyo

it can be inferred that the query vector more influences the proposed method than the adjacency matrix.

Next, looking at the Table 7, result for the entity Q1490 (Tokyo) about the city, nlink-out, nlink-all scores entities about the governor of Tokyo highly, nlink-in, nedit scores entities about the administrative district, and proposed method highly scores entities about headquarters, the administrative district, which is likely to be edited incidentally. The results of all the methods are reasonable as the recommendation result for the editing to the original entity. However, from the viewpoint of increasing the number of edits, the proposed method which recommends more minor items is considered useful.

5   Conclusion

In this paper, we have proposed a method to predict entities in KG that are likely to be edited using editing history. To this end, we have proposed a novel score that takes into account its popularity and recent edits. We have conducted experiments to compare the proposed method with some baseline methods. The experimental results showed that the proposed method could detect small but rare edits on entities, while the baselines using the number of links could detect entities that were constantly edited. This suggested that the proposed method and simple baselines using link numbers are complementary, and it is useful to make better predictions if we combine both of them. Next, the experiment recommends entities to be edited in relation to the entity for which the edit was made, method using the number of links and PageRank tends to score the entities, which are high-level concepts and unlikely to be edited to follow the source entity, but the proposed method was able to recommend many entities that could be said to be relevant and should be edited in both the person and city cases.

In the future, we plan to conduct additional experiments on different datasets to see the general applicability of the proposed method. Besides, we plan to evaluate how useful is the proposed method in the context of KG maintenance.

Acknowledgements. This paper is based on results obtained from the project, "Research and Development Project of the Enhanced infrastructures for Post-5G Information and Communication Systems" (JPNP20017), commissioned by the New Energy and Industrial Technology Development Organization (NEDO), JST CREST Grant Number JPMJCR22M2, and JSPS KAKENHI Grant Number JP23K24949.

References

1. Akiba, T., Sano, S., Yanase, T., Ohta, T., Koyama, M.: Optuna: a next-generation hyperparameter optimization framework. CoRR **abs/1907.10902** (2019). http://arxiv.org/abs/1907.10902

2. Berberich, K., Vazirgiannis, M., Weikum, G.: T-rank: time-aware authority ranking. In: Leonardi, S. (ed.) WAW 2004. LNCS, vol. 3243, pp. 131–142. Springer, Heidelberg (2004). https://doi.org/10.1007/978-3-540-30216-2_11

3. Bordes, A., Usunier, N., Garcia-Duran, A., Weston, J., Yakhnenko, O.: Translating embeddings for modeling multi-relational data. In: Burges, C.J.C., Bottou, L., Welling, M., Ghahramani, Z., Weinberger, K.Q. (eds.) Advances in Neural Information Processing Systems, vol. 26, pp. 2787–2795. Curran Associates, Inc. (2013). https://proceedings.neurips.cc/paper/2013/file/1cecc7a77928ca8133fa24680a88d2f9-Paper.pdf

4. Cimiano, P., Paulheim, H.: Knowledge graph refinement: a survey of approaches and evaluation methods. Semant. Web **8**(3), 489–508 (2017). https://doi.org/10.3233/SW-160218

5. Galárraga, L., Razniewski, S., Amarilli, A., Suchanek, F.M.: Predicting completeness in knowledge bases. In: Proceedings of the Tenth ACM International Conference on Web Search and Data Mining, WSDM 2017, pp. 375–383. Association for Computing Machinery, New York, NY, USA (2017). https://doi.org/10.1145/3018661.3018739
6. Jeh, G., Widom, J.: Scaling personalized web search. In: Proceedings of the 12th International Conference on World Wide Web, WWW 2003, pp. 271–279. Association for Computing Machinery, New York, NY, USA (2003). https://doi.org/10.1145/775152.775191
7. Niklaus, C., Cetto, M., Freitas, A., Handschuh, S.: A survey on open information extraction. In: Proceedings of the 27th International Conference on Computational Linguistics, pp. 3866–3878. Association for Computational Linguistics, Santa Fe, New Mexico, USA, August 2018. https://www.aclweb.org/anthology/C18-1326
8. Page, L., Brin, S., Motwani, R., Winograd, T.: The PageRank citation ranking: bringing order to the web. In: Proceedings of the 7th International World Wide Web Conference, Brisbane, Australia, pp. 161–172 (1998). citeseer.nj.nec.com/page98pagerank.html
9. Pelgrin, O., Galárraga, L., Hose, K.: Towards fully-fledged archiving for RDF datasets. Seman. Web **12**(6), 903–925 (2021). https://doi.org/10.3233/SW-210434
10. Piscopo, A., Simperl, E.: What we talk about when we talk about wikidata quality: a literature survey. In: Proceedings of the 15th International Symposium on Open Collaboration, OpenSym 2019. Association for Computing Machinery, New York, NY, USA (2019). https://doi.org/10.1145/3306446.3340822
11. Shi, B., Weninger, T.: ProjE: embedding projection for knowledge graph completion. CoRR abs/1611.05425 (2016). http://arxiv.org/abs/1611.05425
12. Vrandečić, D., Krötzsch, M.: Wikidata: a free collaborative knowledgebase. Commun. ACM **57**(10), 78–85 (2014). https://doi.org/10.1145/2629489
13. Wijaya, D.T., Nakashole, N., Mitchell, T.M.: CTPs: contextual temporal profiles for time scoping facts using state change detection. In: Proceedings of the 2014 Conference on Empirical Methods in Natural Language Processing (EMNLP), pp. 1930–1936. Association for Computational Linguistics, Doha, Qatar, October 2014. https://doi.org/10.3115/v1/D14-1207. https://www.aclweb.org/anthology/D14-1207
14. Xie, R., Liu, Z., Jia, J., Luan, H., Sun, M.: Representation learning of knowledge graphs with entity descriptions. In: Proceedings of the Thirtieth AAAI Conference on Artificial Intelligence, AAAI 2016, pp. 2659–2665. AAAI Press (2016)
15. Yadav, V., Bethard, S.: A survey on recent advances in named entity recognition from deep learning models. In: Proceedings of the 27th International Conference on Computational Linguistics, pp. 2145–2158. Association for Computational Linguistics, Santa Fe, New Mexico, USA, August 2018. https://www.aclweb.org/anthology/C18-1182

Automatic Extraction of RML-star Mappings from Property Graphs

Julián Arenas-Guerrero$^{(\boxtimes)}$ and Paola Espinoza-Arias

Universidad Politécnica de Madrid, Madrid, Spain
`julian.arenas.guerrero@upm.es`

Abstract. Exposing heterogeneous data as RDF knowledge graphs is usually done with declarative mapping languages. However, the creation of mapping rules is an arduous task, which in the case of relational databases can be mitigated with the automatic extraction of mapping rules. For property graphs, it is convenient to map them to RDF-star which provides quoted triples as a more natural representation for edge properties. Nevertheless, the automatic extraction of declarative mappings from property graphs to RDF-star remains unstudied. In this paper, we address this problem using the recently proposed RML-star mapping language. We implement and validate the approach with the LDBC Social Network Benchmark.

1 Introduction

There are two prevalent models for graph data management: the Resource Description Framework (RDF) and property graphs (PGs). The interoperability between the two models is currently the focus of ongoing research [14]. One of the proposals that brings RDF closer to PGs is RDF-star [10]. Specifically, PGs allow to assign properties to nodes and edges, but edge properties in RDF (also known as statement-level metadata) are intricate [14]. RDF-star reconciles both graph data models with quoted triples, which is a more natural representation of edge properties in RDF.

Direct mappings between PGs and RDF-star [10] were proposed. However, transforming PGs to RDF-star typically involves using a domain ontology or vocabulary, which requires customized mappings. An established approach to express customized mappings is declarative mapping languages such as the RDF Mapping Language [12] (RML). RML allows to declare transformations from heterogeneous data to RDF organized in a domain vocabulary. Recently, RML-star [4] was proposed to view PGs as RDF-star.

The flexibility of declarative mapping languages such as RML-star comes at the cost of time-consuming mapping development [13]. To mitigate this, a solution is to write mappings in a semi-automatic way. First, an initial version of the mapping is obtained with automatic extraction (i.e., bootstrap) from a source database; the generated mappings reflect the behavior of a direct mapping [15]. Then, this mapping is manually edited to structure it according to a domain

© The Author(s), under exclusive license to Springer Nature Switzerland AG 2025
P. Delir Haghighi et al. (Eds.): iiWAS 2024, LNCS 15342, pp. 298–303, 2025.
https://doi.org/10.1007/978-3-031-78090-5_25

vocabulary. Mapping bootstrapping from relational databases to RDF has been widely studied [6,13,15]. However, there are no works on the automatic extraction of declarative mappings from PGs to RDF-star, which we address in this paper.

2   Background

Mapping Bootstrapping from Relational Databases. In many cases, RDF graphs are created from relational databases, for which the RDB to RDF Mapping Language [8] (R2RML) was recommended by the World Wide Web Consortium (W3C) in 2012. Prior to the publication of this standard, D2RQ [5] already provided a tool to automatically generate a default mapping by analyzing the schema of a relational database. The inception of R2RML motivated further works. BootOX [13] and MIRROR [15] generate R2RML mappings that produce RDF graphs in accordance with the W3C Direct Mapping Recommendation [2]. Under some assumptions such as schema normalization, these systems additionally exploit relational patterns to derive further implicit information like subclass-of relationships. Calvanese et al. [6] recently contributed the most comprehensive and up-to-date mapping patterns catalog. The fact that our work is on graph-to-graph instead of relational-to-graph mapping facilitates preserving the structure of the source PG.

PG to RDF. Tomaszuk et al. [17] proposed the PGO ontology to describe PGs and an algorithm to transform them into RDF using PGO, without customized mappings. ProGOMap [9] automatically generates declarative mappings from a PG to an ontology. However, PGO and ProGOMap do not consider RDF-star as in our work. Hartig [10] provides a direct mapping from PGs to RDF-star which we reuse in our bootstrapping approach. There are also works in the opposite direction, from RDF to PG. Angles et al. [1] provides direct mappings that do not consider customized transformations and G2GML [7] is a declarative mapping language from RDF to PG, but both proposals omit RDF-star.

RML-star. RML-star [4] is an extension of RML for generating RDF-star from heterogeneous data. In our work, we bootstrap RML-star mapping rules from a PG. A mapping rule in RML-star is known as a triples map (TM). Each TM has one logical source, e.g., a Cypher query. A TM also has term maps which are functions defining how to generate RDF terms. Term maps can be subject, predicate or object maps. Quoted triples in RML-star are generated with star maps that reference another TM which produces the quoted triples. If required, a join can be defined between the logical sources in the TMs involved in the generation of the quoted triples.

3   Automatic Extraction of RML-star

This section presents an illustrative example of the automatic extraction of RML-star mappings from a PG and the mapping generation procedure.

3.1   Illustrative Example

Figure 1 shows the source PG (stored in the Kùzu graph database) which consists of four nodes with the label User. Edges define the Follows relationship between users, for example, in the context of a social network. There are two node properties, name and age, and one edge property, since.

Listing 1 depicts the bootstrapped RML-star mappings in the YARRRML [11] syntax. The mapping uses the Cypher query language to access the Kùzu database. The first set of rules in the User TM transforms the nodes (User) into resources and node properties (name and age) into datatype properties. The User_Follows_-User TM transforms edges (Follows) into object properties. Finally, the User_-Follows_User_quoted TM transforms edge properties (since) into subject quoted triples.

Listing 2 shows the generated RDF-star graph. The triples in lines 4, 6, 8 and 10 are generated by the User TM; the triples in lines 5, 7 and 9 by the User_Follows_User TM; and the triples in lines 11–14 by the User_Follows_-User_quoted TM.

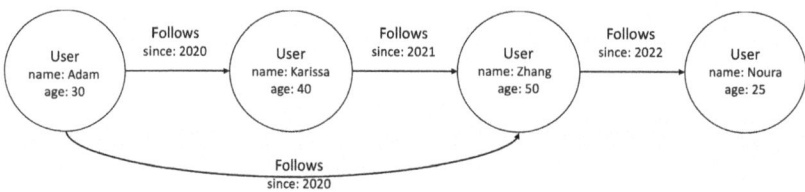

Fig. 1. Source PG based on an example from the Kùzu documentation.

```
1  mappings:
2    User:
3      sources:
4        query: MATCH (x:User) RETURN DISTINCT OFFSET(ID(x)) AS x_User_id, x.name AS name,
             x.age AS age
5        referenceFormulation: cypher
6      subject: ns:User/$(x_User_id)
7      predicateobjects:
8      - [rdf:type, ns:User]
9      - [ns:name, $(name)]
10     - [ns:age, $(age), xsd:integer]
11   User_Follows_User:
12     sources:
13       query: MATCH (x:User)-[r:Follows]->(y:User) RETURN DISTINCT OFFSET(ID(x)) AS
             x_User_id, OFFSET(ID(y)) AS y_User_id, r.since AS since
14       referenceFormulation: cypher
15     subject: ns:User/$(x_User_id)
16     predicateobjects:
17     - [ns:Follows, ns:User/$(y_User_id)]
18   User_Follows_User_quoted:
19     sources:
20       query: MATCH (x:User)-[r:Follows]->(y:User) RETURN DISTINCT OFFSET(ID(x)) AS
             x_User_id, OFFSET(ID(y)) AS y_User_id, r.since AS since
21       referenceFormulation: cypher
22     subject:
23       quoted: User_Follows_User
```

```
24    predicateobjects:
25    - [ns:since, $(since), xsd:integer]
```

Listing 1. Automatically extacted RML-star mapping in YARRRML syntax.

```
1  @base <http://example.com/ns#> .
2  @prefix rdf: <http://www.w3.org/1999/02/22-rdf-syntax-ns#> .
3  @prefix xsd: <http://www.w3.org/2001/XMLSchema#> .
4  <#User/0> rdf:type <#User>; <#name> "Adam"; <#age> "30"^^xsd:integer;
5            <#Follows> <#User/1>, <#User/2> .
6  <#User/1> rdf:type <#User>; <#name> "Karissa"; <#age> "40"^^xsd:integer;
7            <#Follows> <#User/2> .
8  <#User/2> rdf:type <#User>; <#name> "Zhang"; <#age> "50"^^xsd:integer;
9            <#Follows> <#User/3> .
10 <#User/3> rdf:type <#User>; <#name> "Noura"; <#age> "25"^^xsd:integer .
11 << <#User/0> <#Follows> <#User/1> >> <#since> "2020"^^xsd:integer .
12 << <#User/0> <#Follows> <#User/2> >> <#since> "2020"^^xsd:integer .
13 << <#User/1> <#Follows> <#User/2> >> <#since> "2021"^^xsd:integer .
14 << <#User/2> <#Follows> <#User/3> >> <#since> "2022"^^xsd:integer .
```

Listing 2. Generated RDF-star graph with the bootstrapped mappings.

3.2 Mapping Generation

The bootstrapping process consists of three types of mapping rule extraction, which are described next. The description of the steps are linked to the corresponding TMs of the RML-star mapping of the illustrative example (Listing 1).

Node to Resource and **Node Property to Datatype Property**. This extraction generates the User TM. First, find all node labels (by posing queries to the PG); then, for each node label, find their property labels (with queries to the PG as well) and create a TM as follows:

- The logical source is a PG query that uses the node label and node property labels to retrieve the ids of the nodes together with the node property values. The reference formulation is the PG query language of the source database.
- The subject map is a template with the node label (constant) and the node ids (reference to the logical source).
- Add a predicate-object map to create the resource, with rdf:type as the predicate value and the node label as the object value.
- For each node property add a predicate-object map to create the associated datatype property. The predicate is the node property label and the object is the associated reference in the PG query, optionally accompanied by its XSD datatype (this is similar to the natural mapping of SQL values [8]).

Edge to Object Property. This extraction generates the User_Follows_User TM. For each node label found in the former step, use it as the source node label to get associated edge labels and target node labels and create a TM as follows:

- The logical source is a PG query that uses the edge label and the source and target node labels to retrieve the ids of the source and target nodes together with the edge properties.
- The subject map is a template with the source node label (constant) and the source node ids (reference to the logical source).

– Add a predicate-object map to create the object property. The predicate is the edge label and the object is a template with the target node label (constant) and the target node ids (reference to the logical source).

Edge Property to Quoted Triples. This extraction generates the User_-Follows_User_quoted TM. For each edge found in the previous step, create a TM as follows (if it has edge properties):

– The logical source is the same as the one in the associated *edge to object property* TM.
– The subject is a star map that references the associated *edge to object property* TM, which produces the quoted triples. It is not necessary to specify a join condition since the logical sources are the same.
– For each edge property add a predicate-object map to annotate the quoted triples. The predicate is the edge property label (constant) and the object is the associated reference in the PG query, optionally accompanied by its XSD datatype.

4   Implementation and Validation

Implementation. We implemented the approach in Python for the Neo4j and Kùzu [18] graph databases. The syntax of the bootstrapped mappings is YARRRML [11], as it is more user-friendly than the turtle-based syntax of RML and the idea is to facilitate manual editing of the mappings. To be able to use the bootstrapped mappings, we also implemented connectors for Neo4j and Kùzu in the knowledge graph construction system Morph-KGC [3]. The reason to use Morph-KGC is that it is the only RML system that supports RML-star mappings at the time of writing, and it is also implemented in Python as our bootstrapper. The implementation is available on GitHub[1].

Validation on the LDBC Social Network Benchmark. We employed the LDBC Social Network Benchmark [16] to validate the approach. We used the dataset with scaling factor 1, loaded it into Kùzu, and extracted the RML-star mappings (37 TMs) with our implementation. We then used the generated mappings with Morph-KGC to create the RDF-star graph and manually validated its correctness. The bootstrapped mapping is available in the GitHub repository.

5   Conclusion

In this work, we addressed the problem of automatic generation of RML-star mappings from PGs. The bootstrapped mappings encode edge properties as quoted triples, which is a more natural representation than other statement-level metadata approaches in RDF. Our solution reduces human efforts to map PGs to RDF-star using a domain vocabulary. This can be done semi-automatically by first bootstrapping the RML-star mappings and then manually editing them

---

[1] https://github.com/arenas-guerrero-julian/pg2rml-star.

to consider the vocabulary. We implemented the approach in Python for the Neo4j and Kùzu databases, made it openly available, and validated it using the LDBC Social Network Benchmark.

Acknowledgments. This work was partially supported by the Euratom Research and Training Programme 2019–2020 under grant agreement No 900018.

References

1. Angles, R., Thakkar, H., Tomaszuk, D.: Mapping RDF databases to property graph databases. IEEE Access **8**, 86091–86110 (2020)
2. Arenas, M., Bertails, A., Prud'hommeaux, E., Sequeda, J.: A direct mapping of relational data to RDF. W3C Recommendation (2012)
3. Arenas-Guerrero, J., Chaves-Fraga, D., Toledo, J., Pérez, M.S., Corcho, O.: Morph-KGC: scalable knowledge graph materialization with mapping partitions. Seman. Web **15**(1), 1–20 (2024)
4. Arenas-Guerrero, J., Iglesias-Molina, A., Chaves-Fraga, D., Garijo, D., Corcho, O., Dimou, A.: Declarative generation of RDF-star graphs from heterogeneous data. Seman. Web (2024)
5. Bizer, C., Seaborne, A.: D2RQ-treating non-RDF databases as virtual RDF graphs. In: ISWC (2004)
6. Calvanese, D., Gal, A., Lanti, D., Montali, M., Mosca, A., Shraga, R.: Conceptually-grounded mapping patterns for virtual knowledge graphs. Data Knowl. Eng. **145**, 102157 (2023)
7. Chiba, H., Yamanaka, R., Matsumoto, S.: G2GML: graph to graph mapping language for bridging RDF and property graphs. In: ISWC (2020)
8. Das, S., Sundara, S., Cyganiak, R.: R2RML: RDB to RDF mapping language. W3C Recommendation (2012)
9. Fathy, N., Gad, W., Badr, N., Hashem, M.: ProGOMap: automatic generation of mappings from property graphs to ontologies. IEEE Access **9**, 113100–113116 (2021)
10. Hartig, O.: Reconciliation of RDF* and property graphs. CoRR (2014)
11. Heyvaert, P., De Meester, B., Dimou, A., Verborgh, R.: Declarative rules for linked data generation at your fingertips! In: Gangemi, A., et al. (eds.) ESWC 2018. LNCS, vol. 11155, pp. 213–217. Springer, Cham (2018). https://doi.org/10.1007/978-3-319-98192-5_40
12. Iglesias-Molina, A., et al.: The RML ontology: a community-driven modular redesign after a decade of experience in mapping heterogeneous data to RDF. In: ISWC (2023)
13. Jiménez-Ruiz, E., et al.: BootOX: practical mapping of RDBs to OWL 2. In: ISWC (2015)
14. Lassila, O., et al.: The OneGraph vision: challenges of breaking the graph model lock-in 1. Seman. Web **14**(1), 125–134 (2023)
15. de Medeiros, L.F., Priyatna, F., Corcho, O.: MIRROR: automatic R2RML mapping generation from relational databases. In: ICWE (2015)
16. Szárnyas, G., et al.: The LDBC social network benchmark: business intelligence workload. Proc. VLDB Endow. **16**(4), 877–890 (2022)
17. Tomaszuk, D., Angles, R., Thakkar, H.: PGO: describing property graphs in RDF. IEEE Access **8**, 118355–118369 (2020)
18. Xiyang, F., Guodong, J., Ziyi, C., Chang, L., Semih, S.: Kùzu graph database management system. In: CIDR (2023)

Exploring the Role of UML in Data Modelling for NoSQL Databases: Position Paper

Mohammed el Habib Maicha[1]([⊠]) and Jaroslav Pokorný[2,3]

[1] Laboratoire d'informatique et de Mathematique, UATL, Laghouat, Algeria
`mh.maicha@lagh-univ.dz`
[2] Faculty of Mathematics and Physics, Charles University, Prague, Czech Republic
`jaroslav.pokorny@matfyz.cuni.cz, pokorny@savs.cz`
[3] Škoda Auto University, Mladá Boleslav, Czech Republic

Abstract. This paper reviews the use of Unified Modelling Language (UML) for data modelling in NoSQL databases, highlighting its benefits and limitations. It identifies trends in UML's application for NoSQL data structures and suggests future research directions, focusing on innovative modelling techniques that address NoSQL's unique challenges.

Keywords: Unified Modelling Language · NoSQL databases · data modelling · visual representation

1 Introduction

In recent years, the use of NoSQL databases has witnessed a surge in popularity owing to their adeptness in handling vast volumes of unstructured and semi-structured data [1, 2]. Unlike traditional relational databases, NoSQL systems offer flexible and dynamic schemas that enable efficient storage and retrieval of complex data structures [3]. However, creating an effective data model for a NoSQL database is challenging due to the lack of a standardized schema and the diversity of data structures supported by different NoSQL databases [4].

UML, a widely adopted modelling language, provides a comprehensive set of notations and diagrams for visualizing, specifying, constructing, and documenting the components of a software system. By employing UML, data modelers can create clear representations of NoSQL data structures, which facilitates communication among team members and stakeholders. This paper aims to explore the role of UML in NoSQL data modelling, examining how it has been used to model data in various NoSQL databases and identifying the benefits and limitations of this approach.

The remainder of the paper is organized as follows. Section 2 presents relevant existing surveys and studies. Section 3 explores some specific design methods for NoSQL databases based on UML. Section 4 is devoted to planning the systematic literature review (SLR) study. Section 5 describes the literature review process used in this paper. Analysis results are discussed in the main Sect. 6. Finally, Sect. 7 provides conclusions and topics for future works.

P. Delir Haghighi et al. (Eds.): iiWAS 2024, LNCS 15342, pp. 304–310, 2025.
https://doi.org/10.1007/978-3-031-78090-5_26

2 Relevant Existing Surveys and Studies

The literature on NoSQL data modelling reveals various methodologies and tools that facilitate the design of NoSQL databases [4–6]. Nevertheless, few studies have systematically analyzed how UML can be used for modelling in this context. Most existing research focuses on transforming traditional database designs into NoSQL models tailored to specific case studies. Only a limited number of works have explored UML's potential to standardize NoSQL data modelling.

Existing surveys [7–11] have generally discussed data modelling in NoSQL systems without delving into specific UML-based approaches. The lack of a comprehensive analysis has left gaps in understanding how UML can be applied effectively in this rapidly evolving field. This paper fills this gap by reviewing the application of UML in NoSQL data modelling, analyzing its strengths, weaknesses, and opportunities for improvement.

3 Specific Design Methods for NoSQL Databases Based on UML

Research on UML-based design methods for NoSQL databases typically focuses on three levels of representation: conceptual, logical, and physical. Conceptual modelling involves creating high-level representations of data structures, often using class diagrams or entity-relationship (ER) models. Logical modelling refines these representations into specific schema designs tailored to the characteristics of NoSQL systems, such as document-oriented, graph-based, or key-value databases. Physical modelling addresses how data will be stored and accessed within the database system.

Most studies emphasize logical-level modelling, where UML helps to map complex data structures into understandable formats. This approach is particularly beneficial for document-oriented and graph-based NoSQL databases, where data relationships are intricate and dynamic. However, UML's traditional notations can struggle to represent the flexible and often schema-less nature of NoSQL data. This limitation suggests the need for adapting or extending UML to better suit NoSQL environments.

4 Planning and Conducting the Systematic Literature Review (SLR)

To conduct a thorough SLR, we followed established guidelines to identify, evaluate, and interpret relevant research on UML in NoSQL data modelling. The review process included three main phases: identifying the need for the study, planning the review protocol, and systematically collecting and analyzing primary studies.

1. **Need for an SLR Study**. Effective application development in big data requires rigorous modelling. Despite the recognized importance of this modelling phase, there is a lack of widely accepted methodologies for NoSQL systems. Our goal is to investigate and provide a detailed SLR of current efforts in NoSQL data modelling, focusing on adherence to established norms and standards.

2. **The SLR Protocol**. Prior to commencing the SLR, it is imperative to establish a research protocol to prevent potential conflicts of interest among researchers [12].

Consequently, our protocol is structured as follows: firstly, we have delineated specific developmental objectives along with supporting arguments to explicate our contributions. Subsequently, in an effort to distil the existing evidence on big data modelling using UML, we have formulated five research questions.

- **Objectives and justifications**. The primary aim is to present the most pertinent research on NoSQL database modelling and identify trends and gaps related to big data concepts—source models, target models, and the 4Vs (volume, variety, velocity, veracity). This SLR aggregates almost all studies on UML-based NoSQL database modelling to benefit both industry and academia.
- **Research questions.** We formulated five questions to guide the review:
  RQ1. What types of NoSQL databases are covered in the research?
  RQ2. What representation levels are used in NoSQL database modelling methodologies?
  RQ3. How do these methods address the 4Vs?
  RQ4. How have these methods been evaluated?
  RQ5. What are the trends and gaps in big data modelling and management?

5 Literature Review Process

The following steps were necessary to compile an exhaustive list of studies on the topic of interest: finding primary studies, selecting potentially relevant studies, applying inclusion criteria to primary studies, and extracting and synthesizing the data.

5.1 Identification of Primary Studies

We identified potential studies by applying search strings related to NoSQL, data modelling, and UML across academic databases such as Google Scholar and Semantic Scholar. This initial search yielded a substantial number of documents, which were then filtered based on relevance and inclusion criteria.

5.2 Selection and Analysis of Relevant Studies

Studies were selected based on their focus on NoSQL data modelling using UML. We categorized the studies according to the types of NoSQL databases they addressed (e.g., document-oriented, graph-based) and the levels of representation used (conceptual, logical, or physical). The final analysis aimed to provide insights into how UML is used across different types of NoSQL systems and identify common challenges.

5.3 Data Synthesis and Reporting

Data extracted from the selected studies were synthesized to answer key research questions related to UML's application in NoSQL data modelling. The results were then reported in a structured format, highlighting trends, gaps, and opportunities for future research.

6 Analysis Results

This section provides an analysis based on the research questions through bibliometric analysis, a comprehensive literature review, and a discussion of trends and gaps.

6.1 Bibliometric Analysis

We conducted a bibliometric analysis to collate information on authors, publication details, impact metrics (H-index and SJR), and publication outlets. Key findings include:

- Research on UML-based NoSQL database modelling has increased over time, with a notable peak in 2018.
- Prior to 2013, relevant studies were not identified.

The distribution of the studies reveals the extensive involvement of 54 researchers from 15 countries [13–20], highlighting the international scope of research in NoSQL database modelling. Prominent contributions came from European nations such as Spain, Italy, and Germany, as well as from North American and Asian countries, including Canada, South Korea, and China. Additionally, multi-country collaborations underscore the global interconnectedness of this research area, with significant efforts originating from Brazil, Malaysia, France, and others. This geographic diversity reflects the widespread interest and importance of NoSQL databases, as researchers from diverse cultural and technological backgrounds bring unique perspectives to the development and evaluation of NoSQL data modelling approaches. The broad representation of nations and collaborative efforts emphasize the relevance of this research field across various technological ecosystems, underscoring the shared goal of advancing database design and implementation practices worldwide.

6.2 Systematic Literature Review

This review addresses the research questions RQ1, RQ2, and RQ3.

RQ1. *Types of NoSQL databases*

The analysis categorized studies into two groups: those addressing all NoSQL databases ("All") and those focused on specific types ("OneType"). Document-oriented databases are the most frequently studied, with nine studies, while key-value databases are not represented. Figure 1a illustrates the distribution of methods per database treatment, and Fig. 1b details the number of works per NoSQL type.

RQ2. *Levels of representation*

The review identified the levels of representation (conceptual, logical, and physical) used in NoSQL database modelling. Document-oriented databases predominantly use logical representation, whereas graph-type databases primarily utilize conceptual representation. Figure 2 presents the levels of representation by NoSQL database type.

RQ3. *Considerations for the 4Vs*

Non-functional requirements, such as scalability and consistency, are crucial for addressing the 4Vs of big data. Despite their importance, these requirements are less frequently considered compared to functional requirements. Only six studies address non-functional aspects to some extent.

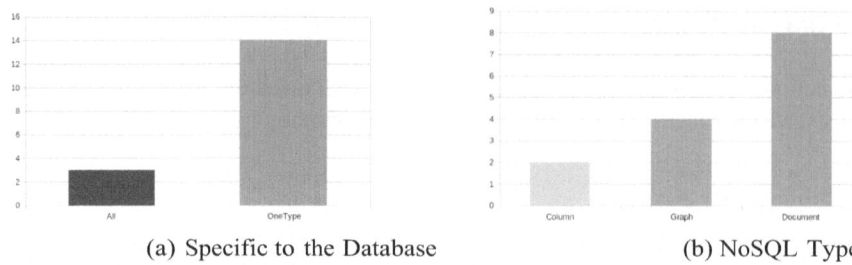

(a) Specific to the Database   (b) NoSQL Type

Fig. 1: (a) Number of works per database treatment; (b) Number of works per NoSQL type

Among the 4Vs, "volume" is the most commonly addressed concept, with several studies incorporating it into their design methods. For instance, some methods include performance considerations, such as a workload-based conversion process, while others focus on integrity, particularly in maintaining logical data consistency across replicated clusters.

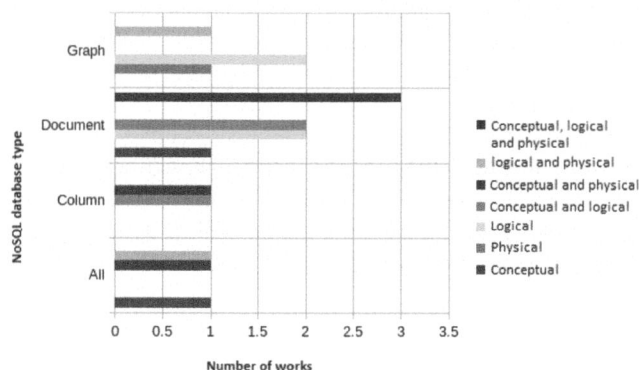

Fig. 2. Representation Levels by Type of NoSQL Databases.

6.3 Discussion

This section addresses RQ4 and RQ5.

RQ4. *Evaluation methods*

Evaluation approaches vary, including experimentation, illustrative examples, and comparisons with established methods. Many methods lack comprehensive evaluations, as depicted in Fig. 3. Some studies include plans for future evaluation or present preliminary use cases rather than extensive assessments.

RQ5. *Trends and gaps*

Future research directions include:

- Enhanced evaluation methods for proposed techniques.
- Automatic or semi-automatic implementation of methods.

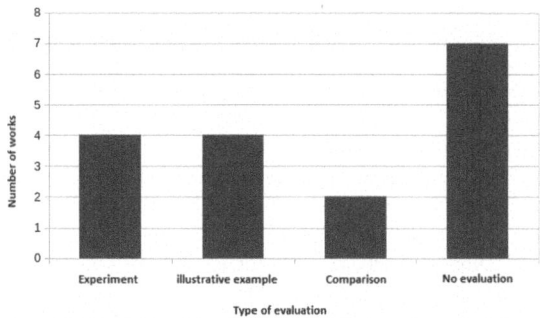

Fig. 3. Number of studies by type of evaluation

- Expansion of methods to include more features (vertical) or types of databases (horizontal).

As additional findings, the following information has been identified in the reviewed articles:

- Most studies present results at conceptual, logical, and physical levels.
- Document-oriented models are most frequently studied at the logical level.
- There is a need for methods that facilitate transitions between different NoSQL models and reduce manual effort in schema development.

7 Conclusions

In this paper we conducted a systematic literature review on UML-based big data modelling, revealing key insights: most studies lack validation with real-world data, and the velocity aspect of big data is often ignored. The ER model is commonly used at the conceptual level, while document-oriented models dominate at the logical level. A major gap identified is the lack of evaluations of proposed methods.

As NoSQL databases rise in popularity for managing complex data, they still lack some strengths of relational databases, particularly in balancing consistency and availability. Future research will focus on updating the review and addressing these gaps in NoSQL database modelling.

References

1. Gandomi, A., Haider, M.: Beyond the hype. big data concepts, methods, and analytics. Int. J. Inform. Manage. **35**(2), 137–144 (2015)
2. Davoudian, A., Chen, L., Liu, M.: A survey on NoSQL stores. ACM Comput. Surv. **51**(2), 1–43 (2018)
3. Krommyda, M.K., Kantere, V.: The big data era: data management novelties for visualizing, exploring, and processing big data. In: Analyzing Future Applications of AI, Sensors, and Robotics in Society, pp. 87–103. IGI Global (2020)
4. Atzeni, P., et al.: Data modeling in the NoSQL world. Comput. Stand. Interfaces **67**, 103–149 (2020)

5. McConnell, C.C., et al.: Efficient denormalization of data instances. US Patent App. 16/740,081 (2020)
6. Mior, M.J., et al.: NoSE: Schema design for NoSQL applications. IEEE Trans. Knowl. Data Eng. **29**(10), 2275–2289 (2017)
7. Hecht, R., Jablonski, S.: NoSQL evaluation: a use case-oriented survey. In: 2011 International Conference on Cloud and Service Computing, pp. 336–341. IEEE (2011)
8. Gil, D., Song, I.-Y.: Modeling and management of big data: challenges and opportunities. Future Gener. Comput. Syst. **63**, 96–99 (2016)
9. Asaad, C., Baına, K.: NoSQL databases–seek for a design methodology. In: Abdelwahed, E., Bellatreche, L., Golfarelli, M., Méry, D., Ordonez, C. (eds.) Model and Data Engineering. MEDI 2018. LNCS, vol. 11163. Springer, Cham (2018). https://doi.org/10.1007/978-3-030-00856-7_2
10. Roy-Hubara, N., Sturm, A.: Design methods for the new database era: a systematic literature review. Softw. Syst. Model. **19**(2), 297–312 (2020)
11. Martinez-Mosquera, D., Navarrete, R., Lujan-Mora, S.: Modeling and management big data in databases—a systematic literature review. Sustainability **12.2**, 634 (2020)
12. Kitchenham, B.: Procedures for performing systematic reviews. In: Keele, U.K. (ed.) Keele University, vol. 33, pp. 1–26 (2004)
13. Daniel, G., Suny´e, G., Cabot, J.: UMLtoGraphDB: mapping conceptual schemas to graph databases. In: Comyn-Wattiau, I., Tanaka, K., Song, IY., Yamamoto, S., Saeki, M. (eds.) Conceptual Modeling. ER 2016. LNCS, vol. 9974. Springer, Cham (2016). https://doi.org/10.1007/978-3-319-46397-1_33
14. De la Vega, A., et al.: Mortadelo: A model-driven framework for NoSQL database design. In: Abdelwahed, E., Bellatreche, L., Golfarelli, M., Méry, D., Ordonez, C. (eds.) Model and Data Engineering. MEDI 2018. LNCS, vol. 11163. Springer, Cham (2018). https://doi.org/10.1007/978-3-030-00856-7_3
15. Roy-Hubara, N., et al.: Evaluation of a design method for graph database. In: Gulden, J., Reinhartz-Berger, I., Schmidt, R., Guerreiro, S., Guédria, W., Bera, P. (eds.) Enterprise, Business-Process and Information Systems Modeling. BPMDS EMMSAD 2018 2018. LNBIP, vol. 318. Springer, Cham (2018). https://doi.org/10.1007/978-3-319-91704-7_19
16. Gomez, P., Casallas, R., Roncancio, C.: Automatic schema generation for document-oriented systems. In: International Conference on Database and Expert Systems Applications. Springer, pp. 152–163 (2020)
17. Feng, W., et al.: Transforming UML class diagram into cassandra data model with annotations. In: 2015 IEEE International Conference on Smart City/Social-Com/SustainCom (SmartCity), pp. 798–805. IEEE (2015)
18. Li, X., Ma, Z., Chen, H.: QODM: a query-oriented data modeling approach for NoSQL databases. In: 2014 IEEE Workshop on Advanced Research and Technology in Industry Applications (WARTIA), pp. 338–345. IEEE (2014)
19. Hamouda, S., Zainol, Z.: Document-oriented data schema for relational database migration to NoSQL. In: 2017 International conference on big data innovations and applications (innovate-data), pp. 43–50. IEEE (2017)
20. ElHabib Maicha, M., Ouinten,Y., Ziani, B.: UML4NoSQL: a novel approach for modeling NoSQL document-oriented databases based on UML. Comput. Inform. **41.3**, 813–833 (2022)

Railway Systems' Ontologies: A Literature Review and an Alignment Proposal

David Camarazo[1,2(✉)], Ana Roxin[2], and Mohammed Lalou[2]

[1] Railenium, Famars, France
`david.camarazo@railenium.eu`
[2] Laboratoire Informatique de Bourgogne (LIB), Université de Bourgogne, Dijon, France
{`ana-maria.roxin,mohammed.lalou`}`@u-bourgogne.fr`

Abstract. Railway systems are complex systems whose design and construction require many cooperating actors. Multiple models have been produced to reduce semantic heterogeneity and enable cooperation across many companies and persons. However, each model created has its own point of view regarding the railway domain and uses its own vocabulary. Therefore, it is necessary to investigate ways to align those models and to ease cooperation between actors. This paper first identifies the main ontologies proposed in the last two decades. Then, we study and compare those models and analyse the difficulties when aligning them. The results regarding our attempts to align identified railway ontologies are thus discussed.

Keywords: railway systems · railway ontologies · alignment framework · semantic heterogeneity · semantic interoperability

1 Introduction

Multiple projects have been initiated to develop semantic models to assist the complex conception of railway system. Those models aim to give a common vocabulary with an unequivocal interpretation for every actor implied in the design of railway systems. Since no model has taken hold, model heterogeneity and unclear interpretations of railway terminology exist. Aligning the different models is essential to ease cooperation across companies working on railway systems.

The research issues addressed in this paper are the evaluation of existing ontologies for the railway domain and the evaluation of existing tools for automatic ontology alignment. We think that the evaluation of automatically extracted ontologies, ontology reuse and evaluation, and automatic alignments are common in every field that uses knowledge engineering. As such, the research issues we address pertain to all domains involving knowledge engineering for

© The Author(s), under exclusive license to Springer Nature Switzerland AG 2025
P. Delir Haghighi et al. (Eds.): iiWAS 2024, LNCS 15342, pp. 311–319, 2025.
https://doi.org/10.1007/978-3-031-78090-5_27

complex systems and aiming to interoperate heterogeneous existing knowledge specifications using alignment tools. Our methodology for evaluating existing ontologies can be easily reused for evaluating ontologies from another domain. The same goes for our methodology for evaluating the existing alignment tools.

The rest of the paper is organised as follows: Section 2 presents the fundamental notions about ontology and ontology alignment, Sect. 3 evaluates railway domain ontologies. Section 4 evaluates ontology alignment tools and discuss our results. The last section concludes the paper and provides several future research directions.

2   Background Definitions - Ontologies and Alignments

We define an ontology as a "formal, explicit specification of a shared conceptualisation" according to the definition [10]. From [5], conceptualisation refers to "an intentional semantic structure which encodes the implicit rules constraining the structure of a piece of reality". We say an ontology is formal, meaning it is written with a syntax that defines a domain's semantics and prevents ambiguous interpretation. Also, an ontology is explicit as it states explicitly the different relations and classes of a shared conceptualisation. Furthermore, it explains implicit knowledge shared in a general agreement.

An ontology is built using logical formula [2] with a vocabulary divided into two sets: classes **C** and properties **P**. An ontology has a terminological scheme, a TBox, and a set of assertions called ABox.

We follow the definition provided by [12] regarding ontology alignments. An ontology alignment is the output of an ontology matching process. An ontology matching can be seen as a function $matching(O_1, O_2, A', p, r)$. Where O_1 and O_2 are the ontologies we are trying to align, A' is a set of already existing alignments, p is a set of parameters (e.g. threshold, metric, filter) for ontology matching, and r is a set of external resources that can be required for ontology matching. An ontology matching process produces an ontology alignment between classes or properties from O_1 and O_2.

3   Ontologies for Railway Systems' Modelling - Identification and Evaluation

3.1   Presentation of the Models

The following paragraphs present the existing ontologies for specifying railway domain knowledge. More specifically, we selected the ontologies identified during the Linx4Rail European project, as, to the best of our knowledge, it is the only European project that has addressed the issue of building a global railway domain ontology. Given our scope to align existing railway ontologies to form a semantic continuum for railway knowledge, we seek to build upon ontologies already considered for alignment, as with the Linx4Rail project. Our ontology selection is further completed with ontologies found through keyword searches on Google Scholar and Linked Open Vocabularies https://lov.linkeddata.es/dataset/lov/about/. We used the keywords "railway domain ontology" and "railway ontology". Our efforts allowed us to find, in addition to the ontologies proposed in Linx4Rail, the ontology RaCoOn [11].

ERA. It is an ontology created by the European Union Agency for Railways and models knowledge about the legal sector and railway-related use cases. Compared with the other ontologies considered, this one is the smallest regarding classes and properties. Additionally, ERA proposes an important hierarchy between classes.

IFC Rail. It is a subpart of the IFC (Industry Foundation Classes) model. IFC Rail is one of the most complete we found. The associated ontology contains thousands of classes and properties with many redundancies. Moreover, the hierarchy between classes is more horizontal than the hierarchy we have found in the other ontologies.

Rail System Model. It is the rebranded and more complete version of the Rail Topology Model (RTM), which has become the Rail System Model (RSM). The associated ontology is reasonably large for humans. However, it does not cover essential parts of infrastructure and has redundant properties. We note that RSM proposes a well-organised hierarchy between classes.

Eulynx. It is a model created by the EuLynx consortium. The implemented version of the ontology is relatively large. It covers an essential part of infrastructure but still lacks more specific classes about rail classes. The proposed hierarchy is rich, giving relations between classes and has a depth of six levels.

TransModel. It is a model sponsored by the European Comity of Normalisation and has been approved as a European standard. The implemented ontology associated with TransModel is the largest regarding the number of classes and properties. Then again, the ontology contains a lot of redundant properties. Additionally, some classes do not represent railway infrastructure concepts. The underlying hierarchy is considerable, presenting rich taxonomy for the various classes.

X2Rail-4. It is a project for studying various railway themes. The model is grounded in European Railway Traffic Management System (ERTMS) standards. On the one hand, the number of classes is reasonable (around one hundred). On the other, we note many redundant properties. We also note that the hierarchy presented by the model is "weak" and does not establish many relations between classes. Moreover, the model does not include other properties or relations to add relevant semantics to the classes.

RaCoOn. It is an ontology developed by the University of Birmingham. The ontology size is reasonable for humans based on the number of classes. There are fewer properties than in the other ontologies, but it is important to note that there are almost no redundant properties. The hierarchy is rich and introducing important class relations.

OntoRail. It is a federation of railway ontologies for different projects (ERA, Eulynx, IFC Rail, RSM, TransModel, X2Rail-4). It uses Simple Knowledge Organisation System (SKOS) vocabulary to express relationships between ontology elements. At the time of writing, Ontorail is an ongoing project.

3.2   Evaluation of the Related Ontologies

After introducing the main ontologies, it is time to evaluate those implemented and available for free download.

First, considering OntoRail as a federation of railway ontologies, it is a direct answer to our problem as an attempt to align various railway vocabularies. However, it presents severe limitations to achieve our goal of creating an automated method to verify the modelling process. The SKOS relations do not formally specify semantic relations between terms. Moreover, in the case of OntoRail, we can not directly map SKOS relations with formal relations. In fact, in OntoRail, "related_match" serves as a way to describe an equivalence relation or a synonym relation.

Considering the discussion above, we now have seven free models implemented as ontologies: ERA, Eulynx, IFC Rail, RaCoOn, RSM, TransModel, and X2Rail-4. We have considered the various criteria provided by Noy et al. [6] for their evaluation.

The Table in 1 recaps different measures studied on previously mentioned ontologies. To ease the reading, we use the abbreviations below: (i)The reasoning result section sums up the result obtained when we reason over the ontology (more details below). The "OK" mention indicates the reasoner has successfully ended its inference task, and the ontology is consistent. The "OOM" mention stands for "Out Of Memory" and means the reasoner could not infer all implicit knowledge successfully. Finally, "inconsistent" means the reasoner found the ontology inconsistent. (ii) OP for Object Property. (iii) DP for Data Property. (iv) Ratio(%) I/CA: per cent ratio between the number of instances and the number of class assertions. It allows us to measure the extent to which ontology instances belong to ontology classes, thus identifying if there are orphan instances. This ratio is lower for manually constructed ontologies (i.e. ERA and RaCoOn) and higher for the automatically generated ontologies (i.e. 211 for TransModel). A higher value for this ratio should be interpreted as an insufficient number of class axioms to allow for a satisfying classification of instances. (v) Ratio (%) SBO/C: per cent ratio between the number of rdfs:subClassOf relations and the number of classes. It gives a hint about the richness of the taxonomy. (vi) Ratio (%) OtherP/P: per cent ratio between the number of various properties and the number of domain/range properties. This allows us to see if the ontologies contain axioms a reasoner can exploit or if the ontology relies only on domain/range axioms.

We use three symbols to evaluate the corresponding criteria for qualitative criteria: check, tilde, and cross. For the quality section in Table 1, a check means that the criterion is overall respected with few (between 1 and 3) or no counterexamples; a tilde implies that the criterion is overall respected but has many counter-examples (more than 3 counterexamples but the criterion is

still respected by the large majority of classes). The cross means too many counterexamples exist to consider the criterion respected. While we are aware this
evaluation lacks precision, it revealed sufficient data for our current study and
allowed us to illustrate the difficulties faced when choosing between ontologies.
Therefore, this section translates our point of view regarding the problems we
encountered when trying to use the ontologies identified. We admit this analysis
may be partially subjective, but we argue it still highlights concrete and real
issues present in the ontologies studied. For the "Scope" section, the check sign
indicates that more than three terms are related to the corresponding infrastructure component. The tilde sign means at least one term related to the element
but less or equal to three. Finally, the cross sign means that no terms about
the corresponding component exist. We now describe the various quality criteria
we considered for our evaluation: (i) Readable URIs: check if an entity's URI is
readable by a human being. Following the W3C point of view, detailed in [1],
URIs being meant to identify resources on a global scale, we argue it is best for
ontology alignment and reuse to have human-readable URIs. In fact as noted in
[6], concepts must be referred to using clear names. Since labels are not manda-
tory and vary in clarity, we believe it is best to use URI. (ii) Acyclic classes:
check no class is a subclass of another class that represents the same concept.
(iii) Unique classes: Check that a label corresponds to exactly one class (there
are no classes with the same label; the contrary would introduce confusion).
(iv) Unique properties: Check that a label corresponds to exactly one property
(there are no properties with the same label). (v) Relevant label: check labels are
readable by a human being and refer to a railway class. (vi) Naming convention:
check a naming convention is respected.

Table 1 summarises our evaluation of the examined ontologies.

ERA, Eulynx, IFC Rail, RSM, TransModel, and X2Rail-4, have been implemented for the project OntoRail. Therefore, they contain class cycles. This is
due to meta-classes defined in the OntoRail vocabulary and redefined in OWL.
Regarding ontologies that have been automatically built from models, they contain a lot of duplicates, classes without names, with unreadable names, or with
names that do not refer clearly to railway classes. Moreover, their URIs are
processes strings without human meaning. Finally, we see that manually built
ontologies, ERA and RaCoOn, have the highest expressivity and specify more
properties other than domain and range properties. This fact suggests that the
knowledge from these ontologies can be exploited by a reasoner for automated
tasks such as verification.

To have a complete overview of the railway domain, our work must also
consider the scope of the evaluated ontologies. Table 1 clearly illustrates that
finding a complete and well-structured ontology is hard. While an automatically
generated ontology can be interesting regarding its scope, which is the case for
Eulynx, IFC Rail, and X2Rail-4, the underlying TBox model presents design and
structural issues and does not expose rich semantics. Moreover, no properties
are defined other than domain and range properties except in TransModel. We

Table 1. Table summarising the above ontologies' evaluation

Criterion	Sub-criteria	ERA v3.0.0	Eulynx 09/03/2023	IFC Rail v2021-02-01	RSM v1.2	TransModel v6.56	X2Rail-4 v2022-01-13	RaCoOn
General	Classes	68	1163	1368	227	2209	551	426
	Object Properties	150	2110	3220	190	3666	1766	70
	Data Properties	300	0	8	0	21	0	12
	Individuals	12	5863	4589	1050	6582	3268	73
	Annotations	41	115	105	106	448	95	20
	DL Expressivity	ALUHIQ(D)	AL	AL(D)	AL	AL(D)	AL	ALCROIF
	Manually created	yes	no	no	no	no	no	yes
	Reasoning result	OK	OOM	OK	OK	Inconsistent	OOM	OK
Class Axioms	rdfs:subClassOf	44	921	497	196	2855	52	460
	Other Axioms	0	0	0	0	0	0	9
Object Property axioms	OP_Domain	140	2110	3220	191	3849	1766	60
	OP_Range	145	2110	2309	191	3849	1766	59
	OP_Other	39	0	0	0	0	0	35
Data Property axioms	DP_Domain	291	0	8	0	8	0	10
	DP_Range	294	0	8	0	21	0	9
	DP_Other	129	0	0	0	10	0	3
Individual axioms	Class Assertions	10	11085	7468	1914	13917	5069	27
	Other Assertions	0	0	0	0	6834	0	46
Ratios	Ratio(%) I/CA	83,33	189,1	162,74	182,3	211,44	155,11	36,99
	Ratio(%) SBO/C	64,71	79,19	36,33	86,34	129,24	9,44	107,98
	Ratio(%) OtherP/P	16,18	0	0	0	0,13	0	21,59
Quality	Readable URIs	✓	X	X	X	X	X	✓
	Acyclic classes	✓	✓	✓	✓	✓	✓	✓
	Unique classes	✓	✓	≈	✓	✓	≈	✓
	Unique properties	✓	X	X	X	X	X	✓
	Relevant labels	≈	≈	✓	≈	✓	✓	✓
	Naming convention	≈	X	≈	≈	X	✓	≈
Scope	Rail	✓	X	✓	✓	≈	✓	✓
	Signalling	≈	✓	≈	X	X	✓	✓
	Power Supply	X	≈	✓	X	X	≈	X
	Telecommunication	X	✓	✓	X	X	X	X

noted this issue for all three ontologies generated automatically from XMI or UML models *i.e.* Eulynx, IFC Rail and X2Rail-4.

4   Railway Systems' Ontologies Alignments

4.1   Manual Alignments

We aim to experiment how to establish alignments between some of those ontologies. We first manually defined alignments between RaCoOn and ERA ontologies because they are the only ontologies correctly conceived, with precise semantics and human-readable.

We identified alignments between classes. Fifteen relations between classes were identified. Those relations are in our gitlab https://gitlab.com/c4m4r4z0/railway-ontologies-alignment/-/blob/main/railwayAlignments.ttl?ref_type= heads. Some relations can be trivially found by comparing the class labels. We can create an equivalent relation between classes if the labels are identical, except for their naming convention. However, this basic approach does not suffice for a thorough alignment. When labels contain similar words or classes with similar ancestors, we must look at the classes' comments, if any, to establish equivalency or hyperonymy relations.

We then investigated the different properties of the two considered ontologies. They are present in our gitlab https://gitlab.com/c4m4r4z0/railway-ontologies-alignment/-/blob/main/railwayAlignments.ttl?ref_type=heads. Given the differences   in   design,   fewer   alignments   were   defined,   and only one owl:equivalentProperty relation was identified. The main difficulties come from the fact that different design choices were made in each ontology. For example, some elements are modelled as properties in one ontology and as classes in the other.

4.2   Automatic Alignments

We now aim to experiment automatic alignment method. Let us first present existing alignment tools from the literature we evaluated, and then we will discuss each in detail. We want to align ontologies using automated tools to save costly expert consultations, which can be laborious. In this work, and to compile a list of automated alignment tools, we have examined two critical sources [3,9]. We have identified three tools that are available for free download and may be customised to use with different datasets, namely, Limes, LogMap, and OnAGUI[1]. We introduced selected alignment tools for evaluation. We will now discuss each tool. We begin with Limes, which is highly configurable. First, we can align ontologies using string similarity or semantic proximity following word-net hierarchy [8]. Once this choice is made, we have different computing methods to compute the similarity between terms. When the computing method has been selected, we must specify a threshold between 0 and 1 to filter out results with a similarity score too low to be relevant. From what we observed, we obtained interesting results with a threshold of around 0.7. A threshold less than 0.5 outputs too many irrelevant results, while a threshold higher than 0.85 provides mappings only when terms are almost identical. Similarity computing method also has a significant impact on results. We have retained four measures with many pertaining scores without too many errors. The cosine and the Ratcliff methods are best for string measures. The Li, Leacock and Chodorow measures are the best semantic measures. However, even with those parameters, we observe many issues in the results. First, Limes does not provide the nature, *i.e.* the type of mapping relation. This requires extra manual labour to sort the mappings between equivalences, "is a" or "subclass of" relation. We also observe duplicate results that modelling particularities in our ontologies can explain. Moreover, since the ontologies may contain irrelevant labels, we can find absurd output mappings. Therefore, asserting reliable and definitive rules regarding correct methods and thresholds is challenging. What we have for now are only heuristics.

Considering LogMap, it is straightforward to use and compute many pertaining mappings. Its internal optimisation to automatically filter irrelevant results decreases the manual labour required to establish proper alignments. Moreover, the framework can compute three types of relations: "equivalent", "more specific than", and "more general than", which helps to understand the calculated mappings. With LogMap, we note that if the trust degree is below 0.2 for a given alignment, the output seems incorrect, linking classes with no semantic

---

[1] Respectively https://dice-research.org/LIMES, https://www.cs.ox.ac.uk/isg/tools/ LogMap/ and https://github.com/lmazuel/onagui?tab=readme-ov-file.

relations. We also observe that the relation type can be incorrect if the trust degree is below 0.6.

For OnAGUI, thanks to its user interface, domain experts familiar with computer science find it straightforward to use. This makes it easy to import source ontologies, export results or manually edit mappings. However, it does not provide the nature of the relationships in the computed mappings, and the user must select a threshold to filter the results. The tool indicates by a colour code which mappings are most relevant, and accordingly, the best threshold value is 0.75. We have found out that the tool is helpful to establish obvious relations between classes that have similar labels automatically. However, we can already see that the tool mixes equivalent relations with hyperonymy relations. Moreover, some relations seem wrong regarding the classes definition.

Unsurprisingly, and regarding the Ontology Alignment Evaluation Initiative (OAEI) results [9], LogMap is the more mature tool. We can select data sources to align, and it returns mostly relevant results. The number of errors is less than five for each alignment task we did. With other tools there are so many errors that it is difficult to correct them manually. It is also important to note that since our ontologies present several issues and limitations regarding their design, other tools may have trouble loading them or computing readable mappings. We have stored the results of our experimentations with the different tools in a GitLab https://gitlab.com/c4m4r4z0/railway-ontologies-alignment/-/tree/main.

5 Conclusion and Future work

With our experiments, we obtained 62 alignments. They are available for download in https://gitlab.com/c4m4r4z0/railway-ontologies-alignment/-/tree/main.

Our methodology first considered defining such alignments manually. Given the complexity of the considered ontologies, this task took a lot of work (many hours). We then turned to automatic alignment tools. Following our evaluation, LogMap was the best performer, identifying many proper alignments without too many mistakes within a few minutes.

We also draw important conclusions from those experiments: (i) ontologies automatically extracted from UML models are difficult to reuse as they expose little semantics. (ii) there is no ideal tool or methodology to automatically align ontologies - it all depends on the domain addressed and the scope identified. (iii) given the complexity of the knowledge domain, as there is no unambiguous and unique knowledge representation, there won't be unique and standard alignments. Alignments have to be reviewed and discussed with experts from the domain, representing a first step towards more solid ontology interoperation approaches.

In future work we aim to pay specific attention to the ongoing work regarding the railML ontology development and its mappings with ERA and IFC4Rail ontologies [7]. Building upon these alignments, we aim to define and implement a federation among railway ontologies by reusing existing architectures such as FOWLA [4]. Coupled with a semantic enrichment module, such federation can serve as a basis for an automated approach to verify railway systems' modelling processes through the different phases.

References

1. Ayers, D., Völkel, M.: Cool URIs for the semantic web. Working Draft W3C (2008)
2. Baader, F.: Description logics. In: Tessaris, S., et al. (eds.) Reasoning Web 2009. LNCS, vol. 5689, pp. 1–39. Springer, Heidelberg (2009). https://doi.org/10.1007/978-3-642-03754-2_1
3. Bergman, M.: 30 active ontology alignment tools (2018)
4. Farias, T.M., Roxin, A., Nicolle, C.: FOWLA, a federated architecture for ontologies. In: Bassiliades, N., Gottlob, G., Sadri, F., Paschke, A., Roman, D. (eds.) RuleML 2015. LNCS, vol. 9202, pp. 97–111. Springer, Cham (2015). https://doi.org/10.1007/978-3-319-21542-6_7
5. Guarino, N., Giaretta, P.: Ontologies and knowledge bases. In: Towards Very Large Knowledge Bases, pp. 1–2 (1995)
6. Noy, N.F., McGuinness, D.L., et al.: Ontology development 101: a guide to creating your first ontology (2001)
7. Olsen, L.C.: Ontology in Norwegian digital infrastructure model (dim) project. In: 45th RailML Conference (2024)
8. Pedersen, T., Patwardhan, S., Michelizzi, J., et al.: WordNet: similarity-measuring the relatedness of concepts. In: AAAI, vol. 4, pp. 25–29 (2004)
9. Pour, M.A.N., et al.: Results of the ontology alignment evaluation initiative 2022. In: 17th International Workshop on Ontology Matching (2022)
10. Studer, R., Richard Benjamins, V., Fensel, D.: Knowledge engineering: principles and methods. Data Knowl. Eng. **25**(1-2), 161–197 (1998)
11. Tutcher, J., Easton, J.M., Roberts, C.: Enabling data integration in the rail industry using RDF and OWL: the RaCoOn ontology. ASCE-ASME J. Risk Uncertainty Eng. Syst. Part A Civil Eng. **3**(2), F4015001 (2017)
12. Xue, X., Yang, C., Jiang, C., Tsai, P.-W., Mao, G., Zhu, H.: Optimizing ontology alignment through linkage learning on entity correspondences. Complexity **1–12**, 2021 (2021)

Combining GraphSAGE and Label Propagation for Node Classification in Graphs

Dolly Sharma$^{(\boxtimes)}$ (ID), Sonia Khetarpaul (ID), Chinmayi Verma (ID), and Prateek Jain (ID)

Department of Computer Science and Engineering, Shiv Nadar Institution of Eminence Deemed to be University, Delhi-NCR, Greater Noida 201314, Uttar Pradesh, India
dolly.sharma@snu.edu.in

Abstract. In node classification tasks, traditional methods like LPA-GCN struggle with scalability and sensitivity to label noise. We propose LPA-GraphSAGE, combining the Label Propagation Algorithm with GraphSAGE's sampling and aggregation techniques to address these challenges. Our model outperforms LPA-GCN in accuracy and efficiency, reducing computational costs. Its inductive capabilities also enable effective handling of dynamic graphs with new nodes. Experiments on benchmark datasets confirm that LPA-GraphSAGE is a robust and scalable alternative for node classification in complex graphs.

Keywords: graphs · message passing · information diffusion · scalability

1 Introduction

Graph-structured data analysis is crucial in areas like social networks, bioinformatics, and recommendation systems. Node classification, which assigns labels based on node attributes and graph structure, faces challenges in scalability, computational efficiency, and sensitivity to noisy labels, as seen in methods like LPA-GCN [1]. Addressing these issues is essential for large, noisy datasets. Graph Convolutional Networks (GCNs) learn node representations by aggregating local features but struggle with scalability due to full-batch training and suffer from over-smoothing in deeper layers. While mini-batch training and attention mechanisms mitigate these problems, GCNs [3,5] still face limitations with large graphs. GraphSAGE, an extension of GCNs, enhances scalability by using sampling to aggregate features from fixed-size neighborhoods, reducing computational costs and preventing over-smoothing. It also supports inductive learning, making it suitable for dynamic graphs. We propose LPA-GraphSAGE, which combines the label propagation of LPA with the scalability of GraphSAGE. Key contributions include:

P. Delir Haghighi et al. (Eds.): iiWAS 2024, LNCS 15342, pp. 320–326, 2025.
https://doi.org/10.1007/978-3-031-78090-5_28

1. Higher accuracy on large datasets (95.90 ± 0.06 on CoAuthor-Phy vs. 94.86 ± 0.14 for LPA-GCN).
2. Greater robustness to label noise, with improved accuracy on noisier datasets like Citeseer (74.06 ± 0.12 vs. 65.76 ± 0.13 for LPA-GCN).
3. Reduced computational complexity and better accuracy on datasets like Cora (86.53 ± 0.22 vs. 80.70 ± 0.25 for LPA-GCN).

2   Literature Review

Node classification in graph-structured data has advanced from traditional methods like the Label Propagation Algorithm (LPA) [2,4] and graph kernels to modern Graph Neural Networks (GNNs). LPA propagates labels through connected nodes but struggles with noisy or sparse labels, while kernel methods like the Weisfeiler-Lehman kernel are computationally expensive and less scalable for large datasets. Graph Convolutional Networks (GCNs) [3,5] have become popular for node classification by aggregating local features but are limited by scalability and over-smoothing in deeper layers. Graph Attention Networks (GATs) partially address these issues with attention mechanisms but add computational complexity. GraphSAGE [8,9], introduced by Hamilton et al., improves scalability by sampling fixed-size neighborhoods and using diverse aggregation functions, enabling efficient training on large graphs and inductive learning for unseen nodes. Hybrid methods like LPA-GCN, while combining label propagation and feature learning, still face scalability challenges, making GraphSAGE a more robust framework for large, dynamic graphs.

3   Background and Proposed Approach: LPA-GraphSAGE

This section provides background on LPA-GCN and introduces the proposed LPA-GraphSAGE framework, which combines the Label Propagation Algorithm (LPA) [2,4] with GraphSAGE for robust and scalable node classification. LPA-GCN [1] consists of three components:

I. **Label Propagation Algorithm (LPA):** LPA is a semi-supervised algorithm that propagates labels based on node similarity. The algorithm works as follows-
   (a) **Initialization:** Assign initial labels to nodes, where labeled nodes retain their labels, and unlabeled nodes receive random or null labels.
   (b) **Propagation:** Iteratively update each node's label to match the most frequent label among its neighbors.
   (c) **Convergence:** Repeat until labels stabilize. The output is a set of initial labels for embedding generation.
II. **Graph Convolutional Networks (GCN):** GCNs generate node embeddings by aggregating features from neighboring nodes. GCN operates in the following manner:

(a) **Feature Aggregation:** Aggregate neighboring node features using a convolution operation.

(b) **Embedding Update:** Update node embeddings by combining the node's own features with the aggregated neighborhood features. The embedding of a node v after k layers is given by:

$$h_v^{(k)} = \sigma \left(\sum_{u \in N(v)} \frac{1}{e_{vu}} W_k h_u^{(k-1)} + b^{(k)} \right)$$

where $N(v)$ is the set of neighbors of node v, e_{vu} is a normalization constant, W_k and $b^{(k)}$ are learnable parameters, and σ is a non-linear activation function.

III. The final embeddings are used for classification via a fully connected layer with softmax activation. Cross-entropy loss and backpropagation are used to train the model (Fig. 1).

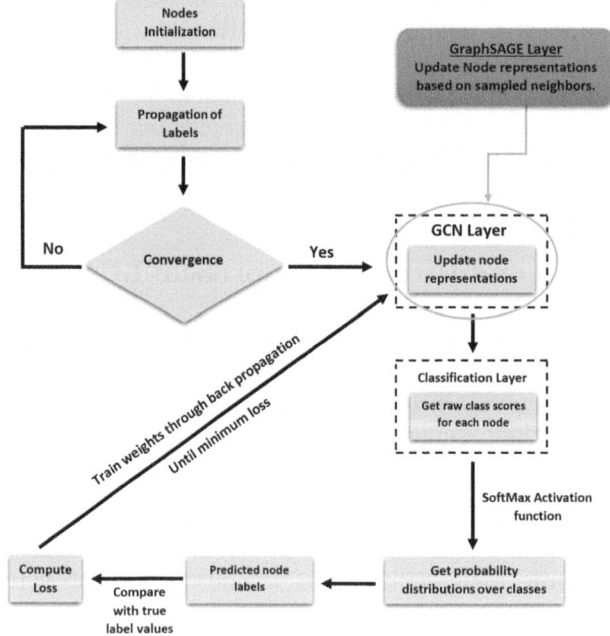

Fig. 1. Comparision between LPA-GCN and LPA-GraphSAGE implementation.

3.1 Architecture Overview of Proposed Algorithm

LPA-GraphSAGE consists of two key components:

I. **Label Propagation Algorithm (LPA):** Explained in previous section.
II. **GraphSAGE:** A GNN framework that generates node embeddings by sampling and aggregating features from a fixed-size neighborhood, enabling scalable learning. The process includes:
   (a) **Neighborhood Sampling:** Sample a fixed-size set of neighbors for each node.
   (b) **Feature Aggregation:** Aggregate the features of the sampled neighbors using an aggregation function (e.g., mean, LSTM, or pooling).
   (c) **Embedding Update:** Update the node's embedding by combining its own features with the aggregated neighborhood features.

Formally, the embedding of a node v at layer k is computed as:

$$h_v^{(k)} = \sigma(W^{(k)} \cdot \text{AGGREGATE}^{(k)}(h_u^{(k-1)}, \forall u \in N(v)) + b^{(k)})$$

where $N(v)$ is the set of neighbors of v, AGGREGATE is the aggregation function, $W^{(k)}$ and $b^{(k)}$ are learnable parameters, and σ is a non-linear activation function (e.g., ReLU).

The final embedding $h_v^{(K)}$ after K layers is used for node classification.

3.2   Final Classification

Node embeddings are classified using a fully connected layer with softmax activation, trained via cross-entropy loss and backpropagation. Input: Node embeddings $H = h_v, \forall v \in V$; Classifier: Fully connected with softmax; Training: Cross-entropy loss with backpropagation.

4   Datasets

There are 5 datasets used in the paper whose descriptions are given below followed by statistics for all datasets in node classification in Table 1.

   I. **Cora:** A citation network [6] where nodes are papers and edges are citations, with seven classification categories.
  II. **Citeseer:** Similar to Cora, nodes are papers with citations as edges, classified into fields like AI and ML.
 III. **Pubmed:** A biomedical citation network [6] with nodes representing articles labeled by topic.
  IV. **Coauthor-CS:** A computer science co-authorship [7] network where nodes are authors labeled by research fields.
   V. **Coauthor-Phy:** A physics co-authorship network [7], with nodes representing authors and edges as co-authorships.

5   Experiment

The experiments assess LPA-GraphSAGE's performance in node classification tasks. Transductive scenario where labels are known for some nodes, with full access to the graph and node features. We used 20% for validation, 20% for testing, and the remaining for training. Model is trained for 1000 epochs using the Adam Optimizer, and test accuracy is reported. L2 regularization and dropout are applied to minimize loss. Accuracy is calculated as the ratio of correct predictions to total predictions, using a 95% confidence interval. Experiments run on 1 NVIDIA GeForce GTX 1650 Ti, Intel i7-10750H CPU, and 16 GB RAM. Hyperparameter tuning optimizes learning rate, dropout rate, and layers based on the validation set. The hyperparameter settings used in experiments are listed in Table 2.

Table 1. Statistics for all datasets for node classification

	Cora	Citeseer	Pubmed	Coauthor-CS	Coauthor-Phy
#nodes	2,708	3,327	19,717	18,333	34,493
#edges	5,278	4,552	44,324	81,894	2,47,962
#classes	7	6	3	15	5
Dimensions of features	1,433	3,703	500	6,805	8,415
Intra-class Edge Rate	81.0 %	73.6 %	80.2 %	80.8 %	93.1 %
Labelled Node Rate	5.2 %	3.6 %	0.3 %	1.6 %	0.3 %

Table 2. Hyper-parameter settings used for all datasets

	Cora	Citeseer	Pubmed	Coauthor-CS	Coauthor-Phy
#hidden layers	32	16	32	32	32
#GCN layers	3	2	2	2	2
#LPA Iterations	5	5	1	2	3
LPA Weight	10	1	1	2	1
L2 Weight	1×10^{-4}	5×10^{-4}	2×10^{-4}	1×10^{-4}	1×10^{-4}
Dropout Rate	0.2 %	0.1 %	0.1 %	0.2 %	0.2 %
Learning Rate	0.05	0.2	0.1	0.1	0.05

5.1   Results and Discussion

We compare the performance of LPA-GCN and LPA-GraphSAGE on five benchmark datasets: Cora, Citeseer, Pubmed, Coauthor-CS, and Coauthor-Phy.

Table 3. Experimental results

Dataset	LPA-GCN	LPA-GraphSAGE
Cora	80.70 ± 0.25	**86.53 ± 0.22**
Citeseer	65.76 ± 0.13	**74.06 ± 0.12**
Pubmed	82.37 ± 0.07	**84.37 ± 0.06**
Coauthor-CS	90.55 ± 0.10	**92.84 ± 0.10**
Coauthor-Phy	94.86 ± 0.14	**95.90 ± 0.06**

The results show LPA-GraphSAGE outperforms LPA-GCN across all datasets, demonstrating improved scalability, robustness to label noise, and strong performance in dynamic graphs. These results confirm LPA-GraphSAGE as an effective solution for node classification in large and evolving graph structures (Table 3).

6   Conclusion and Future Work

LPA-GraphSAGE merges LPA with GraphSAGE to overcome the limitations of GCNs in large graphs and label noise. With the help of experiments we were able to show the that efficient neighbor sampling reduces computational overhead, thus improving the scalability. The algorithm could enhanced resistance to label noise through feature aggregate and supports embeddings for unseen nodes in dynamic graphs. Overall, the proposed algorithm outperforms LPA-GCN in accuracy and efficiency across benchmark datasets. We believe that LPA-GraphSAGE is suited for large, evolving graphs like social and biological networks which could be heterogeneous. The real-world applications (example fraud detection) need to be further explored.

References

1. Wang, H., Leskovec, J.: Combining graph convolutional neural networks and label propagation. ACM Trans. Inf. Syst. **40**(4) (2021). Article 73
2. Li, Q., Wu, X.-M., Liu, H., Zhang, X., Guan, Z.: Label efficient semi-supervised learning via graph filtering. In: 2019 IEEE/CVF Conference on Computer Vision and Pattern Recognition (CVPR), Long Beach, CA, USA, pp. 9574–9583 (2019). https://doi.org/10.1109/CVPR.2019.00981.
3. Kipf, T.N., Max, W.: Semi-supervised classification with graph convolutional networks. In: Proceedings of the 5th International Conference on Learning Representations (2017)
4. Huang, Q., He, H., Singh, A., Lim, S.N., Benson, A.R.: Combining label propagation and simple models out-performs graph neural networks (2020). arXiv preprint arXiv:2010.13993
5. Xu, K., Hu, W., Leskovec, J., Stefanie, J.: How powerful are graph neural networks? In: Proceedings of the 7th International Conference on Learning Representations (2019)

6. Sen, P., Namata, G., Bilgic, M., Getoor, L., Galligher, B., Tina, E.-R.: Collective classification in network data. AI Mag. **29**(3) (2008)
7. Oleksandr, S., Maximilian, M., Aleksandar, B., Stephan, G.: Pitfalls of graph neural network evaluation. In: Neural Information Processing Systems Workshop on Relational Representation Learning (2018)
8. Oh, J., Cho, K. Bruna, J.: Advancing GraphSAGE with a Data-driven Node Sampling, ar5iv.labs.arxiv.org
9. Alaoui, D., Riffi, J., Abdelouahed, S., Aghoutane, B., Yahyaouy, A., Tairi, H.: Deep GraphSAGE-based recommendation system: jumping knowledge connections with ordinal aggregation network (2022)

Author Index

GPSR Compliance

The European Union's (EU) General Product Safety Regulation (GPSR) is a set of rules that requires consumer products to be safe and our obligations to ensure this.

If you have any concerns about our products, you can contact us on ProductSafety@springernature.com

In case Publisher is established outside the EU, the EU authorized representative is:

Springer Nature Customer Service Center GmbH
Europaplatz 3
69115 Heidelberg, Germany

The manufacturer's authorised representative in the EU is Springer
Nature Customer Service Centre GmbH, Europaplatz 3, 69115 Heidelberg,
Germany. If you have any concerns regarding our products, please
contact ProductSafety@springernature.com

Printed and bound by CPI Group (UK) Ltd, Croydon, CR0 4YY
29/04/2026
02099532-0008